PARADISE OF THE DAMNED

Also by Keith Thomson

Born to Be Hanged

7 Grams of Lead

Twice a Spy

Once a Spy

Pirates of Pensacola

PARADISE OF THE DAMNED

THE TRUE STORY OF AN OBSESSIVE QUEST FOR EL DORADO, THE LEGENDARY CITY OF GOLD

KEITH THOMSON

Little, Brown and Company
New York • Boston • London

Little, Brown and Company
Hachette Book Group
1290 Avenue of the Americas, New York, NY 10104
littlebrown.com

First Edition: May 2024

Map by Jeffrey L. Ward
Additional illustration credits located on page 369.

ISBN 978-0-31-649700-8
LCCN 2024933209

Printing 1, 2024

MRQ

Printed in Canada

For Darla

Happiness is only to be found in El Dorado,
which no one yet has been able to reach.

—Spanish proverb

CONTENTS

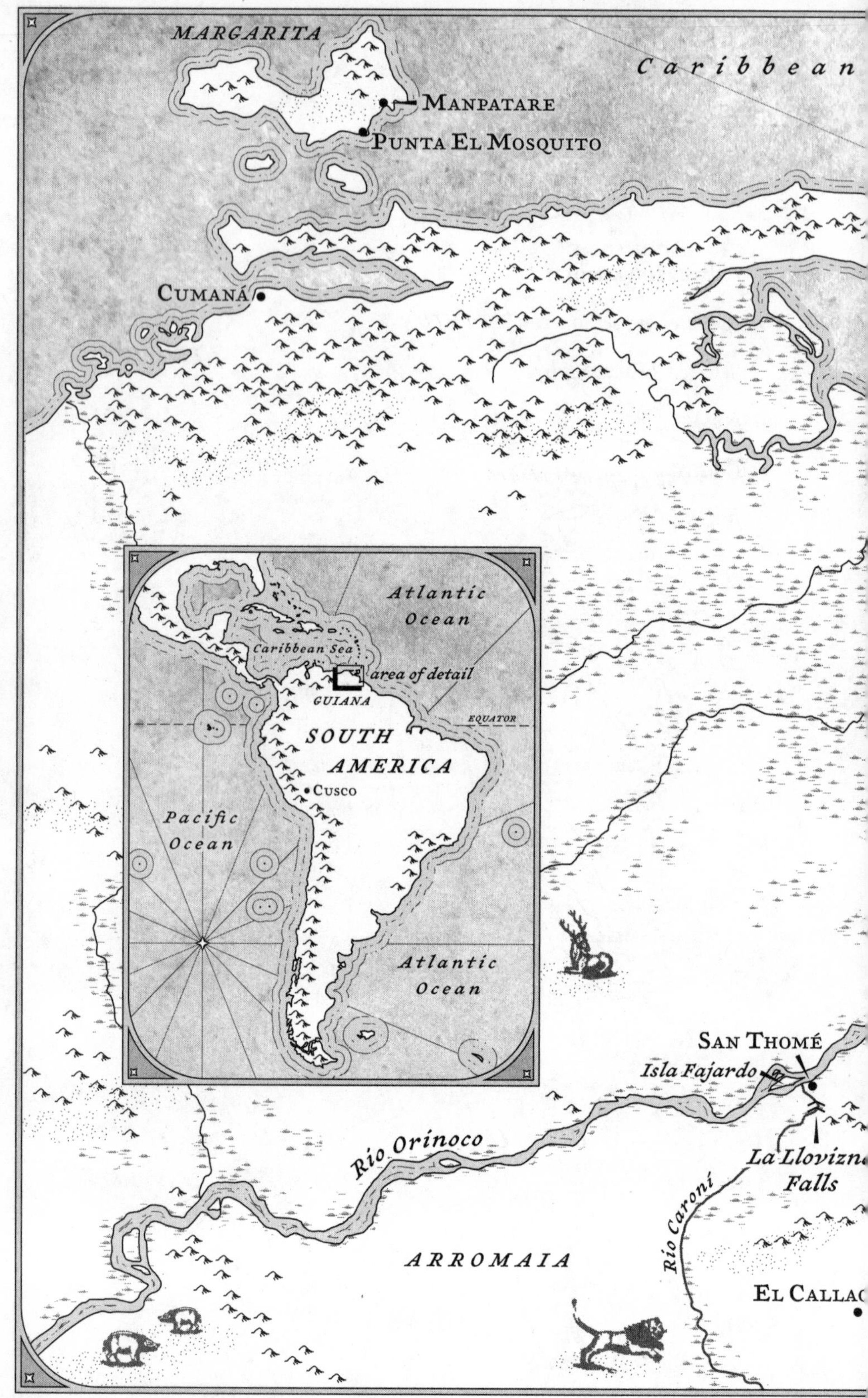
MARGARITA
Caribbean
MANPATARE
PUNTA EL MOSQUITO
CUMANÁ
Atlantic Ocean
Caribbean Sea
area of detail
GUIANA
EQUATOR
SOUTH AMERICA
Cusco
Pacific Ocean
Atlantic Ocean
SAN THOMÉ
Isla Fajardo
Rio Orinoco
La Llovizn
Falls
Rio Caroní
ARROMAIA
EL CALLA

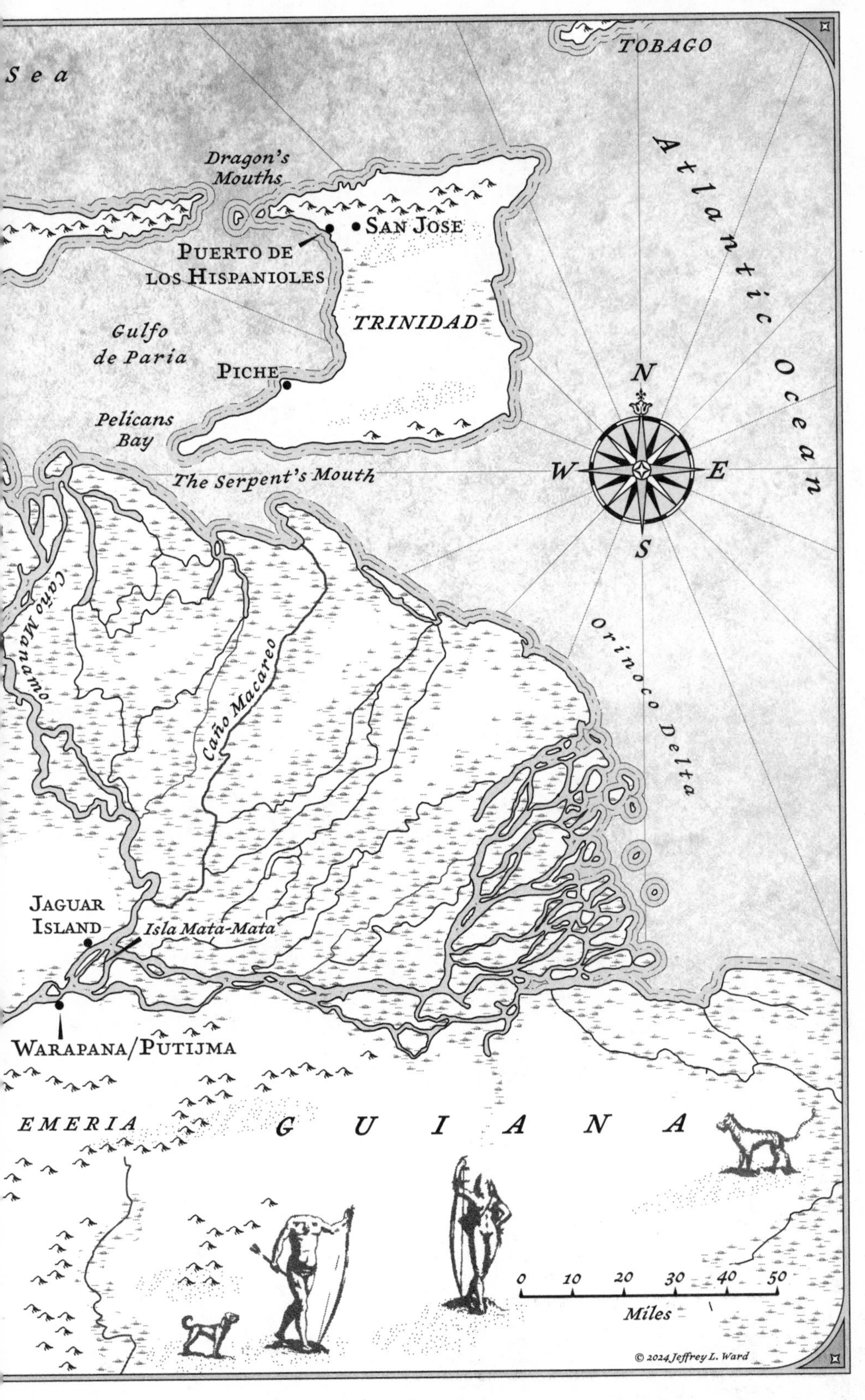
Sea
TOBAGO
Atlantic Ocean
Dragon's Mouths
SAN JOSE
PUERTO DE LOS HISPANIOLES
TRINIDAD
Gulfo de Paria
PICHE
Pelicans Bay
N
W
E
S
The Serpent's Mouth
Caño Manamo
Caño Macareo
Orinoco Delta
JAGUAR ISLAND
Isla Mata-Mata
WARAPANA/PUTIJMA
EMERIA
G U I A N A
0 10 20 30 40 50
Miles
© 2024 Jeffrey L. Ward

PARADISE OF THE DAMNED

1
THE GOLDEN MAN

THE SUN WAS literally roasting Juan Martín de Albujar to death. It wouldn't kill him, though. The hunger would do him in first. Or so he thought as his canoe drifted down a vast, uncharted river somewhere in the Amazon jungle.

He hadn't eaten for days, not since the gunpowder store exploded and the blame fell on him, the munitions master. There's nothing a munitions master can do about a wind-tossed spark, but General Silva needed a scapegoat in order to abort the expedition, and it was imperative that the conquistadors get out of the jungle immediately: between the crocodiles, jaguars, and "savages"—their term for the Indigenous peoples—Silva and his 140 men wouldn't have survived another day without gunpowder. If not for the sudden dearth of it, he likely would have shot Albujar. And he certainly would have executed him on the spot if the munition master's many friends hadn't pleaded for mercy. In a compromise of sorts, Silva dumped him into a canoe without any provisions and sent him floating down a river in Guiana (an expanse comprising parts of modern Guyana, Suriname, Brazil, French Guiana, and Venezuela).

From Albujar's point of view, it was the opposite of mercy: a slower, more tortuous death than a bullet. If he were to go ashore—assuming the crocodiles let him past—he stood to become supper for the jaguars before he could find anything to eat himself. The lush jungle, paradoxically, offered almost nothing in the way of food. If he could elude predators, he might be able to track down a rodent. Still, he would have to contend with scorpions, tarantulas, and the fourteen-inch-long centipedes that killed the tarantulas. Not to mention the hundred-odd species of venomous snakes, including the Amazon's deadliest, the fer-de-lance, or spearhead, named for the way it attacks when disturbed (and because it has the sensitivity of a hair trigger, it's disturbed frequently).

Even the flora could kill a man—the wispy razor grass hanging from the branches, sharp enough to slit a throat, or the aptly named strangler fig roots dangling everywhere. But the greatest obstacle Albujar would face was ordinary, nontoxic flora: the roots, branches, vines, mosses, leaves, and lichens fighting for every last inch of free space that offered access to the odd ray of sunlight managing to squeeze through the forest canopy. Collectively they were impassable, the true king of the jungle, making rivers the only practical way of getting anywhere. Therefore, Albujar's best hope—his only hope, really—was to stay in the canoe and pray he came upon civilization of some sort.

As it transpired, he came upon a group of "savages." Or, rather, they came upon him, snatching him from the canoe so quickly that he couldn't be sure whether they were real or the latest concoction of his heat- and starvation-induced delirium. Next thing he knew, they were marching him blindfolded through steamy rainforest to an undisclosed location. Or maybe they had disclosed it; he couldn't understand a thing they were saying.

The march continued for the remainder of the day, the entire day after that, and then for another twelve days, with Albujar likely forced to endure step after excruciating step on bleeding, blistered feet while rain-and-perspiration-dampened breeches chafed the insides of his thighs to bloody pulp and the mosquito bites riddling the rest of his body were slashed into open sores by the underbrush. The overhang, which the blindfold prevented him from ducking, was worse. And those difficulties were mere trifles compared to the terror: what would happen to him when they finally got wherever they were going? The savages were known to be extremely hostile to outsiders. The Aztecs, for example. When a stranger wandered into their midst, their standard practice was to take him to the top of one of their pyramids, slice open his chest, and wrench out his still-beating heart before ritually sacrificing him.

At noon on the fifteenth day of the march, Albujar's captors peeled off his blindfold, revealing stone and adobe homes as far as he could see. "Manoa," they said, their first word he'd recognized. It meant "lake," and, more pertinently, it was the name of a gold-rich city supposedly built by Incas who'd fled the conquistadors in Peru. Manoa had not only been General Silva's objective but also that of dozens of other expeditions over the previous forty years, beginning in 1529, when conquistadors started hearing tales of the emperor who annually coated his body in turpentine and then rolled around in powdery gold dust, gilding himself, before canoeing to the center of a lake, diving in, and sloughing off the gold as an offering to the gods. *El hombre dorado,* the Spanish took to calling him. The golden man. The moniker soon became an alternative name for his empire, the existence of which was entirely plausible; twice already in the sixteenth century, comparable dominions had been discovered in the New World: the Aztecs' Tenochtitlán (modern-day Mexico City) by Hernán Cortés in 1519, and the Incan City of the Sun, Cusco (in Peru), by Francisco Pizarro in 1533.

Those were small towns, however, Albujar saw now, compared to Manoa, which was so vast that it took him and his captors a day and a half to walk through it—no doubt heading for the pyramid where he would die. On the way he saw tens of thousands of small but solidly built homes, their residents naked save for body paint and substantial gold ornaments suspended from their ears, noses, and necks. They were all agog too: he was the first white man they'd ever seen. Ultimately his party came to a palace, where, to his surprise, rather than die, he was invited to stay as an honored guest.

The ensuing months amounted to an extended vacation in a tropical paradise for him, his hosts catering to his every whim. During that time, he learned their language and used it to compile material for the report he planned to deliver to his countrymen, primarily about the emperor, whom the Manoans called Inca. Compared to Inca, Midas had merely a passing interest in gold. Inca's palace was brimming with it: the guards' armor, the tableware, even the pots and pans in the kitchens. The halls were lined with life-size golden and silver statues of every living thing in the kingdom, even the trees. Outside lay more gold still, piled like logs left to be burned. And the lake ritual wasn't just an annual affair: every single day, Inca slathered his body—not with turpentine but with a whitish balsam of the Amyris plants and Calophyllum trees—before his attendants blew fine powdered gold dust onto him using hollow canes.

At the end of Albujar's seventh month in Manoa, when he prepared to go home, Inca allowed him to take as much gold as he could carry. The haul would translate into tremendous wealth and power for Albujar. Even better would be the look on General Silva's face.

Inca's men guided Albujar back to the Orinoco, at which point his return to civilization might have been a straightforward few days' canoe ride. Soon into his journey, though, he was attacked by Orenoqueponi tribesmen, who stole all the gold Inca had given him save for some beads inside a pair of large, dried gourds—the thieves must have assumed they were merely canteens.

El Hombre Dorado

Albujar spent seven years in their captivity, until earning enough of their trust that he was able to escape. After finding his way to the Atlantic, he gained passage to the Spanish colony of San Juan, Puerto Rico. Although he couldn't have been more grateful for his deliverance, without Inca's gifts he was just a disgraced munitions master with a preposterous story. Worse, he'd contracted a tropical disease, and he was dying.

Only after receiving the sacrament on his deathbed did he speak of his Manoa experience. As wild as the tale was, his confessor was inclined to believe it because of the El Dorado rumors coupled with the fact that, for fear of being turned away from the gates of heaven, Christians tended not to utter false last words. (For that reason, a fundamental principle of testimony in law at the time was *Nemo moriturus praesumitur mentire*—a dying person is not presumed to lie.)

When Albujar died, the two gourds he'd bequeathed to the church were opened and found to be full of gold beads. At once, his tale became as good as gospel—and nearly as widespread, launching myriad new expeditions into Guiana in search of El Dorado. Those efforts would eventually lead to a haul of more than two hundred thousand pounds of gold, enough to replace the copper on the Statue of Liberty twice and carrying a present-day purchasing power relative to income of $100 billion.

By 1592, however, nothing had been found in Guiana, which wasn't altogether surprising given the difficulty of locating a city in an uncharted wilderness the size of Europe, where the landscape often made it impossible to see more than a few feet in any direction. If El Dorado were a needle, the haystack would cover three acres. But that didn't deter the English courtier commonly known as Sir Walter Raleigh—but herein as *Ralegh,* his own most frequent spelling of his family name. (In his lifetime, which predated standardized spelling, he occasionally signed *Rauley* or *Rauleygh* but never *Raleigh.* Nonetheless, the city, county, mountain, and brand of tobacco named after him all spell it that way.)

Walter Ralegh's signature

Having studied the conquistadors, Ralegh believed he could find El Dorado by using a tool they'd never tried: humanity. Take, as a typical example, the very first expedition, in 1529: the conquistadors had clamped iron shackles around the necks of their "porters"—the Indigenous people they forced to carry their supplies—and then tied one shackle to the next, forming a human chain. Whenever a porter grew too tired or otherwise couldn't keep pace, the conquistadors swung an axe or a sword and decapitated him, causing his body to fall away, whereby they could proceed without losing either the time to unfasten the shackle or the shackle itself. Ralegh believed that by instead befriending the "Guianans"—his term for the territory's Indigenous peoples—and offering them Queen Elizabeth's protection, "infinite numbers of souls may be . . . freed from the intolerable tyranny of the Spaniards" and, in the bargain, "the queen's dominions may be exceedingly enlarged, and [England] inestimably enriched." The same policy, as he saw it, had yielded a mutually beneficial partnership with Native Americans in Virginia, which he'd founded in 1585.

To mount an expedition to Guiana, he just needed Elizabeth's approval, ordinarily a simple matter: he wasn't just her favorite courtier; he was her captain of the guard and, arguably, her best friend. Because of his relationship with another woman, however, she'd just put him in prison.

2

THOSE DAINTY HANDS WHICH CONQUERED MY DESIRE

THE TROUBLE HAD started in 1581 when Ralegh, then a twenty-seven-year-old army captain, left the battlefield in hope of winning royal favor, just a whiff of which could substantially change his life. For instance, if Queen Elizabeth were to grant him one of her scores of patents (official permissions). With the patent to license vintners, he would collect £1 per year from anyone wanting to retail wine in England, netting himself £1,000 a year, more than he could earn in a lifetime as a soldier. And if he could stay in favor, the world was his for the asking: the queen also granted patents for exploration and colonization, with the patent holder keeping a share of the land and the riches. Ralegh longed, as he put it, "to seek new worlds for gold, for praise, for glory."

First, he had to gain access to Elizabeth, which could be nearly as difficult as discovering one of those worlds. At all times she was surrounded by fifteen hundred to two thousand courtiers seeking her attention in much the same way trees, ferns, and lichens in the jungle grappled for access to sunlight. Ralegh determined that getting a court position was his best bet, but that, too, was

Sir Walter Ralegh

a challenge. Among several requirements was education, and his was limited: he'd distinguished himself at Oxford but had left well shy of graduation to go to war, first in France on behalf of persecuted Protestants, and next in Ireland, where England was trying to suppress the Desmond Rebellions. Then again, his eight years of military service might be seen at court as more valuable than an Oxford degree. He'd earned a reputation for utter indifference to danger and, perhaps even more valuable, as a soldier who could be counted on to get a job done, however repugnant. The siege of the Irish fort in Smerwick in 1580, for example: at its successful conclusion, Ralegh and another captain perfunctorily carried out their commander's orders to "put to the sword" the fort's six hundred defenders.

At court, however, it was more important to be good-looking. According to the courtiers' second Bible, *The Book of the Courtier* by Count Baldesar Castiglione, "Outward beauty is a true sign of inner goodness . . . just as with trees the beauty of the blossom testifies to the goodness of the fruit." Ralegh didn't protest. By all accounts, he was handsome; it was another box he could check. Leveraging his relation to a connected half brother and/or a late aunt who had once been Lady of the Bedchamber (the queen's personal attendant), he secured the position of esquire in the Body Extraordinary, a group of 150 young men on call to perform minor chores for which they received no pay.

Now he was one of two thousand courtiers vying for Queen Elizabeth's attention, all of them splendidly groomed, coiffed, and attired, and at the ready with flowery attestations of their devotion to her—her catnip—should they manage to get within earshot. At first they looked on the newcomer as a potential ally, which is to say, a stepping stone. But when he opened his mouth, they heard—or, from their perspective, they were subjected to—his Devonshire drawl: it sounded as if he were speaking through a mouthful of straw. Worse, it meant he was from Devon, way down on the southeastern coast, important to shipping and commerce but, for the most part, a backwater full of pirates, smugglers, and hog farmers. On occasion, granted, Devonians made it to court, but always they had the good sense to do something about that accent. For this upstart's own good, thought the courtiers, he had better be the son of a viscount or an earl with a misguided affinity for the sea.

They looked into it—one needn't go far at court to get that sort of information: the place was a living, breathing social register. The Raleghs, they learned, were a wealthy and distinguished Devonshire family. Once upon a time. In recent generations, though, the family had been, according to an authoritative source, "buried in oblivion, as though it had never been." The Raleghs no longer owned their farmhouse nor the land they tilled. They were little more than commoners. Ghastlier still, Walter was the youngest of five sons; he'd be lucky to inherit a hog pen.

He would be well-advised, therefore, to go back to the army. Or, really, to go anywhere other than Queen Elizabeth's court, where the prerequisite for success—more than education, more than looks, more than connections, more than anything—was social standing. "It nearly always happens that both in the profession of arms and in other worthy pursuits the most famous men have been of noble birth," explained the *Book of the Courtier.* The correlation between bloodline and virtue was the same as "in trees, the shoots of which nearly always resemble the trunk." Men of ignoble birth, on the other hand, "lack that stimulus and fear of shame, nor do they feel any obligation to advance beyond what their predecessors have done."

In sum, Ralegh stood a better chance of becoming queen himself than of being looked upon as anything other than an upstart by his fellow courtiers. Which both galled him and stoked his ambition: he wouldn't just sail off to seek new worlds; he would leave the damned elitists gagging on his wake.

For the time being, though, failing to distinguish himself at court for anything other than his accent, he needed to retool. Although he maintained that "no man is esteemed for colorful garments except by fools and women," he began with a visit to the tailor's, overextending himself for an extravagant wardrobe featuring the finest and most meticulously sewn silks lined with lavish furs and studded with pearls. He added a pair of large pearl earrings, and more pearls still to adorn his hair, which received nearly the same level of attention from a cosmetologist that marble did from Michelangelo.

When he returned to court, likely even the most flamboyant fops agreed that the upstart's new getup was ostentatious, pathetically nouveau riche, and, most grievous of all, a violation of their fundamental guiding principle: a courtier should at all times carry himself with a graceful nonchalance. Granted, Queen Elizabeth attired herself in an orgy of bright colors, gems, and frills, but that was her signature style, enabling her to outshine everyone else, and it suited her: she was, effectively, the sun.

On the day of Ralegh's return, according to the lone existing report, by English historian Thomas Fuller, the queen was taking a walk in the Greenwich Palace gardens, accompanied by the usual throng of courtiers jostling for proximity. At one point she came upon "a plashy place"—or, a mud puddle—and "seemed to scruple going thereon." Enter Captain Ralegh "in good habit (his clothes then being a considerable part of his estate)." He "cast and spread his new plush cloak on the ground whereon the Queen trod gently." Taken by the gesture, she rewarded her new sartorial soulmate with several new suits.

There are concerns about the validity of Fuller's report: he wrote it eighty years after the fact, and he was known to embellish. Also, there's no mention of the cloak incident by contemporaneous court sources, for whom relatively quotidian details like the state of Queen Elizabeth's bedsheets merited a ream of coverage. Not long after that damp day in Greenwich, however, Ralegh fashioned a new seal for himself depicting his battle helmet and his family's coat of arms held aloft by a cloak spread out like a pair of eagle's wings. Clearly a cloak had some significance to him.

In any case, from that point, his career took flight. Elizabeth had likely heard of him before, of his heroics in Ireland. In person, surely the tall and darkly handsome young soldier wasn't impeded by her affinity for tall, dark, and handsome young soldiers. There were enough of those at court for a battalion, but none were as bright, glib, or well-read as Ralegh. His curiosity about the world was insatiable: since boyhood,

Ralegh "cast and spread his new plush cloak on the ground whereon the Queen trod gently."

he'd gone through books the way other people did oxygen. Elizabeth was especially struck by his geopolitical insights. Quickly, according to future secretary of state Robert Naunton, "she took him for a kind of oracle," which "nettled" all the courtiers.

For Ralegh it was delicious; by turning their pretensions on them, he'd beaten them at their own game. To capitalize, though, he would need to maintain the queen's favor, which was even more challenging than winning it. Courtiers in her inner circle were required to romance her, done for the most part by celebrating her in words—poetry, music, and tributes—as though she were the love of their lives. Because, at forty-eight, she was older than many of their mothers, and since she was nearly synonymous with virginity (one of the reasons Ralegh's colony would be named Virginia), it was a game. But at the same time, it wasn't. The mere hint that one of her favorites had an outside attachment inflamed her jealousy, at which point, as one of them put it, "came a storm from a sudden gathering of clouds, and the thunder fell in wondrous manner on all alike." As much as they were afraid of her, however, they were enchanted by her. "She did fish for men's souls," wrote one of them, "and had so sweet a bait that no one could escape her network."

Ralegh plunked down his soul, extolling Elizabeth as his "life's joy" and his "soul's heaven above" in poems he wrote for her, tapping talent that would one day place his name on the short list of poets suspected of secretly writing Shakespeare's plays. And he had no shame in laying it on—for instance, waxing about the royal "eyes which set my fancy on a fire," auburn curls that "hold my heart in chains," "those dainty hands which conquered my desire," and "that wit which of my thought does hold the reins!"

As a result, wrote a visitor to court, the queen was believed "to love this gentleman now beyond all the others." She was even taken with Ralegh's Devonshire accent, affectionately using it herself to call him "Water." By 1583, the unofficial title of "Royal Favourite" was his, and it had lavish benefits, including the wine patent as well as a rent-free residence—and not just any residence, but Durham House, the elegant, 250-year-old, centrally located riverside palace where Elizabeth herself had once lived.

He went on to accrue more patents and properties, as well as official titles, including lord warden of the stannaries (the tin-mining counties of Devon and Cornwall), a significant post not only for its salary, £3,000 per annum, but because Devon and Cornwall were responsible for England's standing as the principal supplier of tin in the Western world. Next, he became lord and governor of Virginia,

Queen Elizabeth I

although he'd never set foot there: after Elizabeth granted him the patent to explore the territory in 1584, she was unwilling to part with him. In 1587, to keep him closer still, she made him captain of the guard, a job that entailed overseeing her protection day and night.

On the balance, Ralegh was pleased: in an era when courtiers spent their days fighting for a monarch's attention and ordinary subjects spent months contriving to get even a moment's proximity, the position was as influential as any that didn't come with a throne. Still, court life could be confining to someone who burned to seek new worlds, much less the unquenchably curious sort who didn't so much as see a corner without feeling compelled to learn what was around it. And despite his elegiac avowal that the fifty-four-year-old queen was "my true fantasy's mistress," the thirty-three-year-old bachelor's eye wandered.

Enter the twenty-two-year-old Elizabeth Throckmorton, known as Bess, one of the ten to twelve Gentlewomen of the Privy Chamber, or ladies-in-waiting—personal assistants to the queen chosen for their looks and lineage. Although there were exceptions, one other prerequisite was virginity, which Elizabeth required ladies-in-waiting not only to maintain while in her service but also to rejoice in, as she did. And because she wanted them to be free of loyalty to anyone but her, as little as a dalliance risked her wrath. Marriage, therefore, was off the table for them unless she consented. In most cases, there was a better chance of convincing her to pitch her crown into the Thames.

Still, Walter and Bess wanted to marry—and, in 1591, they needed to: she was pregnant. Asking Elizabeth's permission wouldn't merely be rhetorical, however; it would mean expulsion from court. At the least. Several courtiers' affairs had landed them in prison. Also, per the 1536 Treason Act, it was a capital offense for a person of royal blood to wed without the sovereign's consent. Because Bess's stepsister, Lady Jane Grey, had been queen (albeit for just nine days, in 1553, before she was beheaded), her blood was royal enough.

Nevertheless, in deference to propriety, the couple wed, exchanging vows covertly, on November 19, before returning to court as though nothing had happened. The bride availed herself of the right corsets or farthingales (early hoop skirts)—pregnancy concealment was something of a sixteenth-century cottage industry—and Elizabeth suspected nothing. A few months later, Bess contrived an excuse to go to her brother's country house, where, on March 29, 1592, she gave birth to a boy, Damerei (a variation of the surname D'Amerie on a branch of the Raleghs' family tree connecting them to Henry II).

Bess Throckmorton

Finally, having hired a discreet wet nurse, she returned to court. The Raleghs' cover-up appeared to have succeeded.

It had an Achilles' heel, though: the legion of courtiers perpetually on the prowl for information they could use to subvert one another. Chief among them was First Earl of Salisbury Robert Cecil—"Pygmy," Elizabeth called him, on account of his small stature and a back hunched from scoliosis. Cecil's outsized mind and his genius for politics had made him an exception to her rule of favoritism based on physical attributes, earning him a knighthood in 1591. Now, at twenty-eight, he'd just become the youngest-ever member of the Privy Council, the body of nineteen noblemen who oversaw most of the kingdom's daily operations.

When Cecil asked him about the rumors of a secret wedding, Ralegh replied, "If any such thing were [true,] I would have imparted it unto yourself before any man living." Calling God as his witness, he added that his love for Queen Elizabeth relegated the notion of another woman to nonsense. In Cecil's experience, however, Ralegh's definition of truth was whatever was most expedient to attaining his objective. The personal motto on Ralegh's winged-cloak seal, *Amore et Virtute* (with Love and Virtue), was in the same category as the mercurial Elizabeth's motto, *Semper Eadem* (Always the Same), or that of her father, Henry VIII, who'd had six wives and executed two of them: *Coeur Loyale* (Loyal Heart).

Cecil resolved that the queen would hear all about the secret wedding—albeit from someone other than him, so he wouldn't be exposed to the fallout. Consequently, in late May 1592, both Walter and Bess Ralegh were placed under house arrest for two months—he at Durham House and she, as far as is known, somewhere in London that had a courtyard—before being imprisoned in the Tower of London for however long the queen needed to decide what to do with them.

3

ENGLAND OR INDIA OR ELSEWHERE

William the Conqueror built the Tower of London fortress as a royal residence in 1078, but his successors thought it was better suited for use as a prison. Over the next four centuries, they added concentric hexagonal ramparts, a moat, and a small city's worth of buildings, including the one in which Walter Ralegh found himself in 1592, the Garden Tower—or, the Bloody Tower, as everyone had called it since 1483, when two young princes were held and allegedly murdered there by their uncle, Richard of Gloucester, enabling him to succeed their father, King Edward V. Bess Ralegh, meanwhile, was placed "somewhere else" in the Tower complex. Details of baby Damerei's whereabouts are even murkier.

Although both Walter and Bess were permitted servants and spacious quarters—he had a two-room apartment with a view of the Thames—their imprisonment was anything but comfortable due to the continual sensation of impending catastrophe. Despite their vast network of courtiers close to Queen Elizabeth, they were unable to glean anything of her thinking, save that an apology was in order. Walter instead wrote a letter to Elizabeth in which he lamented being unable to behold her "like Venus, the gentle wind blowing her fair hair about her pure cheeks, like a nymph, sometimes sitting in the shade like a goddess, sometimes singing like an angel." He received no response.

As a follow-up, he tried poetry, which had never failed to move her. In "The 21st (and last) Book of the Ocean to Cynthia," a 543-line requiem that is now widely considered a masterpiece, he portrayed her as Cynthia, goddess of the moon, who controls the Ocean—i.e., Water, Elizabeth's pet name for him. Their relationship meant everything to the Ocean, but unfortunately "Her love hath end: my woe must ever last." Ralegh sent the completed work to Cecil, who, he hoped, would give it to the queen. Instead, Cecil stuck it on a shelf in his country house, where it would collect dust for three centuries.

Next, Ralegh turned to a more reliable means of appeasing Elizabeth: money. Along with the throne in 1558, she'd inherited a £227,000 national debt that made paying bills a perpetual struggle—one that the Irish rebellion and ten years of war with Spain hadn't helped. On September 8, 1592, three months into Ralegh's stay in the Tower, one of his privateering (state-sanctioned piracy) fleets returned to England having captured the *Madre de Dios,* a Portuguese merchant ship practically swollen with valuable cargo, including 537 tons of spices and chestfuls of gold, silver, pearls, and ambergris, a sperm whale intestine secretion literally worth its weight in gold to perfume manufacturers. The queen was entitled to the privateering standard one-tenth of the proceeds, £14,100, but Ralegh added his own share to hers, giving her a total of £80,000. To put that figure in context, the construction cost of the most luxurious royal palace of the day, Henry VIII's Nonsuch—so known because no such palace equaled its magnificence—was £23,000. Certainly the sum was "more than ever any man presented Her Majesty," Ralegh told an associate, adding, "If God had sent it for my ransom, I hope Her Majesty of her abundant goodness will accept it."

She did accept it. Yet she left him in the Tower to brood over what more he could have done to placate her, eventually leading him to the idea of capitalizing on his privateers' 1584 capture of Pedro Sarmiento de Gamboa, the governor of Patagonia and author of the 1572 landmark *Historia de Los Incas* (History of the Incas). Ralegh had held Sarmiento for ransom but treated him as an honored guest and fellow gentleman adventurer rather than a captive, allowing him to stay at Durham House and even introducing him to Queen Elizabeth. The two men developed a convivial rapport, meanwhile, delighting in conversing in Latin before Ralegh switched to fluent Spanish, which he had learned in order to avail himself of New World intelligence only available in books like *Historia de Los Incas*. It allowed him and Sarmiento to have the sort of long, deep conversations possible only between kindred spirits. Or so the Spaniard thought. In fact, Ralegh was acting, his objective being to gather more intelligence, and in the trove he would wheedle was the story of munitions master Juan Martín de Albujar.

In 1592, Ralegh's first step to El Dorado was reconnaissance, as always—"Prevention is the daughter of intelligence," he liked to say. It would be especially important in Guiana, given the Spanish military presence. Fortunately, the Tower of London didn't prohibit inmates from interviewing privateers and hiring them for transatlantic reconnaissance missions. Once he'd dispatched them, however, he could do little more than wait for their return—months, at best. As if he didn't have enough suspense already.

The conditions didn't help; a drought and uncommonly high September temperatures dried up the Thames. And then there was the 1592–1593 London Plague, the latest in a series of bubonic epidemics that had begun with the Black Death in 1346. It would claim the lives of one in ten of the city's two hundred thousand residents, resulting in an almost constant toll of church bells. Although Ralegh was permitted to have guests, none came, everyone with means having hightailed it out of town.

Its cooler temperatures notwithstanding, October prolonged his hell, then immeasurably deepened it with the death of his son, Damerei. It's unknown whether the seven-month-old was a victim of the plague, infant mortality (which claimed 27 percent of English babies at the time), or something else. His parents' thoughts and the details of their lives during that difficult interval are similarly lost to history, save that even Walter's rivals sympathized. As Robert Naunton remarked, "Sir Walter Ralegh was one that, it seems, fortune had picked out . . . to use as her tennis-ball, thereby to show what she could do."

Two months later, some combination of compassion, elapsed time, and the advent of Christmas seemed to soften Elizabeth. Walter was freed on December 13, and Bess on December 22, although both were still banished indefinitely from court. That was fine with Bess, who wanted to move to Sherborne Castle, the Dorset country estate Walter had long coveted before Queen Elizabeth gave it to him—just a few months prior to the marriage flap. Set in the shallow valley of the River Yeo and surrounded by a serene deer park, the property included the quintessential medieval palace replete with moat, drawbridge, and quartet of three-story spires. Bess saw it as a chance to start a new life away from court. Queen Elizabeth continued to exert a gravitational pull on Walter, however. According to his friend, the playwright Ben Johnson, the issue was that Ralegh "esteemed fame more than conscience."

Eventually, though, he came around, embracing country life—even after the old castle proved to be drafty and gravity-challenged. He and Bess set to work building a new home on the other side of the river, and not just any home but a four-story brick mansion that would conjure palaces of old, at the same time embracing modernity with innovations like a plaster facade, tall windows to admit an extraordinary amount of daylight by era standards, and fresh water pumped in from a nearby spring. Next, the Raleghs augmented the estate's sweeping lawns with a network of terraces and walkways dotted with New World flowers, and they added cedar trees—brought as seedlings from Virginia—to the surrounding woods.

They made their most significant addition to Sherborne in October 1593, a son named Walter. Wat, as they called him, was christened on November 1 at a nearby country church straight out of a storybook. By Christmas, ensconced at Sherborne with a loving and beloved wife and a healthy newborn son, Walter Ralegh arguably had anything a man could want. Unless that man wanted to seek new worlds for gold, praise, and glory.

And the gold was now less a want than a need. The costs of improving and maintaining Sherborne were exceeding Ralegh's diminished means, much of his income having previously come from privateering operations that needed to be authorized by the queen—with the proceeds having gone into his Virginia colonization effort, some £40,000 he'd yet to recoup. He still had his official posts, like lord warden of the stannaries and its £3,000 salary, and his wine patent wouldn't expire for twenty-six years, but Elizabeth could easily reassign those. And her successor almost certainly would: not a small concern. At sixty-two, she was well past her expiration date per era norms. Aristocrats who made it past twenty-one had an average life expectancy of forty-three, two years more than commoners. That advantage, however, didn't extend to royals, who tended to perish a decade earlier than their subjects. As it happened, Elizabeth's four predecessors—Henry VIII, Edward VI, Jane Grey, and Mary I—lived to an average age of thirty-three exactly, with Henry the longevity champ at fifty-five.

Accordingly, in December 1593, Walter sought a return to court, a strong possibility provided that the answer to any one of the following questions was yes: Had Elizabeth been mollified by the passage of time—a year and a half since his arrest? Had England's stagnation abroad given her an appreciation for his colonization strategy? During the latest round of Irish strife, had she missed his counsel? Did she miss him?

The answers came in his ensuing pursuit of a vacant Privy Council seat. Not only was he flatly denied, but his effort was widely mocked at court: only Sir Upstart could have overlooked "The Disgrace." To return to favor, Ralegh concluded, he needed something on the scale of El Dorado.

As if on cue, the privateers he'd dispatched months earlier returned to England from Guiana. Their objective had been to locate a Spaniard-free beachhead where he and an expeditionary force could safely land and leave their ships while venturing onto the continent. Unfortunately, the privateers reported, Spanish military presence in the area was pervasive. Still, there was an island eight miles east of the continent that might fit the bill: Trinidad. The Spaniards had a garrison there, but it was nothing Ralegh couldn't take with a couple hundred men, allowing him to secure the island. The privateers had also brought two Natives of Trinidad and two more from the continent, all excited to learn English so they could serve as interpreters on the expedition. Ralegh now had a clear path to El Dorado, or, at least, into the jungle.

Almost as important was a path out: without Queen Elizabeth's willingness to defend El Dorado once he'd discovered it, he would essentially be discovering it for Spain. But even if the queen was thoroughly smitten with his plan, her financial headaches would preclude her from paying for any of it. Before approaching her, therefore, he needed to privately raise the requisite £60,000. And to do that, he needed buy-in from Bess.

She recognized the financial urgency. Their family life at Sherborne Castle hadn't just been the antidote to court she'd hoped for, however; it had exceeded her fondest dreams. In addition, their union had solidified to the point that when they were apart, she felt "dis-severed from him." At such times, she said, "a hermit's cell" was "fit for me and my mind." And then there was their son, on the cusp of toddlerhood. Wat would miss his father—and very possibly lose him altogether: twenty-four of Ralegh's reconnaissance men had died just in minor skirmishes with the Spaniards. How much higher would that figure have been had they actually set foot in the deadly Amazon jungle, where he planned to spend months?

Hoping to find a less perilous solution, Bess looked to Robert Cecil, her confidant—or so he'd led her to believe. "I hope for my sake you will rather draw Sir Walter towards the east than help him forward toward the sunset," she wrote in September 1594, referring to Guiana by its direction alone in order to maintain the strict secrecy of the destination, lest rival explorers horn in. Cecil, by that point, knew all about the plan to explore in Guiana—or "England or in India or elsewhere," as Ralegh had cryptically been referring to it in his fund-raising effort.

In addition to Cecil, Ralegh had solicited Charles Howard, who, as lord high admiral, had led England to victory against the Spanish Armada in 1588. In assessing the proposed Guiana expedition, Howard could see a cautionary tale in Virginia, where achieving profitability in corn, wheat, and tobacco crops would at best be a long haul. The crop in Guiana—gold—was more immediate, though, and far more enticing. Howard was in, as was Cecil, who no doubt told Bess his hands were simply tied.

With such influential men backing the enterprise, it would be politically difficult for Queen Elizabeth to withhold letters patent, the official authorization to explore on her behalf. With rising confidence Increasingly confident, Ralegh began equipping a fleet and recruiting personnel for a yearlong voyage. Since crew compensation

Sir Robert Cecil

came in shares of plunder, he was hampered by the need to keep his destination secret. Still, within a few months, he managed not only to enlist 150 men but also to provision five ships.

As it transpired, Queen Elizabeth was sold on the idea—so much so that she encouraged twenty-year-old aspiring explorer Robert Dudley to mount his own El Dorado expedition. As much as she was aware of the importance of the secret behind Ralegh's cryptonym, "England, India, or Elsewhere," she was invested in Dudley's prospects. His late father and namesake had been her lifelong friend and, as was widely speculated, her lover. In his own account of their discussion, the younger Dudley wrote that the queen, unsettled by his original plan of preying on Spanish ships in the Atlantic, advised him only to sail to the West Indies instead. Yet a preponderance of evidence suggests that her recommendation was much more specific, for instance, the account of the same proceeding by the expedition's blunt pilot, Abram Kendall, stating that the reason Dudley headed for Guiana was "he had order to do from Queen Elizabeth."

Dudley posed a formidable threat to Ralegh. As it happens, a description of Dudley by one of their contemporaries might well be one of Ralegh: "A person of stature tall and comely, also strong, valiant, famous at the exercise of tilting [jousting], singularly skilled in all mathematic learning, but chiefly in navigation and architecture, a rare chemist, and of great knowledge of physics." A critical difference between the two men was means. Although Dudley was the Earl of Leicester's illegitimate son, he'd inherited the bulk of the Leicester estate, including the grand Kenilworth Castle in Warwickshire, the home of five King Henrys, from IV to VIII, before Queen Elizabeth gave it to Leicester. To outfit his expedition, Dudley simply had to go to the goldsmith's and make a withdrawal. And he was able to afford the very best seamen, like Kendall, who'd served as pilot for legendary explorer Sir Francis Drake.

On November 21, 1594, Dudley's fleet weighed anchor at Plymouth, the Devonshire port city where the English Channel broadens before joining the Atlantic. Ralegh happened to be at Plymouth too, readying his own fleet and, for the most part, languishing while waiting on his letters patent from the palace. Possibly he suffered the indignity of being on the pier that day while crowds of onlookers oohed and aahed at the spectacle of the wind filling Dudley's pristine sails and sending his four splendid vessels flying toward the New World.

Robert Dudley

Elizabeth's maddening heedlessness aside, Ralegh worried that even if Dudley and his men utterly failed to find El Dorado, they would treat the Guianans poorly, prejudicing them against England and upending his own plan. Dudley also might simply beat him to El Dorado—if the governor of Trinidad and veteran El Dorado hunter Antonio de Berrío didn't beat both of them. Ralegh's reconnaissance team had learned that after coming within a hairbreadth of the golden city in 1591, Berrío was planning a new expedition. And if not him, then another Englishman who'd managed to get wind of Ralegh's plan and was now mounting his own expedition, Thomas Heaton, mayor of Southampton, shipowner, and privateer with a nose for prizes.

The rest of November 1594 came and went with Ralegh pacing the Plymouth piers waiting for his letters patent, the delay eating at his soul. Queen Elizabeth finally took official action on December 6, authorizing Cecil to issue a document permitting "our servant Sir Walter Ralegh" to "offend and enfeeble the King of Spain and his subjects in his dominions to the uttermost" and "to discover and subdue heathen lands not in the possession of any Christian prince." Ralegh noted with chagrin that he was no longer the queen's "trusty" and "well-beloved" servant he'd been in his Virginia commission. Surely, though, the sentiment was crowded out by relief: the document constituted his letters patent. He could ready his fleet.

He benefited from an exuberant three-hundred-man crew of professional seamen complemented by many of his friends, trusted associates, and fellow gentleman adventurers. By December 21, 1594, they had food, water, and everything else they needed. Except wind. There wasn't enough to put out a candle, much less to sail. On December 24, after three days of the same, Ralegh wrote Cecil, "This wind breaks my heart."

He returned to Sherborne to celebrate Christmas Eve with Bess and Wat, but it was difficult to take his mind off the rival expeditions "bound to the wars," as he put it. Christmas passed without the gift he'd prayed for—wind—as did the rest of December and then the entire month of January 1595, by the end of which it was easy to imagine Robert Dudley swinging a machete in the dark jungle, splitting stalk after vine until, all of a sudden, he glowed golden in the reflection of El Dorado.

But even if Dudley had taken a wrong turn and wound up in, say, India, any more delays could derail Ralegh altogether; each passing second was a tick of the clock toward the rainy season in Guiana, which began in May, made exploration impossible by July, and persisted into October. As it stood, since Ralegh was personally paying for his crew's daily provisions, the delay had cost him nearly everything he had. If he were to die in Guiana, he lamented, he would be leaving Bess and Wat to live on £150 a year—less than a tenth of Sherborne's annual costs.

As the maddeningly still air continued into February, he began to have reservations about going. "In the winter of my life," he wrote, here he was leaving his family to undertake an expedition "fitter for boys less blasted with misfortunes, for men of greater ability, and for minds of better encouragement." But as sailors like to say, a good wind can sweep away any of life's frustrations, and on Thursday, February 6, 1595, finally, such a wind filled Ralegh's sails.

4
THE UNLUCKY BASTARD

In 1588, Robert Dudley matriculated to Oxford at all of thirteen years old and bowled over his classmates and instructors alike with his mathematical ability. Yet the first thing any of them said about him was, "He's Leicester's bastard." Indeed, his father, the First Earl of Leicester, also named Robert Dudley, had been married to someone else on August 7, 1574, when his lover, Lady Douglas Sheffield, gave birth to the junior Robert—Robyn, they called him. Leicester lovingly raised Robyn, referring to him as "my lawful son." On September 4, 1588, when Leicester died without any legitimate children, his colossal estate went to fourteen-year-old Robyn. Although the boy's illegitimacy precluded him inheriting the title of Earl of Leicester, he now had an unofficial title: Luckiest Bastard in England.

Bent on a greater distinction, Robyn threw himself into books, studying navigation and naval warfare and becoming an expert on both despite having no actual experience at sea. That stood to change on November 6, 1594, in Southampton, when, at the age of twenty years and two months—ten months shy of the Royal Navy's minimum for a captain—he took command of the sleek, custom-built, thirty-gun, 200-ton *Bear*. His fleet also included the 180-ton *Bear's Whelp* and a pair of pinnaces (small, two-masted boats), the *Frisking* and the *Earwig* (names that are run-of-the-mill by the standards of English ship nomenclature set by, among others, the *Happy Entrance,* the *Carcass,* the *Spanker,* and the *Cockchafer*).

Dudley's crew consisted largely of veteran seamen, rough-and-tumble salts whose lives had been a series of hardships and struggles. As he gave orders for them to weigh anchor and sail the 120 miles of English Channel to Plymouth—where they would anchor briefly before crossing the Atlantic—it was natural to wonder whether they would obey him and, in general, how they would respond to a lucky bastard of a greenhorn who, past his teenage years by a matter of weeks, had become their admiral by virtue of a sack of Daddy's silver. In fact, most of the crewmen were impressed by both his maritime acumen and his aplomb; he'd had their adherence almost from the moment he first set foot on deck.

He did not, however, have beginner's luck. The crew had reason to expect his top-notch fleet to cover the 120 miles from Southampton to Plymouth in a day or two, but, for lack of wind, the journey took thirteen days, a pace just north of a third of a mile per hour. An average swimmer could have done it in half the time.

On November 21, after anchoring briefly at Plymouth—the same port where Walter Ralegh remained in limbo—Dudley sailed out to the Atlantic, where his luck didn't get any better. That night, he was awakened prematurely by the extreme pitching and rolling of his ship. A glance out the stern windows of the captain's quarters supplied little in the way of information; darkness at sea can seem like immersion in India ink. It's easy to imagine Dudley winching his way topside, where everything that wasn't tied down flew from one side of the deck to the other with each mountainous wave. In the fleeting intervals between those three-hundred-thousand-pound masses of water slamming into the hull, and when the shrieking gale dipped to a mere howl, he could hear Kendall shouting orders. While trying to carry them out—to reef the sagging sails, for example—the men on deck struggled to maintain their footing in gelatinous seafoam that had the effect of oil on decks that would have been slippery even without the fusillade of rain. Simultaneously, they had to watch out for waves capable of sweeping them to oblivion and wind-loosed chunks of rigging heavy enough to crack their skulls open. And those men, arguably, had it better than their shipmates belowdecks, furiously working the pumps in the bilge (the lowest part of the hull, where water collected) while forced to breathe dank air that reeked of urine, vomit, and rotting rodent carcasses. At the same time, all around them, planks and boards whined, the hull seemingly one wave away from collapsing into kindling; it was as though the ship were pleading for a return to port—in which case she would have been seconding Dudley's officers.

Dudley concurred. His *Bear* and one of the pinnaces managed to reach Plymouth safely, with the *Bear's Whelp* and the second pinnace landing in Falmouth, forty miles east. Undaunted by the experience, he sent orders to the *Bear's Whelp* to weigh anchor again as soon as possible and then meet him in the Canary Islands (off the coast of northwest Africa), where the fleet could reprovision before starting across the Atlantic.

The *Bear* set sail on December 1, catching a strong wind and proving to be the gazelle Robyn had hoped for, which is to say, a privateering vessel capable of both seizing any Spanish merchant ship—which his patent permitted him to plunder—and escaping any Spanish man-of-war. The same wind, however, lofted a wave onto the *Earwig*, swamping the pinnace, and before her crewmen could pump her, she was on the way to the sea bottom without hope of recovery.

Lunging for lifeboats or anything else that might float, the men tried to get to the *Bear*. Later, when they assembled on the *Bear*'s deck, they discovered that no one had died—which, as it happened, was the best that could be said for the expedition to that point.

Writing off his difficulties as garden-variety "misfortune," Dudley was confident that the law of averages would catch up to the company, meaning good luck was only a matter of time. His men were less sanguine. Sailors were as superstitious as anyone in human history. It was bad luck to stir tea with a knife, they believed; it stirred up trouble. Turning a loaf of bread upside down once it had been sliced was thought to have the same effect. Whistling while at sea was also a problem: it provoked the winds. In contrast, a cat aboard ship, an albatross flying overhead, and an odd number of fishing nets were among many indicators of good luck; the Dudley expedition was woefully short of such portents.

Next, the captain and crew of the *Bear's Whelp* decided to go rogue, capturing "two great and rich galleons" before returning to England to spend their prize money. On reaching the Canaries in late December 1594, however, all Dudley knew was the *Bear's Whelp* crew had failed to rendezvous with him. Left to assume the worst after twelve days passed without any sign of them, he set sail for Trinidad, where, he was convinced, his luck would turn—although he wouldn't dare voice the sentiment given sailors' belief that, while at sea, it was bad luck to say "good luck."

If nothing else, he was well ahead of his rivals. Little is recorded of Thomas Heaton's expedition save that the Southampton mayor would make it back to England a year later with only a couple of trunkfuls of tapestries and other "Indian stuff" to show for his efforts, leading to his imprisonment for debt. Walter Ralegh, meanwhile, didn't depart England until three weeks after Dudley's ships sailed for Trinidad.

Although Ralegh made decent time to the Canaries, when he landed at the island of Tenerife, on February 20, 1595, six of his eight ships were missing. Among them was the *Lion's Whelp*, the frigate supplied by Lord High Admiral Charles Howard. Her commander, the expedition's vice admiral, George Gifford, was a friend of Ralegh's as well as a cousin of Bess's. He was also a scoundrel who'd routinely sold out his friends—and, on one occasion, as will be seen, a cousin. Although Ralegh trusted him, it wasn't out of the question that Gifford had absconded with the Lord High Admiral's frigate and that she was now a pirate ship.

Ralegh had even more reason to mistrust Captain Amyas Preston, who was in command of four of the other missing vessels. In fact, just like the captain and crew of the *Bear's Whelp* in Robert Dudley's fleet, Preston and his men had gone rogue.

Also unaccounted for was the galliot (a small, flat-bottomed merchant ship) captained by Lawrence Keymis, one of Ralegh's closest friends. Tall, lean, with a perpetual squint in one eye, the thirty-year-old Keymis looked the part of a sea captain. Unfortunately, he was anything but. A native of landlocked Wiltshire, Keymis had gone to Oxford's Balliol College in 1581 at sixteen, winning a reputation as a brilliant mathematician and alchemist. After earning his degree, he stayed on at the school to lecture until 1588, when he was offered a job providing navigational, mineralogical, and other scientific data for Ralegh's privateering and colonial ventures. While working together, Keymis and Ralegh grew close. Eventually the unmarried Keymis moved into Durham House so as to maximize his time in its alchemy lab, and in the years that followed he took on additional responsibilities, including running the household, administering the wine patent, and, now, commanding the galliot.

At first his disappearance didn't overly concern Ralegh. Nor did those of the other five vessels. Ships disappeared as often as keys, nearly as often reappearing within a day or two, typically just catching up after losing sight of the rest of the fleet in darkness or a storm. For that reason, fleets prearranged a rendezvous point—in this case, Tenerife, one of the best meeting spots on earth; not only was it the centermost and, at 785 square miles, the largest of the Canaries, but its seemingly limitless panorama of turquoise Atlantic and periwinkle sky made an incoming vessel easy to spot, even after dark, as moon and starlight fringed the translucent wavetops, demarcating inbound craft. At night, as one sailor put it, objects at sea "seemed to swim in a sparkling sea of fire," and with each furrow a ship cut into the waves, "sparks, flying like glowing iron when struck with a heavy hammer, momentarily lighted up its immediate surroundings."

Over the next three days there, Ralegh spotted several inbound craft. None were his. Two proved lucrative prizes for him: a Belgian vessel transporting wine and a Spanish ship laden with firearms. Given the urgency of getting to Guiana, though, he would have happily traded the plunder for his own ships, or even for an explanation for their absence, which he was finding increasingly hard to fathom: the sailing from England had been nothing but smooth. The *Lion's Whelp* and Captain Preston's quartet of ships might have been delayed in getting out of Plymouth, he thought. But what the devil could have happened to Keymis? Ralegh had last sighted the galliot off the coast of Portugal before dark. Could the Spaniards have had something to do with her disappearance? Possibly, but if they'd attacked the galliot that night, his crewmen probably would have heard gunfire and seen the muzzle flashes.

More likely, Keymis had struck a rock or run aground, either of which could put the galliot out of commission for weeks while she underwent repairs. But the most likely explanation, and the most troublesome given Ralegh's decision to place Keymis in the command of the galliot, was that her crew had mutinied and turned pirate. Lawrence was one of the finest scientific minds in England, but he could be a diffident intellectual, the antithesis of the red-blooded commander to whom men responded best—those aboard the galliot especially, most of them the professional infantrymen Ralegh had brought along to attack the Spanish garrison on Trinidad.

On February 24, 1595, his fifth day at Tenerife, Ralegh still had only the two vessels he'd arrived with, his own—presumably the two-hundred-ton *Bark Ralegh*—and veteran naval commander and privateer Robert Crosse's bark (or barque, a broad term encompassing ships with square sails on the first two masts and a triangular fore-and-aft sail on the third). Three days later, Ralegh was no closer to an explanation for the absence of the other six ships, and he was beginning to feel an urgency to cross the Atlantic without them. It would be painful to leave Keymis behind, though, and utterly reckless to go to Trinidad without soldiers; lacking an infantry, he would have almost no chance of securing the island.

The next day, February 28, Ralegh woke and looked out the row of windows in the captain's cabin, eagerly anticipating the sight of the galliot bobbing beside him. He saw only the same bark that had been anchored there all week. As for the horizon: no sails. Seeing no other choice, he gave orders for the two barks—now the entirety of his fleet—to set sail for Trinidad.

5

ALL THAT GLISTERS

On January 31, 1595—four weeks before Ralegh left the Canary Islands—a dark line materialized on the horizon ahead of Robyn Dudley's westbound ships. As they drew closer, the line grew wavy, like a sea serpent—which could hardly be ruled out, given the run Dudley and company had been on. Their luck had gone from bad—the difficulties departing London—to worse, with lost vessels and a series of failures to seize Spanish ships on the way to the Canaries, and then to horrific: the fiercest storm in nearly a century while they were on their way out of the islands. As they drew closer to the line, however, its hue brightened to a neon yellow-green, and its irregularities sharpened to mountain peaks and lusciously verdant valleys. The men realized that it was the answer to all their recent prayers: Trinidad.

The island seemed to welcome them as they sailed toward it, exuding moist air perfumed by a galaxy of brightly colored flowers. Its towering trees, vines, and seemingly every other variety of flora on earth were packed tightly together and collectively pulsing, throbbing, and chirping. Europe in comparison, with her sedate plains and woods, was a charcoal sketch. As the vessels neared shore, the bustle revealed itself to consist of countless birds improbably navigating the maze of shoots and boughs, most of them unlike anything the Englishmen had ever seen—for instance, the scarlet ibis, which makes the brightest flamingo look downright pasty.

As soon as they landed—on February 1, at a beachy southwestern inlet named Curiapan (today, Icacos Point)—it seemed that their luck had finally begun to turn. They were met by a group of islanders whose canoes were laden with chickens, tobacco, nuts, fruits, and vegetables they hoped to trade for beads or fishhooks. Better still, the islanders were Arawaks, the "friendly savages," according to the Spaniards, as opposed to the Caribs, hostile cannibals undeserving of Christian commiseration and fit only for enslavement or extermination. (At the time, the names "Carib" and "Cannibal" were used interchangeably.)

Dudley would later describe the Arawaks as "a fine shaped and a gentle people, all naked and painted red, the commanders wearing crowns of feathers." In addition to the paint—actually, a form of insect repellent—they had tattoos, including a stripe above their eyebrows sprouting perpendicular lines, like a comb, and, rising from each corner of their mouths, a line resembling a mustache half curled at the end, reaching to the temples. Surprisingly, the skin peeking out from beneath all the paint and ink was no darker than that of Spaniards or Italians. Far and away the Arawaks' most remarkable feature, however, was the gleaming half moons of gold hanging from each of their necks. When asked about his, one of them replied, "Calcuri"—the one Arawak word known to all the Englishmen, and the one they'd been hoping for months to hear. It meant "gold."

After finding an Arawak who could speak Spanish, a man named Balthazar, Dudley asked where the calcuri came from. A mine eight or nine miles down the coast, Balthazar said matter-of-factly, adding that he would be happy to guide the Englishmen there. Although the day was oppressively hot and they were suffering from the physical deterioration attendant to months of confinement in a ship, they told him there was no time like the present.

Dudley, who one sailor noted was "unaccustomed, God knows, to walking on foot," impressed his men by leading the arduous march, for the most part through deep sand. The men were even more impressed by the mine, in which gold sparkled everywhere, like a starry night. Each delirious Englishman gathered as much of the ore as he could. They would still have to leave tons behind, but that fell into the category of desirable problems.

Moved to officially claim the island for England, Dudley ordered his smith to forge a lead plaque inscribed with the queen's coat of arms and the message *Robertus Duddeleius, Anglus, filius illustrissimi Comitis Leicestrencis*—Robert Dudley, Englishman, son of the illustrious Earl of Leicester. Next, at the head of a triumphal procession that included trumpeters and drummers, Dudley held up the plaque, wrapped for the occasion in a white silk scarf fringed with silver lace, then affixed it to a tree by the mine's entrance while his men cried out, "God save our Queen Elizabeth."

Trinidad, however, had been discovered by Christopher Columbus (to the extent that an already inhabited island can be credited as a discovery) during a Spanish-sponsored expedition in 1498. As far as the Spaniards were concerned, the island remained under their control, and any Johnny-come-latelies who had a problem with that could speak to the Spanish soldiers in the garrison at San José de Oruña (today, St. Joseph), just a few miles inland. Dudley had had every intention of sacking the San José garrison, enabling him to secure the island and leave his ships behind while he went off to explore the continent. But he hesitated now for two reasons. First, he was hearing that there were as many as three hundred Spanish soldiers in San José, too great a force for his to engage absent the *Lion's Whelp* crew. Second, it no longer made sense for him to explore the continent on this expedition: as soon as Queen Elizabeth laid eyes on all the gold he'd found, she would send the entire Royal Navy to take Trinidad, allowing him to go to South America and search for El Dorado at his leisure. He decided instead to return to his ships the following morning and weigh anchor for England, meaning he just needed to keep the gold out of the Spaniards' hands overnight.

That evening, he and his men made camp at Curiapan—which he renamed Pelicans Bay, because, of all things, as he recorded, "it was very full of pelicans." Almost immediately after they'd gone to sleep, there was trouble: what appeared to their sentinel to be forty to sixty lit matches, held at eye level, emerging from the jungle. Advancing Spanish soldiers, he feared. Creeping closer for a better view, he ruled out soldiers. The matches were disembodied. He realized, to his horror, that they were held by ghosts.

In his place, most of his comrades would probably have arrived at the same conclusion; at the time, the existence of supernatural entities such as fairies and elves was almost as widely accepted as that of dogs and cats. More than merely believing in witches, Europeans had tried, convicted, and burned more than two hundred thousand of them over the past three centuries. In 1595, King James VI of Scotland, soon to succeed Queen Elizabeth on the English throne, was twenty-eight years into a reign devoted in large part to hunting such "detestable slaves of the Devil," as he termed them in *Daemonologie,* his exhaustive book about ghosts, wizards, spirits, demons, werewolves, and, mainly, witches and the scourge of witchcraft. More than six thousand of his eight hundred thousand subjects in Scotland were tried as witches, with as many as four thousand executed. At that rate, were James ruling the modern United States, 2.5 million witches would be tried with 1.6 million put to death.

The Dudley expedition had faced witches too. Or, possibly, sea devils. The men weren't sure which, though they were sure that one or the other was responsible for the storm that hit them on their way out of the Canaries. Accordingly, in Pelicans Bay now, the sentinel raised the alarm. Rallying to defend themselves and their gold, however, Dudley and company discovered that the camp was surrounded by neither ghosts nor witches but rather fireflies.

In the morning, the gold was still there, but there was a problem with it. Having conducted an acid test, Dudley's assayer reported that it was marcasite, a fool's gold similar to pyrite, and worth even less. There was no point in even loading it onto the ships. In his 1600 memoir, Dudley would quip, "All is not gold that glistereth," an expression that had been immortalized in 1598 with the production of *The Merchant of Venice*. In 1595, he was less blithe, but, as ever, he was resilient. He asked Balthazar about the softer, somewhat yellower, and more valuable sort of calcuri. The Arawak said he knew all about that calcuri: it came from a "much to be esteemed" mine in Orocoa, he said, two hundred miles south in the Orinoco River Delta.

If Balthazar expected the Englishman to jump for joy, he was disappointed. Dudley was aware of what amounted to the local tradition of waxing about distant gold mines as a means of getting rid of persecutors, a designation for which his men qualified. What exactly they did in Trinidad is lost to time—theft, rape, and sadism were standards on such expeditions—but Acting Secretary of State Robert Cecil would be incensed when he learned of it, necessitating a formal apology from Dudley. Because the treacherous and labyrinthine Orinoco Delta—16,852 inundated square miles, each practically identical to the next—was one of the best places on the planet to send persecutors one hoped never to see again, Dudley was circumspect. That is, until Balthazar offered to guide him and his men to the gold mine himself, on pain of death if he failed.

6

A CANOEFUL OF GOLD

On March 7, 1595, two weeks after Robert Dudley decided to go to Orocoa, Walter Ralegh was eight days into the 3,100-mile voyage to Trinidad, sailing at a brisk 140 miles a day, three times the average transatlantic pace. But it didn't seem brisk. Thinking about the race with Dudley—or the other race, with the rainy season—could turn a second into an eon. And if he tried not to think about it, he was likely to find himself puzzling over the fates of Keymis and the other missing captains and crews. Not exactly a diversion.

Nor was the scenery: water and sky, day after day. The shipboard routine, similarly, rarely changed: the crew was divided in half by two-to-four-hour "watches," with one watch sleeping while the other contended both with decks that required no end of scrubbing and scraping and with cumbersome sails perpetually in need of setting, reefing, furling, unfurling, striking, drying, and mending. Sleep offered a refuge, but one often thwarted by the activity and elements topside and, belowdecks, by the foul stench resulting from the pissdales (basins that served as urinals), the bilge, the rats, the rats' excrement, the dead rats, and the hundred sweaty men who typically went months without bathing. Further, it was always clammy down there; no matter the quality of the caulking, the planks in the overhead decking were never truly watertight. Seawater leaked in through the scuppers (drains on the deck) even in good weather; in bad, it poured in, permeating the oakum and seams, which never quite dried. Clothes, too, stayed wet for days on end, meaning that when it was cold, there was no getting warm. For most of the men, therefore, the refuge of sleep required dangling in the lower deck's putrid, inky darkness on a sopping too-narrow hammock—at best. Otherwise, their beds were deck boards or atop cargo or wherever they could find space. Officers benefited from large, airy quarters and mattresses; Ralegh's cabin was as spacious as most bedrooms on land, adorned with art and furniture upholstered in green silk, including a plump bed with gilt dolphins for legs. Still, in bed, he might roll over onto a drowned rat or, worse, a live one.

For the third of the crewmen who were literate, books could blunt the shipboard tedium—Ralegh himself always traveled with a fresh crateful. So could songs and chanteys; music was to morale as wind was to sails. Fiddlers, drummers, pipers, and trumpeters were ubiquitous at sea, and prized. There's no mention of music in Ralegh and company's accounts of the voyage, but food was never mentioned either, and presumably they had that too—and it was terrible: salted meat and biscuits, the latter weevil-free some of the time, and almost always hard enough for use as a bludgeon.

Ralegh at least had the option of good dinner companions, including several of his fellow gentlemen adventurers as well as many of his kinsmen, including his nephew, John Gilbert, and cousins John Grenville and Budockshed "Butshead" Gorges. He also enjoyed the company of a harder element, the men with whom he'd collaborated on privateering ventures over the years, like Jacob Whiddon, a fellow Devonian whom he considered his "most valiant and honest" officer. The thirty-five-year-old Whiddon didn't mind getting his hands dirty, allowing him to compile an extensive privateering résumé including command of the ship that captured Pedro Sarmiento de Gamboa in 1584. It was also Whiddon whom Ralegh had trusted with the critical mission to reconnoiter Trinidad in 1593.

One other notable member of that briny cadre was Robert Calfield, a thirty-seven-year-old infantryman turned privateer captain who'd been instrumental in the capture of the *Madre de Dios* as well as the mayhem once she was brought into Dartmouth, in September 1592, when her valuable cargo began to dwindle at the hands of drunken crewmen happy to trade a chunk of ambergris to local tavern owners for another tankard of ale. Calfield and his unruly mates snuck into the ship's cargo holds to help themselves to plunder so often that their candles started five different fires. And no one had been able to control them, not even their commander, the venerable Martin Frobisher, widely admired for his repeated attempts to find the Northwest Passage. No one, that is, except the man whose imprisonment had necessitated Frobisher's hire: Walter Ralegh. Things were so bad in Dartmouth that Robert Cecil urged Queen Elizabeth to temporarily release his rival from the Tower of London, and although she'd only recently imprisoned him, she acquiesced. Upon Ralegh's arrival at the port, Cecil marveled, "All the mariners came to him with such shouts of joy as I never saw"—and, immediately, the chaos was transformed into the richest prize in English history.

When he had the opportunity to spend time with these men, Ralegh left behind the ostentation and arrogance with which he armored himself at court, allowing him to enjoy a camaraderie born of years of shared struggles and triumphs, of having shed blood together, and of a willingness to die for one another. While none of these hardened privateers would have dared characterize their feelings for one another as love—much less discuss their feelings—that's what it was, and it gave them an appreciation for the monotony and the stale biscuits.

That said, brothers fought and familiarity bred contempt, more readily on ships than on land because of the confines and the unrelenting time together, which could give undue prominence to something as picayune as the way a man cleared his throat. Over the course of a transatlantic crossing, that *ahem* could irritate a shipmate to the point he considered the sole remedy to be heaving the offender overboard. Even before departing England, Captain John Burgh—second-in-command of the expedition that netted the *Madre de Dios*—regarded a duel as the solution to what he thought of as John Gilbert's childish excuses. The contest did in fact provide relief, though not in the way Burgh had hoped: Gilbert accepted the challenge, chose rapiers, and killed him.

Little wonder that during Atlantic crossings the daily ration for each man typically exceeded a gallon of beer or a pint of rum, notwithstanding the fact that such liberal quantities tended only to make matters worse.

Back on Trinidad, despite a good hundred Arawaks having corroborated Balthazar's claims of the wealth of Orocoa, Robyn Dudley's men were unwilling to go there. The problem wasn't the journey through perilous jungle so much as having to take it in small open boats, a necessity since their ships couldn't manage the shallow inland waterways. Dudley eventually convinced thirteen men to accompany him, but only to face a new round of backlash from the rest, who refused to stay behind under the strict pilot, Abram Kendall. Perceiving that they would mutiny if anyone but he himself oversaw them, Dudley turned the leadership of the inland expedition over to his cousin, Thomas Jobson, a veteran Colchester seaman who'd served as a captain under Francis Drake.

At dawn on Saturday, February 22, 1595, Jobson departed Trinidad with twelve or thirteen men in a small boat, sailing the eight miles west to the continent and then another hundred down its coast into the Orinoco Delta, where myriad Orinoco River distributaries fan out into a forty-mile-wide confluence with the Atlantic. Balthazar directed the party onto one of the smaller waterways, which was like a corridor through the rainforest, and a world removed from anything Jobson and his men had ever experienced. Wherever they looked they found rich, robust abundance: fish, fowls, and, of course, the verdure. Even the disagreeable insects—lantern flies bigger than hummingbirds and locusts bigger than most birds—spoke to a preternatural plenitude. It was almost inconceivable that this magnificently fertile land wasn't coursing with veins of gold.

The Englishmen were astonished yet again during a stop at a Warao village, a cluster of simple straw houses that stood in marked contrast to the exquisitely crafted cedar canoes, some as long as fifty feet, for which the tribe was renowned (Warao means "boat people"). The residents were uncommonly diminutive, the men barely over five feet tall and the women closer to four, all with sinewy physiques on full display save for the odd loincloth or shawl. Their eyebrows were plucked bare—replaced with tattoos of curved lines, matching the designs inked at the corners of their mouths—but otherwise they were exceptionally unkempt, in both their persons and their homes, perhaps the source of the Arawak expression "as dirty as a Warao." Many were also afflicted with boils and sores resulting from chigoe fleas that flourished in the mire beneath the village. The insects' predilection for burrowing into human feet and buttocks to lay eggs left the villagers dappled with bluish spots the size of peas—egg capsules containing hundreds of eggs—and gruesome ulcers where larvae had already emerged.

What astonished Jobson and company, however, wasn't anything they saw but rather the question posed to them by the village's chieftain: *Would you like a canoeful of gold?* If so, he added, he would have someone row to the gold mine in Orocoa, fifty miles upriver. The Englishmen didn't need to deliberate over the offer.

The chieftain's canoe returned later bearing nothing, however, except a message from his opposite number in Orocoa, whose name was Armago. If the visitors wanted gold, Armago had said, they should come themselves. In the scheme of things, Jobson had no reason not to go. It would be respectful, possibly even the foundation for a trade partnership. He and his men returned to their boats, with Balthazar guiding them.

At the appointed meeting spot, a riverbank outside Orocoa's village, Armago arrived with a hundred men in canoes, a show of force rooted in his suspicion that the Englishmen would try to steal his gold. "By force," he warned them, they would have "nothing but blows." But if they returned with hatchets, knives, and Jew's harps, he said, he would happily open a gold mine to them. Gold was so prevalent in the region that men routinely sprinkled their bodies with gold dust, he added. And that was nothing compared to the "great town called El Dorado" farther inland.

Armago's claims seemed too pat, especially his use of the Spanish name for the great town, and Jobson's mistrust was fired. As though sensing as much, the chieftain gave him a sample, three or four half moons, each wrought in pure gold and weighing at least a quarter of an ounce. It was enough that Jobson and his companions were eager to return to Trinidad to test it. If it were in fact gold rather than marcasite, they would race back with goods to trade for more.

They hadn't gotten far on their return voyage when Balthazar inexplicably ran off, leaving them deep within a maze of lookalike rivers, tributaries, and inlets, each with more twists and curves than a large intestine, rendering compasses utterly useless. Given their dwindling supplies, Jobson and his companions knew one wrong turn could easily mean death. And even if they lucked onto the best possible route back to Trinidad, without a guide, they would be subject to predators, in particular the Caribs, who, they believed, would regard them as a feast.

They managed to retrace their path back to Orocoa, where they asked Armago for a new guide. The chieftain happily complied, but not long into their second attempt to return to Trinidad, that guide abandoned them too. By then, however, they'd figured out how to read the tidal flow in the rivers, and they were able to follow it back to the Atlantic, reaching Trinidad on March 10. During the last three days of the return journey, they'd hadn't had a drop of fresh water, on top of which they were "almost dead from famine," as Dudley recorded, and in "very pitiful condition."

As soon as he heard about Armago, Dudley was ready to load up the boats with hatchets, knives, and Jew's harps. But his men steadfastly refused to go back to the Delta, this despite it being within the rights of his commission to hang them if they didn't. Having had time to mull it over, their mistrust of Amargo was too great. The result of the acid test was irrelevant; of course the chieftain would use actual gold to bait them back. And once they'd brought the goods he wanted, they could expect to be riddled with arrows.

Dudley was convinced. To fully exploit Guiana, he realized, he would need to return with ample personnel. Toward that end, he weighed anchor for England.

7
OYSTER TREES

IN 1492, THE *Niña, Pinta,* and *Santa María* covered the thirty-seven hundred miles from the Canary Islands to the Bahamas in thirty-six days (not including a twenty-seven-day stretch that the fleet spent on Gran Canaria while repairing the *Pinta*'s rudder), which was relatively rapid. A century later, despite significant advances in navigation and sturdier rudders, transatlantic crossings still averaged a good three months. By reaching Trinidad on Sunday, March 22, 1595, Walter Ralegh completed the crossing in just twenty-two days, an auspicious start to the expedition if not a record. On his order, anchor chains rattled from the ships, and thousands of pounds of steel struck Pelicans Bay with the resounding boom that was the exclamation point at the end of a journey.

He allowed his men time to recuperate from the voyage. Never big on rest himself, however, he began plotting an attack of the Spanish garrison in San José de Oruña, and, on March 27, the company's fifth day in Trinidad, he took to his small barge accompanied by veteran privateer Jacob Whiddon and a handful of others to gather intelligence from the island's Indigenous peoples. Oddly, none of the islanders had come to greet the ships at Pelicans Bay. In the Caribbean, typically, Natives raced to greet Europeans in order to trade for

Niña, Pinta, and *Santa María*

fishhooks, hatchets, and so forth. And here, Ralegh had had reason to think, he and his men would be treated to an especially spirited welcome: during his reconnaissance voyage in 1593, Whiddon had made a friend of Cantyman, one of the island's most influential chieftains, who said that all of Trinidad's tribes prayed for the day the English would come and liberate them from their Spanish oppressors.

Ralegh sailed the barge up the island's western coast, landing and then hiking inland at Puerto de los Hispanioles (now Port of Spain,

Trinidad's capital city), where, having boned up on the local tribes, he expected that he and his companions would find plenty of Carinepagotos. But even at the most popular watering places, there was no one. At least as far as he and his companions knew—perhaps the islanders were following them the whole time, concealed by the rainforest. Between all the chirping and bleating and the veritable cliff walls of foliage, the Englishmen might have been none the wiser had a marching band been tailing them.

It wasn't until the fifth night of their barge tour that they saw evidence of human life: a bonfire on shore. Even better, Natives were gathered around it. As soon as the Natives spotted the barge, however, they bolted into the woods, effectively vanishing. Which mystified Ralegh and his companions. Could the islanders' reticence now be rooted in mistreatment by Dudley's men?

The barge tour continued into a second week without another Native sighting, not even at the port of Parico (modern Cedros, seventy miles down Trinidad's western coast from Puerto de los Hispanioles). Little more than a year earlier, related an incredulous Whiddon, this place had been "a seat of Indians."

From Parico, the party sailed twenty miles north to an especially barren coastal area known as Piche, where the Iaio people lived by a lake of "pitch," a naturally occurring tar English seafarers used to protect their hulls from shipworms and rot, so much so that they were known the world over as "Jack Tars," or just "Tars." At one time the English had made their own pitch, boiling the sap out of pine trees, but they quickly depleted their forests, forcing them to buy it from other countries. By 1595, they were paying £3 per twenty-eight-gallon barrel; the two hundred gallons required for a single ship cost more than a skilled tradesman earned in an entire year. It stood to reason that the Iaio would never leave such a valuable commodity unattended.

While landing, Ralegh's companions were astonished by "oyster trees" along the shore: mangroves that appeared to sprout the prized mollusks by the hundreds. Ralegh himself already knew about such trees, having read about them in explorer André Thevet's account of his experiences in France Antarctique, a settlement in modern Rio de Janeiro. Pliny the Elder had also written about oyster trees in *The Natural History, Volume XII,* Ralegh recalled. (Later Ralegh and his men would discover that the oysters actually originated in the sea, attached themselves to tree branches during high tide when the trees were submerged, then remained on the branches after the water fell.)

The lake itself was equally amazing, a mile and a half around and brimming with high-quality tar, more of it than the entire Royal Navy could use in a thousand years. Known today as Pitch Lake, it is the largest of five such natural asphalt deposits on earth, and Ralegh is universally credited for its discovery, though Dudley had already been there, and of course the Iaio lived there. Usually. On that day, disturbingly, the Iaio village was deserted, its residents having missed an opportunity to trade their tar for enough fishhooks and hatchets for a lifetime. Between the pitch lake and the oyster trees, the New World had suddenly redefined "possible." A lake full of gold was hardly a stretch. But Ralegh's plan of finding gold was predicated on collaboration with the Natives. Where were they?

On April 4, thirteen days into the barge tour, he still had no idea. That stood to change, though, when a small group of Spanish soldiers at Puerto de los Hispanioles waved down the barge, offering a sign of peace. They were a detachment from the San José de Oruña garrison assigned to guard the port, they said, and eager "to enter into terms of peace." A fantastic development, Ralegh thought. The Spaniards would only seek a suspension of hostilities if they doubted their ability to match up to his force, 120 men at present. Accordingly, he decided to attack their garrison as soon as possible—before Spanish

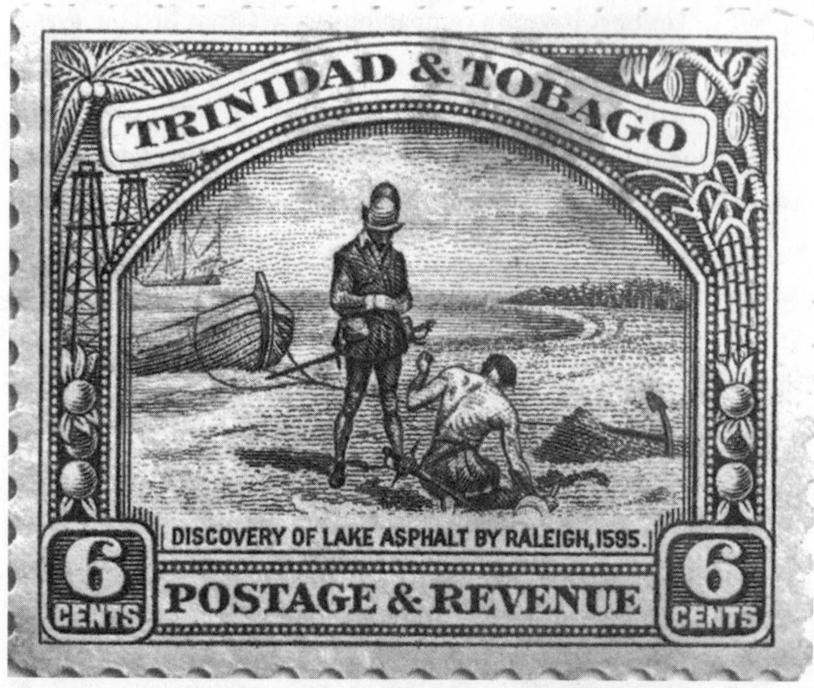

reinforcements could arrive from the Caribbean island of Margarita, 140 miles west.

First, though, information being the better part of his valor, he invited the Spaniards to the *Bark Ralegh*. Nine came aboard, including Governor Antonio de Berrío's nephew, Roderigo de la Hoz, bearing gifts of fowl, venison, and local fruits. Ralegh served a feast and, hearing that his guests had been unable to get wine to the island lately, let his casks flow. As he would record, "a few draughts made them merry," and soon, as he'd hoped, they were telling tales of their El Dorado quest.

Feigning only mild interest in the golden city—he'd claimed to have been en route to relieve his Virginia colonists when extreme weather drove him to Trinidad—he asked whether there was really anything to that old story. Absolutely, the Spaniards said, going on to

Antonio de Berrío

crow about Manoa's vast riches and the determination and masterful detective work of their governor, Antonio de Berrío, who was now poised to lead them into the golden city.

Ralegh was pleased to learn there was no truth to the rumor that Berrío had died. In 1593, when Whiddon and his privateers had anchored off Trinidad, Berrío invited them to come ashore and reprovision, giving them his word that they would be safe. But when they landed, his soldiers ambushed them, killing eight. Ralegh could now look forward to avenging those men, starting with the governor himself.

He reconsidered, though, as his intoxicated guests went on to detail "the ways and passages" through Guiana to El Dorado. An inconsequential detail he'd heard years earlier suddenly became very consequential: a Spanish captive's story of meeting Berrío's maestre del campo—or, camp master—who'd just come from Guiana with forty plates of pure gold, Guianan swords decked and inlaid with gold, and gold-coated feathers, among other such valuables that Berrío would be sending to King Philip. Given Berrío's singular knowledge of the area, Ralegh realized, he could be of far greater value alive than dead, possibly even as a partner in an expedition.

Ralegh dashed off a letter to him. "I have arrived at this port with much desire to see you and to discuss with you my affairs, or service to His Majesty King Philip," he wrote, adding, "I beg you on no account to refuse this visit." So that Berrío would trust that his intentions were peaceful, Ralegh enclosed a gold ring, a token of friendship, along with effigies of the Virgin Mary and Saint Francis, evidence of his Catholic concord.

No sooner had the Spanish soldiers gone and the letter been dispatched than Whiddon's Trinidadian friend Cantyman arrived at the *Bark Ralegh* along with a second prominent chieftain, both bent on convincing Ralegh to kill Berrío and destroy the town he'd founded, San José. They had to use the cover of darkness to canoe out from the island, they told Ralegh, as Berrío had made it known that any Native who spoke to the Englishmen would be hanged and quartered—divided into quarters while still alive, either by a sword or by four galloping horses each tied to one of the victim's four limbs. Already, two of their people had been executed in that fashion, the chieftains added. On behalf of all of Trinidad's tribes, they beseeched Ralegh to avenge them.

Perhaps detecting his reticence, they appealed to his sense of justice with a catalog of Berrío's abuses. It was nothing Ralegh hadn't heard before—enslavement, rape, theft, ransacking hallowed ancestral graves for gold and silver—until they arrived at Berrío's signature persecution, which he'd recently inflicted on Trinidad's five other chieftains: after imprisoning Natives, the Spaniard would have them stripped, chained together, and starved, all to maximize their suffering a few days later when he prepared the meat before them, the tender strips emitting a pleasant hiss as they were laid on the hot grill, crackling with increasing intensity as they crisped, and popping here and there as they threw off bits of fat. Meanwhile, the savory smoke wafted across the confinement, tantalizing the captives. When the bacon reached the perfect golden-brown, however, Berrío didn't let them eat it. Instead, he dropped the still-sizzling strips onto their bare flesh, scalding them. The hot oil adhered the meat to their skin, and their chains forestalled their efforts to cast it off.

Vengeance was in order after all, Ralegh decided, on top of which it would make a bold statement that England was the Natives' friend and ally. Adding in the security he would gain for his ships by taking control of the island, the benefits outweighed Berrío's intelligence value. The same night, with a hundred soldiers in tow, he set upon the Spaniards guarding Puerto de los Hispanioles, several of whom he'd just entertained aboard his ship. This time, once his force overwhelmed their post, he "put them to the sword," as he would record. In an era when "sanctity" and "human life" seldom found their way into the same sentence, killing sentinels was considered the best means of preventing them from warning of an attack.

Meanwhile, Robert Calfield, who'd ranked as a lieutenant colonel in the infantry, led sixty of the English troops to San José de Oruña, seven miles east. The three-year-old town—consisting of a few dozen homes, a church, a Franciscan convent, and the garrison—was nestled at the base of Trinidad's Northern Range, affording it the natural protection of the eighteen-hundred-foot Mount Tabor to one side

Ralegh moves on San José de Aruña

and the potent San José River to the other. Thanks to Cantyman, Calfield and his sixty troops knew of what amounted to a back door to the town, on its outskirts. Soon joining them there with the other forty men, Ralegh decided to postpone the attack until daybreak, when most of the soldiers in the garrison would still be asleep, and there would be just enough darkness remaining to veil his company's advance—yet enough light for the Englishmen to see what they were shooting at.

A few hours later, as the sun peeked out from behind the Northern Range, they launched themselves toward the garrison. The only details of the ensuing confrontation are Ralegh's. The Spaniards, he wrote, "abode not any fight after a few shot" and surrendered. A mistake, at least in hindsight, because most of them were quickly, as he put it, "dismissed," which, based on post-incident reports by Spanish colonial officials, was another way of saying "put to the sword." The same reports had the Spanish death toll at seventeen, with sixteen of the soldiers escaping to Margarita. Ralegh also took two prisoners, Antonio de Berrío and Alvaro Jorge, a Portuguese lieutenant who'd begun his military career more than fifty years earlier, serving under prominent conquistador Hernán Pérez de Quesada before becoming Berrío's longtime right-hand man.

The sun rose soon after, revealing San José's uniquely beautiful setting, a backdrop of mountains clad in forest so dense and vivid that they appeared to be draped in green velvet. And the town itself was something of a paradise, especially its gardens, with richer and more fertile soil than anywhere else on the island yielding uncommonly robust papaya, watermelon, and sugarcane. But any thought Ralegh had of sparing San José was dispelled by the sight of the five chieftains who'd been subjected to Berrío's bacon torture; still

Ralegh liberates the five Trinidadian chieftains

chained together, they were "almost dead of famine," as he recorded, "and wasted with torments." San José became a uniquely beautiful setting for a fire.

Afterward, Ralegh assembled all the island's chieftains, showed them a portrait of Queen Elizabeth, and told them she was "a great cacique [chieftain] of the north" who had sent him to *Cairi*—he used their name for Trinidad, from the Carib "place of the hummingbird." She sought to free them from the Spaniards, he added, and defend them from further tyranny and oppression.

A Spanish spy would report that Ralegh "handled these caciques with great courtesy and gentleness, contrary to their expectation, at the same time setting them free and giving them . . . the best treatment and reception possible," and he won them over to the point that they had no idea how they could ever repay him. As it happened, he had something in mind: help finding El Dorado. And he was ready to get underway: although the four ships under Amyas Preston were still no-shows, both Gifford's *Lion's Whelp* and Keymis's galliot had landed at Puerto de los Hispanioles that day (the former having been delayed in leaving England, the latter slowed by weather), giving him a total of 250 men.

The chieftains were forthcoming, but their knowledge of El Dorado was at best secondhand, as opposed to that of Ralegh's captive, Antonio de Berrío, who had all but knocked on Manoa's front gate on his most recent inland expedition. As Ralegh knew, however, it would have been a challenge to get Berrío to share any of the details on the best of days, whereas on that day, his nephew, Roderigo de la Hoz, had been killed, and the idyllic town he'd founded and named after his beloved late wife had been reduced to ashes. Nonetheless, Ralegh asked that Berrío be brought to him.

8

IF THE SNOWS OF THE ANDES TURNED TO GOLD

Antonio de Berrío was not in high spirits, unsurprisingly, when English soldiers brought him before Walter Ralegh—presumably in the *Bark Ralegh*'s great cabin, the windowed dining and meeting room atop the stern. But melancholy may have been the Spaniard's default setting rather than a consequence of recent events: while his officer's bearing remained intact—he stood tall and erect, shoulders squared, chin held high, back ruler-straight—the corners of his mouth appeared to have sagged over the course of his sixty-eight years, mirroring the contours of his droopy mustache. And then there were his eyes, fixed in a look of entreaty, as though he were silently imploring God, who'd put him through so much, to give him a break just this once.

As Ralegh had done in 1584 with Patagonia governor Pedro Sarmiento de Gamboa, he treated Berrío as an honored guest rather than a captive, inviting him to sit at the dining table and share in a feast. By way of introduction, Ralegh maintained the fiction that he'd been on his way to Virginia to provide relief to his colonists when driven off course by a storm—which he now regarded as a stroke of good fortune—aside from the unfortunate hostilities attendant to their nations' animosity, of course—because it had afforded him the opportunity to meet the illustrious Antonio de Berrío and hear firsthand about his adventures.

The flattery didn't necessarily warm the Spaniard, but it opened him to sharing a story or two, leading Ralegh to conclude that he was in the presence of "a gentleman of great assuredness and of a great heart." Over the next few days, while Ralegh's men felled a swath of forest and began constructing a fort at Pelicans Bay, he continued meeting with Berrío, and each adventurer began to see something of himself in the other, such that a friendship blossomed—at least in Ralegh's telling. A Spanish official would offer a much different version of the Berrío-Ralegh tête-à-tête, reporting that the Englishman threatened to "deliver up . . . Berrío to the Indians to be slain by bowshot, and [Berrío's lieutenant] Alvaro Jorge to be hanged, if they did not declare the way to [El Dorado]."

By both accounts, though, Ralegh did eventually steer the discussion toward El Dorado, and he learned that his captive had married into the quest. A soldier from a family of them, Berrío had served Spain with distinction in the Italian wars of the 1550s and in the Spanish effort against the Barbary corsairs a decade later, along the way winning the hand of María de Oruña, a niece of conquistador Gonzalo Jiménez de Quesada, the founder of Bogotá who had devoted much of his life to finding El Dorado.

When Quesada died in 1579, he left Berrío his fortune along with the exploration rights he'd been granted by King Philip II. Typically, such a grant extended not only to the recipient but also to an heir of his choosing, so long as the heir agreed to its terms—namely, that the king received a fifth of the gross proceeds of anything valuable obtained, such as precious metals, gems, and slaves, or, if the items came from a tomb, half. Quesada's bequest was unusual in that, to claim so much as a peso, Berrío had to commit to continuing the El Dorado quest. Fifty-two at that time, Berrío had settled into the governorship of the Alpujarra, a cluster of villages on the breathtaking southern slopes of Spain's snowcapped Sierra Nevadas, where he, María, and their seven children were happily rooted. He uprooted them, moving everyone to Bogotá to organize his El Dorado expedition.

As a next step, it was critical for him—as it would now be for Ralegh—to learn from both the successes and the failures of previous expeditions, and then weave seemingly innocuous details from those efforts into actionable intelligence. The first case worth studying was the very first expedition, in 1529, led by Ambrosius Dalfinger, a twenty-nine-year-old German who came to Coro (on northwestern Venezuela's Caribbean coast) to govern the colony Spain had licensed to the Welser family, powerful merchant bankers from Augsburg. Hearing local lore of a gold-rich city somewhere in the continent's interior, Dalfinger convened two hundred Spaniards with wildly disparate backgrounds—aristocrats, peasants, artisans, soldiers—all willing to go without pay and risk their lives for a share of the Natives' wealth that his grant of governorship permitted him to plunder. Some were simply seeking adventure. Most were of the ilk—the lesser aristocrat's second son, the failed artisan—whose desperation might have just as easily nudged them onto a pirate ship. "[Conquistadors] are the sort of men who have no intention of converting the Indians [to Christianity] or of settling and remaining in this land," wrote Gonzalo Fernández Oviedo y Valdés, a conquistador himself before becoming one of the era's foremost historians. "They come only until they get some gold or wealth in whatever form they can obtain it. They subordinate honour, morality and honesty to this end, and apply themselves to any fraud or homicide and commit innumerable crimes."

Assisted by several hundred "porters"—the Natives shackled at the neck until their failure to keep pace resulted in their decapitation—the Dalfinger expedition headed west, coming to village after town where they received gold as a "tribute"—really, an attempt to forestall the bloodbath, rape, and enslavement that had become conquistador staples. In Colombia, the Cindahuas people gave Dalfinger nine pounds of fine gold, worth £360, enough at the time to buy seventy-five horses. Over the next two years, he accumulated more and more gold, but his progress was slowed by the deaths of most of his troops—from fever, mosquito-borne illnesses, and starvation—and then ended by a poisoned arrow to the neck, giving him the distinction of being the first in a long line of El Dorado seekers killed by Natives.

On the Atlantic side of the continent, meanwhile, fifty-one-year-old conquistador Diego de Ordáz appeared to have found a more providencial path. As a captain in Hernán Cortés's conquest of Mexico, Ordáz had achieved great wealth and influence, but he longed for Cortés's fame, and he thought he could achieve it along the populous Orinoco River, which flows fourteen hundred miles, mostly across Venezuela, from the Sierra Parima Mountains to the Atlantic. Yes, the area was a steamy, unnavigable, lethal morass. That was to its credit, Ordáz believed, because, as a Spanish theologian put it, "A father with an ugly daughter gives her a large dowry . . . and this is what God did with that difficult land, giving it much wealth in mines so . . . he would find someone who wanted it."

Ordáz's conviction was validated by local tales of a kingdom at the base of a mountain near the Orinoco's confluence with the Meta River—in eastern Colombia, some five hundred miles west. The inhabitants wore clothes, Ordáz was told, and rode from one gold-drenched establishment to another on llamas. In his ensuing attempt to find them, in 1531, he battled waterfalls, Natives, hunger, and disease that combined to claim the lives of most of his 280 men, but as was often the case in the conquest of the Americas, the aforementioned difficulties were mere trifles compared to rival conquistadors. When one of them claimed Ordáz and company were encroaching on his allotted territory—and fired cannons to repel them—Ordáz saw no choice but to pack up and sail to Spain to plead his case to the Council of Indies. He died en route, in 1532, likely having been poisoned by one of his rival's agents.

Ordáz's quest was then embraced by his lieutenant, Alonso de Herrera, whose exploration of the Meta in 1535 was plagued by the usual deprivations and disease as well as vampire bats, which, as their name would suggest, swoop onto a prospective victim, then typically pierce his neck with stiletto-like incisors before chewing away a flap of flesh and drinking his blood. Still Herrera made progress, encountering increasingly splendid cities until, when it seemed he might find people riding llamas around the next corner, he was struck by five or six poisoned arrows, one of them running through his mouth. During the six days that followed, he began to rave and bite his hands, for no reason apparent to his men, whose desperate efforts to find an antidote were ultimately in vain. Yet his death wasn't for naught, they believed: the savages wouldn't have been trying to repel him from nothing. Surely, El Dorado was nigh.

Thinking along the same lines, at least five potent expeditionary forces swarmed into the region over the next three years, most famously the four hundred soldiers under the command of intrepid German knight Georg Hohermuth, also known as Georg von Speyer. His was a force out of a Hieronymus Bosch painting: big, bearded men with plumed helmets, damask breeches, and thigh-high leather boots, many of them riding mighty warhorses and everyone bristling with gleaming shields and weapons, including lightweight Toledan steel swords and potent battle maces, with the whole lot preceded

Poisoned arrows

by musicians playing trumpets and tambourines. In short, absurdly inappropriate for the New World. Soon, all but fifty of them were dead—of fever, illness, starvation, and poisoned arrows—an attrition rate that was typical of the new expeditions.

After "suffering as much misery and privation . . . as any Christians had ever previously suffered," wrote one participant, the five companies limped out of the wilds decimated and destitute. Yet they'd found just enough—a golden statuette, a temple, a compelling witness—to substantiate the stories they'd heard of a local priest-king who smeared his body with turpentine, layered on gold dust, and, "thus golden and resplendent," paddled a raft onto a great lagoon, accompanied by "music and songs of the immense multitude of people who covered the slopes that surrounded the lagoon." It didn't seem at all far-fetched. Lake worshippers all over the continent were known to anoint themselves with turpentine or turtle fat and then adhere sparkly flecks of mica. Only one question remained: where was the golden man?

In 1541, taking "the slopes that surrounded the lagoon" to mean that the lagoon sat by a mountain, Gonzalo Pizarro led 340 Spaniards and 4,000 Native attendants down Ecuador's Coca River to Sumaco. Having served in the conquest of Peru under his older half brother Francisco Pizarro and then governed there for a decade, Gonzalo, now thirty-one, was as seasoned as any conquistador ever to seek El Dorado. And as notorious, both for handing out death sentences to Incas for even a whisper of dissent and for the rape of their queen, Cura Ocllo.

The Sumacans, Gonzalo was certain, knew the way to El Dorado, yet they told him they'd never heard of it. So he tortured them, and when that failed to elicit information, he had several of them torn apart by dogs. The rest he bound to the top of platforms resembling giant grills and left them to roast over a fire until they told the truth. These tactics eventually netted him confirmation that he was going the right way and should continue.

As he did, the tribes he encountered, having heard about his treatment of the Sumacans, gave him the same directions, leading to an expedition as arduous as any in history, with his Native "guides" forced to hack paths through unending dark, rainy, snake-intensive clots of forest, the sort that dulled machete blades and debilitated muscles twenty minutes into a twelve-hour slog. Soon the guides had all either fled or died, leaving the conquistadors to fend for themselves. Procuring the most basic sustenance was a problem: the Spaniards were forced to eat their horses, then their saddles, and then their dead. And as they attempted to advance, according to an observer, "the thorns and matted underwood of the dense forests (which they had to cut by blows of their axes) cruelly tore them, and made them look as if they had been flayed." Meanwhile, their shoes and clothing disintegrated. After what amounted to a two-year golden-goose chase, a defeated Pizarro was one of the eighty naked and skeletal survivors dragging themselves out of the jungle. Remarked another observer, "It seemed as if a charnel-house had given up its dead."

The good news, thought conquistadors eager to take the baton, was that Pizarro had systematically ruled out much of the western half of the continent. Among that next wave of explorers was María de Berrío's uncle, Gonzalo Jiménez de Quesada, a lawyer who'd become a conquistador in 1536 when he marched out of Santa Marta (in northern Colombia) with five hundred to eight hundred men. At each town he came upon, Quesada insisted on "giving good treatment to the Indians." That is, unless they refused to cooperate after they'd been read *El Requierimento,* Spain's official four-hundred-word demand that they submit at once to Spanish authority, per God's will. Most of the time, *El Requierimento* was accepted. When it wasn't, in Tunja, eighty miles northeast of Bogotá—possibly because the Chibha-speaking Muisca chieftain didn't understand Spanish—Quesada administered the penalty the document had laid out: "With the help of God, we . . . shall make war against you in all ways and manners that we can." (To indemnify themselves against prosecution, the Spaniards had added that "the deaths and losses which shall accrue from this are your fault.") The spoils were 1,925 pounds of fine gold, worth £77,000, enough to build three of King Henry VIII's unsurpassed Nonsuch Palaces.

But it wasn't enough for Quesada. As Incan leader Manco Inca said of the conquistadors, "Even if the snows of the Andes turned to

Nonsuch Palace

gold, still they would not be satisfied." Hearing of *el hombre dorado,* Quesada decided to continue ahead and find the golden city, the rainy season be damned. According to one of his men, flooding forced them "to advance like fish through the water by day and climb into trees to sleep at night." All the while they were ravaged by jaguars, black flies, ticks, and cattle worms that bored into their skin, creating red pus-filled lumps the size of golf balls that were risks to disseminate bacterial infection through the bloodstream. The result was as many deaths as on any expedition in the history of New World exploration.

Yet Quesada continued to pursue El Dorado for nearly four decades, until 1572, when, at sixty-three, he staggered out of Guiana following a three-year expedition on which he'd lost another three hundred men and eleven hundred horses, contracted leprosy, and provided the basis for the title character of Miguel de Cervantes's *Don Quixote*, published in 1605. Nevertheless, he took action to ensure the perpetuation of his enterprise by bequeathing Antonio de Berrío of his governorship, exploration license, and steady revenue stream of Muisca tributes. Along with his brother, Hernán Pérez de Quesada, Gonzalo Jiménez de Quesada had also added a second major clue to the El Dorado canon, a reliable Native report that a cordillera (mountain range) east of Colombia—where Diego de Ordáz had focused his search—was the backdrop for the golden man's ritual swim.

Notable among the explorers who rushed to find that cordillera was German nobleman Philipp von Hutten, a veteran of the Hohermuth expedition. In August 1541, von Hutten and a large force marched inland from Coro toward the eastern foothills of the Andes Mountains. They wandered around the continent for the better part of three years, starving to the point that their survival hinged on finding enough ants to eat. Eventually they realized they'd been going in circles, but not for nothing: when they climbed a mountain to reorient themselves, they glimpsed a city built along a grid, with one house that greatly surpassed the rest in size. According to their guides, the house belonged to a chieftain, who had numerous golden statues the size of children—and he was hardly the wealthiest chieftain in the area; others lived in an even richer town a short distance away.

Before they could investigate, the explorers found themselves under attack by the town's advance guard, with von Hutten himself taking a lance to the ribcage. He and his men lacked the numbers, he realized, to do anything other than run for their lives. Nonetheless, when he made it back to Coro, in 1545, the report of his progress dazzled everyone, especially the new governor, Juan de Carvajal. Longing to find El Dorado himself, Carvajal had von Hutten arrested on a trumped-up charge and then beheaded—slowly, with a worn machete. Carvajal's own expedition was forestalled, however, when he was found guilty of murdering von Hutten and then was executed himself, in 1546.

The conquest of the New World was put on hold from 1550 to 1559 while Spain debated its morality, ultimately deciding that the "naturally inferior savages" benefited from Spanish tutelage as well as from conversion to Christianity, both of which were easier to achieve if they were first enslaved.

Over the following decade, a slew of new El Dorado hunters followed in von Hutten's footsteps, circuitous though they were, with a combination of trial and error (mostly the latter) enabling them to pinpoint the mountainous Guiana Highlands (encompassing modern Venezuela east of the Orinoco River, west-central Guyana, and northernmost Brazil), inasmuch as an area twice the size of Texas can be pinpointed. In 1569, one of those hunters, Juan Álvarez de Maldonado, heard credible reports of a "land of gold" with "provinces inhabited by people clothed in cotton, and all having rites and ceremonies like those of the Yungas in Peru." Although he couldn't find it, he became convinced that it had been founded by Incas who'd fled eastward after Francisco Pizarro's slaughter of thousands of their higher-ups and the seizure of their emperor, Atahualpa, in the 1532 Massacre of Cajamarca (in northern Peru).

Among the explorers to take up the Incan thread was Pedro Maraver de Silva, an Andalusian who'd emigrated to Peru, where he became a wealthy businessman, married into even greater wealth, and started

The execution of Atahualpa

a family. In 1568, after learning of a people near the Orinoco River "who were so rich that all the furnishings of their houses were of gold and silver," he sailed to Spain to apply for a license to conquer them. On his ensuing expedition, which began in July 1569, he marched into the Guiana Highlands with 140 men, who, almost immediately, began to desert. Even his two trusted lieutenants absconded, along with his entire store of wine, leading to more desertions and leaving him with too small a force to resist the incessant Native attacks.

Shortly into his second expedition, in 1576, Silva was abandoned by the entirety of his force and then he died, along with his two young daughters, at the hands of Caribs. The same fate soon befell all his deserters, save a number who succumbed to disease first. Yet Silva's exploration career was not the complete tragedy it seems, at least from the standpoint of the El Dorado conquest: his decision to maroon his munitions master during his first foray allowed a European to lay eyes on Manoa for the first time—if the story of Juan Martín de Albujar is to be believed.

According to one of Albujar's contemporaries, Spanish priest and historian Juan de Castellanos, the munitions master resided in Manoa for seven years (rather than seven months, as in the retelling that reached Ralegh), during which he taught his hosts modern military techniques, led them to victories against their enemies, and was rewarded with several houses, servants, and wives. Notably absent from Castellanos's reporting is an abundance of gold: the Manoans, Albujar had told him, were "gente pobre"—poor people.

To get to the truth, Antonio de Berrío dug through the chancery in San Juan, Puerto Rico, where Albujar had reportedly died. There he found a copy of a sworn deposition of the munition master's deathbed confessor, and it led him to a revelation.

9
THE EL DORADANS

MANOA WASN'T MERELY a city the Incas had built after their flight from Peru, Berrío learned. Instead, it was their point of origin. Cusco, the grand and spectacular City of the Sun, therefore, was merely a territory they'd gone and conquered, an outpost in comparison to Manoa. As Berrío would impart to Ralegh, "For the greatness, for the riches, and for the excellent seat, [Manoa] far exceedeth any of the world, at least of so much of the world is known to the Spanish nation."

Early in 1584, after two years of preparation in Bogotá, Berrío set onto Los Llanos—the vast tropical plains east of the Andes—to find the golden city. With him were a hundred men, the majority in boats and the rest following along the banks on horseback. Straightaway, twenty of them deserted to join one of the six rival El Dorado expeditions, each sanctioned by local authorities despite the fact that Berrío had the exclusive exploration rights. He could have sued to stop the other companies, but that would have entailed returning to Bogotá to get summonses, tracking down the other expeditions to deliver the summonses, and then trusting their commanders to drop everything and come to a hearing. He decided instead to simply beat them to El Dorado.

He took the fourteen-hundred-mile-long and aptly named Río Negro, the world's largest "blackwater" river, nomenclature derived from the water's resemblance to black tea, a result of decaying leaves, vegetation, bark, and other organic matter. Of the expedition's first months, during which he and his men and horses ventured six hundred miles into Guiana, he would relate, "I crossed the plains, passing mighty rivers and swamps, through many lands peopled by Indians, who were idle and naked and unacquainted with metals." And then, after reaching the Orinoco River, "by the Grace of God and his Glorious Mother . . . I discovered the Cordillera." Not just any cordillera but the (henceforth capitalized) Cordillera, the mountain range near the border of modern Guyana and Venezuela that, as Berrío added, had been "so ardently desired and sought for seventy years past and which has cost the lives of so many Spaniards." By his reckoning, no other range fit the story of the golden man ceremony, which reportedly took place in a lake surrounded by mountains. Moreover, it was the same range in which Philipp von Hutten and his men had seen a substantial city before repulsed.

As Berrío advanced toward the Cordillera, his force too came under attack—by four thousand Native warriors. The Spaniards were outnumbered forty to one, but as it transpired, four thousand men with bows and arrows were no match for a hundred with guns and swords. After taking several of the warriors captive and questioning them, Berrío learned that if he advanced to the far side of the Cordillera, he would find a gold-rich metropolis on the shore of a seven-hundred-mile-long saltwater lake.

He started across the range, but with all his supplies and munitions, ascending even the most hospitable of the mountains was impossible. And his captives couldn't—or wouldn't—show him an alternative route. Figuring he could find a waterway that cut through the Cordillera, he continued down the Orinoco River. Along the way, disease hit, quickly reducing his force to just thirteen able men, who found themselves face-to-face with a thousand Native warriors. With thirteen guns to the Natives zero, Berrío had a chance of shooting his way past them. But then what? He would still need to make it through the Cordillera to reach the great towns, whose inhabitants were unlikely to welcome him warmly and willingly load his boats with gold.

Deciding instead to get reinforcements, he retreated to Bogotá, reaching the city in May 1585. Rather than resting after seventeen months in the wild, he jumped right into recruiting personnel for a new expedition. Convinced he was on the verge of finding El Dorado, men signed on in droves, enabling him to return to the Cordillera a few months later with an abundance of provisions, ammunition, and optimism.

Over the next three years, the company roamed the seven-hundred-mile mountain range in search of an Orinoco tributary that cut through to Manoa, but to no avail. Concluding that such a tributary would lie past the Cordillera, Berrío ordered his men to construct a fleet of canoes for a more expansive search of the Orinoco. The men resisted. Because the Orinoco branches into more than four hundred different rivers and two thousand lesser water-courses over an area of 366,000 square miles (twice the size of Spain), it was easy for them to imagine themselves slogging through the bug-infested steam bath for another three years. Berrío tried to inspire them with reminders of the "great riches" and the place in history awaiting them. He found himself speaking to their backs; they were going home. Unable to survive long without their help, he followed them.

Fortunately. Because, on his return to Bogotá, he learned that King Philip II had appointed him governor of the new Spanish province of El Dorado that encompassed most of Guiana. The position imbued him with sweeping power to dedicate state resources to research, staffing, and exploration.

On March 19, 1590, the now sixty-three-year-old Berrío returned to Guiana in command of an elite force of seventy Spanish soldiers in twenty canoes and twenty rafts. Trailing them on the banks of the Orinoco were another forty Spaniards, a party of Native guides, and 220 horses. One other notable member of the expedition was Berrío's thirteen-year-old son, Fernando. Within a year, the force had dwindled to just sixty-two Spaniards and a few horses—thirty-four of the elite troops deserted, everyone else died either from disease or from attacks by hostile Carib tribes, and all the canoes were destroyed on Orinoco rocks. Berrío had yet to find the passage through the Cordillera, and now the rainy season was upon him, forcing him and his companions into winter quarters for four months.

Hunkering down proved to be a boon: for a change, the Caribs viewed the Spaniards as trading partners, and in the course of their commerce they presented Berrío with a number of gold plates—mainly pectoral plates, worn as symbols of high lineage—and beautifully crafted golden artifacts. They also gave him the route through the Cordillera: a river known as the Caroní, which rose from the northern slopes of a mountain range known as the Sierra Pacaraima (a name derived from the sandstone peaks' resemblance to Native baskets called *pacara*) and ran seven hundred miles straight up the continent before flowing into the Orinoco. By continuing west on the Orinoco to the province of Arromaia, the Caribs assured Berrío, he could pick up the Caroní and reach Manoa in just four days.

Berrío ordered the remaining horses killed for two reasons, both to deprive his men of the opportunity to go home prior to the fulfillment of their objective, and, on a more practical level, to be salted and then eaten during what would be a long and arduous journey—if everything went well.

For once, it did. In August 1591, Berrío and his company reached Arromaia, found the mouth of the Caroní exactly where the Caribs had said it would be, and started up the river. They quickly ran into a massive impediment. Either the Caribs hadn't mentioned or hadn't known about the cataracts, now known as Salto La Llovizna, or Llovizna (Spray) Falls. Among them was a wall of water sixty-five feet high stretching from one bank of the Caroní to the other. To reach Manoa by boat, Berrío would have to go over the cataracts, which, as far as he could tell, couldn't be done. Nor could he ascend the cliffs to either side of the falls, at least not while carrying supplies and munitions. Also, the surrounding woods were thick and spiny, so dense with prickles, thorns, and briars that it would be a job to penetrate them even on flat ground.

As it happened, Berrío was lucky he didn't find a way over Llovizna Falls, because just beyond them lived the bellicose Ewaipanoma, headless men with faces on their chests. So he was told afterward by Morequito, the Arromaian king renowned in conquistador circles for his recent visits to area Spanish settlements, when he'd brought a "great store of plates of gold" to trade for goods for his kingdom. Daily the settlers had thrown feasts for him, celebrating him as "one of the greatest kings or Lords of Guiana."

And even if Berrío had defeated the Ewaipanoma, Morequito went on, he would have had to face an equally vicious warrior tribe consisting solely of women, the Amazons. The Amazons weren't news: beginning with Columbus, the conquistadors had heard no shortage of stories about them. Gonzalo Pizarro's lieutenant Francisco de Orellana actually saw female warriors during his 1542 discovery of the river thereafter named, not coincidentally, the Amazon.

Still, Berrío was circumspect. If Amazons are human, he asked Morequito, how do they reproduce? They tolerate the company of men once a year, the king explained, in a monthlong festival of feasting, dancing, drinking, and sex. Often the women conceive, and whenever one delivers a son, he's sent to live with his father, while daughters stay with the tribe.

Berrío remained skeptical about the Amazons as well as the Ewaipanoma, but as long as they were susceptible to bullets, he was sanguine about his prospects on the far side of Llovizna Falls. While plotting an overland route that circumvented the cataracts, though, he fell into a series of conflicts with Morequito and the Arromaians, whom he believed were in cahoots with his chief El Dorado rival, Francisco de Vides, the governor of Cumaná. Ultimately, Berrío ordered Morequito's execution, the idea being to force the "savages" into submission. But as the old Spanish saying goes, "El hombre propone y Dios dispone"—essentially, Man plans, God laughs. Morequito's death spurred a brutal Arromaian vendetta. Which the Spanish might have been able to withstand if not for their latest bout with a deadly tropical disease.

With no viable option but to retreat, Berrío went seventy miles east on the Orinoco to the river-crisscrossed province of Emeria (now the Delta Amacuro state, in eastern Venezuela), a hundred miles shy of the Atlantic, close enough that he was able to send a request to Margarita for reinforcements.

Two months later, the reinforcements had yet to arrive, and yet another tropical disease outbreak was forcing Berrío to bury his remaining men one after the next. He was loath to abort the expedition, but as more men died and more days passed without any sign of reinforcements, there was no choice. He ordered the survivors into the boats and sailed east for the Atlantic, then north to Margarita, where he planned to get reinforcements himself.

When he reached the island, early in the fall of 1591, Berrío found out that the reinforcements he'd sent for had long since departed for Guiana. But rather than follow their orders to rendezvous with him in

Emeria, they'd continued up the Orinoco and raided Arromaia, capturing three hundred Arromaians and selling them into slavery. He also learned that, while he'd been away, his beloved wife, María, had died.

His return to civilization only went downhill from there. Hearing how close the Berrío expedition had come to Manoa, his host, Margarita's governor, Juan Sarmiento de Villandrando, sent a letter to King Philip. Antonio de Berrío was failing, Villandrando wrote, going on to propose that he himself instead direct the El Dorado effort.

Word of Berrío's progress, meanwhile, inspired a slew of new Spanish expeditions into Guiana. As the governor of the El Dorado province now, Berrío had the legal authority to equip a force to chase after these competitors, arrest them for encroaching on his exploration rights, and throw them in jail. But as long as he was going to the trouble of equipping a force, he figured, he might as well reprise his effort to get over Llovizna Falls and find Manoa.

He began by moving his base of operations to Trinidad, because, as he explained in a letter to King Philip, it was just a one-day journey from the island to the mouth of the Orinoco, and from there less than twelve days to the Caroní River, the threshold of El Dorado. He went on to ask Philip for money; the three previous expeditions had cost him more than a hundred thousand ducats (about £50,000), depleting not only his entire inheritance, but his daughters' dowries.

Not long after he sent the letter, his archrival, Francisco de Vides, arrived from Spain with a royal commission that declared Vides governor of the New Andalucia province, which included the area Berrío had been exploring and extended all the way east to Trinidad and the neighboring island of Tobago. The commission also granted Vides the exclusive rights to explore the New Andalucia province, meaning Berrío was out. As for the beautiful town of San José de Aruña he'd just built on Trinidad and named in honor of his late wife, it too fell within Vides's jurisdiction. Berrío was thereby evicted.

Feeling as though the ground were giving way beneath him, Berrío grabbed on to a loophole in the royal commission: he could still stake a claim to Manoa if he were the first explorer to identify its precise location. By the same logic, he could also hold on to San José de Aruña, arguably, but for the moment Manoa was everything. He threw together a team of thirty-five men under his loyal maestre del campo, Domingo de Vera e Ibargüen, and sent them up the Orinoco.

Vera returned five months later, in May 1593, with gold trinkets that had been presented to him as gifts by Guianan chieftains. The ore, the Guianans had told him, came "from a province not passing a day's journey off" where there was "so much gold as all yonder plain will not contain it" and the people have "many eagles of gold hanging on their breasts." The chieftains also supplied Vera with Manoa's precise location: just south of the Macureguarai and Gaygapari provinces, which sat on the far side of Llovizna Falls. They even provided him with a way to get around the falls on foot.

Berrío was jubilant: he now had more than enough to stake his claim to Manoa. He still needed funds to go there, but, in light of Vera's discoveries, that seemed only a matter of asking. As it happened, the very first wealthy patron Berrío pitched was so impressed that he immediately sent his own expedition to search beneath the Macureguarai and Gaygapari provinces, altogether cutting out Berrío. "The devil himself is the patron of this enterprise," Berrío wrote in November 1593 from San José, where he was now technically a squatter.

But he didn't give up, dispatching Vera to Spain to plead their case to King Philip in person. Berrío also sent his son Fernando, now sixteen, to Bogotá to drum up additional support. Both efforts paid off. Late in 1594, Fernando wrote his father that he would be returning to Trinidad with a large force no later than March 1595. And in Spain, Vera's El Dorado pitch was garnering widespread attention from both municipal and private investors. Consequently,

Ralegh and Berrío

when ships came into view from Trinidad in March 1595, Berrío was overjoyed—until learning that they were English.

On the receiving end of Berrío's tale, Ralegh was fully aware that, to preserve his chances of winning the race to El Dorado, the self-possessed Spaniard was not being entirely forthcoming, for instance in his claim that he was unable to tell "the east from the west." Otherwise, it was difficult for Ralegh to distinguish the truth from the fiction. But he did have a means of gauging the overall utility of what he'd heard: the Virginia colony relief mission had just been a cover story, he confessed to Berrío, adding that, actually, he'd been planning all along to seek El Dorado, which was why he'd sent Jacob Whiddon to Trinidad the year before.

Hearing this left Berrío "stricken into a great melancholy and sadness," according to Ralegh. Because the older man had been duped, certainly. But also, perhaps, because he'd recognized Ralegh as a kindred spirit—not merely an intrepid adventurer but an "El Doradan," the sort of adventurer whose reality is victimized by his dreams of what lies over the next mountain, whose appetite for glory can never be sated, and who thus becomes a resident of a place that cannot exist.

Hernán Cortés had been the El Doradans' primogenitor. After his 1521 conquest of Tenochtitlán, one of the largest and most spectacular cities in human history to that point, Cortés kept searching for more and better for nearly three decades, gradually depleting his fortune and ultimately dying penniless. Diego de Ordáz was an El Doradan too, and possibly the inspiration for the expression *dormirás cuando estés muerto*—you can rest when you're dead. Ordáz commemorated the completion of one expedition by planning the next, despite having achieved fabulous wealth and prestige, and even when he died, while sailing to Spain to litigate a territorial dispute, his quest lived on with the followers who assumed his license, including Alonso de Herrera—until it doomed him too. Berrío's uncle-in-law, Gonzalo Jiménez de Quesada, was a classic El Doradan, having forsaken the life of a king for a squalid camp tent. As was Francisco Pizarro. After taking Cusco in 1532, Pizarro wrote, "This city is the greatest and the finest ever seen in this country or anywhere in the Indies." Yet his monomaniacal pursuit of more such cities never ceased—until his death eight years later, at the hands of his own countrymen during a petty power struggle.

Gonzalo Jiménez de Quesada

And then there was Berrío himself. Now sixty-eight, he'd spent a total of seven years in South American swamps and jungles, losing every last ducat of his fortune—and his wife. All he had left was his children and grandchildren, who needed him—in Bogotá, a thousand miles away. Yet here he was on the island of Trinidad, illegally, fighting tooth and nail to go on a fourth expedition. He couldn't help himself; it was an addiction. If in the adventures of the El Doradans, and in the account of what should have been Berrío's golden years, Ralegh wasn't hearing a cautionary tale—if he hadn't gleaned that El Dorado was a paradise of the damned—well, then, the Englishman simply needed more information. The expedition "would be labor lost," Berrío spluttered, on top of which Ralegh and his men would "suffer many miseries."

Ralegh was all ears, though he feigned nonchalance, egging on Berrío. To begin with, said the Spaniard, Ralegh wouldn't be able to enter the ludicrously shallow rivers in Guiana with the smallest of his ships. But even if he somehow procured more suitable craft, he wouldn't be able to carry a fraction of the provisions necessary to sustain his company—unless he secured the Natives' cooperation. And good luck with that! On sight of him, they would turn and run. If he attempted to follow them home, they would burn their villages and then disappear into the jungle. Also, the very last thing they would do was relinquish any gold—that was per a recent decree by their chieftains after Vera had come away with the trinkets that had half of Christendom drooling and descending on Guiana. Gold, the chieftains had come to realize, would be their undoing.

But all that aside, Berrío said, there was no time to get to Manoa; it was nearly winter in the southern hemisphere: the rains were about to swell the rivers, ratcheting up the current to the point that stemming it was impossible. If Ralegh were to go to Guiana anyway and make camp for the winter, he would be overtaken by Domingo de Vera and his two thousand Spanish soldiers. Either way, an inland expedition was a fool's errand.

To Berrío's dismay, his admonitions seemed only to galvanize the Englishman. In fact, Ralegh found the knowledge of the obstacles empowering. With one exception: the distance. Manoa was at least two hundred miles farther inland than he'd previously believed, meaning two to three additional weeks of rowing against currents that would be strengthened by early winter rains. The extra distance would also push the expedition that much farther into the rainy season, and—since his food supplies couldn't last over such a journey—necessitate that the company reprovision in the jungle. If the men had any idea, they would refuse to go. Against his better judgment, Ralegh decided to keep it to himself.

10

HE WHO DOESN'T DIE WILL GO CRAZY

The Orinoco Delta is a maze twice the size of Massachusetts. Ralegh's task of finding a way through it, in order to reach the Orinoco River itself, was complicated by the fact that it was entirely uncharted save in the heads of Guianans who canoed there. To learn what he could from them, he deployed two reconnaissance parties, one led by John Douglas, the ship's master (responsible for sailing operations), the second by Jacob Whiddon.

Douglas returned with news of "four goodly entrances" to the Orinoco River from within the Delta. But those four waterways all had the same problem: they were just six feet deep in places, far too shallow to accommodate even the smallest of the English ships. Ralegh dispatched three more reconnaissance parties, one of which found a route to the Caño Manamo, the Orinoco's primary northern distributary, but it, too, appeared to be too shallow for the English vessels. The men had been unable to find out for sure on account of cannibals in the vicinity. If they didn't turn around that instant, their guide said, their boat would become the landing spot for a flock of poisoned arrows.

Ralegh turned to Berrío, whom he was planning to bring along on the inland expedition; the hope was that the Spaniard would provide reliable counsel rather than watch his own blunders repeated, prolonging his agony. Berrío had little to add to what he'd already said, that sailing ships through the Delta was impossible. The Englishmen could instead go in small boats, but then they would have no protection from the elements—or from poisoned arrows. Regardless, Ralegh had too few suitable craft, just his barge and a pair of wherries (rowboats) that together could accommodate thirty men if he really packed them in—or far too little space for the bare-minimum force of a hundred men he would need, not to mention their piles of equipment, weapons, and ammunition. And provisions: they would need at least a month's worth of food and fresh water, Berrío said, more than they could conceivably carry without a ship.

Ralegh acknowledged as much, but he had an idea: what if he used Keymis's dilapidated galliot? Berrío must have scoffed. Yes, the galliot could accommodate a hundred men, maybe one-fifty, but her draft—the minimum depth a vessel needs without its hull hitting the bottom—was twelve feet. In the Delta, she would have six feet at best.

Ralegh saw a potential workaround: by removing her heavy upper deck and superstructures, he could essentially reduce the galliot to a single-level open boat. Might that improve her buoyancy? And while the carpenters were at it, might they increase her maneuverability by adding banks of oars to her sides, as seen on a classic rowing galley?

All pointless, according to Berrío. The problem was the Delta's *barras*—the sandbars. Berrío on *barras* was like a preacher on the topic of temptation. Every single day, members of his own company—who were actually familiar with the Delta—got mired in those barras despite canoes that drew a mere twelve inches. Given the galliot's bulk, if she impacted a barra, she would get stuck, and, as the current swayed her back and forth, small stones within the sand could act like sawblades on her hull. As Ralegh knew, such impediments routinely turned ships into shipwrecks long before they could be freed either by their crewmen or rising tides. Still, he told his carpenters to retrofit the galliot.

They worked for a week, likely forgoing sleep in the race against the rainy season. Ultimately, on or about April 18, the galliot was able to "draw but five foot," as Ralegh happily recorded. He wasted no time before loading sixty men into her, including himself, Whiddon, Keymis, most of the other officers and gentlemen, and his captives, Berrío and Jorge, whose best hope now was that the massive Guiana expeditionary force led by their cohort, Domingo de Vera, would arrive from Spain in time to catch up to the *Ingleses* and mow them down.

Setting sail along with the galliot were the two wherries, the first helmed by Calfield and packed tight with eight men, including Ralegh's cousin Butshead Gorges. The second wherry had nine men led by Ralegh's friend and the expedition's vice admiral, George Gifford. Rounding out the flotilla were the barge and a small boat from the *Lion's Whelp* that had been pressed into service, each carrying ten men.

Guiana sat eight miles ahead, a green-gray ridge on the western horizon. To reach it, the company had to traverse the Gulf of Paria, a glittering blue mosaic of an inland sea that must have appeared a pleasant day sail to the 150 Englishmen staying behind at Pelicans Bay to guard the ships. The men in the boats were informed otherwise, however, by the forceful current and increasingly strong gusts. Soon into the crossing, the last vestiges of the pretty day were chased off by a billowing easterly wind that transformed the gulf into an undulating steely mass and gave rise to large waves—foam-capped walls of water, really—that hit the boats as though trying to flatten them, lashing the white-knuckled passengers with cold froth.

Although the retrofitted galliot was the steadiest of the five vessels, she was Ralegh's greatest worry. To enter the Orinoco Delta, the flotilla would need to navigate the ominously named bottleneck at the Gulf of Paria's base, the Serpent's Mouth. If the easterly wind drove the galliot into a sandbar within the Serpent's Mouth, the current would bury her. Fortunately Ralegh had Ferdinando, a young Warao from a town just below the Delta who regularly canoed through the Serpent's Mouth to sell cassava bread in Margarita. Ferdinando's assurance that he could lead the Englishmen to the Orinoco had won him the job as their pilot for a salary of one knife, one shirt, and one hatchet—a windfall, as far he was concerned; typically he needed to sell a hundred pounds of cassava bread just to get a knife.

He succeeded in getting Ralegh and company through the Serpent's Mouth that afternoon, bringing them to South America's Arabian Coast, a name derived from the Arawak word *Arawabiecie*, meaning jaguar. None of the cats were in sight, thankfully, just glistening mangroves and a rainbow of tropical blooms on the edge of what appeared to be a rich carpet of vegetation covering the continent.

Closer in, the coast lost much of its aesthetic appeal: the mangroves' tangle of roots rose above the waterline, posing a navigational menace as well as trapping rotting detritus dumped into the Atlantic by the Delta. Holding their noses, Ralegh and company managed to circumnavigate the quagmire, bringing them into a tranquil harbor (fronting what today is the village of Capure, in Venezuela's Delta Amacuro state).

Now, they had a choice of four channels, the "four goodly entrances" to the Orinoco. All four connected to what was now the flotilla's immediate objective, the Caño Manamo, a primary Orinoco distributary. The trouble was, along the way to the Caño Manamo, each of the four channels branched off into myriad subsidiaries, which, in the maze of islands and crisscrossing waterways, were often indistinguishable from the channel itself. The men might inadvertently go off course and not realize their error for weeks, at which point the proximity to the rainy season would necessitate a return to the ships in Trinidad.

Because Berrío would have loved nothing better, Ralegh was wary of his counsel and instead looked to Ferdinando, who recommended the Caño Pedernales. As would soon become clear, the Warao had almost no idea what he was doing; the Pedernales was the worst of the four channels, eighty-five miles of hairpin turns through the thickest Orinoco Delta jungle. Had he selected any of the other three channels, the company could have entered the Caño Manamo within fifteen miles.

On the Caño Pedernales, Ralegh and his companions suddenly found themselves swallowed by hot, throbbing, fecund darkness. "All the pictures my imagination had painted in anticipation of the impression [such] a virgin forest would make on me sank like faded shadows into insignificance before the sublime reality," wrote another explorer about his entry to the Orinoco Delta, adding, "In mute delight I stood in front of the mighty giants that had seen hundreds

of years pass by, and yet with the same unimpaired vital powers were pressing their trunks to heaven."

Although Ralegh's account of his own expedition would include no shortage of such balladry, he recorded nothing of his first moments in the Delta, likely because he was preoccupied by the ever-shifting mud flats, shoals, and jagged rocks inches beneath his hull, altogether concealed by the black water. In Ferdinando, he'd believed he had a pilot with back-of-his-hand knowledge of such navigational hazards. But in what quickly became a steamy, aquatic house of mirrors, the Warao lost his way. It had been twelve years since he'd last ventured into the Delta, he admitted to Ralegh, and at that time, he was "very young, and of no judgment."

In desperation, Ralegh turned to Berrío, but if the old man knew how to get to Caño Manamo, he wasn't saying. Instead, with the objective of convincing Ralegh to turn back, he may have shared the maxim the Spaniards had derived from their Guianan pilots: *Quien se va à Orinoco, si no se muere, se volver à loco*, or, "He who goes to Orinoco, if he doesn't die, will go crazy." Berrío almost certainly shared the trick to leaving the Delta, however, the same one Dudley's men had figured out: follow the current back to the Atlantic. Ralegh tried, hoping to backtrack, but his boats were already so deep into the Delta that signs of the ebbs and flows couldn't reach them.

Compasses were only marginally more helpful. Using the instruments to head west effectively carried the flotilla in circles around the islands, which were fringed by tall palms, crabwood, and dragon's blood trees (so called because of their red-pink sap) that blocked the view in every direction. And there were so many islands in such proximity to one another that simply rowing in a straight line became guesswork. While endeavoring to maintain a westerly course around one of the islands, Ralegh found that he was heading north, and yet, somehow, after the next island, south—and on an entirely different waterway. It was beyond confounding.

If only the company could pull over and ask for directions, but the banks were bereft of civilization. It was natural for the men to wonder whether that had anything to do with the creepy surroundings, which included "walking palms," trees that use roots resembling octopus tentacles to move themselves to areas with better sunlight or soil. (By sprouting new roots in the direction they intend to travel and letting the roots behind them die and fall away, the palms can walk sixty-five feet in a year, or more than enough for a gang of them to converge on a village and push it into the river.) Equally unnerving were the pracaxi, monstrous trees supporting masses of leaves that look, freakishly, like feathers. Hence the trees were known by Berrío and his countrymen as *gaviláns*—hawks.

Adding menace to trees were green anacondas, who liked to sun themselves on branches overhanging the water. As long as thirty feet and weighing up to 550 pounds, the snakes could devour a deer in a single gulp. Although anacondas weren't known to eat people, a crewman would be disinclined to sit idly by if one fell into the boat beside him—or onto him. Jumping out was no solution, though, given the Delta's electric eels, which could measure up to seven feet long and discharge up to 860 volts, nearly eight times the voltage of a standard American wall socket. A victim could survive the electrocution, but in his resulting stupor he might easily drown. If the flesh-eating piranhas didn't get him first.

Ralegh and company managed to make it to the end of their first day in the jungle unscathed. But any relief they felt was cut short when night fell—instantly, as if the setting sun had tripped a switch—and creeping from the loam came nocturnal predators they had little chance of seeing before it was too late, including jaguars, scorpions the size of lobsters, and carnivorous bats with three-foot wingspans.

Moreover, the sudden blare of cicadas and crickets seemed to have an urgency to it, perhaps warning the newcomers about whatever was responsible for the far-off shrieking—from the sounds of it, a poor beast with a mammoth vampire bat's incisors sinking in its neck. (In fact, the shrieks emanated from the cat-size howler monkey, which possesses a cavernous larynx and an unusually large hyoid bone—supporting its tongue—that, in tandem, have the effect of a microphone, allowing the animal's territorial calls to carry three miles.)

For such reasons, rather than make camp onshore, the Englishmen preferred to spend the night in the boats. While they slept—or, rather, while they tried to sleep—their sentinels could ensure that the vicinity was free of vampire bats by waving torches. The flames, however, drew mosquitos by the thousands, as well as giant moths—with wingspans of up to fourteen inches—known as white witches by the Natives, who believed them to be the embodiment of lost souls.

A far greater threat was posed by reptiles Ferdinando called "lagartos." The "small" ones, six-to-eight-foot alligators or caimans, could snap off the hand that a dozing crewman had inadvertently draped over a gunwale. They rarely killed anyone, though; they weren't maneaters. But their cousins the Orinoco crocodiles—which grow to twenty-three feet long and weigh half a ton—were another story, as Ralegh and his men would soon find out.

11

UPON THE HARD BOARDS

THE FIRST THREE days in the Orinoco Delta passed for Ralegh and his men without any indication that a human being had been there before them, nor any evidence that they were on the right course. The conditions, meanwhile, made each of those days feel like a week. Having lived in relative luxury for so long, Ralegh realized he'd forgotten how difficult it was to "lie in the rain and weather, in the open air, in the burning sun, and upon the hard boards." Even at sea, his existence had been opulent, with servants catering to his every whim. Now, factoring in his perpetually wet clothing and the men packed into the boats like cards in a deck, he concluded that "there was never any prison in England that could be found more unsavory and loathsome."

On the company's fourth day in the Delta—April 22, 1595—as though heaven-sent, a small dugout canoe materialized from the haze carrying a trio of dark-complexioned men of the Tivitiva tribe, a Warao offshoot. On first glimpse of the flotilla, these three prospective saviors spun their craft around and launched it toward the far bank.

To keep them from getting away, Ralegh leaped from the galliot to the swifter barge. Quickly overtaking the canoers, he tried communicating—presumably via Ferdinando or one of his interpreters—that he meant no harm, that he just wanted to find out the way to the Caño Manamo. Simultaneously, motion in the woods on the far bank caught his eye: an entire crowd of Tivitivas. If they had bows and arrows, he and his men were in grave danger.

Once his assurances had been translated, the canoers appeared to relax, and their tribesmen casually emerged unarmed from the woods and offered to take the company to their village, where their chieftain would provide directions to the Caño Manamo. The invitation wasn't necessarily a positive development, though. Centuries of Arawak, Carib, and Spanish attacks had made the Tivitivas devout recluses; they considered their settlements' remote locations and inaccessibility integral to their survival. In going to the village, the Englishmen risked never leaving. But without the tribe's help, Ralegh and company were likely to wander for a year in this "labyrinth of rivers," as he put it.

Staying in the barge, he left the rest of the flotilla behind and followed the Tivitivas, eventually turning onto a creek that led to their village. Tivitivas typically lived in beehive-shape straw huts supported by stilts built into five-foot-high palm tree stumps. During the rainy season, when the Delta waterways rose twenty to thirty feet and inundated the villages, the alleys between the huts transformed to canals, hence Italian explorer Amerigo Vespucci's choice in 1499 of the name Venezuela (Little Venice) for the region. Like the proverbial fish story, Vespucci's description of the stilts was amended with each retelling to the point that Ralegh fully expected to find the Tivitivas—whose name in turn derived from *tigüe-tigüe,* their onomatopoetic word for sandpiper—living in the trees like birds.

His attention was instead seized by the human skeletons hanging from their huts' crossbeams. When one of their chieftains dies, Ralegh was told, the Tivitivas bury the body, wait for

Late Tivitiva chieftains

the flesh to fall off, then dig up the skeleton and adorn it for display with colorful feathers and all the man's gold jewelry.

While Ralegh and his men waited in the barge, Ferdinando went ashore accompanied by his brother, who had joined him in signing onto the expedition. The two were escorted to an audience with the Tivitiva chieftain, who, it turned out, had no intention whatsoever of helping to orient the English party. Instead, he charged at Ferdinando with the aim of beating him to death. Which the pilot deserved, he raged, for assisting yet another strange nation bent on spoiling the region and destroying everyone and everything in it. Weren't the Spaniards bad enough already?

Ferdinando spun out of the chieftain's way, slipped through the other Tivitivas, and bolted into the woods, where, as ever, he got lost. Utilizing the diversion to flee into the same expanse, his brother managed to find his way to the creek and sprinted toward the barge, shouting that Ferdinando was in jeopardy of being slain. Ralegh immediately grabbed hold of an old Tivitiva villager, who had the misfortune of being within reach, and communicated to the man that he would lose his head if the pilot wasn't returned.

The villager thought about it briefly before calling to the chieftain and begging him to spare Ferdinando. By way of response, the chieftain released a pack of hunting dogs in pursuit of the pilot. A stroke of good fortune, as far as Ralegh was concerned: the barking enabled him to discern Ferdinando's course through the woods. Ralegh then directed the barge to a tree-lined bank where he reckoned the pilot had emerged.

The bank was empty, though. As Ralegh wondered where he'd erred, Ferdinando jumped down from a tree and swam to the barge, making it aboard safely, albeit "half dead with fear." Yet the misadventure may have been for the best, Ralegh thought, looking over the villager he'd taken hostage. As a native of the area, the old man might know the way to the Caño Manamo. In any event, he couldn't be a worse pilot than Ferdinando.

He wasn't, as it transpired; he directed the flotilla onto the Caño Guinamorena, a fifteen-mile-long stretch of spectacularly bright jungle that he knew led directly to the Caño Manamo. But he was unfamiliar with the Guinamorena's shoals, evidently: on the third day out of the Tivitiva village, the galliot ground to a halt, lodged inextricably, it seemed, in the waterway's notoriously thick and otherwise glue-like *lodo,* or clay mire. Not only was the expedition over, Ralegh thought, but until he could find a means of returning his men to Trinidad, sixty of them would have to remain behind with the Tivitivas, living "like rooks upon trees."

He woke the next day in hope that the hull had loosened overnight. Mornings in the Delta had a way of inspiring optimism: the

Treehouses

sweltering, bug-plagued, and seemingly never-ending night had in fact come to an end, with refreshingly cool air in its place and pristine sunbeams that transformed the fresh dewdrops into diamonds, in turn setting the leaves and petals and flowers aglow. At the same time, the joyous chirps and warbles of small birds, flitting about like comets, declared that anything was possible. If nothing else, it was a relief that the howler monkeys had finally shut up.

The galliot remained fixed on the river bottom, though. Ralegh ordered the men to remove heavy items from it, not least of which was the ballast—rocks, iron, gravel, or the like placed in a vessel's hold to counterbalance the effect of the wind, provide additional stability, and keep her sufficiently low in the water when she had no cargo. Relieved of the weight, he hoped, the galliot would rise. She didn't, leading the men to desperate tugging, hauling, and back-and-forth rocking, which worked sometimes. To Ralegh's profound relief, this was one of those times, and—a minor miracle—the craft was undamaged.

At the end of the next day, the expedition's sixth on the continent, the Caño Manamo came into sight. Wonderfully straight, Ralegh thought, an antidote to all the zigs and zags of the Pedernales and the Guinamorena. Also wider, about two miles across, and prettier: clear blue water lined with giant, old-growth trees straight out of a fairy tale. "As goodly a river as ever I beheld," he said.

He revised his assessment the moment the boats actually entered the channel: the current hit them like a stampede, a function of floodwater and discharge from the Orinoco—which, with a volumetric flow rate of thirty-nine thousand cubic meters per second, ranks as the world's third most powerful river, trailing only the Amazon and the Congo. Rowing in still water, the men could advance the flotilla at a speed of seven or eight miles an hour. But against such a strong current they would be lucky to go a mile and a half an hour, meaning that over what might be a hundred miles to the Orinoco, they could expect seventy hours of back-breaking rowing. On foot, they could cover the distance in half the time, if not for the swampland, and never mind the predators. The only real option, as Ralegh saw it, was for everyone to put their backs into it.

Everyone meant *everyone*, even the gentlemen for once, hour-long shifts at the oars that amounted to heavy lifting, the discomfort exacerbated by rising heat and, of all things, the fairy-tale trees, which blocked the breeze that might have cooled the men, yet offered almost no protection from the scorching sun. The boats became skillets; in each, rowers teetered on the brink of fainting, and their will evaporated.

More troubling, from Ralegh's vantage point, provisions were running low, and the company was unhappy about it. As another

English commander would observe of underfed men, "Nothing emboldens them sooner to mutiny." Either with the aid of his interpreter or on his own, Ralegh instructed the Tivitivan pilot to assure the men that they were just two days from the Orinoco. It was a white lie intended to boost morale, and it worked.

The two days passed without any sign of the great river, however. Ralegh had the pilot promise that tomorrow would be the day. Again, the subterfuge succeeded in keeping the oars moving. But the next day, the expedition's ninth, when the pilot said, "Good morning," the men thought he was lying. Forget El Dorado. They'd begun to doubt that they would ever see the Orinoco. They rowed on only because of the possibility of food and fresh water ahead—there was certainly none behind.

Ralegh wanted to reward them, but instead he had to cut their rations, and soon after, when the water supply was exhausted, he was forced to subject them to a blazing thirst magnified by the reminder of their deficit everywhere they looked. Drinking the brackish river water, though, would kill them sooner and in far more gruesome fashion than drinking nothing.

Mercifully the day finally came to an end. But the flotilla had to keep going through the night, in a race against starvation and dehydration; a few hours of sleep could be the difference between living and not. They didn't waste time doling out rations either, though that wasn't by choice. Gifford reported that he'd spent all his wherry's provisions; Calfield's boat, too, was out. Collectively the company was down to crumbs.

Ralegh saw new depths of despair in his men. At the same time, the current was getting violent, seemingly trying to break them. Just one more day, he told them, and they would have all the food and drink they wanted. But now they saw his optimism as a tragic flaw. He appealed instead to their vanity: if they turned back now, he said, "the world would laugh." Not a bad scenario, from their standpoint, because it would mean they'd made it out of this inferno. If only because turning back guaranteed starving to death, they continued at the oars.

Finally, the scenery began to change. Fruit dotted the trees and, as Ralegh reported, "We saw birds of all colours, some carnation, some crimson, orange tawny, purple, green" and pale blue. Likely they were parrots, macaws, maroodis, and powis, a type of land fowl. What mattered was that they were within firing range. For the first time in three days, the men had a meal.

But not much of one. As a result, the Tivitivan pilot suggested a nearby Arawak village, where, he'd heard, Spanish soldiers had found provisions during their flight from Trinidad following the attack of San José de Oruña. The English could now expect the same, he said: bread, hens, fish, and wine. Pointing ahead to a small branch of the river—probably the Caño Guara—the old man said that if they went in the smaller boats, they could be there and back in six or seven hours.

Ralegh, with no reason to doubt the Tivitiva, switched from the galliot to the barge for the excursion, taking eight musketeers as well as the pilot. Gifford and Calfield came too, in their wherries with four men apiece. Having been persuaded by pilot that the village was just around the corner, they brought no food or water. A mistake, they realized after they'd rowed three hours without seeing so much as a hut. Not to worry, the pilot said. The village was just a little farther.

After another three hours of rowing with no village in sight, Ralegh had to wonder if he'd inadvertently taught the pilot to say "just a little farther" in response to any question. His men were even more unsettled by the pilot's other claim, that Spanish soldiers from Trinidad had found provisions in the village. How did he know that? Was he in league with the Spaniards? If so, he could expect a mountain of beads and fishhooks for delivering a party of *Ingleses,* much less the *Ingleses* who'd burned their idyllic San José de Oruña to the ground and put two-thirds of their comrades to the sword. Their suspicion boiling over, Gifford and Calfield and the others demanded to know where the village was. Just a little farther, the pilot said once again—and then, when pressed, that it was "just four reaches more," a reach being the Waraos' smallest unit of measurement for distance.

After rowing four reaches without any sign of the village, and then another four reaches—forty miles in all since departing the Caño Manamo, Ralegh estimated—the men wanted to give up. Right after hanging the pilot. As Ralegh saw it, there was only one argument for keeping the Tivitiva alive: without him, they had no chance whatsoever of finding their way back to the Caño Manamo, especially now that night had fallen.

The old man begged them to believe that the village sat just beyond the pair of upcoming bends. Proceeding went against Ralegh's better judgment, especially since the river had started to narrow; so many trees limbs now hung over the boats that the men needed to slash them out of the way with their swords in order to advance, a problem both on account of the exertion and because, on a night that was "as dark as pitch," as he put it, they might bring down a tree boa or an anaconda onto themselves. Ultimately the growling in their stomachs was a persuasive argument for going a bit farther, then farther still, until, after midnight, a light appeared in the distance. Left to pray that it didn't belong to Spanish soldiers, Ralegh and his companions rowed toward it.

A dog's barking cut through the night. Another dog joined in, then several more. Pets of the Arawak villagers, it turned out. Despite the hour, the villagers welcomed the Englishmen (or they dared not be unwelcoming to the firearm-toting strangers), offering to put them up for the night in their chieftain's house. He was on a journey to the Orinoco, they explained, to trade the Caribs for gold, cotton, and young women.

Ralegh gratefully accepted the villagers' offer, and they served him and his men bread, fish, hens, and what he described as an "Indian drink"—possibly cachire, a wine made either from the mauritia palm or cassava. Alcohol was certainly in order for the men after hearing about the chieftain's *four-hundred-mile* journey to the Orinoco: even if, as they hoped, the villagers had meant a *round trip* of four hundred miles, the company still had two hundred miles to row before reaching the river, or another two weeks at their present pace. Ralegh had either been grossly underestimating the distance, his men realized, or, far more grievous, intentionally understating it. Fortunately for him, their ire was softened by the villagers' mention of the gold on the Orinoco.

Everyone rested soundly that night and awoke the next morning—the inland expedition's tenth day—in paradise. "On both sides of the river," wrote Ralegh, "were the most beautiful country that ever mine eyes beheld." After trading with the villagers and starting back toward the Caño Manamo laden with provisions, he marveled at how what had appeared the night before to have been "nothing but woods, prickles, bushes and thorns" was in fact an expanse of "plains of twenty miles in length, the grass short and green" with "groves of trees by themselves, as if they had been by all the art and labour in the world so made of purpose." The river was equally spectacular, abounding with strange and wonderful fish, and deer came to feed on its banks as though drawn by "a keeper's call."

While the party paused to delight in this latter-day Eden, one of the men jumped into the water for a swim only to find himself between a crocodile's jaws. All that's known of him, per Ralegh, is that he was Black, "a very proper young fellow," and, now, in quite a predicament: whereas a human tears into meat with 162 pounds

The "largarto" attack

per square inch of bite force, the crocodile's jaws deliver 2,980 pounds per square inch, more than any animal on earth, including the great white shark. To escape, a man must generate force sufficient to lift a pickup truck off himself. In other words, the proper young fellow had no hope of escaping without help from his companions. Their lone option was to shoot the crocodile, but the intricate, multistep process of loading a musket required a half minute in the best of circumstances. Before they could even react, the beast devoured their comrade and disappeared underwater.

Among the surviving crewmen, the incident raised several issues that amounted to a single question: "Should we go home?" When they rejoined the flotilla on the Caño Manamo later in the day, the rest of the company was asking the same question. Turning back to the ships against Ralegh's orders would constitute mutiny, a hanging offense. They deliberated on it nonetheless, but without arriving at a definitive answer.

Tabling the question in order to return to the oars, they once again found themselves rowing toward a destination that, if it existed at all, seemingly grew farther away the farther they went. Meanwhile, their ever-wet clothing scraped their limbs to putty, the sun scalded the rest of their hides, and every stroke either added a new blister or ruptured an existing one. When their provisions began to dwindle, yet again, they had the answer to their question: "Aye."

12

PATIENCE CONQUERS PAIN

A MUTINY COULD GIVE Vice Admiral George Gifford the admiralty, as well as the lion's share of the expedition's proceeds attendant to the position. The price would be steep—his fifteen-year friendship with Walter Ralegh. It would hardly be the first time, though, that Gifford had cashed in a friend.

One of many examples was the business with the philosopher's stone, a small object God had given Adam that could turn ordinary metal into gold—or so people had believed for centuries. In 1586, Gifford, then thirty-four, claimed that with ample funding for research and development, he could manufacture his own philosopher's stone. He anticipated investors would be skeptical, in no small part because of his reputation: although he was a member of Parliament who'd inherited not one but two splendid country manors—Weston-under-Edge in Gloucestershire, and Ithell in Hampshire—he was perpetually running out of money and resorting to questionable methods of making more. So he fronted the philosopher's stone venture with his (and Bess Ralegh's) upstanding cousin George Throckmorton. When the project failed to produce any gold—save the £80 Gifford was paid for his part—Throckmorton was left to absorb the backlash.

Gifford's most notorious swindle had taken place a few years earlier, in 1583, when he was a royal bodyguard as well as a star jouster at Queen Elizabeth's annual Accession Day tournament. Seeking to capitalize, he convinced a pair of influential Frenchmen that he could use his proximity to the queen to assassinate her, and they gave him a £200 down payment. That was the end of it as far as he was concerned, but what smacked of a regicide plot to authorities landed him in the Tower of London.

The charges were eventually dropped for lack of evidence, freeing Gifford to perpetrate more ruses. Often he was caught, but nearly as often he was able to extricate himself by leveraging his family connections and considerable charm: even though he'd accepted money to murder her, Elizabeth would knight him in 1596. His roguery would continue until his death, in 1613, when a contemporary would write, matter-of-factly, that his loss "would have been less, both for himself and his posterity, if he had gone thirty years ago."

Yet Gifford had a remarkable work ethic for a rake. Undoubtedly it was instrumental in his success as a jouster. Jousting was pageantry, but it required serious martial training. Any young jouster "must have seen his blood flow and felt his cheek crack under the blow of his adversary, and have been thrown to the ground twenty times," wrote one medieval expert. "Thus will he be able to face real war with the hope of victory." Struggle, Gifford came to believe, went hand in hand with progress. When he was imprisoned in the Tower of London, he emblazoned his wall with the adage that might have been his credo: *dolor patientia vincitur*—patience conquers pain.

Although Gifford's forbearance had so often gone into criminal activities, Ralegh had been willing to bet that, in Guiana, it would go toward reaching El Dorado. To right his ledgers, Gifford needed a golden city as much as Ralegh himself did. And surely, Gifford recognized that he couldn't get there without Ralegh.

To fix the troops' morale, the company needed a break, Ralegh told Gifford on April 27, 1595, their eleventh day on the continent. Thinking that the troops would enjoy being dry for a change, Gifford took nine men and rowed his wherry upriver ahead of the flotilla in search of a bank where he could build a bonfire. He found something better: four Arawak canoes headed toward him, one of them brimming with loaves of freshly baked bread.

Mouths watering, he and his men started toward the canoes, spurring the Arawaks to turn away and race off. They were afraid, Gifford knew, but he expected that would change when they saw the hatchets, fishhooks, and beads that could be theirs in exchange for just a crust of their bread. Exhorting his men to "try the uttermost of their strengths," he pursued the Arawaks, whittling away at the gap between them before two of the canoes suddenly veered onto a creek and seemingly disappeared.

With no hope of escaping the wherry, the two remaining canoes pulled onto the nearest bank. But not to surrender. Instead, the four canoers jumped out of their craft and bolted into the jungle. Gifford and his men banked their wherry, leaped out, and gave chase, finding themselves in an especially thick and damp expanse of woods. Which was fortuitous, as it allowed them to pick up the Arawaks' trail.

In the contest that followed, the Arawaks benefited from superior physical fitness and what amounted to home-field advantage. But the Englishmen had guns, which proved pivotal, with the Natives deciding to surrender rather than press their luck against the bullets tearing apart everything in the vicinity. Still, both parties won: the Arawaks had been on their way to Margarita to sell their bread; now they would earn far more for it, while saving themselves a long and perilous journey. And the Englishmen not only avoided starvation but also acquired pivotal intelligence: the two canoes that had gotten away were carrying a trio of Spaniards, a gentleman, a refiner, and the soldier assigned to protect them.

Of the bread, Ralegh would write, "Nothing on earth could have been more welcome to us [other than] gold." Full bellies changed the mindset of his men: once again they were keen on El Dorado, whatever the distance. But before proceeding, Ralegh wanted to know more about the three Spaniards, particularly the refiner, whose job was to use a combination of pressure, intense heat, and a variety of chemicals to extract gold from ore, typically brown, iron-stained rock or white quartz. Why, Ralegh wondered, would the Spaniards send a refiner up this godforsaken river unless they'd already found gold?

Berrío knew the gentleman, who certainly wouldn't bring a gold refiner into this lethal morass just for the company. Naturally, Berrío said nothing of this to Ralegh. Ralegh still had the option of asking the refiner himself, though. Along with Gifford and Calfield, Ralegh hunted for the other two canoes, soon finding them on a bank along the same creek they'd disappeared down earlier. Their passengers were gone, presumably into the adjacent woods. While Gifford and Calfield searched the woods, Ralegh inspected the canoes, finding a "good quantity of ore and gold" in them. Perhaps it had been too much for the Spaniards to carry. If so, he had reason to hope that they'd opted to hide in the vicinity until it was safe to return to the canoes.

Something drew him to a nearby thicket. Wading into the dark sea of stems and leaves, he led with his musket, protecting himself from men who at any moment might lunge at him from behind a bush. He also had to look out for hazards on the ground, like fer-de-lances and pinkfoot goliaths. The former, one of the world's deadliest snakes, is easily identified by its cream-colored underside, but it rarely exhibits its underside, instead using the olive, gray, and brown scales on its dorsal side to blend into the forest floor. Similarly, the latter, a tarantula that grows to twelve inches in diameter—or large enough that it can eat birds—is given away by its baby-pink feet, but only from below, since its top side is swathed in forest-brown fur. What Ralegh stepped on was more remarkable than either creature: a handcrafted Native basket containing quicksilver, saltpeter, and several other items he recognized as implements for testing metals, all of them sprinkled in dust from ore that had been recently refined. It was a refining kit—a strong clue, to say the least, that the refiner was still in the area.

Although unable to find him in the thicket, Ralegh availed himself of the flotilla, ordering one of the boats to land. To offset the beleaguered crewmen's reluctance to plunge into the dangerous expanse of forest in pursuit of Spaniards likely to shoot them on sight, he offered a £500 bonus for the capture of any one of the fugitives. The men then followed him into the woods—in hindsight, a tactical error: while they were away, the three Spaniards tiptoed out of their hiding place and stole away in one of the canoes.

The search wasn't entirely fruitless, though: Ralegh did turn up the Arawaks who'd been serving as the Spaniards' guides, and, in them, he saw not only intelligence sources but also potential allies—especially after they confessed to being surprised, given the Spaniards' tales of the barbarous *Ingleses*, that they weren't being eaten. Instead, to their amazement, the English had provided them with meat and, more amazing, gifts. Per his standard practice, Ralegh gave each of them "some thing or other," as he put it, presumably fishhooks and beads.

Although Martino, the Arawaks' leader, had served as the Spaniards' guide, he had no interest in doing them any favors. Every day, he explained to Ralegh, the Spaniards had forcibly taken Arawak wives and daughters and "used them for the satisfying of their own lusts." It was astonishing, he added, that the English hadn't straight away charged into his village to do the same thing. Keeping to himself that it took a Herculean effort on his part to prevent that, Ralegh let the Arawaks conclude that gentlemanly treatment of women was a uniquely English practice—"Nothing got us more love among them," he would write. It would pay significant long-term dividends.

In the short term, he was able to secure Martino's services as the expedition's new pilot. Martino's predecessors, Ferdinando and the old Tivitiva, were sent home in a canoe along with provisions, a payment of "such things as they desired," and a letter intended for the company guarding the ships in Trinidad—which the duo would deliver.

Not only did Martino know the waters well, he was also a veritable encyclopedia of the Spaniards' gold-hunting operations in the area, including all the places they'd searched and those they *should* have searched. He offered to take Ralegh to the best of the lot. While intrigued, Ralegh was unnerved by a harbinger of the rainy season: the rivers were rising "with such speed," he wrote, that "if we waded them over the shoes in the morning outward, we were covered to the shoulders homeward the very same day."

Resuming their ascent of the Caño Manamo, he and his companions were presented with the sight of a pair of peaks rising above the horizon that heralded the Orinoco River (probably the Peluca and Paisapa, part of the Imataca range spanning two hundred miles of the border between modern Guyana and Venezuela), in turn sparking a celebration in the boats. As though Mother Nature found the men's joy infectious, the wind picked up, allowing them to cool off for the first time in recent memory and, better still, to use their sails.

The next day—May 2, the sixteenth of the inland expedition—Ralegh and company reached the Orinoco River, which appeared to be flowing with coffee and cream rather than water, a function of sediment produced by erosion in the Andes, on the far side of the continent. Otherwise, given its scale, the men might have believed they'd taken a wrong turn and come to the Atlantic Ocean; on average the Orinoco is nearly four miles wide, and, in spots, as many as fourteen.

The arrival was an occasion for a party, or might have been if not for the men's hunger. The land was far more populous than any they'd passed to this point, meaning provisions would be readily at hand—if the population cooperated. Along the fifty miles of Orinoco that now stood between the Englishmen and their objective, Arromaia, lived several hostile tribes, including the Arora, who were notorious for both their poisoned arrows and their propensity for firing them at Spaniards. As Ralegh noted, "the party shot endureth the most insufferable torment in the world, and abideth a most ugly and lamentable death, sometimes dying stark mad, sometimes their bowels breaking out of their bellies, and are presently discolored, as black as pitch, and so unsavory, as no man can endure to cure them, or to attend them." What chance was there that he and his men would be given a pass just because they were armed white Christians from a *different* part of Europe?

They were presented with a litmus test later that day in the form of a trio of passing canoes that, on sight of the flotilla, turned and bolted. But when Ralegh's interpreter shouted that the company was not Spanish but English, the canoers—who were Nepoyo, an Arawak offshoot—stopped at once, came aboard the galliot, and presented Ralegh with the turtle eggs they'd collected that day along with all the fish they'd caught. News of his kindnesses to the Arawaks on the Caño Manamo had preceded him upriver.

The eggs, as big as oranges, had likely been laid by matamata turtles, which are among the world's largest freshwater turtles. Their nearly flat heads and long necks give them each the appearance of a snake that has hijacked a turtle shell—an extremely revolting snake, that is, with a face full of protuberances, warts, and knobs placed seemingly at random, like malformations, and a tubular horn rising from the tip of its snout. The Englishmen ate the eggs anyway. According to Ralegh, they were "very wholesome meat, and greatly restoring."

The Nepoyos promised to bring more provisions in the morning. In the meantime, they said, just a short way up the Orinoco bank was a cream-colored beach where the Englishmen could find more turtle eggs by digging in the sand 80 to 140 paces from shore. The flotilla anchored there for the night and unearthed thousands of eggs, resulting in a well-fed crew electrified by the proximity to El Dorado.

13

TRUE REMEDIES OF POISONED ARROWS

Day seventeen on the continent—May 3, 1595—began with breakfast delivery: fruit, bread, fish, and wine brought ashore by thirty or forty of the Nepoyos, who preceded Toparimaca, their chieftain and, at the moment, from Ralegh's perspective, the single most important person in the universe. Ralegh desperately needed an experienced Orinoco pilot to keep the company out of trouble on the way to Arromaia, which amounted to a fifty-mile minefield of sandbanks and hull-shredding rocks, not to mention the Arora tribe's poisoned arrows.

In the resulting summit, it's likely the two leaders sat on sturdy, exquisitely carved oak armchairs inside the lavish, embroidered pavilion Ralegh had brought from England for such occasions. Straight away he found common ground on the topic of wine: Toparimaca was something of an oenophile, as it happened, and he ranked wine from Spain as his greatest joy "above all things." Ralegh immediately ordered the bottles of Spanish wine he had among his provisions and presented them as a gift to the chieftain. Toparimaca was moved to invite Ralegh and his captains to his village to try Nepoyo wine, which he also gave a rave review. Gathering that it was the local version of a peace pipe, Ralegh was only too happy to accept.

In the galliot, he and Whiddon, Gifford, and Calfield followed Nepoyo canoes five miles up the Orinoco to their port at Arowacai—Nepoyo for "Jaguar Island"—and then another mile and a half on foot to a flourishing hillside village surrounded by gardens and a pair of large ponds, where the residents fished. There Toparimaca proudly presented Ralegh and his officers with a ten-to-twelve-gallon earthenware pot of piwari, a cassava-based wine.

Refusing the chieftain's largesse would be to spurn his friendship, but the Englishmen might have felt inclined to do so after learning how piwari was made: Nepoyos—typically women—chewed on pieces of charred cassava bread, allowing their saliva's amylase enzyme to turn the starch into sugars, instigating fermentation. Once they'd ground the bread to mush, they spat it into a trough along with the accumulated saliva. Any insufficiently granulated pieces of bread were fished out, rechewed, then returned to the trough, with the resulting mixture spiced and left to ferment. Preparing a twelve-gallon pot required a full day of such chewing, and because the tribe drank piwari frequently, it was rare to see a Nepoyo woman older than thirty who still had a single good tooth.

Another piwari welcome ritual was underway that day, and seeing it quashed any hope the Englishmen had of merely making the appearance of swallowing the spittle. From an earthen pitcher, women from the village ladled three cups of piwari to both a visiting chieftain and a Nepoyo captain, who each lay in a cotton hammock. One man drank a cup, then it was the other's turn. When both had finished their three cups, the women ladled three more.

Ralegh and his captains lowered themselves into hammocks of their own, likely with all the joy of getting into a cold bath. It could have been worse, though. The Arawaks, Ralegh noted, "beat the

Winemaking

bones of their Lords into powder, and their wives and friends drink it all in their several sorts of drinks." After drinking the piwari, he wrote, "It was very strong, with pepper and the juice of diverse herbs and fruits" yet "very clean and sweet." It left him and his men "reasonably pleasant."

Toparimaca was delighted, and the next morning—May 4, day eighteen of the inland expedition—he loaned his guests several of his men, including his older brother, who was such an experienced Orinoco pilot that he could breeze up and down the river even on the darkest night. The new day also brought favorable conditions, including an easterly wind strong enough that the English boats could fly their sails.

As the flotilla proceeded upriver, passing the island of Assapana (known today as Chivera), the woods began to thin out, revealing banks Ralegh described as "perfect red"—from iron oxidation—and lined with "blue metalline" rock (likely oxidizing manganese). His cousin Butshead Gorges was a member of the detachment that ascended the banks to see what new menaces awaited the company. They found flat grassland, dotted by hardwood trees and palms and stretching to the horizon like an emerald sea. According to the pilot, this was the great floodplain of the Orinoco, which extended all the way to the mountains of Cumaná, at the top of the continent.

The trees were the hazards. As one explorer would put it, "Almost every tree . . . lodges its own more or less dangerous species of ant." The Englishmen particularly needed to watch out for bullet ants, which deliver the most painful sting of any insect on earth, comparable to that from a gunshot. Initially. The burning sensation lasts far longer.

But better that than the sting of arrowheads; the Arora archers could also be concealed within the trees. In another of his attempts to dissuade Ralegh from proceeding, Berrío warned that there was no way to reverse the effects of their arrows' poison, which was thought to be made from a mixture of the stinging ants and snakes' teeth. Oh, how the conquistadors had tried to obtain a cure, he related. First with bribery, then torture, and then experiment after experiment in which they sacrificed several of their own people—not to mention countless savages. Failing, many Spaniards had resorted to covering themselves head to toe in quilted cotton padding despite both triple-digit temperatures and the measure's questionable effectiveness.

Once again, Berrío's scare tactics backfired. As Ralegh put it, "There was nothing whereof I was more curious, than to find out the true remedies of these poisoned arrows." What the conquistadors ought to have done, he realized as the flotilla resumed its course upriver, was share a ten-to-twelve-gallon earthenware pot of piwari with the Nepoyos. One of the Nepoyos who'd thereby bonded with the Englishmen—likely Toparimaca's brother, the pilot—confided to Ralegh that the poison, known as urari, was made from a bush rope called urari-yè (part of the family that yields one of assassins' historical favorites, strychnine). Urari's effects could be mitigated, he added, by administering an extract from a root known as tupara. If a victim could then withstand twenty-four hours of pain and convulsions and abstain from sating the seemingly lethal thirst caused by the poison, he would survive. (As it happens, the modern remedy for strychnine poisoning also involves withholding fluid, in combination with medications that lower brain activity so as to spare the victim the bulk of the aforementioned suffering.)

Ralegh and company covered ten miles that day, reaching the province of Warapana and anchoring for the night at the island of Ocaywita (probably the modern Isla Iguana), which, at five square miles, was one of the smaller islands they'd seen on the Orinoco. Many of the land masses on the river were astonishingly large; the biggest, Isla Tórtola, is 119 square miles, or five times the size of Manhattan. The Englishmen waited on Ocaywita through the next day while two of the Nepoyos went to the mainland to smooth things over with Putijma, the local chieftain and a staunch ally of the late king of Arromaia, Morequito.

Putijma's recent experiences with Europeans had done nothing to foster his hospitality: first Antonio de Berrío had come in and executed Morequito, then Berrío's would-be reinforcements from Margarita enslaved and dragged off three hundred Arromaians. The mere appearance of a white face now might be grounds for Putijma's archers to let arrows fly. But once briefed, Ralegh and company hoped, the chieftain would come and welcome them with a pot of piwari. The greater hope was that he would assure their safe passage over the thirty remaining miles to Arromaia. But for whatever reason, Putijma opted against the trek from his village to the river, leaving Ralegh and his men to continue up the Orinoco with the fear that every movement on the banks signaled an arrow streaking their way.

Their disquiet was prolonged by an especially potent current running against them. To contextualize the Orinoco's discharge rate of 39,000 cubic meters of water per second: the Taj Mahal is 39,500 cubic meters. And 39,000 cubic meters is just the Orinoco's average; the rate is considerably greater during the first week in May, when Ralegh is believed to have begun his ascent of the river. As he'd noted in late April, each day the current grew more forceful and the water higher. Now, everywhere he looked, he found new harbingers of "winter," as the locals called it. Some were benign, like the melancholy warbling of the tree frogs and the sudden appearance of winged ants (which the Natives regarded as a delicacy). More ominous were the "dark and dismal clouds" that rolled in on shifting winds and, according to one explorer, "rested like black walls on the distant mountains." And then there was the "vivid summer lightning that . . . played all night and covered the whole cupola of Heaven with an almost phosphorescent blaze."

By early June, the sky would resemble a dam burst, and the verdant plains to either side of the Orinoco would be under water as deep as sixty-five feet. Because the current would be in his favor, Ralegh could expect the return journey to take just ten days, or half the twenty he'd spent so far. That left him only two weeks to find Manoa.

14

CALLED FOR BY DEATH

On May 8, 1595, day twenty-two on the continent, the appearance of a pair of gray-blue mountains—the Sierra Piacoa and Sierra Imataca—declared that the company had reached Arromaia, at long last. The more momentous landmark was the "great anchor" left behind by Pedro de Silva in his haste to quit the jungle in 1569. There's no record of whether the rusty bulk, weighing at least a ton, sat on an Orinoco bank or protruded from the river itself. Either way, it was as magical as a bestowal from the Lady of the Lake. Suddenly the stories weren't just stories; somewhere in the vicinity, General Silva's munitions master, Juan Martín de Albujar, had been plucked out of the river and taken to Manoa. The Englishmen would hardly have been surprised now to see Manoans paddle past in a canoe riding low in the water under the weight of heaps of gold.

A short distance upriver, Ralegh sought to drop his own anchors at the port known as Morequito, named after the executed Arromaian king (today it is part of the bustling Guayana City, three miles east of the Orinoco's confluence with the Caroní River). The plan was to dispatch the pilot to seek out Morequito's successor, Topiawari—who is often and understandably confused for Jaguar Island's chieftain, Toparimaca, even in contemporaneous reports.

The "maca" at the end of the latter's name serves as a mnemonic: *Topuremacka*, in the Macusi language, means "make them pleased," as in, make them wine.

The hope was that Topiawari would lend the Englishmen guides, without whom they had no chance of crossing the Cordillera and reaching Manoa; even if they'd had precise directions, they were unlikely to survive the journey absent the Arromaian king's blessing. His subjects, the Orenoqueponi, were renowned throughout Guiana as the foremost manufacturers of urari. They delivered the poison not only on arrows but also on darts fired through elaborately crafted, six-foot-long wooden blowguns topped by what appeared to be a pair of devil's horns, though in fact were fangs of an agouti, a lapdog-sized relative of the guinea pig. Positioned so as to counter warping, the fangs were one of several innovations that extended the weapon's effective firing range to a hundred yards, equal to that of the English muskets.

While Ralegh's men readied their anchors, a fleet of Orenoqueponi canoes appeared, blazing across the two-mile-wide stretch of river, on course to meet the English boats. As the canoes drew closer, Ralegh saw that their passengers were not tribesmen eager to trade food for beads, as he might have hoped, but rather, warriors armed with massive bows, which were lethal at a range twice that of their blowguns.

Before drawing a single arrow from a quiver, however, the Orenoqueponi canoes turned around and scattered. Had the warriors sized up the opposition and decided their poison would best be deployed from concealments? Seeing a new opportunity for diplomacy, Ralegh ordered his men to give chase. The swifter boats, capitalizing on their superior number of oarsmen, caught a canoe with five or six warriors and brought them back to Ralegh. As one of his crewmen would record, "[Ralegh] embraced them, and made show of much love towards them, and of desiring their friendship." He also gave them gifts—mirrors, combs, knives, and so on—to make them "understand that he did not come to do evil, but to win their friendship." Then he released them to convey those sentiments to Topiawari.

Left on tenterhooks awaiting the king's response, Ralegh anchored at the port, a tropical paradise, but also a collection of trees, hills, and rock formations that the Orenoqueponi warriors could use as cover for an onslaught if, as he had reason to suspect, they'd merely made a show of accepting his embraces and gifts. As night fell, he and his men faced a struggle to sleep, with each whine of a mosquito easily mistaken for the sound of an incoming blow dart.

Morning eventually came—and went, to Ralegh's dismay, without any sign of Topiawari. Just before noon, though, Ralegh heard something. A mob, it sounded like. As his men scrambled into a defensive posture, dozens of Orenoqueponi—men, women, and children—approached, bearing not weapons but gifts: venison, pork, chicken, bread, wine, and various fruits, including pineapple, which Ralegh would dub "the prince of all fruits." (He was not alone in his infatuation with the pineapple: it would have a role in future English exploration when Elizabeth's successor, King James, tasted one from Guiana and declared it "too delicious for a subject to taste of.")

The Orenoqueponi also brought their king, Topiawari, who explained to Ralegh that he would have come sooner, but he'd had to walk fourteen miles from his village, Orocotona (possibly the present-day town of Los Negros, in Bolívar, the largest of Venezuela's twenty-three states), and, as was quite evident, he was very old. A hundred and ten, he said. Nevertheless, he was sharp, and he lived up to his reputation as "the wisest of all the Orenoqueponi," according to Ralegh, who added, "I marveled to find a man of that gravity and judgement, and of so good discourse [despite] no help of learning nor breed."

Topiawari presented additional gifts, including small parakeets and a cat-sized animal called a *cassacam*, which Ralegh described as "barred over with small plates somewhat like to a rhinoceros, with a white horn growing in his hinder parts, as big as a great hunting horn, which they use to wind instead of a trumpet." It was a particularly exciting acquisition because he'd recently read Spanish physician Nicolás Monardes's claim that "a little of the powder of that horn, [when] put into the ear, cureth deafness." (The animal is known today as an armadillo, the horn that grows on its hinder parts is actually a tail, and Monardes's assertion has yet to be substantiated.)

In addition to gifts, Topiawari had grievances, beginning with the execution of his nephew and predecessor, Morequito. On that note, Ralegh quickly moved the proceedings to his embroidered pavilion, not for its comfort as much as to prevent Topiawari from catching sight of Morequito's executioner—Berrío—and jumping to the conclusion that the English were in cahoots with the Spaniards.

Once inside the pavilion, Topiawari told of how the Spaniards had arrived in Arromaia, put him on a chain, and dragged him "like a dog" around his kingdom for seventeen days, demanding that his subjects pay a ransom including a hundred gold plates for his release. Implicit in his polemic was a question: How were the English any different from the Spanish?

Ralegh was quick to reprise the pitch he'd given the chieftains on Trinidad, this time emphasizing "her Majesty's greatness, her justice, her charity to all oppressed nations" and "the rest of her beauties and virtues." Queen Elizabeth had sent her soldiers to Guiana, he told Topiawari, to defend the Guianans and "to deliver them from the tyranny of the Spaniards." Topiawari listened attentively, expressing "great admiration."

To ascertain how the English might be of service to Arromaia—and learn the way to Manoa—Ralegh asked about Topiawari's domain and the neighboring areas, steering the conversation to the

Ralegh meets with Topiawari

Pacaraima mountains on Arromaia's southern border, beyond which, he suspected, lay Manoa.

At the mention of the mountains, Topiawari let out a great sigh. His eldest son had died there, he said. Clearly he didn't relish the topic. Ralegh would come to interpret the sigh as an effort by the old man to loose an "inward feeling of the loss of his country and liberty, especially for that his eldest son was slain in battle . . . whom he most entirely loved." For the time being, Ralegh asked about the towns on the far side of the mountains. Long ago, Topiawari said, when he was young, "there came down into that large valley . . . a nation from so far off as the sun slept." They called themselves the Epuremei, he added, but he preferred the pejorative, *Oreiones*.

Ralegh was transfixed. Although Berrío believed the Incas had originated in Manoa, conventional wisdom was that they'd founded the city only after fleeing Peru—where the sun set. Also in Peru, the conquistadors had taken to calling the Inca nobles "Orejones"—Big Ears—on account of the cylindrical plugs, as large as two inches in diameter, that they wedged into their pierced earlobes. The Epuremei wore large red coats, Topiawari went on, and hats of a crimson color. Another indication Ralegh was on the right track. The Manoans were said to wear clothing, unlike other South American tribes.

The Epuremei killed as many of the region's Native inhabitants as there are leaves on the trees, Topiawari continued. His son was chosen to lead a great Orenoqueponi force to go to the aid of their over-the-mountains neighbors, but the army of invaders was so large it couldn't be counted. Or resisted. The Epuremei seized the fertile lands at the base of the mountains, offering themselves a commanding view of the infinite plains. There, they built a town called Macureguarai that was now full of impressive and expansive multistory houses.

Supposedly, Macureguarai was the gateway to Manoa: Berrío had said that he and his men had tried to get there but were forced to run for their lives when an Epuremei force set fire to the savanna—which was covered by dry and highly flammable grass five to six feet high. According to Topiawari, Macureguarai now served as the Epuremeis' first line of defense against invasion from the nations on the north side of the mountains; Inca kept an army of three thousand men there at all times. Inca, Ralegh knew, was the Manoans' term for their emperor, same as their Incan forebears. As for the force of three thousand men: the number wasn't quite the fifteen thousand that explorer Philipp von Hutten had claimed were guarding the impressive city he stumbled upon in 1541, but because the Epuremei were raining arrows on him and his men at the time, couldn't he be forgiven for overestimating?

Ralegh was left with just one question: where exactly was Manoa? Before he could get an answer, Topiawari brought the meeting to an abrupt conclusion. He needed to go home, he said. Ralegh tried to persuade him to stay just a bit longer, but Topiawari couldn't spare the time. He had "far to go," on top of which it was hot, he was "old and weak, and every day called for by death." Ralegh persisted, inviting the king to stay the night. Topiawari declined but promised that they would meet again. First, though, as a foundation for an alliance of their peoples, he wanted Ralegh to explore Arromaia. Ralegh was pleased to have license to nose around.

The next day—May 10, his twenty-fourth on the continent—he and his men headed west on the Orinoco toward the vaunted Caroní River, the route through the Cordillera that had taken Berrío six years to find. The morning had brought a breeze strong enough for them to sail rather than row. Better, Topiawari had given them an excellent guide, his twenty-year-old son, Caywaraco. If conditions remained favorable, Caywaraco told Ralegh, the company would need four or five days to reach the friendly Cassipagotos village located just north of Macureguarai, some forty miles up the Caroní. If, as Ralegh suspected, Manoa sat a few days past Macureguarai, he stood a good chance of at least getting a glimpse of the golden city before the rains necessitated that he turn back to Trinidad.

Weaving around a handful of tiny islands, the flotilla sailed three miles before anchoring for the night at the five-square-mile Isla Fajardo, a mile off the Orinoco's southern coast and parallel to the mouth of the Caroní. As they made camp, the men had to shout to one another to be heard over what Ralegh called a "great roar and fall" emanating from the Caroní. The cataracts, he assumed.

In the morning, the company sailed into the Caroní's mouth, which Ralegh estimated was "as broad as the Thames at Woolwich," or half a mile (he was spot-on). Immediately, the current punted the boats back onto the Orinoco. Ralegh and the eight oarsmen in his barge redoubled their efforts, yet over the next hour they were unable to row "one stone's cast." There was reason to hope they could make better progress closer to shore, but as they discovered, the current along the eastern bank was equally ferocious. The western side was more of the same. Concluding that every part of the river was impassable, Ralegh decided to make camp in hope that the current would calm down overnight.

It didn't. In the morning, the cataracts were roaring with laughter, it seemed, at his designs. To have any chance of crossing the Cordillera so close to the rainy season, he realized, he would need to know the overland route that circumvented Llovizna Falls, the same one the Manoans would have used to march munitions master Juan Martín de Albujar to their city. Berrío had to know it from his own attempt to reach the city. Might he now direct Ralegh? Might the opportunity to finally solve the riddle and lay eyes on Manoa provide the old Spaniard a measure of fulfillment, or even the peace of mind that would allow him to live out his remaining years somewhere other than a boiling, bug-ridden jungle? Not a chance. Berrío expected either Vera's expeditionary force to arrive from Spain or his son Fernando's from Bogotá, if not both, at which point Ralegh would become his prisoner.

But Topiawari's son, Caywaraco, had another means of discovering the way across the Cordillera. With Ralegh's leave, he trekked to the village to see what he could find out. The young guide returned the following morning—May 12—accompanied by Canuria's chieftain, Wanuretona, who gave Ralegh the full honored-guest treatment: a crowd of subjects carrying a bevy of provisions and gifts, all of which Ralegh would have traded, along with Sherborne Castle, for the route to Manoa. To get that, though, he would have to win over Wanuretona.

He launched into his standard "Queen Elizabeth's aim is to free Guiana from Spanish tyranny" speech, and in Wanuretona he found his most receptive audience to date. Not only did the Canuria chieftain loathe the Spaniards but he also burned to team up with the English and three neighboring tribes—the Cassipagotos, Eparagotos, and Arawagotos—against the Spaniards. And after finally driving the Spaniards away, Wanuretona hoped, the English-Guianan force could go to work on the Epuremei in Macureguarai, against whom his people had a long-standing grudge.

Ralegh said he would be willing to go and reconnoiter Macureguarai. He just needed a way around the falls. Easy, said Wanuretona, proceeding to detail a pass through the Curaa Mountains (now the Serranía de Imataca). It was telling that, suddenly, for the first time in weeks, Berrío was forthcoming with information. He had his lieutenant, Alvaro Jorge, take Ralegh aside and let him in on the "great silver mine" near the very bank where they were standing. To access the overland route to Macureguarai, Jorge said, Ralegh would need to get back onto the Caroní and risk spending the remainder of his fleeting time battling the current. Why would he want to do that when he could instead mine a king's ransom in silver nearby?

Heartened by the Spaniards' attempts to dissuade him, Ralegh couldn't get back onto the Caroní soon enough. But when he did, the water was deeper by another four or five feet, its current seemingly fired from a giant cannon. Against it, as he would write, "it was not possible by the strength of any men, or with any boat whatsoever, to row." At the same time, the leaden sky looked like it was about to come crashing to earth. Though he was loath to concede, it was time to return to Trinidad.

15

VERY FINE

Ralegh decided to risk staying in Arromaia for an extra day or two, long enough to at least size up the opposition, Llovizna Falls, which lay twenty miles up the Caroní. After anchoring the flotilla at the river's edge, he scaled the steep bank along with Calfield, Gifford, and six other men, bringing them onto savanna that was extraordinarily vibrant, seemingly a function of all the rain. Fording six-foot-tall blades of grass, they made their way to a hilltop that offered a view of the falls. But where the falls ought to have been, they saw, as Ralegh recorded, "smoke that had risen over some great town."

Mist, he realized, when a gentle easterly wind slid it aside as though it were a curtain, revealing "a series of ten or twelve overfalls," each one "as high over the other as a church tower" and lined with neon-green trees cloaked in orchids and other flowers that flourished in the constant moisture. To either side of the falls were cliffs as precipitous as any he'd ever seen—but, maybe, climbable.

Such rock formations were nothing unusual for the Guiana Highlands, as his guide, Caywaraco, could attest. The region abounded with "tepuis" (houses of the gods, in his language), tree-stump-shaped mountains of Precambrian quartz arenite sandstone that rose from the ground as sharply as buildings. Among them,

150 miles south, was the Auyán Tepui, down the sheer face of which spills Angel Falls, the world's tallest uninterrupted waterfall, at 3,212 feet—more than twice the height of the Empire State Building. (It's a testimony to the expanse and density of the Highlands that a natural wonder of such enormity wouldn't be discovered until 1933, and then only by a pilot flying high overhead.)

Ralegh was more interested in the surprisingly navigable riverbanks. He could proceed to the falls on foot, he realized, then attain the mountain pass to Macureguarai, the gateway to Manoa. That is, if he could figure out a way to scale the cliffs to either side of the falls. Advancing to a neighboring hilltop for a better vantage, he saw sheets of foam thrown off by the cataracts, in turn delineating rocky plateaus on the cliff faces that he and his men could use to stairstep their way up.

Caywaraco warned against even thinking about it. Their presence would draw the thousands of Epuremei soldiers stationed at Macureguarai, he said, far too many for them to repel, their firearms notwithstanding. And even if Ralegh's charm were to prevail with the Epuremei, diplomacy would be of no use with their neighbors, the bellicose Ewaipanoma, the headless people with faces on their torsos who wielded bows and clubs thrice the size of the Orenoqueponis'.

Long before Berrío had told him about the Ewaipanoma, Ralegh had read about such creatures in *The Travels of Sir John Mandeville*, the memoir in which the explorer wrote of men "showing nothing of neck or head . . . but they have their eyes in front of the shoulders, and in the place of the breast a mouth open." The book had been dismissed as fiction until the discovery of the East Indies corroborated much of Mandeville's reporting. Nevertheless, Ralegh considered the Ewaipanoma to be a "fable." Reading his doubt, Caywaraco avowed that he'd once seen an Ewaipanoma himself, and over the years Topiawari's warriors had seen the headless men repeatedly, with the brutes having killed hundreds of Orenoqueponi.

Still, Ralegh was willing to take his chances on the other side of the falls. Because he was an "ill footman," as he put it, he couldn't make the voyage himself, but he trusted his cousin Butshead to go in his stead. In dispatching him, along with thirty-three other men, Ralegh shared Canuria chieftain Wanuretona's instructions: once they reached the town of Amnatapoi, they would find guides able to take them to a village called Capurepana, at the foot of the Serranía de Imataca. The chieftain there, Haharacoa, was Topiawari's nephew and could guide them over the mountains to Macureguarai.

Butshead's detachment didn't get far before the sky opened, dropping masses of water the likes of which he and his companions had never imagined. And what had been a gentle easterly wind ratcheted up to a gale so powerful that it uprooted even stout, ten-story trees that had stood for centuries; they in turn took entire swaths of forest with them as they boomed to the ground. The gusts, meanwhile, transformed the oversized raindrops into darts. One salvo caused the men—who lacked protection from the elements beyond their sopping doublets and breeches—to cry out in pain. The precipitation was a trivial matter, though, compared to the sheet lightning, an electrical discharge within a cloud that gives it the appearance of a blindingly bright sheet. It was a common phenomenon in the tropics, but to the uninitiated, it was Armageddon, a transformation of the "whole vault of heaven into a fiery hemisphere," as one of them put it.

When Butshead's party rejoined Ralegh, the Caroní had begun overflowing its banks, spilling onto the adjacent plains. To advance, Ralegh conceded, there was no choice but to wait until after the rainy season. Crestfallen, he gave the order for the company to return to Trinidad.

The Caroní rocketed the boats downriver, with little to no effort required on the part of the men. Reaching the Port of Morequito in Arromaia the next day—May 17, 1595, the company's thirty-first on the continent—Ralegh sent a messenger with an invitation for Topiawari to meet and lay the groundwork for a return expedition to Manoa. There was every reason to expect that the meeting would cost a valuable day, or more, given that the aged king lived fourteen miles inland.

Luckily, Topiawari happened to be nearby, and within a few hours, he was seated across from Ralegh in the pavilion, surprised to learn of the Englishman's interest in "the golden parts of Guiana." Or, at least, acting surprised. He hadn't imagined the English would try to go there, he said, given the time of the year and the inadequacy of their force. Had they succeeded in reaching Manoa, he added, they would now "be buried there." He cited as evidence an advance on Macureguarai a few years earlier by a three-hundred-man Spanish force: the city's defenders set the long, dry grass on fire, forcing the Spaniards to run for their lives (this had to be the incident Berrío had told Ralegh about, when Epuremei had ignited the savanna in order to repel him and his men). Even with far more men and weapons, Topiawari continued, any move on Manoa would be doomed without the support of the Orenoqueponi and the rest of Guiana's tribes.

Trying to win that support, Ralegh argued that the Guianans stood to benefit if the English could gain Manoa: Inca, the Manoan emperor, had to know of the conquistadors' brutal treatment of his predecessors in Peru, and certainly he was aware of the Spaniards' actions since then, the wanton destruction of entire nations under the pretense of serving God. Inca would see England as a natural ally, if not a means of protecting himself and his people "in their just defensive wars against the violence of usurpers." On the other hand, Ralegh went on, if the Spaniards were to get to Manoa first, their firepower would be decisive; they would conquer Manoa and subjugate both the Epuremei and the Guianans. Accordingly, he asked, if the English were to return with ample reinforcements after the rainy season, would Topiawari and his people help them attain Manoa?

Eagerly, the king said. And they would "desire nothing of the gold or treasure, for their labors, but only to recover women from the Epuremei"—so many of their wives and daughters having been snatched away by their over-the-Cordillera neighbors. Between that and the depredations of the Spaniards, he lamented, Arromaia's population was dwindling. When the English returned, he promised to rally his warriors and lead them across the Cordillera himself—but on one condition: in the interim, Ralegh had to leave fifty soldiers behind to protect Arromaia from the Spaniards.

Ralegh had a total of just fifty soldiers with him—the bulk of the inland company being tradesmen, laborers, and rowers—and he needed all of them to ensure a safe return to Trinidad. Still, he considered leaving a few behind, and he presented the option to them. His nephew John Gilbert and his cousin John Grenville were among several keen to stay under Calfield and establish an English garrison. Ultimately, though, Ralegh was against it. As he explained to Topiawari, they lacked the tools to construct a proper fortress, as well as the gunpowder, ammunition, and most everything else that would be necessary for them to repel the Spanish attack that was a certainty if the English took up a position in Guiana.

In that case, the English needed to forget about Manoa, Topiawari said, because within a few days of their departure, the Epuremei would preemptively invade Arromaia, destroy it, and execute him. If he wasn't assassinated first by the Spaniards. Ever since dragging him around like a dog for seventeen days, they'd been scheming to remove him from power and replace him with his nephew, Eparacano, a

Hispanophile now going by Don Juan. News of the nascent Guianan-English alliance would only fuel their fire.

While sympathetic, Ralegh suspected that both the Epuremei and the Spaniards would be thwarted by the same weather currently constraining his own forces. He pledged to return to Guiana after the rainy season with two thousand English soldiers. Or at least, he said, he would try. Mounting an expedition of that magnitude wouldn't be easy, especially since his backers' return on investment from this one was little more than an armadillo.

With an eye toward placating those backers, he asked Topiawari about the gold plates, and how exactly the Manoans managed to extract the ore from the hard stone he'd seen. "Most of the gold which they made in plates and images was not severed from the stone," the king said. Instead, by the lake on which their city sat, "they gathered it in grains of perfect gold and in pieces as big as small stones." With remarkable specificity, he went on to explain how Manoan goldsmiths then fabricated the plates: they added just a small "part of copper, otherwise they could not work it" and then "they used a great earthen pot with holes round about it, and when they had mingled the gold and copper together, they fastened canes to the holes, and so with the breath of men, they increased the fire till the metal ran, and then they cast it into molds of stone and clay."

Topiawari wasn't merely convincing: on the basis of this encounter, Ralegh could tell Queen Elizabeth that with the colonization of Guiana alone, she could compensate for her grandfather's oversight—in 1489, before reaching terms with Queen Isabella of Spain, Christopher Columbus's younger brother Bartholomew had presented King Henry VII with a map of the world and offered the West Indies to England. Still, Ralegh knew, Elizabeth would need more than his report of a 110-year-old Guianan's secondhand knowledge. Which Topiawari could understand. For that reason, evidently, he took Ralegh to a secret gold mine.

In the sweeping account of the Guiana expedition Ralegh would go on to publish, he would say nothing about such a mine. Instead, he would describe a valley near Llovizna Falls, where he and his men "never saw a more beautiful country, nor more lively prospects, hills raised here and there over the valleys, the river winding into diverse branches, the plains adjoining without bush or stubble all fair green grass." There were "deer crossing in every path" as well as "birds towards the evening singing on every tree," and, fittingly in this Eden, "every stone that we stooped to take up promised either gold or silver by its complexion." Lacking any mining tools beyond their daggers, however, the men couldn't extract more than the odd loose stone.

It stands to reason that Ralegh included that episode as a cover story for the gold mine he actually did visit, the details of which needed to be kept secret. What may be the expedition's most important episode would thus be lost to history if not for the records of a Spanish spy, a corroborating report by a Spanish official, and Ralegh's private correspondence.

Of the spy, all that's known is that he or she lived in London and opted to work for the Spaniards before hearing the gold mine story directly from Ralegh's mouth and retelling it in a handwritten document delivered to the Spanish embassy. It began with Topiawari ferrying Ralegh and a number of his men to an embankment—likely on the Caroní River—a few miles from the port in Arromaia. Taking shovels and a pickaxe, Topiawari disembarked, allowing only Ralegh and his two most trusted captains to accompany him. If word of what they were about to see reached Spanish ears, the king explained, it would cost him his life. Not even his son Caywaraco could know about the mine.

Ralegh ordered twelve of his musketeers to stay behind and stand guard before he, Keymis, and the second captain—probably Calfield—followed Topiawari to a mountainside a mile inland. Finding the spot he wanted, the old man swung his pickaxe, loosing a clod of turf and revealing what appeared to be grains of yellow sand within a vein of white quartz just below ground level. Ralegh had no reason for excitement; it could be gold, but more likely it was marcasite—or even, simply, yellow sand.

If it weren't *muy fino* gold Topiawari declared, he would forfeit his own life. Now he was speaking the language Ralegh had learned as lord warden of the stannaries—or miner-in-chief. *Muy fino*—"very fine," in Spanish—was twenty- or twenty-two karats (a karat being a measure of purity, with twenty-four representing 99.9 percent gold and only negligible traces of other minerals).

As Ralegh also surely knew, an old miner's rule of thumb was that visible gold within ore practically guarantees high-density gold. And if the gold vein indeed ran through the mountain, there would be similar displays nearby. There were plenty, said Topiawari, kneeling to collect the divot and replace it so that the area appeared undisturbed. When he finished, he rose, advanced a few paces, and hacked away another clump of earth, exposing more gold-flecked quartz. A third test produced more still.

Ralegh wished he had the requisite tools to test the depth and expanse of the ore, or even to extract adequate samples from the quartz. Unfortunately, it would have been easier to cut into a brick; the mineral's name is derived from the German *quarz*, which translates to "hard." Using Topiawari's pickaxe, he was at least able to break off a few pieces he could have tested.

If it was in fact very fine gold, he asked Topiawari, why not work the mine? The king replied that he "did not dare to attempt such a thing for fear of the Spaniards." If they found out about the mine, they would kill him for having concealed it from them, then seize the mine for themselves. The gold was far more valuable to him as incentive for the English to save his people from Spanish persecution. Accordingly, his worst-case scenario was that the Spaniards would find out about the mine before the English could return to Guiana.

Which is exactly what happened, according to a report by a local Spanish official. A few months later, when Spaniards captured and interrogated one of Ralegh's crewmen, they learned that Topiawari came to Ralegh "declaring to him that there was much gold in that country" before taking him three miles inland to prove it. Following the excursion to the gold mine, the crewman added, the English and Arromaians celebrated with a feast. In his published account of the expedition, *The Discoverie of the large and bewtiful Empyre of Guiana*, Ralegh mentioned neither the excursion nor the feast, but his private correspondence dovetailed with the Spanish reporting—for example, his letter to Cecil detailing gold found "at the root of the grass."

During his final days in Arromaia, Ralegh said in the *Discoverie*, he was merely trying to cement the English-Guianan alliance by gaining Topiawari's promise that he and his people would become servants of Queen Elizabeth. And Topiawari was inclined to give his word, provided Ralegh help him with another issue: even if the Spaniards and Epuremei left him alone, the reality was that, at a hundred and ten years old, he was unlikely to live to see his people and the English achieve their aims. Therefore, he wanted his designated successor, Caywaraco, in the loop. At Topiawari's request, Ralegh agreed to bring Caywaraco to England so that the boy could learn the ways of the Europeans.

Concluding the published account of his time in Arromaia, Ralegh wrote, "Having learned what I could . . . and received a faithful promise of the principallest of those provinces to become servants to her Majesty and to resist the Spaniards if they made any attempt in our absence . . . I then parted from old Topiawari." As the flotilla pulled away from Arromaia, he added, he was pleased to see the king and his subjects wearing the twenty-shilling gold coins—featuring a likeness of Elizabeth—he'd given them as a token of English friendship.

Finally, he reported that among the Arromaians waving goodbye were two of his crewmen. The first was twenty-three-year-old Francis Sparrey, a gifted chronicler charged with compiling a report of the area replete with sketches. Sparrey had also been supplied with hatchets and the other usual trinkets to trade for information in Macureguarai, or in Manoa if he could make it that far. The second crewman was Hugh Goodwin, an adventurous sixteen-year-old cabin boy with a flair for languages; he wanted to learn the local tongues in order to serve the return expedition.

Now all Ralegh had to do was get off the continent ahead of the floodwaters, Spanish bullets, and Aroran arrows, then sail across the Atlantic during hurricane season, and, perhaps most challenging of all, mount a return expedition.

16

STONES THE COLOR OF GOLD

To back a second Guiana expedition, Acting Secretary of State Robert Cecil and Lord High Admiral Charles Howard would almost certainly need a return on their investments in the current effort, a pile of gold at a minimum. Taking into account the twenty-shilling coins Ralegh had given the Arromaians and the gold ring he'd sent Berrío as tokens of friendship, he was going home with less gold than he'd had at the outset—especially if, as he feared, the samples he'd taken from Topiawari's mine were nothing but marcasite.

He could still argue that Manoa was now within his grasp, but it was easy to imagine the dispassionate Cecil countering by asking whether, in the history of El Dorado expeditions, a single explorer returning empty-handed from the jungle had ever said anything else. Ralegh's claims wouldn't be bolstered by the fact that Cecil thought of him as the consummate lily-gilder—even before Ralegh had sworn up and down that the news of his marriage to Bess was merely a malicious rumor. Hence, to mount a second expedition, not to mention pay his way out of the debt incurred on this one, Ralegh had to improve his bottom line.

An opportunity presented itself in Warapana on May 19, 1595, twenty miles and two days into the company's return to Trinidad.

When the flotilla had stopped in the province on the way up the Orinoco, the local chieftain, Putijma, couldn't—or wouldn't—make time to see Ralegh. But this time the Englishman's reputation—his kindness to the Arawaks, his alliance with Topiawari—preceded him. Putijma greeted him and his men with open arms, invited them to stay in his village, and offered to take them to a hallowed mine full of what he described as "stones of the color of gold." Because Putijma hoped that his son, like Caywaraco, could accompany Ralegh to England, there was good reason to believe that the stones' composition would match their hue.

That night, the Englishmen happily availed themselves of Warapanan hospitality, slept it off, and, the next morning, met Putijma for an excursion to the mine, which was located on Mount Iconuri (the modern name and location of which is unknown). The chieftain led Ralegh and a small detachment across meadows warmed by a golden sun that seemed propitious given all the rain the past three weeks.

Unfortunately, the same injury that had made Ralegh an "ill footman" a week earlier began to nag him now. He was given a sorely needed respite when the party stopped for lunch at a lake, and Putijma's guides caught "great fishes as big as a wine pipe" (the wooden cask known as a "pipe" contained 176 gallons, about four times the capacity of a standard bathtub). Next they adroitly transformed a pair of sticks and some dry grass into a crackling fire to cook the meal. But despite the "most excellent and wholesome meat"—which, the Englishmen learned, was not fish but rather manatee—and a generally restorative interlude, Ralegh couldn't continue to the mountain mine.

Sending Keymis and six other Englishmen ahead with Putijma, he returned to the harbor with the rest of the detachment, rejoined the main body of the company in the flotilla, and resumed the descent of the Orinoco. The plan: pick up Keymis and the others downriver that afternoon and then lade the galliot with "stones the color of gold" that the party had collected in Putijma's mine.

At the appointed place and time, though, there was no sign of the Keymis party. It was reasonable to conclude they'd been waylaid; things went wrong in Guiana practically as a rule. On the other hand, Keymis's absence could be a positive development; he was, after all, a first-rate alchemist. There was no one more capable of making the determination that the mine merited an extra expenditure of time.

Hoping to put the delay into his credit column, Ralegh left two men at the rendezvous point to wait for Keymis, sent the rest of the flotilla downriver to the port by Jaguar Island (where he'd shared piwari with Toparimaca), then took his barge to the nearby "Mountain of Crystal." According to Berrío—back in Trinidad, before he'd quit talking—its peak had entire swaths of pink and white crystals, including diamonds and other precious stones that "shined very far off."

Sailing down an Orinoco offshoot known as the Winicapora (probably the modern Caño José), Ralegh and the handful of men with him soon saw the mountain, which, he would write, "appeared like a white church tower of an exceeding height." From its peak rushed "a mighty river which toucheth no part of the side of the mountain" and fell "to the ground with a terrible noise and clamor, as if 1,000 great bells were knocked one against another." Those details would earn Ralegh credit, albeit as "Walter Reilly," for the discovery of Mount Roraima, which, at 9,220 feet, is the highest of the Pacaraima tepuis, a group of sandstone mountains that stand at right angles to the forest floor. Mount Roraima indeed shimmers with minerals, including huge chunks of white and pink quartz that practically blanket its Valley of Crystals—the inspiration for Arthur Conan Doyle's 1912 novel *The Lost World*. But because Mount Roraima sits two hundred miles south of the Orinoco, it's almost impossible that Ralegh even glimpsed it. Instead, he was probably admiring the Sierra de Imataca and its two-hundred-foot Salto El Mono—or, Monkey Falls.

Impressed in any case, he and his companions went ashore at Winicapora—a town that shared the name of the river—in hope of finding someone to guide them to the mountain. It happened to be a feast day there; all the Winicaporans were, as Ralegh recorded, "drunk as beggars." Another European explorer would note that "the quantity of liquor drunk on such an occasion is enormous; and as there would not be a sufficient number of vessels in the largest household of an Indian chieftain to contain it, a canoe is generally taken from the river, rendered water-tight, and filled with their beverage." The villagers wouldn't stop drinking until the canoe was empty, or when "the greater number lie senseless on the ground or in their hammocks."

A similar scene in Winicapora made securing a guide problematic, on top of which, Ralegh discovered, the Mountain of Crystal was a several-day trek under the best of circumstances. But the excursion wasn't a complete loss: the Winicaporans invited the Englishmen to join the party, and the hot, weary visitors appreciated the refreshment, especially the pineapple wine. They couldn't stay long, though, needing to be back at the Orinoco rendezvous point by nightfall.

Soon returning to the barge, they headed upriver—or, rather, they tried to. A vicious gale and current beat the craft back, and masses of thunderheads and preternaturally hard showers blotted out the remaining daylight. For the first time on the expedition, Ralegh was "heartily afraid." Not until the storm let up the next morning was he able to reach the rendezvous spot.

And still there was no trace of the Keymis party. Only in the rosiest scenarios now, Ralegh thought, was his friend still alive. In hope of finding him, he exhorted his companions in the barge to row back toward Putijma's village in Warapana. The rain-swelled Orinoco was less a river now than an avalanche. Throwing everything they had into each stroke, the men advanced the barge at half the rate at which they could have crawled on all fours.

Meanwhile, they tried to get the attention of the Keymis party with gunshots that may or may not have risen above the tumult of water and wind. For twelve hours they proceeded in this fashion, stopping only when darkness left them no choice. Long after the physical toll of the preceding twenty-four hours ought to have plunged him deep into slumber, Ralegh was kept awake by grief over his friend's apparent death. Sleep finally came, but it was interrupted by a gunshot rippling over the adjacent savanna. Ralegh opened his eyes to find the sun already up and, straight out of a dream, Keymis and his six men, all alive and well.

In gratitude for the rescue, Keymis vowed to change the name of the Orinoco River to the Raleana. (Despite his tireless efforts both in his writing and cartographic output for years to come, the name wouldn't catch on.) Ralegh would have preferred gold; Keymis had none, and his explanation was confounding: "Putijma pointed to [Mount Iconuri], making signs to have me go with him," he said. "I understood his sign and marked the place, but mistook his meaning." The chieftain wanted to show him and his men a waterfall, Keymis thought. Intent instead on the mine, the Englishmen continued ahead, somehow losing Putijma as well as their way, thus never so much as glimpsing the vaunted stones the color of gold.

Ralegh nevertheless celebrated his reunion with Keymis, landing on Isla Mata-Mata, namesake of the snake-headed matamata turtles, and making a feast of the armadillo given to him by Topiawari. By necessity, it was a brief celebration. As Ralegh explained, "Our hearts were cold to behold the great rage and increase of [the] Orinoco."

For a while the river worked on their behalf, propelling the barge eastward at ten times the speed she'd managed on the westward leg. The now-familiar red banks and blue mountains blurred past, and the party reached Jaguar Island in just two days. Unfortunately, there could be no piwari this time: as they rendezvoused with crews of the galliot and the other three boats, thunder instructed them they shouldn't waste time even in catching up.

They hurried back into their vessels and, against the gathering storm, raced to the Orinoco distributary they'd ascended five weeks earlier, the Caño Manamo. The storm—"the bitterest of all our journey," according to Ralegh—won. Because of the resulting turbulence, which appeared likely to slam the boats into rocks and shoals, Ralegh recognized it was no longer possible for the flotilla to return to Trinidad via the Caño Manamo, save as flotsam. But the adjacent Orinoco offshoot, the relatively placid Caño Macareo, appeared to be a viable alternative: the same hundred miles to the Atlantic as the Manamo, but wider and straighter, which is to say, more navigable.

Unfortunately, it was also shallower, as Ralegh discovered after it was too late to turn back. The water was at most six feet deep, he judged while hurtling downriver in the galliot, whose hull would impact the bottom at a depth of five feet. He and his crewmen barely dodged one catastrophe in time to face the next—and that was before the break of the latest storm to earn their title of Mightiest-so-Far. The sopping darkness effectively blindfolded them, eliminating any chance of circumnavigating the submerged rocks. "I protest before God that we were in a most desperate state," Ralegh would write.

There was no choice but to leave the galliot behind. But how could he possibly fit her sixty crewmen into the four smaller boats, each already overcrowded with nine or ten men? As it turned out, the sixty crewmen couldn't get off the galliot fast enough before wedging and contorting themselves, one on top of the next, into the boats. And so, "all very sober, and melancholy, one faintly cheering another to show courage," as Ralegh recorded, he and his men left the galliot behind, "put ourselves to God's keeping, and thrust out into the sea."

17

TO OFFEND AND ENFEEBLE THE KING OF SPAIN

ON THE GULF of Paria, at nine o'clock on the morning of May 28, 1595, nine days into their return from Guiana, Walter Ralegh and his ninety-five men—bedraggled, drenched, and stuffed into four small boats—sighted the island of Trinidad and, shortly thereafter, their ships, bobbing at anchor on Pelicans Bay, just as they had been six weeks earlier. "There was never to us a more joyful sight," Ralegh wrote. "Now that it hath pleased God to send us safe to our ships, it is time to leave Guiana to the sun, whom they worship, and steer away towards the north."

To bolster the chances of a return expedition the following July, however, he considered first steering west, to the island of Margarita, where Spaniards forced the Indigenous Guaiqueríes to dive as deep as forty-seven feet to the ocean bottom and fill baskets with oysters. In the fifteenth and sixteenth centuries—often called the "Pearl Age"—pearls were worth as much as ten times their weight in gold, and the island of Margarita was literally synonymous with the gem, "margarita" being the Latin word for "pearl." By relieving the Spaniards of their ill-gotten pearls, Ralegh could fulfill the privateering duty detailed in his letters patent from Queen Elizabeth, "to offend and enfeeble the King of Spain and his subjects in his dominions to the uttermost" and, at the same time, put the expedition in the black, making a sequel more palatable to his backers.

At Pelicans Bay on or about May 29, 1595, just a day after their return from Guiana, Ralegh ordered his men to weigh anchor. Margarita sits 135 miles northwest of Pelicans Bay as the crow flies, but a hundred miles farther for vessels forced to traverse the fang-like inlets and outcroppings of the channel known as the Bocas del Dragón (Dragon's Mouths), which runs between the Gulf of Paria and the Caribbean.

A little over a week later, on the night of June 7, moonlight enabled lookouts on Margarita to discern the English fleet bearing down on their port city of Manpatare (now Pampatar). Having heard about the band of *Ingleses* from Spanish soldiers who'd escaped Trinidad after the attack on San José, the Spaniards on Margarita were prepared: their governor, Pedro de Salazar, had sealed all means of entry to Manpatare save a single gate. Should the *Ingleses* attempt to pass through it, they would face the fire of the fifty entrenched musketeers with orders "to await the enemy to the last man, or until the enemy should be exterminated."

Ralegh had options for neutralizing the Spanish musketeers, however, including a newly popular flying mortar consisting of a small container of gunpowder and either musket balls or bits of shrapnel, all packed tightly inside, like the seeds in a pomegranate—hence its name, *grenade,* the French word for pomegranate. To deploy one, an English grenadier had to light it and then get close enough to the Spanish defenses to lob it—easier said than done through a squall of musket balls and, potentially, the Spaniards' own grenades. Deploying the weapons was so risky that privateering crews would come to offer substantial cash rewards to each man who threw even a single grenade at the enemy.

In Margarita, Ralegh thought, it was too risky. Not that he'd suddenly developed an aversion to risk; there was simply no reason for it when he and his men could instead waltz into the comparatively defenseless Spanish royal pearl fishery on the tiny Isla de Coche, ten miles southwest of Manpatare.

The Spaniards had thought of that too, though: Ralegh's attempts to land boats on the islet resulted in a torrent of Spanish defensive fire, the capture of three of his men, a hasty retreat, and the unhappy conclusion that his future did not include pearls.

But he wasn't out of fundraising ideas. Sailing back up to Margarita, he landed at Punta El Mosquito, on the island's southern coast, and released Alvaro Jorge with instructions to go to Manpatare and procure a ransom of fourteen hundred ducats (£700) for his boss, Berrío. Jorge succeeded in reaching the city and obtaining the money, but Governor Salazar stepped in and prevented him from taking it to Ralegh.

After waiting another two days at Punta El Mosquito, a dreary wasteland of scrub and cacti with no shortage of its bloodsucking, disease-bearing namesakes, Ralegh had soured on Margarita. He'd also identified a superior target fifty miles southeast, Cumaná. The longtime Spanish trading settlement was English privateers' prototypical target: a small-to-midsize city where they could anchor far enough away to evade detection before mounting a surprise attack overland. And a privateer couldn't ask for a better date to attack; June 23 was one of the longest nights of the year in the southern hemisphere, a boon for an invasion force advancing under cover of darkness. It also happened to be Saint John's Eve, the night of celebration prior to the Feast Day of Saint John the Baptist, meaning the Spaniards would be preoccupied.

The invasion force would still have to contend with soldiers in the pair of formidable fortresses guarding the bayside city, but Ralegh had a workaround for those thanks to the newest member of his company, Caywaraco. Topiawari's son wasn't just familiar with Cumaná; he knew its defenses in microscopic detail, including an overlooked mountain road that led directly into the city. The road was considered treacherous by the locals, but for men who'd just logged six weeks in the Guiana jungle, it would be a pleasant stroll.

That night, according to an official Spanish report, a force of 210 English soldiers, musketeers, and pikemen under the command of the pirate *Guaterral*—a common contemporaneous Spanish rendition of "Walter Ralegh"—landed a mile west of the Cumaná and proceeded to take the "devilish road" inland. The city's residents were entirely unaware of the threat until Guaterral and his men "attacked with the fury of demons."

Seventy Spanish soldiers—as many as could be rounded up on short notice during the Fiesta de San Juan Bautista—realized that it would be folly to try to fight off the invaders. Instead, the Spaniards gathered in the small fortress at the base of the city, and, when the *Ingleses* came within firing range, they loosed three volleys of musket fire. Not in rapid succession, though. To ready his matchlock arquebus, a soldier had to strike a match and light a slow-burning rope, then precisely prepare and load gunpowder into the pan before loading the musket ball into the barrel and using a ramrod to properly seat it. Only after eighteen additional steps could he fully cock his hammer (lest he "go off half-cocked," in which case his weapon wouldn't fire), find his target, aim, and, finally, pull the trigger. He might fire once per minute on a good day, as opposed to a night when his eyes and lungs were full of acrid smoke pouring out of sixty-nine other arquebuses in a dark, enclosed space. And presumably the rate of fire was even less rapid on a holiday celebrated in large part with feasting and wine.

By the time the Spanish soldiers had fired their three volleys, the English had attained higher ground, an elevated part of the city known as Guana Quintera. Still, the three volleys had added up to some two hundred lead balls as big as marbles traveling a thousand feet per second and capable of penetrating helmets and upper-body armor. Six Englishmen fell dead; more were wounded. By climbing onto the tile rooftops, however, Ralegh and company were able to reduce their exposure as well as to fire down at the Spanish soldiers in the fortress.

In response, the Spaniards ran, altogether abandoning the key defensive position, which must have been hard for the Englishmen to make sense of—prior to the paroxysm of gunfire behind them and the whines of hundreds of incoming projectiles: musket balls, mainly, and some arrows. Most cracked into adobe walls and tiles, filling the air with plaster dust. Several found their targets, though, one breaking the leg of the English drummer boy, another one killing Robert Calfield. Three other Englishmen also died.

At this point, per English privateers' prototypical plan, either the invasion force should have been on the verge of seizing control of the defensive fortifications or the Spaniards should have surrendered. But as Ralegh could plainly see, his force was well within the effective firing range of the larger of the city's two fortresses, which was manned by the Spanish soldiers who'd abandoned the smaller one. And now they could take their time finding their shots and reloading. The Englishmen's position—on rooftops lacking parapets or anything else to shield them—was now as bad as any in Cumaná, and getting worse still, with Spanish reinforcements streaming into the city from a third fortress, the existence of which was news to Caywaraco.

With no other choice, Ralegh and company leaped off the roofs and ran for their lives. Emboldened, Spaniards emerged from the big fortress, chased after the *Ingleses,* and "shot them down at their pleasure," as governor of Cumaná Francisco de Vides would report. Before driving the invaders into the sea, Vides's force killed forty-eight of them. Many more, he supposed, would die from the poisoned arrows the defenders had delivered.

Of the Englishmen lucky enough to reach the bay, several missed the departing landing craft and had to swim to the ships, requiring them to first cast off their armor and abandon their muskets—an armaments bounty for the Spaniards—and then dodge Spanish bullets fired at their backs. Of the 160 men who made it back to the fleet, at least 25 would succumb to their wounds over the next few days, among them Jacob Whiddon and Ralegh's cousin John Grenville, who'd wanted to stay behind in Arromaia.

During that interval, as the fleet lingered off the coast of Cumaná, Ralegh attempted one more cash grab, again trying to ransom Berrío. His opposite number in the negotiation was Governor Vides, Berrío's longtime nemesis—it was Vides who'd evicted Berrío from San José de Oruña in Trinidad. Vides loved the idea of Berrío being held captive on an English ship; he probably would have paid Ralegh to keep the old man. If only to cover himself in Madrid, though, the governor negotiated, offering the English drummer boy, whose broken leg had prevented his escape from Cumaná. On June 28, five days after the battle, Ralegh concluded that that was as much as he would get.

Berrío was released, the drummer boy hobbled back to the English fleet, and Ralegh tried to come up with a new plan. Any hope he had of raiding small-to-midsize Spanish Main cities—for example, Rio de la Hacha and Santa Marta—had been left in Cumaná with the piles of English corpses and armaments. Raiding Spanish ships was another story. But as his men continued to die postbattle, his assault force dwindled, along with his chances of taking a Spanish ship of any consequence. Bereft of alternatives, he gave orders to set sail for England.

Not long into the voyage, however, a pinnace and four ships' worth of reinforcements nearly ran into him: off the coast of Cuba on July 13, the fleet crossed paths with the squadron commanded by his onetime partner in the Guiana expedition, Captain Amyas Preston. Back in May, after two months of delays getting from England to the Caribbean, Preston had opted to go a-raiding on the Spanish Main rather than rendezvous with the fleet in Trinidad, a dereliction of duty that surely infuriated Ralegh. With the extra manpower in Guiana, Ralegh might have been able to move on Manoa. But here was Preston now, better late than never, with a force of three hundred men fresh off an impressive sneak attack on Caracas as well as a successful blockade of Havana. They'd even done well in Cumaná, landing on May 21 and extracting a large sum of money from the inhabitants in exchange for a promise not to plunder the city or burn it down. With Preston and his men, Ralegh could not only make short work of a Rio de la Hacha or a Santa Marta but also demand a ransom to leave. He might even be able to take a shot at the Spanish treasure fleet.

On a morning one week into preparations, though, he awoke to find no sign of Preston's squadron, which could be explained by one of the scores of reasons ships typically separated overnight. But when Preston failed to turn up in the ensuing days, it seemed more likely that he'd sighted a sail during the night and given chase, once again abandoning his commitment. Lingering bad blood from the partnership would bring Ralegh and Preston to the verge of a duel in 1602. For now, Ralegh again gave orders for the fleet to return to England.

18

KINGS OF FIGS AND ORANGES

On Sunday, September 6, 1595, half a century before the advent of universal spelling, Bess Ralegh wrote, "Sur hit tes trew I thonke the leveng God Sur Walter is safly londed." Her intent was to communicate, "Sure it is true, I thank the living God, Sir Walter is safely landed." Word of the fleet's arrival in Plymouth had just reached her at Sherborne Castle, and she was relaying the news to Robert Cecil. Walter had returned, she added, "with as gret honnor as ever man can, but with littell riches."

On receipt of her letter, Cecil wrote to an influential courtier that Ralegh had "come home well and rich." Either the acting secretary of state had been thrown by Bess's orthography or, more likely, he recognized a need to cast the best possible light on the fact that Ralegh had come home broke. But the courtiers saw through Cecil's spin. A September 25 letter from one to another shared the analysis of Lord High Treasurer William Cecil, Robert's father: "Sir Walter Rawley is returned with an assured loss of his bravest men . . . His wealth, in my Lord Treasurer's opinion 'tis made little."

Two days later, the same courtier reported that Ralegh's backers were trying to convince Queen Elizabeth that Sir Walter had done her a great service by discovering the wealth of Guiana and in "making known to that nation her virtues, her justice." They proceeded to present the case—one Ralegh had made for them in his forty-page treatise "Of the Voyage for Guyana"—that she send a return expedition with sufficient strength to colonize Guiana. The effort would be honorable and profitable, they contended. And crucial: if England didn't do it, Spain would, and with El Dorado's vast riches added to his coffers, King Philip would "be able to trouble the better part of Christendom." Without gold, as Ralegh liked to say, Philip and his predecessors would merely be "kings of figs and oranges."

The group sparked Elizabeth's interest only in meeting the prince Sir Walter had brought home, Caywaraco, son of Topiawari, king of Arromaia. Her consideration of a return voyage would hinge on Ralegh's gold samples. Already, several of his crewmen had flocked to London assayers with samples of their own from Trinidad. The peals of laughter at Whitehall belonged to the Ralegh detractors who'd heard the assayers' analysis: "marcasite, and of no riches or value." Exactly as Ralegh had warned the crewmen. Those samples were from the same calcuri mine Robyn Dudley had momentarily imagined would spur the queen to send the Royal Navy to Trinidad.

Ralegh, meanwhile, sought appraisals of his own samples by three assayers whose impartiality was universally regarded as beyond reproach. He would be happy with ore that was 0.0033 percent gold, or high average. Ore that was 0.05 percent would rate as spectacularly high grade. According to the assayers, the first of the three samples had 13.67 percent gold, or nearly three hundred times as much gold as found in spectacularly high-grade ore. The second sample was 26 percent gold, more than five hundred times as much as spectacularly high grade, and the third even better, at 30.4 percent.

But in an England still smarting from a 1577 scandal when a privateer's find of fourteen hundred tons of fool's gold had tested as "high-grade gold ore," the assayers' verdicts on the Guiana samples were written off either as rigged or the latest bit of Sir Walter's fabulism. As the joke went, an ounce of such high-grade gold and four pence gets you a loaf of bread (the cost of a loaf of bread otherwise: four pence). If Guiana really had high-grade gold, said Ralegh's detractors, surely he would have brought home more of it, or at least a witness: an explorer of Antonio de Berrío's renown and gravitas would have gone a long way toward corroborating Ralegh's claims. That Sir Walter would trade away Berrío for a drummer boy? It strained credulity.

Some of the more charitable courtiers accepted the assayers' findings but dismissed their significance based on skewed samples: the chieftains who'd given the ore to Ralegh wanted to extricate themselves from the Spaniards' yoke. What wouldn't they do to lure English forces to Guiana?

A third faction at court believed Ralegh was too soft and effete to go to Guiana himself, that he'd simply purchased the ore from the Barbary Coast. They maintained that he'd then holed up in Cornwall the whole time he purported to be abroad, weaving the expedition story from whole cloth.

Ralegh found himself on the defensive against such "malicious slanders." He would have brought home more ore, he explained, if not for the fact that in Guiana, it occurred in white quartz, which, as anyone familiar with the strength of the mineral would attest, makes the extraction of ore exceedingly difficult, "especially by us who had neither men, instruments, nor time."

Hoping that the people who mattered most—Queen Elizabeth and her privy councillors—would now grasp Guiana's potential, he returned to Sherborne Castle in late October, just in time to join Bess in celebrating their son Wat's second birthday. The lodge was now fully completed, adorned with deer statuary (a play on the name Ralegh, derived from the Old English *ra leah,* meaning "a meadow for deer"), and even more spectacular than Walter could have hoped. Yet a few days later, in a letter to Cecil, he referred to Sherborne as "a desolate place." What it lacked was news of the return expedition. "What becomes of Guiana I much desire to hear," he added, "whether it pass for a history or a fable."

His letters said nothing of his return to family life, which doesn't rule out the possibility that he was delighting in the autumnal fireworks show of his thousand acres of woods, meanwhile bouncing a giddy Wat on his knees and basking in Bess's love. Indeed the couple's correspondence over the course of their lives tells a story of unremitting passion and profound devotion to each other. The surviving letters that form the historical record for that interval, however, have Ralegh only going back to London, rowing up and down the Thames day and night to rally support for his return to Guiana, and attending church daily—perhaps praying for divine assistance.

Which seemed essential now that Berrío's capable maestre del campo Domingo de Vera and the bottomless-pocketed Robyn

Sherborne Castle

Dudley were both fitting out new expeditions. Forget winning the race to El Dorado; if either rival explorer reached Arromaia ahead of Ralegh, his efforts to win over Topiawari could well be for naught. As it was, a rumor was swirling through Guiana that Ralegh's "company were all slain, and [his] ships sunk at Cumaná." Neither Berrío nor Francisco de Vides, both of whom were jockeying for influence in Arromaia, saw any reason to refute the rumor.

Meanwhile, at El Escorial, King Philip's new 330,000-square-foot palace outside Madrid, Walter Ralegh was considered a godsend—by Domingo de Vera, who was able to rile up King Philip with news that Guaterral's pirates had invaded Trinidad, destroyed the idyllic town of San José de Oruña, slaughtered dozens of His Majesty's loyal subjects, and kidnapped the august governor of the El Dorado province, Antonio de Berrío. As a result, the greatest of all His Majesty's prizes, the golden city of Manoa, was about to fall into English hands.

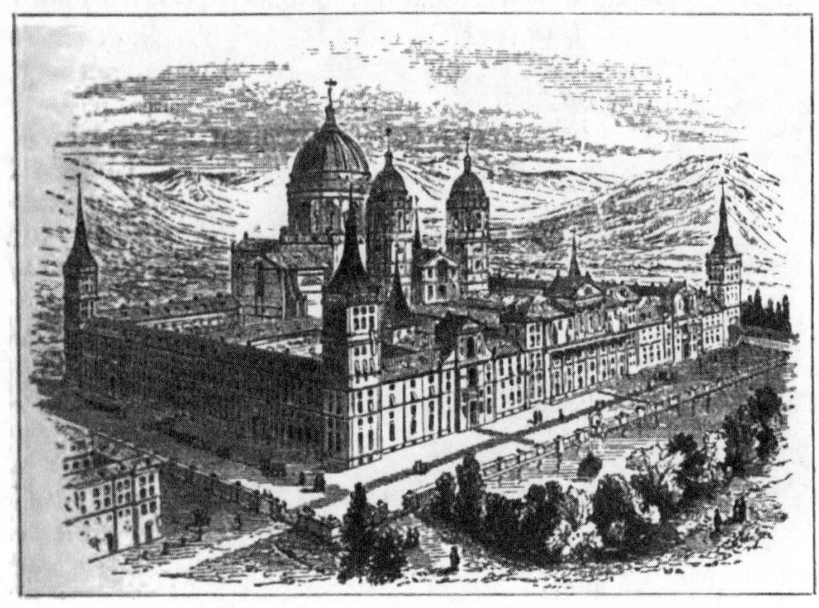

El Escorial

A concerned Philip committed seventy thousand ducats (£35,000, or enough to build one and a half Nonsuch Palaces) and six hundred unmarried soldiers, promising another four hundred married troops if Vera could also bring their wives and children to Guiana as part of a colonization effort.

Seeing the extra manpower as crucial to the advance on Manoa, Vera scrambled to find more ships. In the port city of Seville, he delivered a speech about the marvels of El Dorado that reverberated across the grand plaza, thrilling the gathered populace, who contributed five ships and five thousand ducats to the new expedition. Beating Guaterral and the *Ingleses* to El Dorado became a cause célèbre in Spain; one after another, war heroes, noblemen, and clergy joined the fleet, which would set sail from Sanlúcar in February. Quickly Vera's force numbered two thousand, excluding women and children.

Back in England, Ralegh could claim at least as many men, all of them warriors promised by Topiawari. But it made no difference. Cecil could not—or would not—buck the prevailing sentiment at court that the whole El Dorado business had been a desperate play by the old upstart to escape his disgrace. By early November 1595, two months after he'd returned from Guiana, Ralegh realized that mounting a new expedition ahead of the rainy season—or ahead of Vera—would require a minor miracle.

He got one a few days later in the return to London of privateer George Popham, who'd captured a Spanish ship carrying letters sent from South America to Spain. The headliner was one Vera had written a year earlier to King Philip detailing a visit to Guiana during which a chieftain presented him with a good deal of gold "from a province not passing a day's journey off, where there are so many Indians as would shadow the sun, and so much gold as all yonder plain will not contain it." Another of the captured epistles, penned by Spanish army official Rodrigo de Caranca, added that those Indians had "many eagles of gold hanging on their breasts," and that a Spaniard traded a hatchet to them for "an eagle that weighed 27 pounds of good gold." A third writer told of a "giant all of gold, of weight 47 quintals [4,700 pounds], which the Indians there held for their idol." Caranca also discussed Topiawari as part of his analysis that the Spaniards should emulate Ralegh's approach. Continuing their aggression in Guiana "would fill up those plains with Indians to fight us," he said, whereas "if we came in peace, we should enter and be well entertained of them."

"You may perceive by this relation that is no dream which I have reported," Ralegh wrote Cecil from Sherborne on November 12, going on to estimate the forty-seven-quintal golden idol's value at no less than £100,000. He beseeched Cecil to encourage Queen Elizabeth to act before King Philip's ramp-up precluded the option. Even "if I be thought unworthy to be employed, or . . . because of my disgrace all men fear to adventure with me," he argued, the queen should send someone else for the good of England.

Two weeks later, still at Sherborne when he needed to be in Plymouth fitting out ships, Ralegh sent Cecil another letter, warning, "If the winter pass without making provision, there can be no victualling in the summer, and if it be now foreslowed, farewell Guiana forever!"

Cecil finally swung into action, first by diverting Dudley's new expedition, probably by exerting influence as one of the enterprise's principals and by stoking Queen Elizabeth's unease over her young protégé's safety. The *Bear* and the *Whelp* would not weigh anchor again until either late the following year or early 1597, and when they did, they sailed not to Guiana but to China, and Dudley stayed home, having replaced himself with Captain Benjamin Wood. Fortuitously. Wood and his crew would never be heard from again.

Cecil's next step, lobbying Queen Elizabeth for a new El Dorado expedition, began by taking Captain Popham's letters to the Privy Council along with Ralegh's map of Guiana, which included the supposed location of Manoa. The privy councillors were more interested in the home front, specifically encroachments by the Spaniards, who in the preceding summer had followed a series of devastating raids on Cornish port cities with the construction of a new armada. The councillors were further preoccupied with England's ongoing conquest of Ireland, in crisis after as many as seven hundred English troops had been killed by the forces of rebel leader Hugh O'Neill, the Earl of Tyrone, during the Battle of Clontibret the past March.

In late November 1595, as time ran out on mounting a new expedition before the next rainy season, Ralegh glumly reflected that all his efforts in Guiana had been for naught, and that he'd "returned a

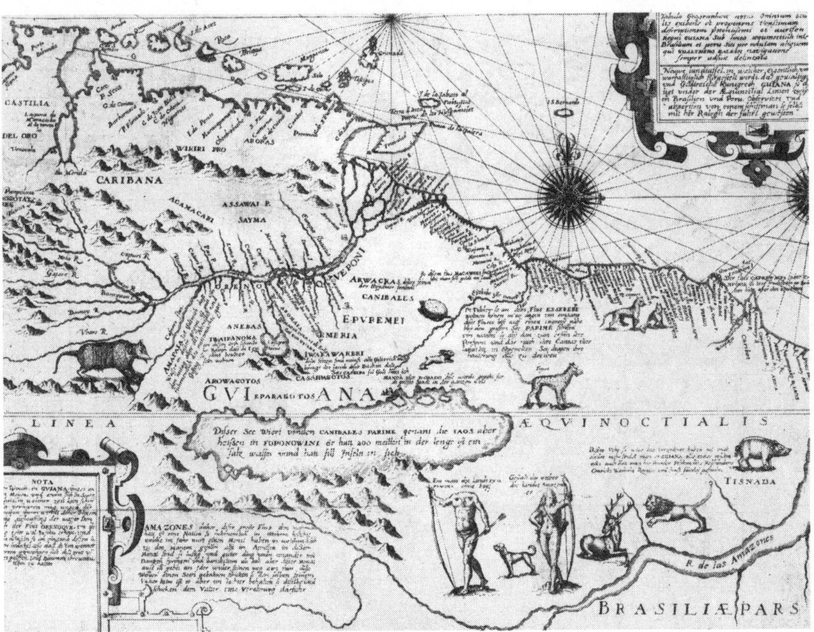

Ralegh's map of Guiana

beggar, and withered." But he still had two valuable commodities: his pen and paper. He devoted the rest of the year to writing an account of the expedition in the hope that he could transform public opinion and, in turn, Elizabeth's. The result—*The Discoverie of the large and bewtiful Empyre of Guiana, with a Relation of the Great and Golden City of Manoa (which the Spaniards Call El Dorado), Etc. Performed in the Year 1595*—would be a phenomenon.

19

HEADLESS MEN

Ralegh desperately needed to explain his delay to Topiawari, but sending even a brief message to Guiana would cost nearly as much as mounting an expedition. Nonetheless, he argued to Robert Cecil, it was imperative. Cecil agreed, donating a new ship, the *Darling of London,* and asking his father, Lord High Treasurer William Cecil, for £500 in expenses, mostly gifts for Topiawari and other chieftains—friendship dues, effectively.

Next, Ralegh looked to Lawrence Keymis to deliver the message and gifts, and, while in Guiana, to gather an incontrovertibly massive sample of 30.4 percent gold ore. The mathematician threw himself into preparations, enabling Ralegh to go to London and reap the benefits once Queen Elizabeth had read *The Discoverie of the large and bewtiful Empyre of Guiana,* his chronicle of "travels fit for boys less blasted with misfortunes, for men of greater ability, and for minds of better encouragement." The 110-page book was also a case for the colonization of "a country that hath yet her maidenhead, never sacked, turned, nor wrought, the face of the earth hath not been torn, nor the virtue of the soil spent." Whichever "prince shall possess it," he'd written, "that prince shall be lord of more gold, and of a more beautiful empire, and of more cities and people than either the king of Spain or the great Turk."

Published early in 1596, the *Discoverie* was an immediate sensation, seeing multiple printings and three editions by year's end before exploding into foreign languages. Readers paid little attention to the colonization thesis, though. Instead, the book became famous—or, rather, notorious—for the Ewaipanoma, the men who, according to Ralegh, had "eyes in their shoulders, and their mouths in the middle of their breasts." Never mind his disclaimer that he was merely relaying Guianan tales of the Ewaipanoma and that "for mine own part I saw them not." The *Discoverie*'s cartoonish illustration of the headless men didn't help. On the streets of London, a visitor would gather that Sir Walter Ralegh had made the most preposterous claim in history despite the fact, as he himself had noted, that history was saturated with reports of headless men dating back to Herodotus,

Ewaipanoma

who described the Acephali as "men with mouths on their breasts." Needless to say, the courtiers cackled themselves hoarse.

Ralegh's hopes now rested on Keymis's success in Guiana—he set sail from Portland Road on January 26, 1596—and on Antonio de Berrío's failure. The old Spaniard had never quit; as Keymis would put it, "He never would yield under the burthen of his adverse fortune."

Six months earlier, on June 28, 1595, Berrío had found himself at his lowest point to date, having just been traded for an English drummer boy to, of all people, his archrival, Francisco de Vides, the governor of Cumaná. The sixty-eight-year-old could have asked Vides for passage home, to Tunja, so that he could finally be with his children and grandchildren, and Vides would have happily granted the request, given that Tunja was nestled into the mountains eighty miles northeast of Bogotá—that is, well out of the El Dorado fray. But of course Berrío was already plotting a new run at El Dorado, beginning with trying to get passage back to Trinidad—no matter that he was likely to find few if any of his men on the island, most of them having either fled the burning San José de Oruña or been killed by the English. He could work out staffing details as he went. And perhaps Domingo de Vera would finally arrive from Spain with fresh troops.

Rather than provide Berrío with passage to Trinidad, Vides let him sit for a week and a half. It wasn't until July 8, when detaining his adversary any longer risked piquing Madrid, that Vides let him go, but only as far as Margarita. Undeterred, Berrío rounded up ten men on the island, including Alvaro Jorge, and found a vessel to take them all to Trinidad. Once there, Berrío added five more men, the remnants of his garrison force. Next, from the ashes of San José de Oruña, he managed to equip himself and his small band with ample supplies, provisions, and armaments for a new El Dorado expedition.

An old Guiana hand now, he led the party across the Gulf of Paria, through the Serpent's Mouth and the Delta, then up the Orinoco, all without incident. Skirting the Arromaians, Berrío and company landed on the southern bank of the Orinoco at its confluence with the Caroní and ascended a tall, rocky outcrop that had been known as San Thomé de Guayana since the 1570s, when it was the site of a Jesuit mission (today it's San Félix, part of Guayana City). They then wasted no time before getting to work on construction of a fort suitable as a base of operations for a Spanish advance on Manoa, completing it in early 1596, just in time for them to square off with the small force led by Lawrence Keymis.

Berrío's fortress was the latest problem in a litany of them for Keymis, beginning with a harrowing seven-week transatlantic voyage; the lone positive was that his ship, the *Darling of London,* had made it to South America. Landing on March 14, he left her at anchor and, accompanied by an interpreter and nine or ten men, started in a small boat toward the Orinoco—or, as he called it, the Raleana.

As part of his effort to deliver a message of reassurance to the Guianans, he stopped at an Arawak village in the Orinoco Delta. When he offered its residents his hand, they spit into their hands before shaking, a good sign: it affirmed their friendship. Especially pleased to see him was Ferdinando, the cassava bread trader who'd served tragicomically as the 1595 expedition's first pilot. The Spaniards had returned to Guiana in droves, Ferdinando told Keymis, and they'd resumed tormenting any Native who entered their field of vision. As Keymis would report to Ralegh, "the Indians our friends,"

having "earnestly expected our return from England these four or five months," are now "betwixt hope and fear."

Keymis continued upriver with a heightened sense of urgency. Wisely, he didn't bring Ferdinando along as pilot, but he did fill the position with someone Ferdinando had recommended, an elderly man named Gilbert. Although Gilbert knew of a deeper, easier passage through the Delta than any the English had previously found, his hire proved questionable almost immediately, when a storm hit and he was unable to get the boat ashore—for days on end. "Day and night," Keymis wrote, he and his men were "wet and weather-beaten in our coverless boat, which was sometimes ready to sink under us." Able to do little more than try to keep from being flung out of the craft, they grew progressively weak and sick. After a week, the storm lifted, leaving in its wake a brisk but manageable wind that let them sail to Arromaia in just eight days—half the time it had taken the previous year.

Then Keymis's real troubles began. First, on April 14, he and his companions landed at the port of Morequito, and none of the

Arromaians he knew were willing to spit into their hands. Nor would they deign to meet with him. As he would explain to Ralegh, "The time of our return promised at your Lordship's departure from thence [had] expired." Keymis anticipated that as soon as he explained the delay to Topiawari, the astute king would take steps to help, including providing a more substantial gold sample. But Topiawari had died, and most of his subjects had fled Arromaia because of the strengthened Spanish presence coupled with the rumor that Ralegh had been killed during his failed raid on Cumaná. And unfortunately, Topiawari's chosen successor wouldn't be much help: Caywaraco, who'd gone to England with Ralegh, was currently in military school in Flanders.

Keymis still had hope that the two young crewmen who'd volunteered to stay in Arromaia a year earlier, Francis Sparrey and Hugh Goodwin, had made inroads and could spread the message of reassurance to the Guianans just as well. He learned, however, that Sparrey had been captured by Spanish soldiers and taken to Cumaná—where his interrogation apprised the Spaniards of the existence of Topiawari's gold mine—and Goodwin had been eaten by a jaguar.

But all wasn't lost: Keymis could still salvage the expedition by ascending the Caroní River himself and collecting gold samples. From the Orinoco bank where he and his men had made camp, the mathematician now gazed up at the newly constructed stockade atop San Thomé that stood in his way. If he and his men attempted to pass it, Berrío would certainly know both that they were heading for the Caroní and why, and he wouldn't be inclined to do them any favors. Or let them live. With just ten musketeers in one small boat against fifty-five soldiers and six cannons firing down at him, the odds against Keymis were staggering. That didn't bother him: he was willing to take almost any risk for Sir Walter. But even if he and his men managed to get past San Thomé and collect a ton of very, very fine gold, in the process they would almost certainly alert the Spaniards to the whereabouts of Topiawari's mine. That was a risk Keymis couldn't take, especially when he was so close to Mount Iconuri and the chieftain Putijma's vaunted "stones the color of gold," about which the Spaniards were entirely unaware.

Rather than attempting to reach the Caroní, Keymis turned around and sailed for Warapana, intent on finding Putijma, laughing off the misunderstanding last time, and, this time, making it to the mine. As though validating Keymis's decision, the Orinoco whisked him and his men the twenty miles to Warapana in just six hours. Oddly, though, Putijma's village was deserted, and stranger still, embers were smoldering in the hearths; the only explanation was that the villagers had mistaken the Englishmen for Spaniards and run for their lives. The problem, given the recent mass exodus from Arromaia, was the distinct possibility that they would never return; without them, Keymis had little to no chance of finding Putijma's mine.

By an extraordinary stroke of luck, however, Gilbert, the pilot, had been to the Mount Iconuri mine before and could attest to it being "the richest and most plentiful" gold mine in the region—he'd even been in on the ruse Putijma used to keep interlopers away, describing it as the lair of a dragon that devoured anyone who came near. It was one day's journey overland, Gilbert said, pointing at a distant peak Keymis recognized as Iconuri.

They started toward the mountain, but ran into a problem: ten Spaniards who were living in the area, likely prospecting—and not having much luck, judging from their habit of killing Natives who refused to trade them gold and then burning down their villages. If these Spaniards saw the English party sniffing around Mount Iconuri—about which they'd no doubt heard the ridiculous dragon story—they would alert their countrymen in San Thomé, meaning the region's richest and most plentiful mine could be under Spanish control within days. Even worse, they would alert their local benefactor, the young chieftain who'd been rechristened Don Juan and was second in line, after Caywaraco, to succeed his uncle, Topiawari. Because Don Juan would do anything to delay Caywaraco's return from Europe until after he'd taken power, he would be loath to let Keymis and his companions leave Guiana, lest they get word to Caywaraco. Therefore, if his party were to linger in Warapana, Keymis reasoned, "the hope of following this voyage would be buried." It was far better, he decided, that he return to England and facilitate Caywaraco's succession.

But first, so that the results of the expedition wouldn't entirely demoralize Sir Walter, Keymis decided he would procure tobacco. Although Columbus had written about tobacco in Cuba in 1492 and explorer Sir John Hawkins was said to have brought it to England as early as 1565, Ralegh, per his Virginia enterprise, had been widely credited for introducing it to England. As the famous story went, one of his servants, seeing Sir Walter smoking a pipe for the first time and fearing that he was on fire, doused him with a bucket of ale. Ralegh liked smoking, but even had he despised it, he would love the sight of the *Darling of London*'s holds overflowing with tobacco; the proceeds would defray the expedition's cost.

Keymis sailed to St. Vincent, an island 150 miles north of Trinidad well-known for its tobacco crop, finding the Carib tobacco growers there eager to trade him a great store. But day after day, they didn't. Delays, they claimed. Really, one of their slaves confided to Keymis, they were waiting on an opportunity to kill him and his men and then eat them. Keymis and company hurriedly weighed anchor, landing at four other islands, trying and failing to obtain tobacco at each—even at Tobago, which was named for its tobacco. The growers there, evidently, had fled the Caribs.

Ralegh's servant misinterprets smoking

"Thus have I emptied your purse," Keymis wrote to Ralegh in the conclusion of his expedition report, adding, with great understatement, "Sorry I am." He would be sorrier when the report was published and a Carib's statement he'd included to extinguish the public ridicule of Ralegh—"He certified me of the headless men, and that their mouths in their breast are exceeding wide"—instead fanned the flames.

Meanwhile, Domingo de Vera was poised to deal Ralegh a far greater blow. On April 19, 1596, just as Keymis and his men were retreating from Guiana, unbeknownst to them, Vera was landing in Trinidad with far and away the largest El Dorado expeditionary force in history.

A Carib

20

HOW CAN WE FIRE ON OUR BROTHERS?

FINALLY, FINALLY, *FINALLY,* Antonio de Berrío's moment of deliverance was at hand with the arrival of twenty-eight fresh Spanish soldiers at the gate of his San Thomé fortress early in the spring of 1596. That Phelipe de Santiago was one of them was a nice twist of fate. Fifteen years earlier, when the Berrío family had first come to the New World, Phelipe was an orphan they took into their home in Tunja. Antonio and María raised him as their own, watching with pride as he grew into a spirited and resourceful soldier and quickly became a captain. Before Berrío relocated his operations to San Thomé, he decided Phelipe was the perfect overseer for Trinidad and left him in charge there. Likely the young man had now come to report the arrival of Domingo de Vera's massive force at the island and to spearhead the San Thomé troops' advance on Manoa.

Instead, Phelipe had come, as he told his adoptive father, "to expel you from this land, by order of Governor of Cumaná, Francisco de Vides." Berrío could have quibbled over whether Vides's jurisdiction included San Thomé. He also could have given voice to a tempest of outrage, indignation, vexation, and, most of all, hurt after all he and

María had done for Phelipe. It was almost inconceivable that the boy was betraying him—and for Vides, of all people!

But before Berrío could say a word, he had to contend with two dozen bursts of gunfire of which he alone was the target, rather than the fifty-some soldiers in the fortress behind him. It was an age-old tactic: eliminating the commanding officer affected his men the way decapitation does a body. As a pair of musket balls whined toward him, the sixty-nine-year-old instinctively dove back into the fortress. Both shots buzzed past his left ear, harmlessly. He didn't have to give his men the order to return fire. They'd already taken up their arquebuses, found the invaders' officers in their gunsights, and loosed a volley. One of the officers fell dead.

While both sides scrambled to reload, Berrío rethought his position and ordered his men to hold their fire. As he explained, "It's Santiago and them," which his side understood to mean, "How can we fire on our brothers?" Most of the attackers, too, couldn't find it in their hearts to kill their fellow Spaniards. Berrío had concluded as much from their first volley, when the vast majority of their sharpshooters' rounds had sailed well over his head.

He strode out of the gate and straight into the assault force, intent on conversing face-to-face with Phelipe. Within the walls of the fortress, musketeers covered Berrío as much as was possible: if the attackers sought to put a musket ball in the old man's head, they needed merely to tap a trigger. But as Berrío neared them, they lowered their guns, though all around, hands tightened on sword grips just in case.

Berrío spread his arms wide. Phelipe stepped into his embrace. The old conquistador told his onetime protégé that he'd long considered him a good soldier and an honorable man and that now he respected him even more, as he'd followed his commander's orders despite unspeakable personal repercussions. The two walked together for two or three hours, resolving to leave the matter of Vides's jurisdiction open until Domingo de Vera arrived from Spain. Phelipe then returned to Trinidad.

Vides countered by deploying more troops to Trinidad, unwavering loyalists who seized control of the island, cutting off the flow of supplies and correspondence to San Thomé and isolating Berrío. But not for long. On April 19, 1596, Vera's gargantuan fleet finally landed at Trinidad. At once, he and a hundred of his soldiers leaped onto the beach and took back the island in the name of its rightful governor, Don Antonio de Berrío.

Getting two thousand troops through the Delta and up the Orinoco was more of a challenge for Vera, with all the usual difficulties compounded by the fact that many of the soldiers had brought wives and children. He procured forty-four canoes, enough that he was able to dispatch a first wave of 470 settlers. At the outset of their journey, those men, women, and children were ravaged by thick clouds of mosquitos during the daytime, squadrons of gnats after dark, and, perpetually, the bête-rouge (French for "red-beast"), a small scarlet insect that uses its proboscis to drill into the epidermis, where it remains for a day or two, gorging itself from within a lump that is painful and intolerably itchy for the host, lasts up to two weeks, and is exacerbated by wet clothing.

And the bugs were minor annoyances compared to the difficulties that followed. First, as they always seemed to, provisions ran low. Then, on the sixth day of the journey, three hundred Caribs attacked. Although many of the settlers were small-town folk with little combat experience, they had firearms. But even the veteran marksmen had difficulty shooting bulky arquebuses with any accuracy from wobbly canoes, much less reloading in cramped confines with water flying every which way, extinguishing their matches and spoiling their gunpowder. It was enough of a job to dodge the arrows ripping toward them at a hundred miles an hour.

The Caribs killed dozens of the settlers, and in several cases they slashed open a man's chest, plucked out his heart, and ate it—before devouring the rest of him. They were, according to one of the settlers, "voracious for human flesh." Several Spanish women were spared, but only to be carried off by the Caribs for use as concubines. Fortunately, Vera was right behind the settlers with a second wave of a hundred soldiers. But before he could repel the Caribs, he ran into a hurricane that drowned forty of his men and destroyed all but three of his canoes.

Most of the five hundred or so survivors from the two groups wound up having to continue to San Thomé on foot through the snake-and-insect-infested mire. The trek was excruciating for the men, even before they had to carry the children, whose feet were so blistered they could barely stand, much less walk. Nevertheless, in late June or early July 1596, fifty-four days after setting out from Trinidad, the settlers reached San Thomé. Despite their exhaustion, everybody donned their finest clothing for the occasion, and several of them exultantly waved shiny banners.

Now Berrío had sufficient manpower to move on Macureguarai, the gateway to Manoa. Or did he? Reviewing the new arrivals, he felt as though he'd been transported to a gala in Seville. Any general would have been given pause by a crowd of amateurs in lavish attire suitable for a wedding rather than for war. But even if their combat skills belied their appearance, Berrío thought, he would struggle to feed so many mouths. Furious at Vera's failure to bring adequate supplies, he sent the maestre del campo back to Trinidad, where the remaining fifteen hundred Spaniards were also in desperate need of provisions. Over the next eight months there, what Vera characterized as "a long series of hardships"—illness, starvation, and deaths—led to desertions, rebellion, and, ultimately, his fade to obscurity.

In San Thomé, meanwhile, Berrío managed to cull some 250 able men from the transplants. Adding fifty of his existing troops, he sent them to Macureguarai as an advance force while he awaited the next wave of soldiers from Trinidad to commence the invasion of Manoa.

Once the advance force started up the Caroní River, providing for the settlers in San Thomé proved even more difficult than Berrío had feared. His fledgling town had yet to grow the crops needed to sustain itself. The Arromaians, who'd traded him fresh provisions in the past, had largely fled the area. And the new arrivals from Spain proved incapable of procuring food for themselves; they resorted to consuming their fancy leather shoes—and praying that their soldiers would return from Macureguarai with real food.

The soldiers were led by Alvaro Jorge, who, like Berrío, was now well into his sixties. As ever, the ascent of the Caroní was arduous, this time to the extent that, just a few days into it, Jorge died. With him went the troops' discipline. Rather than barter with the riverside tribes for provisions, they helped themselves to whatever they wanted, including women. Any tribesman who resisted was put to death—until thousands of angry tribesmen resisted at once, ambushing the Spaniards and killing all but the fifty who were able to escape to San Thomé.

At the same time, more settlers trickled into the town from Trinidad, an influx that was a double-edged sword for Berrío. He sorely needed reinforcements, but he was still unable to provide for the men, women, and children already under his charge, all hollow-eyed sacks of bones at this point. As it happened, the new arrivals included dozens of priests, but as much as San Thomé stood to benefit from their prayers, Berrío would have preferred a single carpenter. Every time there was a storm—which is to say, constantly, with the rainy season now underway—the thatched roofs blew off the huts he'd slapped together for the settlers, exposing them to the elements.

Insects were a greater concern. Because the first wave of settlers had eaten their shoes, they had been walking around barefoot, enabling sand fleas to burrow into their soles and lay eggs by the hundreds, resulting in painful bumps and lesions. The settlers would experience a measure of relief and revulsion four weeks later, when the eggs hatched and baby sand fleas—which could pass for quarter-inch langoustines—wormed their way out. The more pressing issue was the infection left behind. In San Thomé, the stench of it alone was insufferable—and inescapable, because venturing outside the town's walls meant death at the hands of now vengeful Natives. Soon the settlers began dying on their own, and their rotting corpses piled up. Although the bodies were "as light as if they were made of straw," per one account, the survivors lacked the strength to bury them.

Still, Berrío remained optimistic, maintaining that his soldiers would not only persevere but also learn from their mistakes and reach Manoa after all. Consequently, fifteen or sixteen of the soldiers' wives armed themselves with butcher's knives and snuck toward his house in the middle of the night, intent on assassinating him. A nun talked them out of it, allowing Berrío to face yet another round of insects. Crickets this time, a plague's worth. Their chirps blended into one incessant banshee shriek as they enveloped the settlement, pouring into the huts through windows, doors, and the apertures that roofs had once covered, then gnawing to bits whatever they landed on—chairs, books, clothing, trunks—leaving the settlers with literally nothing.

With Berrío out of reasonable arguments for them to stay in San Thomé, the settlers went home, or, rather, they tried to, throwing themselves into the first boat or canoe they found, even though most of the craft were in deplorable condition, and all lacked pilots. Unsurprisingly, very few of the settlers survived the return journey.

Berrío's dream was shattered. To an El Doradan, however, that means only that reassembly is required. Along with a handful of other diehards, he replaced the roofs on the huts, constructed new furniture, and eked out sustenance. At the end of the rainy season, those efforts were rewarded with the arrival of his son, Fernando—now twenty—from Bogotá. Although nearly two years late, Fernando's timing couldn't have been better considering the thirty fresh troops he brought. And money and supplies, enough that Berrío was able to buy his way back into the hearts of the neighboring tribes, facilitating a healthy and potent Manoa expeditionary force in early 1597.

At long last, the seventy-year-old could have closure, savor having solved the riddle, and see his struggles and sacrifices recast as testament to perseverance. With heaps of gold, he would also be able to compensate his children and grandchildren for his long absence, and, in retirement in Tunja, he could bask in their love. El Doradans can achieve a harmonious balance of adventure and family after all, he would be able to tell Walter Ralegh.

Before the expedition could set out, Berrío fell terminally ill. No one would have been surprised if he managed to shake it off and lead the way into the golden city: Antonio de Berrío had always been impervious to disease, not to mention starvation, drowning, jaguars, serpents, poisoned arrows, blow darts, musket balls, and most every other form of adversity. This time, however, he proved mortal.

Yet even on his deathbed, he had hope of attaining El Dorado: his son Fernando vowed to remain in San Thomé and continue the quest. The old man's response wasn't recorded. Likely he was gratified. Or perhaps he saw it as the prologue to the damnation it proved to be, especially if, after quietly departing the earthly realm a few days later, he was privy to his son's effort. The same qualities responsible for Fernando's two-year delay in reaching San Thomé continually undermined him: he was "slothful," per an official report, and corrupt, costing him his position as governor of San Thomé in 1612. Sharing his father's resilience, though, he won reappointment in 1619 and resumed his search, mounting a total of as many as twenty expeditions by 1622, when he sailed to Spain to rally support for the next one. But he was captured by Barbary pirates and taken to Algiers, where, while awaiting ransom, he died of the plague.

21

RALEGH HATH MADE ME LOVE HIM

In early 1596, Walter Ralegh's path to El Dorado appeared to wind through the Spanish city of Cádiz. After the Spaniards had raided the English port of Penzance the previous August, he'd told any privy councillor who would listen that Queen Elizabeth needed to take the offensive against Spain. Otherwise, the Spaniards would invade England. With his disgrace having been compounded by the laughter still resounding from *The Discoverie of the large and bewtiful Empyre of Guiana,* however, his credibility was such that he might as well have been warning that England would be invaded by an army of headless men.

But on April 24, when the Spaniards took the French port city of Calais and were suddenly just twenty miles across the English Channel, Secretary of State Robert Cecil and his fellow privy councillors rediscovered their appreciation for Ralegh's geopolitical intuition and, accordingly, they urged Elizabeth to attack Spain. A successful raid of Cádiz, they maintained, would both cripple King Philip II's offensive capability and replenish England's drafty coffers: in addition to warships, Cádiz served as the base for the Tierra Firme (Mainland) treasure fleet, which annually carried goods and supplies to the New World before returning to Spain with riches. Elizabeth consented, leading to the assembly of the largest fleet to that point in England's history, a total of 120 ships: 96 English and 24 from another of the Spaniards' enemies, the Dutch.

If the banished Walter Ralegh could be one of the sixteen thousand men aboard the vessels, he could rehabilitate his reputation and thereby revive his El Dorado backers' hopes of a return on their investment. So thought one of those backers, Cecil, who pleaded Ralegh's case to Robert Devereux, the Second Earl of Essex—universally referred to simply as "Essex"—who, along with Charles Howard, was commanding the Cádiz expedition. Essex, who had long been Ralegh's chief competitor for the title of Royal Favourite, seldom ignored an opportunity to undercut him. But in this case, he regarded his rival's singular combination of naval and infantry experience as an asset; he even asked Ralegh to join the war council advising him.

The fleet sailed from Plymouth on June 1, 1596, a veritable forest of masts, rigging, and canvas. A thousand miles and nineteen days later, on a dangerously choppy June 20, Essex, Howard, and company anchored a mile and a half from Cádiz. The famously wealthy city of ten thousand sat on the base of a narrow, six-mile-long isthmus that resembled a compass needle pointing north-northwest. Between the isthmus and the mainland was a harbor shaped like a bottle standing on end, with most of the Spanish ships moored at its base. To get to the Tierra Firme fleet, the English needed to sail east around the tip of the needle and then south through the neck of the bottle, a half-mile-wide strait protected by a pair of Spanish forts. Under fire from the forts, the Englishmen would have to outmaneuver the vessels defending the harbor, including several of Spain's great warships known as the Twelve Apostles.

Four of the Apostles were in Cádiz at the moment, Howard and Essex were told by the crew of an Irish merchant ship that had just left the port. Otherwise, the Irishmen said, there were very few warships. It was hard to imagine that all the lookouts and vessels along the Portuguese coast had failed to spot the largest English fleet ever assembled, but that's exactly what seemed to have happened.

Without question, it was an extraordinary opportunity. Unfortunately, Howard and Essex couldn't agree on how to capitalize. In fact, they couldn't agree on anything. Which was no surprise based on a glance at them, the hawk-nosed and otherwise hawk-featured sixty-year-old lord high admiral together with the sparkly eyed redhead half his age made for a sight gag. In temperament, the conservative Howard and the impulsive Essex were also polar opposites; it was a wonder they didn't physically repel each other.

Considered the second coming of Sir Galahad by both an adoring public and himself, Essex wanted the entire English fleet to charge immediately into the bottleneck in a formidable, magnificent, and glorious assault. Seeing no reason to subject his men unnecessarily to a squall of cannonballs, Howard argued for a more measured approach, beginning by landing and neutralizing the fort on the tip of isthmus. Essex relented, suspiciously easily, piling his men into landing craft and disembarking them—a reckless move, given the violent southerly gusts transforming the waves into battering rams.

Aboard the *Warspite,* Ralegh watched the waves toss about the ordinarily sturdy landing craft as if they were eggshells. Within minutes, several sank, along with their armor-laden passengers. At the rate things were going, the sea would do the Spaniards' job for them. Ralegh dropped into the froth in a skiff, raced over to Essex's ship, the *Due Repulse,* and offered a blunt assessment even though criticizing the thin-skinned and vainglorious admiral could mean a demotion to cabin boy. By landing now, Ralegh said, Essex was risking "the utter overthrow of the whole armies" and "general ruin."

Essex agreed. Landing was a tactical error. Howard's error. But to pause now, he said, would be "esteemed an effect of fear."

Persuading him to hold off, Ralegh jumped back into his skiff and sped to Howard's ship to advance an alternative plan. The lord high admiral approved it, so long as Ralegh directed the effort. Essex for once agreed with Howard.

At the break of the next day, heading up a nineteen-ship vanguard that included Essex's *Due Repulse,* Ralegh's *Warspite* charged into the bottleneck leading to Cádiz's harbor. The Englishmen's high spirits were given pause by a series of distant, deep-throated booms that, a fraction of a second later, were drowned out by the raspy buzz of incoming cannonballs flying a hundred miles an hour. Each twenty-something-pound cast-iron ball could destroy a man if it so much as clipped him. Even if it landed on the deck a dozen feet away and hit a plank, by transferring enough kinetic energy to effectively turn the splinters into bullets, it could still kill him.

The cannonballs originated from the base of the strait, launched from a fortress that was ringed by a moat and heavily manned stone bulwarks, meaning Ralegh had no chance of landing men and neutralizing it. Enough cannonballs smashing through the *Warspite*'s hull would sink her, but his greater concern was a shot to her masts. The larger of the two, the mainmast, although taller and thicker than most trees, could snap like a matchstick if struck near its midpoint. And a shot to its base might topple it, bringing down sails, yards (the spars from which sails are set), and a rain of blocks and sheaves and other pieces of rigging substantial enough to split a man's skull. Deprived of the use of sails, Ralegh would no longer be able to maneuver the ship, leaving her to be jigsawed by the cannons aboard the Apostles, the four gargantuan warships now hurtling toward him along with seventeen several smaller vessels, the lot adding cannon fire to what sounded like a thunderstorm. But it was more than a sound. It was also a shove: Ralegh and his men could feel the force of the hot air in their hair, their stomachs, and their teeth. It stood to reason that they would return fire. Ralegh commanded his cannon crews to hold their fire, though. His musketeers too. Everyone but the trumpeter: following each Spanish discharge that failed to impact the ship, Ralegh had him play a melancholy *wah-wah-wah*, mocking the Spaniards.

The Spaniards had to wonder if the *Warspite*'s commander had lost his mind—which was what he wanted them to think, especially the crew of the *San Felipe*, the largest and most potent of the Apostles. Because the *Warspite* stood no chance in a shootout with the giant warship, Ralegh's best hope of defeating the *San Felipe* was to board her.

First, he needed to clear her decks of musketeers, for whom Englishmen leaping across the watery gap between the two vessels would be like low-hanging fruit. Clearing the *San Felipe*'s decks presented quite a challenge to his own musketeers, however: they would have to fire with extreme precision at a smoke-obscured moving target from a heaving deck, all the while taking fire themselves.

Three hours later, they'd yet to get close enough to the *San Felipe* to fire a single musket ball. Because Queen Elizabeth would be livid if her expensive new man-of-war were destroyed, Essex had forbidden Ralegh from sailing anywhere near the *San Felipe*. Instead, the earl said, he would send over a pair of smaller, nimble flyboats for Ralegh to use to board. Inexplicably, he'd yet to deliver them. Likely, Ralegh thought, Essex was "glory-jockeying," disregarding a battle plan so as to position himself to deliver the decisive blow to the enemy, that moment that would live forever in oil on canvas. Whatever the reason, without the flyboats to board the *San Felipe*, Ralegh was forced into an exchange of broadsides—simultaneous discharges of all the artillery on one side of a vessel. It was exactly the firefight he'd sought all along to avoid—and that was before a second Apostle, the *San Andrés*, joined the fray.

The *Warspite* was clearly getting the worst of it; despite frantic efforts to patch the breaches in her hull, she was sinking. Getting into his skiff, Ralegh dodged Spanish cannonballs, going to the *Due Repulse* and demanding Essex's permission to use the *Warspite* to board the *San Felipe*. It hardly mattered if the *Warspite* burned in the process, Ralegh said, since, as it stood, she was going to sink. Cowed, Essex gave his word of honor that he would second whatever decision Ralegh made. Ralegh knew from experience, though, that the earl's word of honor had an implicit caveat: "Unless I change my mind."

Proceeding with the attempt to board regardless, Ralegh hurried back to the *Warspite* and then drove her toward the *San Felipe* through a herd of cannonballs, some forty-eight having been discharged at once. One of them thumped onto the deck near him. Harmlessly, it seemed, save perhaps snapping a plank or two, but something impacted his leg, boring through bone and tissue, collapsing him to the deck. Through the tear in his breaches, he saw that his calf was "interlaced and deformed with splinters" though not hemorrhaging enough, thankfully, to hold him out of the fight. Struggling to his feet, he discovered he could no longer walk without support—nor would he for the rest of his life. But for the time being, he wasn't hindered from directing *Warspite* ahead, a fresh torrent of cannonballs be damned.

This was definitely madness from the point of view of the men aboard the *San Felipe,* who'd woken up that day without any expectation of engaging the English fleet, much less of keeping a horde of sword-swinging *Ingleses* with a death wish from their decks. Accordingly, the *San Felipe*'s crewmen let the tide carry their vessel onto the sandy shore. The crew of the *Santo Tomás,* another of the Apostles, followed suit. A sound maneuver, from Ralegh's perspective. On shore, the Spanish sailors could more easily protect their ships and themselves.

But rather than mounting any sort of defense, they were simply bent on fleeing; that became clear moments later when both Apostles burst into flames. Rather than lose the two great galleons to the enemy, the Spanish crews had set them on fire—precipitously, though. Before the men could disembark, they found themselves penned in by walls of flame intensified by continual detonations of gunpowder. Tumbling out of vessels and into the sea came "heaps of soldiers," as Ralegh recorded, "so thick as if coals had been poured out of a sack," several of them forced underwater, drowning in the bedlam. At least five other Spanish crews did succeed in destroying their vessels, allowing the incoming English and Dutch ships to breeze past them and capture the harbor.

Thanks to Ralegh's gambit, the English were able to land their infantry. By nightfall, they'd taken the city. Now the invaders could claim the spoils of victory, savor the exhilaration of being fired on without result, and then celebrate. For Ralegh, it would be a badly needed payday, but his wounded leg prevented him from going. Intent on carrying the conquering hero into town, his crewmen hoisted him atop their shoulders. Still, the pain was unbearable.

Remaining on the *Warspite,* he watched his countrymen run past like children on Christmas morning. Among them was Essex, who, in the giddy rush, paid no heed to the fleet of rich commercial vessels, nor the Spanish merchants offering two million ducats (£1 million) as ransom for their cargo. The oversight would allow Spanish soldiers to torch the vessels, leaving the English with zero ducats.

Ralegh's captain's share of the booty from the city was worth £1,769, enough to pay the staff at Sherborne for a year. While it rankled him that other officers who'd merely ridden his coattails came away with much more, he saw the real prize as Queen Elizabeth. "I hope her most excellent Majesty will take my labours and endeavours in good part," he wrote Cecil. "Other riches than the hope thereof, I have none."

As the English fleet sailed back to Plymouth, he would have been pleased to know, his restoration in London was underway thanks to letters sent ahead by his comrades. Another member of the war council wrote that "Sir Walter Ralegh's service was so much praiseworthy as those who were formerly his enemies do now hold him in great estimation." Indeed, as a longtime Ralegh detractor said, "I never knew the gentleman until this time, and I am sorry for it, for there are in him excellent things beside his valour; and the observation he hath in this voyage used . . . hath made me love him."

22

THE CARVING OF THE QUEENE'S MEATE

IT WASN'T JUST a brilliant victory; it was the worst defeat ever dealt King Philip II on his own soil, made worse still when the English force torched Cádiz, burning down nearly half the city. Whoops and cheers could be heard throughout England.

Except at court. Why, demanded Queen Elizabeth, had any of her subjects profited from Cádiz? The expedition was supposed to have been a national enterprise with the proceeds used to defray its cost, which is to say, her cost. Instead, her army had looted the city like a horde of besotted pirates while ignoring a port full of merchant ships, an oversight that enabled Spanish soldiers to set the ships on fire to keep them out of English hands. If the merchants had been willing to pay a £1 million ransom for the vessels, what must their cargo have been worth? £10 million wasn't out of the question.

Even more infuriating to Elizabeth were the vessels that had escaped immolation: the Tierra Firme fleet—the same blasted mainland treasure fleet that had been half the point of the raid—had been spotted in Lisbon a few days later, meaning the two dozen ships must have slipped out of Cádiz right under her men's noses.

Actually, under Sir Walter Ralegh's nose, crowed the courtiers, spinning the reports of his heroics into blame. Essex had returned to court by then—mid-August 1596—and could have corrected the record, but he was too busy absorbing the queen's vitriol for his own gaffes. Not that he would have propped up his rival even in the best of circumstances.

Needless to say, back at Sherborne Castle, Ralegh wasn't receiving any royal riders requesting his presence at the palace for Her Majesty to show her appreciation. Absent such an invitation, different riders would soon appear, requesting his presence in civil court to answer for his unpaid debts.

Meanwhile, he was incurring fresh El Dorado expenses, primarily outfitting a new pinnace, the *Wat* (his son Walter's nickname), to explore the region south of the Orinoco in hope of finding a route to Manoa that was free of both cataracts and Spaniards. The *Wat*'s commander, Leonard Berry, would also be responsible for Anglo-Guianan diplomatic relations, which needed resurrection in light of Topiawari's death as well as the devastating news that the king's son Caywaraco had taken ill at military school and died, leaving the Hispanophile Don Juan as the likely successor. And while in Guiana, if Berry could bring back gold sufficient to restore Ralegh's reputation and coffers, that would be nice too.

When Berry sailed from London's Limehouse docks on October 14, 1596, all of Ralegh's hopes were with him. As much as Ralegh was inclined to leap aboard the *Wat* himself, however, he felt obligated to stay in England: Spain was about to attack again, he believed, and the country needed to act. In his paper "Opinion upon the Spanish Alarum," he made the case for a preemptive strike against King Philip. But the fallout from Cádiz had kicked his credibility back into the gutter; "Opinion upon the Spanish Alarum" could have included the Spanish plan of attack in King Philip's own handwriting and still the courtiers would have cried that the paper was just the latest example of Ralegh's fearmongering and opportunism.

As it happened, King Philip came to Ralegh's aid ten days later, by sending the Second Spanish Armada, with 19,500 men aboard 140 ships, to invade England—just as an epic storm hit. It cost the armada five thousand men and thirty-eight ships, including five Apostles, and forced the survivors to retreat to Spain. The upshot was that Ralegh was again an "oracle," and, over the months that followed, Queen Elizabeth realized that unless she wanted to bet her realm on another deus ex machina defense against the inevitable Third Spanish Armada, she needed such an adviser.

On June 2, 1597, five years after she'd banished Ralegh from court, she invited him back. The forty-five-year-old's sentiments that day were not recorded, though at any moment, while his wherry cut through the murky Thames and wove in and around the barges on the way from Durham House to Whitehall, or as he was admitted to the palace and once again breathed the familiar bouquet of wood polish, old leather, and pomander, it would have been understandable if he expected to suddenly find himself in his Sherborne bedroom, awaking from his recurring dream of a second chance.

Two months shy of her sixty-fourth birthday, Elizabeth wore a bold red wig bedecked with rubies and pearls, emphasizing a face that, as ever, was caked in white makeup (used to conceal pockmarks from her 1562 smallpox bout) but had become a road map of wrinkles since Ralegh last saw her. Of her teeth, one visitor noted, "Many of them are missing so that one cannot understand her easily when she speaks quickly." Per other sources, she had all her teeth; they only appeared to be missing because they'd turned black—something of an epidemic in sixteenth-century England due to the surge in sugar importation. Nevertheless, the courtiers told her, she was "very youthful still in appearance, seeming no more than twenty years of age."

The sole record of the reunion is a letter from Rowland Whyte to another courtier relating that the queen treated Ralegh "very graciously." Perhaps they both savored the rapprochement or the rediscovery of their old friendship, or maybe they said only what was expedient to renew their working relationship. In any case, "in the evening he [rode] abroad with the Queen, and had private conference with her," and at the conclusion of the ride, she restored him to his role as captain of the guard. He also received the coveted dinnertime honor of the "Carving of the Queene's Meate," and, not long after that, as Whyte related, "he comes boldly to the Privy-chamber, as he was wont."

But what Whyte either didn't know or didn't add was that Ralegh's deception still rankled Elizabeth. Also, her coolness—or, at least, her collegiality in place of the old ardor—deprived him of the requisite whip in his new role at court, which amounted to lion tamer. If he were to maintain his tenuous position, let alone return to Guiana, he had to control the pair of lions fighting for supremacy, Cecil and Essex, at the same time collaborating with them on a plan to counter the Spanish threat.

Finding common ground for the two might have been simple. They were close in age—Cecil thirty-three and Essex thirty-one—and they'd spent much of their childhood together: when the First Earl of Essex, Walter Devereux, had died in 1576, his son, the eight-year-old Second Earl of Essex, went to live with the Cecils as their ward. The two boys never developed a brotherly relationship, though, save for squabbling.

The strategizing sessions in 1596 were no different. While the public saw Essex as a war hero, Cecil saw someone who, apart from looking good in a uniform, had possessed no qualifications whatsoever when he was appointed colonel general of the cavalry by Queen Elizabeth, and who, since, had unfailingly opted for whatever tactic

Robert Devereux, the Second Earl of Essex

offered him the greatest opportunity for glory, England's strategic objectives be damned. He was doing it now, calling for the English fleet to blaze into the Galician port city of Ferrol and destroy the Second Spanish Armada ships that had found refuge there after the storm. The Spaniards were simply too well entrenched in Ferrol, Cecil argued, with Ralegh adding that the Spanish defenses would only be bolstered by the summer storms. Essex acknowledged the difficulties but embraced them for the glory they would add to the English victory.

Ralegh's ability to mediate, meanwhile, was constrained by Cecil's mistrust of him and Essex's tendency to filter everything he said for grounds to run to Elizabeth and get him sent back to Sherborne for good. Seeking to at least subtract the circus that was court from the equation, Ralegh invited them to dinner at Durham House, a place

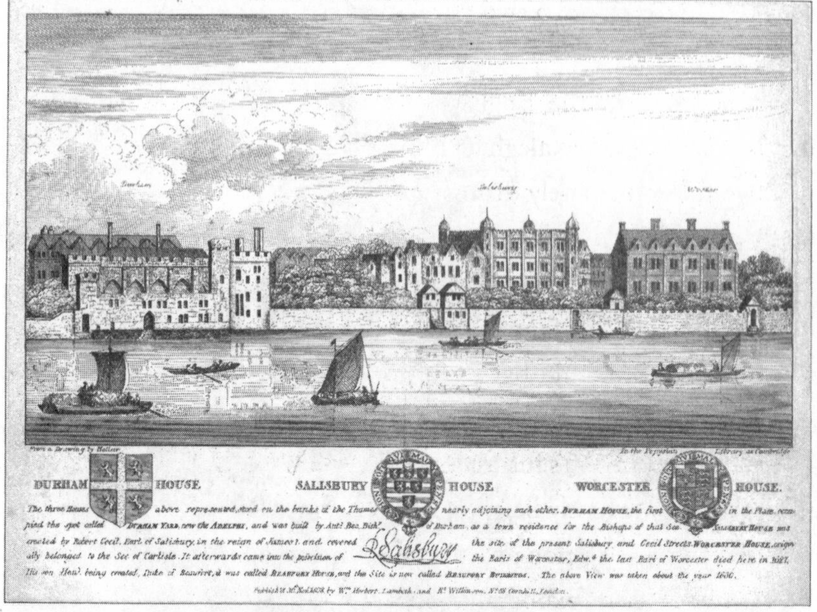

Durham House (left), Salisbury House, and Worcester House on the Thames

that made the impossible seem attainable when people set aside their differences: here, aristocrats in silk stockings and starched linen ruffs were chatting with half-naked Guianans who'd come from the New World with Keymis. There, graceful socialites in the latest couture gowns dined on Ming dynasty porcelain with the very pirates who'd seized it from a Spanish galleon out of Brazil. And everyone joined the leading lights of the arts, science, and exploration in discussing dreamed-of ventures.

Durham House helped insofar as Essex returned the favor at Essex House, then Cecil hosted at Cecil House, and soon the three were regular dining companions. They even caught a show together, Shakespeare's *Richard II*, about a monarch undermined by his favoritism. Just like their boss! They were developing a relationship that, despite the enmity, felt like friendship. Soon, they'd hammered out a two-part Spanish plan they took to Queen Elizabeth.

It began with the English fleet attacking Ferrol—per Essex's insistence. Cecil and Ralegh let him advance the idea, believing Elizabeth would immediately dismiss it for the pitfall it was and instruct them to proceed directly to the second half of the plan, refreshing her treasury by ambushing the Spanish treasure fleet. In her analysis, however, Ferrol was a fantastic opportunity, leaving Cecil and Ralegh to wonder if she would have approved an attack of the moon if her handsome favorite had advanced it.

Suddenly, Ralegh's future hinged on a fraught plan, and his stakes in its success were only heightened with Captain Berry's return from his six-month expedition to Guiana a few days later, on June 20, 1597. Berry delivered an exuberant report of amazingly fertile territory south of the Orinoco, where he'd discovered the Essequibo River. According to the locals, he said, the waterway came "within a day's journey of the lake called Parima, whereupon Manoa is supposed to stand." An impassable waterfall prevented him from seeing the city, but he'd received confirmation from the same locals of its "good store of gold."

Berry's report, in sum, was the same as those of the previous hundred El Dorado expeditions, and it had nothing new Ralegh could use to excite the queen—or anyone other than Berry himself—about a return expedition. And there was new urgency for a return expedition because Spain was on the verge of acquiring the services of Francis Sparrey, the young English crewman who'd stayed behind in Guiana in 1595 and was captured by Spaniards.

According to one of Cecil's spies in Madrid, Sparrey was now trying to barter gold for his freedom. By trading knives, axes, mirrors, and combs in Guiana, he told his captors, he'd amassed a million ducats (£500,000) worth of gold, which he'd buried. He was willing to let

King Philip have 80 percent of it. Ralegh would also hear that Sparrey had found a "sufficient" mine "of which the Spaniard knoweth not." It was easy to conclude that during his stay in Arromaia, Sparrey had learned the whereabouts of Topiawari's mine, meaning the Spaniard was about to know about that too.

As soon as possible, therefore, Ralegh needed to get to Guiana—with a force large enough to beat back the Spaniards. To accrue the necessary political capital, however, he would first have to sail to Ferrol and help Essex execute a dangerously flawed attack plan.

23

THEY DID NOT DEIGN TO TAKE OFF THEIR HATS

On July 13, 1597, three days into the English fleet's five-hundred-mile voyage to Ferrol, Rear Admiral Walter Ralegh's concerns about summertime storms were vindicated by towering thunderclouds, a sea he characterized as "raised and enraged," and wind so strong he needed to lower his sails to keep them from being "rent off the yards." He was in command of four of the fleet's 120 vessels, which all "rolled so vehemently, and so disjointed themselves" that their ribs, stanchions, and transverses splintered, admitting seawater along with rain. On his own ship, the bulkheads burst apart, the brick cook room was "shaken down into powder," and seasickness had a comparable effect on the crew—fatally, in the case of one of the gentleman volunteers. It all added up to the sort of tempest that taught sailors that they and their thousand-ton ships were but balls and jacks in the hands of fate. There was no choice but to return to England.

If they could. No longer able to use either his sails or rudder, Ralegh had his men try dragging her anchor to control their ship. Failing, they "made account to have yielded our souls up to God." With some combination of divine help, improved conditions, and luck, they managed to reach Falmouth three days later, along with most of the battered fleet, including Essex's flagship, which was all but totaled.

While the ships underwent repairs, Ralegh tried again to dissuade the earl from Ferrol, to no avail. The fleet set out anew a month later, on August 17, 1597, and was once again pummeled by foul weather, this time scattering the ships and thereby alerting the Spaniards to the threat to Ferrol. Only then did Essex call off the attack, ordering everyone to sail to the Azores—an archipelago nine hundred miles west of Lisbon—to ambush the Spanish treasure fleet. It was a questionable move now, as England would be left without any naval defense against the very Spanish ships Essex and company were supposed to have destroyed.

Sure enough, while the English fleet was in the Azores—before retreating with little more than barnacles to show for the three-month operation—the Spaniards rallied. When Ralegh landed in Cornwall in late October 1597, he found his countrymen in a panic because the Spanish warships in Ferrol had joined the Third Armada, 136 vessels in all and now bearing down on an England unable to defend herself, as most of Essex's 120 ships had been blocked from the English Channel by a vicious storm.

As it happened, the Third Spanish Armada ran into the teeth of that storm; less than a third of the ships made it home. Still, Queen Elizabeth lit into Essex when he landed, on October 26. How could he have skipped past the Spanish fleet in Ferrol, his primary objective? And even if he hadn't bungled the Azores, if not for the storm, the two of them would now be prostrating themselves before King Philip.

Contrition was in order, but Essex had come to court fuming over the news that Elizabeth had given the earldom of Nottingham to his old nemesis Charles Howard rather than to him. Instead of

begging her forgiveness, he demanded a duel with Howard—or, in recognition of the fact that the lord high admiral was sixty-one, one of his sons. Elizabeth had abolished dueling in 1571, deeming such violence puerile, and she was unwilling to make an exception now. Her response sickened Essex, literally, or so he claimed as he bolted the palace and fled to his country house in Wanstead, where he barricaded himself in his bedroom and buried himself in cloaks and blankets.

He knew what he was doing. Elizabeth begged to take care of him. A few days later, when he returned to London to help her welcome a visiting French delegation, she couldn't have been more grateful. Once again, he was the Favourite, making the courtiers in his orbit that much keener to spread the dirt he dished on his rivals, for instance that Walter Ralegh had faced court-martial in the Azores for attacking the Spaniards without permission. Likely, the versions that resounded through London omitted the fact that Essex himself had levied the charge in a pique after his tardiness forced Ralegh into action without him, depriving him of the glory. And almost certainly the retellings left out the aftermath: when the earl cooled down, he gathered that Ralegh had done nothing wrong and dropped the case. Similarly, there is no record of Essex recounting the solitary thing that went right on the voyage—namely, the capture of a Spanish galleon carrying £50,000 in goods—by Ralegh.

Consequently, on December 21, 1597, when Ralegh went to the House of Lords on a parliamentary matter, the members neither invited him to sit down nor took off their hats, demonstrations of respect customarily extended to any visiting dignitary. To anyone, in fact, but a common servant. The message was clear: "My fortune at court," as Ralegh would put it, was "at a stand."

He needed El Dorado as much as ever, but more than at any other time, it was out of reach. In the ensuing months, all he could get from Elizabeth were thankless official tasks, like arbitrating title disputes wherein any decision was liable to infuriate at least one of the parties, and he was "made mad with intricate affairs and want of means."

King Philip II came to his aid again, this time by dying—in September 1598—creating a power vacuum after a quarter century of his stewardship of Spain's El Dorado effort. At the same time, a seat opened on the Privy Council, an opportunity for Ralegh to steer England toward Guiana. He diligently worked the angles and poured all his remaining political capital into his campaign for the position, but it went to Gilbert Talbot, notable for his collection of titles, including Seventh Earl of Shrewsbury, Seventh Earl of Waterford, and Thirteenth Baron Talbot, along with the subsidiary titles of Sixteenth Baron Strange of Blackmere and Twelfth Baron Furnivall.

Meanwhile, the Dutch had leaped into the breach, sending two ships to Trinidad in December 1597, and, from there, launching four small boats onto the continent as far as the Caroní River, where they would search for gold. If the plan sounded familiar to Ralegh, that was because, according to a member of the expedition, it was based on the descriptions "made by Sir Walther Halley"—presumably in *The Discoverie of the large and bewtiful Empyre of Guiana.*

Ralegh investigated mounting an independent El Dorado expedition, one that need not rely on English military support. By taking the river Berry had found, the Essequibo, he believed he could altogether circumvent the Spanish on the way to Manoa. He entered into secret negotiations with one of the *Discoverie*'s biggest fans, Swedish duke Charles of Sudermania (later, King Charles IX of Sweden), who was willing to commit twelve fully victualed vessels. The secret negotiations weren't secret enough, however: the Spaniards found out about the plan and shored up their defenses in Guiana. To get past them now, Ralegh realized, he would have to go through them. As Sweden lacked the requisite military might, he needed Elizabeth.

She no longer needed him, though. That is, until she ran into trouble in Ireland. At the Battle of Yellow Ford in August 1598, the Earl of Tyrone's forces had killed two thousand English soldiers, spurring uprisings all over the Emerald Isle and presenting her with an acute need for a commander capable of restoring order. Given Ralegh's talents as an organizer, leader, and tactician on top of his extensive combat and colonization experience in Ireland, he was uniquely qualified. Still, she offered the job to Essex.

The earl regarded it as a waste of his time, though. No glory whatsoever. Meeting with her and some of her advisers, including Howard, he suggested she instead appoint Ralegh's cousin, George Carew. Dismayed that the supposed second coming of Sir Galahad was thinking only of himself in the face of a national emergency, Elizabeth chided him for his transparent plan to remove a Ralegh ally from court. Enraged—perhaps because his mind had been so easily read—the earl spun away, turning his back on her. She lunged at him, smacked him in the ear, and shouted, "Go and be hanged!"

In response, he reached for his sword, but before he could draw it, Howard stepped in. Storming off, Essex swore that he "neither could nor would bear such an indignity, nor would have taken it even from Henry VIII," adding that the queen was "as crooked in her mind as in her carcass." Everyone wondered whether she would indeed hang him.

Instead, she sent him to Ireland in command of seventeen thousand men. As the army set off, on a sunny March 27, 1599, Londoners lined up for four miles to cheer the Earl of Essex, their champion, as ever. Poems were recited in his honor, his praises were sung, churches resounded with prayers for his success.

Ralegh could at least derive some consolation from the odyssey of the Dutch, who, on reaching San Thomé, reported that "Governor Don Fernando sent with us on our search his miner, who brought us to all those places . . . Sir Walther Halley had been." Clearly, Antonio de Berrío's son, Fernando, had sent them down a garden path. Unsurprisingly, they found no gold, but, as they related, "we understand from the Indians that there is a place about 6 miles higher up where there ought to be . . . much gold." Stymied by the falls and the threat of poisoned arrows, however, they contented themselves with the discovery of several new rivers before returning to the Netherlands, leaving Fernando de Berrío as Ralegh's primary competitor for El Dorado—if Ralegh could manage to reenter the competition.

Essex effectively lent a hand from Ireland, where, rather than attacking Tyrone's forces in the north, he marched south, frittering away three months on skirmishes and sieges that, in combination with disease, devastated his fighting force. By September 1599, he'd lost thirteen thousand men, and although Elizabeth had expressly forbidden him to strike any sort of truce with Tyrone, he sat with the Irish leader and agreed to a cessation of hostilities—in the queen's name. Which boggled her mind. For what earthly reason, she wrote Essex, had he defied her order?

Deciding to explain himself in person, he raced back to England by boat and then rode through the night, reaching Nonsuch Palace at ten in the morning on September 28. Unable to wait another moment to make his case, he burst into the queen's bedroom, finding the sixty-six-year-old half-dressed and yet to don her wig and makeup. Although mortified, she retained her composure, upbraiding him for his incompetence and then placing him under house arrest for "contemptuous disobedience." By the time of his release, in August of the following year, she'd had him stripped of his official offices, and she wasn't finished. Next, by refusing to renew his patents—the sole source of his income—she plunged him into financial ruin.

On February 8, 1601, he fought back, leading three hundred armed adherents into London to restore his offices and patents and replace Elizabeth with James VI of Scotland. The operation, which would come to be known as Essex's Rebellion, had all the forethought and strategic brilliance of the earl's earlier military campaigns—which is to say, not much. Crown forces quickly quashed it, and two and a half weeks later, Essex found himself on a scaffold outside the Tower of London, his head resting atop a stout wooden block as an executioner stood over him and swung an eight-pound axe. The blade failed to uncouple the earl's head and body, requiring a second and third swing, two more than optimal. Furious on their hero's behalf, the crowd of spectators attacked the axeman.

Ralegh, as captain of the guard, was obligated to attend the execution. He stood far away from the scaffold, watching through an armory window—enjoying a pipe and smirking, according to his detractors. Their shoddy record as reporters lends credence, however, to Ralegh's own account, that he was "sorry that I was not with [Essex], for I heard he had a desire to see me, and be reconciled."

When Essex died, Ralegh wrote, "I shed tears." Tears of joy, his detractors might have been quick to add, believing that, with the earl's subtraction from the competition for the queen's favor, Ralegh couldn't have been unhappy about his prospects.

In fact, all Ralegh could get from the queen in the year that followed was another pile of thankless tasks, including Essex's old job of entertaining visiting French dignitaries. As it happened, though, the French breathed life into his El Dorado campaign—at, of all places, the Beargarden, the popular amphitheater where a thousand spectators wagered on the outcomes of mastiffs fighting a bear or a bull shackled to an iron stake—"a sweet and comfortable recreation fitted for the solace and comfort of a peaceable people," according to the Privy Council. There, between all the barking, roaring, cheering, and blood flying into the gallery, Ralegh likely heard that France's king,

King James

Henry IV, was gung ho about colonizing Guiana. Indeed, on May 8, 1602, Henry would issue letters patent for "the Conquest and Planting of Guiana" under René Maree, Sieur de Montbariot.

Ralegh raced to see Queen Elizabeth; England had to get there first, he argued. As long as Tyrone was making trouble in Ireland, she said, she couldn't spare the men or the ships. But she did need Ralegh to go to sea, to be the governor of Jersey, the largest of the Channel Islands, a four-day round-trip sail.

In that capacity, as he put it, he "laboured like a mule" for more than two years. In hindsight it would be clear that the time might have been better spent at home, guiding his troubled seven-year-old son, Wat. In the short term, though, his service appeared to pay off: in early 1603, when English forces in Ireland pushed Tyrone to the brink of surrender, the queen was finally able to reappraise colonization. But on March 24, 1603, before she could authorize the new Guiana expedition, she died, leaving the throne to her first cousin once removed, King James Stuart VI of Scotland, whose mother she'd had beheaded. At least James was a Protestant, ensuring stability. He was also a great admirer of the Earl of Essex and eager to avenge his death.

24

THE GREATEST LUCIFER THAT HATH LIVED IN OUR AGE

In the opening years of the seventeenth century, while Ralegh had his hands full with discharging official tasks for Queen Elizabeth, other courtiers were making a full-time job of currying the favor of her likely successor, King James VI of Scotland. In 1601, when James asked them to name England's sinners, one of them identified Ralegh as "the greatest Lucifer that hath lived in our age," going on to warn James that Ralegh had been concocting spells to harm His Royal Majesty. Steadfast witch-hunter that he was, James recoiled.

Even more distressing to him were the rumors of Ralegh's atheism. Although Elizabeth had yet to choose him to succeed her, James launched an investigation, placing at its head his cousin, confidant, and reputed lover, the Third Duke of Lennox. In London, Lennox took Ralegh aside and asked whether he was interested in helping to lay the groundwork for the Scottish king's succession. Overwhelmed by court matters at the time, Ralegh reflexively replied that his profound love of and devotion to Queen Elizabeth acted as blinders, precluding him from looking for favor elsewhere. But later, thinking better of his response, he ran it past Robert Cecil. The two had grown increasingly close following the death of Cecil's wife, Elizabeth, in 1597, with Walter and Bess taking Cecil's son, Will, into Sherborne and raising him alongside their own son. When Ralegh asked whether he'd been wise to spurn James's advances, Cecil said that "if the like offer had been made" to him, he would have given the identical response.

In fact, the like offer had been made to him, and he'd embraced it, secretly sending James reams of court gossip, including a full replay of Ralegh's hand-wringing over his Lennox encounter. Cecil was thus in position to refute the atheism charges against Ralegh, whom he knew to be quite religious. The secretary of state could have related how, after his wife's death, when he was lonely, Ralegh cheered him by reminding him of his ever-present companion: "The mind of man is that part of God which is in us." Instead, Cecil said nothing in Ralegh's defense, writing to James only that he couldn't "support a person"—Sir Walter—"whom most religious men do hold anathema."

Yet Cecil ranked as a Walter Ralegh booster compared to Essex, who, until his death in 1601 had been another of James's secret pen pals. As a result of their correspondence, James would come to refer to the earl as "my martyr," by implication branding Ralegh as "my Judas." Still, in April 1603, when the thirty-seven-year-old James was proclaimed king of England, Ralegh was hopeful of forging a working relationship with him. Not only was Ralegh preceded by his reputation as a war hero, colonizer, and foreign affairs savant, he and the new king had a good deal in common: in addition to their shared desire for English prosperity, both were avid scholars and poets.

Soon thereafter, James was traveling from Edinburgh to his coronation in London, his peregrination met in every hamlet by ringing bells, joyous songs, and flower petals lofted into the royal path by schoolchildren. Nights he spent at grand English country estates along the way, including perhaps the grandest ever, Burghley House, the 115-room Tudor mansion in Lincolnshire both designed and built by William Cecil, the First Baron Burghley, who'd died in 1598 and bequeathed it to his son Robert. It was there that Ralegh was granted a royal audience, unaware that the coldly calculating Cecil had stacked the deck against him. It didn't help that James was a snob—"Virtue followeth oftest noble blood," he wrote. Also he disdained the new product with which the low-born Devonian had become synonymous; soon into his reign, James would publish a six-thousand-word *Counterblast to Tobacco,* decrying smoking as "loathsome to the eye, hateful to the nose, harmful to the brain, [and] dangerous to the lungs."

Likely, Ralegh was ushered either into Burghley House's 170-foot-long Long Gallery or the space known to this day as the King James Drawing Room for the life-size statue of himself the monarch gave

Burghley House

Robert Cecil, whom he called his "little beagle." James commenced the interview with one of his puns. "Ralegh," he said. "On my soul, man, I have heard *rawly* of thee." The courtiers all laughed, at least outwardly.

And therein lay opportunity for Ralegh. He could differentiate himself from the corps of royal sycophants with the same brutal honesty Elizabeth had cherished in him. Accordingly, when James remarked that had he not inherited the English throne, he could have taken it by force of arms, Ralegh said, "Would to God that had been put to trial." James took umbrage. "Why do you wish that?" he asked. "Because then," said Ralegh, "you would have known your friends from your foes."

James responded with no more enthusiasm than he would have had Ralegh chanted a witch's spell. Ralegh quickly pivoted to foreign policy, advancing his argument for aggression against Spain, either unaware of or failing to consider that James disliked such hostilities, on top of which he wanted peace with King Philip III. As a result, James probably didn't rush to read the eighteen-page "Discourse touching a War with Spain and the protecting of the Netherlands" that Ralegh had prepared for him. And it's almost certainly no coincidence that, following the meeting, the king granted the Bishop of Durham's request that Durham House—Ralegh's primary residence for twenty years—be returned to the church.

The eviction notice came on May 31, 1603, capping a month in which Ralegh also lost his job as captain of the guard along with the other positions and patents responsible for most of his income. He absorbed the blows with the hope that they would eventually prove mere stumbling blocks and that by perseverance he would win over James. It wasn't enough to be "wise with a wise prince," Ralegh would reflect, "nor valiant with a valiant . . . nor just with him that is just." Instead, a courtier had to adapt himself to suit the prince, he concluded, resolving to make pacificism work as foreign policy. By staying out of wars, after all, England would have that many more men and ships to send to Guiana.

In mid-July, an increasingly hopeful Ralegh rode out to the Berkshire countryside to take part in a royal hunt at Windsor Castle. His optimism could only have been augmented by the excitement of the other riders in their crisp red hunting jackets, everyone tensed in eager anticipation of the bray of the kennel huntsman's horn that would launch them onto the freshly shorn meadow. Before Ralegh could take his mount, Cecil sidled up and said His Royal Majesty wished Sir Walter to stay behind at the castle so the Privy Council could discuss an urgent matter with him.

A new opportunity? Hardly. The privy councillors asked Ralegh what he knew about a plot to overthrow James and replace him with his twenty-eight-year-old cousin, Lady Arabella Stuart. Nothing, Ralegh said. A lie, concluded the councillors, including a newly inducted Henry Howard, the courtier who'd told James that Ralegh was a latter-day Lucifer. They had Ralegh taken back to London and placed under house arrest pending further investigation.

Not incidentally, they were right: he had lied. He had heard about the Arabella Stuart plot from his friend Sir Henry Brooke, the Eleventh Baron Cobham. Like Ralegh, Cobham had been stripped of his income and offices by James. His solution had been to overthrow the king, and he'd found an eager backer in Count Charles of Aremberg (a principality that today is part of Germany). If the Privy Council could make a case that Ralegh knew anything about the plot, he would be found guilty of misprision, the deliberate concealment of knowledge of a treasonable act. That would in turn cast doubt on his plea of innocence to the more serious charge sure to follow: being one of the conspirators himself.

Accordingly, while under house arrest, he walked back his statement, writing the Privy Council that there was something he'd only just recalled, an oddity he'd noticed after Cobham's visit to Durham House a few months earlier: instead of taking his barge down the Thames toward his own residence, Cobham had rowed across the river in the direction of the home of a man believed to be a confederate of Aremberg's. Ralegh acknowledged that he had indeed held a seed of suspicion about Cobham, but nothing actionable, nothing he could have brought to the attention of the authorities.

He sent the note in care of the privy councillor he still trusted above all others, Cecil. Cecil confronted Cobham, asking why he'd been consorting with Count Aremberg. Rather than tell the truth, that he and Aremberg were plotting to overthrow the king, Cobham said Ralegh had recruited him to direct a coup. Almost as soon as the words were out of his mouth, a guilty Cobham tried to take them back. But it was too late. Cecil had what King James had craved: grounds to try Ralegh for treason.

On July 19, 1603, Ralegh's enjoyment of a tankard of ale was interrupted by his arrest, imprisonment at the Tower of London, and the prospect of a trial whose verdict was all but a foregone conclusion: in treason cases, the state had no more interest in giving defendants a fair trial than the Romans did in giving the Christians swords before sending them into the arena against the lions. The court date was less a hearing than a proclamation of the state's might. Not only was the defendant prohibited from having any sort of attorney, he also wasn't privy to the evidence against him until its presentation at the trial. Spontaneous responses left less opportunity for mendacity, the thinking went, and no manner of skill was required to make "a plain and honest defense." If a defendant needed help, the judges would look out for him. In theory. In Ralegh's case, the judges would be the same privy councillors who'd placed him under arrest. At best, he thought, a guilty verdict would leave him as an unemployed forty-nine-year-old swordsman. At worst, dead.

His best course of action, he decided, was to compose a suicide note: "I am now made an enemy and a traitor," he wrote, "by the word of an unworthy man"—Cobham—"who has proclaimed me to be a partaker of his vain imaginations." He preferred to die rather than suffer from the association, he went on, and by taking his own life, he might at least clear his name. Of Cecil, he added, "I thought he would never forsake me . . . I would not have done it to him, God knows."

Either the same day or a day later—July 27, 1603—while Cecil and a group of privy councillors were at the Tower interviewing prisoners, Ralegh asked a guard for a long, thin knife. To stir wine, he said when asked why. Because of the absurdity of the response in combination with his blatant melancholy, the request was denied. Ralegh decided to make do with his table knife.

It was Cecil who found him, lying on the floor, bleeding profusely but still alive. Weakly, with what might have been his last gasp, Ralegh protested his innocence—the truth, as Cecil knew, per the principle of *nemo moriturus praesumitur mentire* (a dying person is not presumed to lie). Therefore, the words ought to have been enough for Cecil to take his friend in his arms, plead with him to cling to life, and beg his forgiveness. But Cecil also knew Ralegh's penchant for theatrics, and at once he saw the long, thin knife gambit for what it was, a way that an expert swordsman might do only superficial damage to himself as part of a desperate sympathy play. The table knife had done no more—"rather a cut than a stab," Cecil would sneer.

Such melodrama might have been effective in the day of Queen Elizabeth. In the court of King James, it merely cast Ralegh as a relic from a bygone era. Three days later, Cecil was unsurprised to receive a note from one of the Tower keepers declaring Ralegh "perfectly whole." The treason trial would proceed.

25

THE HORRIBLEST TRAITOR THAT EVER LIVED

LATE IN THE summer of 1603, there was doubt that Walter Ralegh would live long enough to stand trial. Plague was ripping into London like never before. Twice as lethal as the 1592–1593 edition, the 1603 London Plague would kill a fifth of the city's population of 150,000. In the fall, when the trial was moved out to Hampshire because of it, Ralegh was given a reprieve.

But only to face a greater peril. All along the way, mobs descended on his carriage to decry the vile traitor and throw mud, stones, and tobacco pipes at the Judas responsible for the death of their beloved Earl of Essex. The Tower guards accompanying Ralegh had never seen anything like it, and they doubted he could be "brought alive through such multitudes of unruly people." Ralegh was astonished too, not by his countrymen's odium; that, he dismissed as ignorance of the facts. He simply couldn't believe so many of them would congregate given the risk of contracting the plague.

Ultimately the crowds only slowed his progress; it took five days to cover the sixty miles to Hampshire, where the five-hundred-year-old, flint-and-limestone Winchester Castle towered above a russet countryside. Ralegh was to be tried in the castle's Great Hall, which was new, relatively, having been added by Henry III in the thirteenth century.

At eight o'clock on the morning of November 17, 1603, when the guards prodded Ralegh through the soaring Gothic archway, the cathedral-like Great Hall had been transformed into a courtroom. Still hanging on the rear wall was the castle's centerpiece, a replica of the Arthurian round table with King Arthur's portrait and the names of his knights inscribed at their respective places. Legend had it that Arthur preferred a table without a head so that his men couldn't claim precedence over one another, allowing them to focus instead on the greater good of England. Ralegh must have found that hard to believe.

His minders steered him past an overflowing gallery; spectators often paid more for admission to trials than they did to go to the theater, and this was an especially hot ticket. Many of them had waited outside all night long for the chance to jeer Ralegh now. Slowed by his bad leg, illness, and five draining months of incarceration in the Tower of London, he was drenched by their epithets. He was also assaulted by the sour scent of vinegar; to mitigate the "gaol air" originating from defendants, courtrooms were commonly strewn with the fluid. For the same reason, judges brought small bouquets of flowers to their benches.

Eventually Ralegh was left alone at the bar, where he was allowed to sit on a stool. The proceeding got underway with the entry of the four judges, each in a fur-trimmed violet robe with a starched ruff at the neck and a cincture knotted around the waist. Powdered wigs had recently come into fashion as a means of hiding the open sores and bald patches wrought by syphilis, but they wouldn't be standard judicial attire for another half century. Taking chairs at an elevated dais facing the bar, the judges were joined by seven special commissioners, including Robert Cecil and Henry

Howard. To avail himself of the practice of judicial disqualification based on personal bias or a conflict of interest, Ralegh would have had to wait two centuries.

Next, the clerk of the Crown Office acquainted him for the first time with the charges against him, beginning with participation in the Main Plot (so called to distinguish it from a concurrent conspiracy against the king, the Bye Plot) to assassinate James and replace him with Arabella Stuart. Ralegh was also accused of a plot to murder the king's children, a conspiracy to effect a truce with Spain, another conspiracy to enact English toleration of the papistry, and a scheme to receive illicit payment for all of the above from the Spanish.

When the clerk of the Crown Office finished the recitation, which took some seven minutes, Ralegh entered his plea—"Not guilty"—and was read the names of the twelve men in the jury box and then asked whether he took exception to any of them. "I know none of them," he said, adding that since they were all Christians and honest gentlemen, "I except against none." He would have been wise to except against every last one of them: Attorney General Sir Edward Coke had handpicked them based on their biases and willingness to convict regardless of the evidence. King James reportedly joked that even he would have rued being tried by such a lot.

Next, Coke strode onto the floor to prosecute the case. The sharp-featured, fifty-one-year-old aristocrat was considered the greatest legal mind of his generation—as well as one of the most vituperative men of any generation. At his death in 1634, his wife would say, "We will never see his like again . . . Thank God." Spinning toward the bar, Coke asked Ralegh, "To whom do you bear malice? To the royal children?"

"You tell me news I never heard of," Ralegh replied.

"Oh, sir, do I?" Coke scoffed. "I will prove you the most notorious traitor that ever came to the bar."

Sir Edward Coke

Ralegh was unfazed. "Your words cannot condemn me. My innocence is my defense. Prove one of those things wherewith you have charged me, and I will confess the whole indictment, that I am the horriblest traitor that ever lived, and worthy to be crucified with a thousand torments."

"Nay, I will prove all." Coke radiated confidence. "Thou art a monster. Thou hast an English face, but a Spanish heart." The attorney went on to malign Ralegh's career as one of "devilish and Machiavellian policy" and "the most horrible practices that ever came out of the bottomless pit of the lowest hell." In contrast, Cobham—whom Ralegh had accused of instigating the Main Plot—was a simpleton, "never politician nor swordsman," and utterly lacking experience abroad. Ergo, Coke told Ralegh, "All that [Cobham] did was by thy instigation, thou viper." To use *thou* was condescending; it was how members of the upper class addressed servants, and lest there be any doubt that's what he'd intended, Coke added, "I thou thee, thou traitor." Trying to get under Ralegh's skin, he also called him "the rankest traitor in all England," a "spider of Hell," and, most "damnable" of all, an "atheist."

Ralegh kept his cool. "It becometh not a man of quality and virtue to call me so," he told Coke. "But I take comfort in it. It is all you can do."

The quip silenced the gallery and seemed to shift the momentum. One spectator noted that Ralegh was behaving himself "so worthily, so wisely, so temperately, that in half a day the mind of all the company was changed from the extremest hate to the greatest pity."

Ralegh followed up with an attempt to turn Coke's logic back on him: "Mr. Attorney, you said this [plot] never came out of Cobham's quiver," for "he is a simple man," with "neither love nor a following." Why would a cunning, devilish Machiavellian worth his cloven hooves entrust the overthrow of a kingdom to such a naïf?

As Coke spluttered in search of a response, Ralegh piled on logic, asserting that for much of his career he'd been commissioned "to offend and enfeeble the King of Spain and his subjects." On three separate occasions, he noted, he'd risked his life fighting them. "And to show I was not Spanish, as you term me, I had written at this time a treatise to the King's Majesty of the present state of Spain, and reasons against the peace." He meant the eighteen-page "Discourse Touching a War with Spain and the Protecting of the Netherlands" he'd composed for James and delivered to him when they met at Burghley House. Finally, the paper did him some good, giving the jurors little choice but to dismiss the allegation. "Never any man spoke so well in times past," remarked an observer, "nor would do in the world to come."

But his long-standing bias against Spain aside, Ralegh went on, what sense would it make for him to betray England now of all times, with the country fortified by the union with Scotland, Ireland finally under control, and the Spanish empire at its lowest ebb? And speaking of the alleged betrayal, save for testimony Cobham had recanted, where was the evidence?

Coke had evidence, did he ever. With a flourish, he produced a new letter from Cobham claiming he'd been coerced into recanting his original testimony—by none other than the defendant, Sir Walter Ralegh. Therefore, Cobham said, the original testimony should stand.

Ralegh was astounded, in part by the letter, but mostly by the judges' response to it: they were clearly relieved. As a court reporter noted, the new letter gave them "a great satisfaction, and cleared all the former evidence, which before stood very doubtful."

Coke went on to bolster Cobham's credibility by presenting another document, the deposition of Ralegh's longtime right-hand man, Lawrence Keymis. In it, Keymis had testified under oath that Sir Walter had sent him to coerce Lord Cobham into recanting his original testimony.

Setting Keymis's testimony aside for the moment, Ralegh argued that Cobham's accusation alone was insufficient grounds for conviction based on a law dating back to King Edward VI: "No man shall be condemned of treason unless he be accused by two lawful accusers." Without two witnesses, Ralegh told the judges, "You try me by the Spanish Inquisition."

The presiding judge, seventy-one-year-old Lord Chief Justice of England John Popham, cut him off. The Edward VI two-witness statutes had been repealed in 1553, Popham said. Since then, one witness had sufficed.

Ralegh tried biblical law instead: "At the mouth of two witnesses, or three witnesses, shall he that is worthy of death be put to death; but at the mouth of one witness he shall not be put to death."

The argument wowed the spectators, but the judges were unimpressed. "I marvel, Sir Walter," said one of them, "that you being of such experience and wit, should stand on this point; for many horsestealers should escape if they may not be condemned without witnesses."

In that case, Ralegh said, he would exercise the right afforded a defendant by English common law to confront his accuser. "Good my lords," he said, "let my accuser come face to face and be deposed"—a simple matter of bringing Cobham upstairs from the cell, where he was awaiting his own treason trial. "Were it not for his accusation, all this were nothing . . . Let him avouch any of these things, I will confess the whole indictment and renounce the king's mercy."

Lord Chief Justice Popham fired back a series of laws and statutes, the sum of which was that, yes, a defendant in a treason case could examine witnesses, but only if the prosecutor assented. Since there was a better chance of Coke pausing this proceeding for an appreciation of the defendant's poetry, Ralegh returned to refuting the accusation: Cobham had retracted his original testimony, he said, and in fact no one coerced him into doing so. Instead, Keymis himself had been coerced into confessing that he'd forced Cobham to recant. Turning to the jury, Ralegh explained that Keymis had been held prisoner in the Tower of London for eighteen weeks, then was "threatened with the rack to make him confess." It was a bold claim, one that rocked the Great Hall at Winchester Castle and would have scandalized any Protestant: only the Catholics resorted to torture.

"Keymis was never on the rack," privy councillor-cum-special commission member Henry Howard blurted out. "The king gave charge that no rigor should be used."

"Was not the Keeper of the Rack called for," Ralegh asked, "and he threatened with it?"

"We told [Keymis] he deserved the rack," another privy councillor clarified, "but we did not threaten him with it." Several of his colleagues were disturbed by the revelation. One grumbled, "It was more than we knew."

Turning to the twelve men in the jury box, Ralegh begged them to put themselves in his shoes and then asked whether they would be "contented on such presumptions to be delivered up to be slaughtered, to have your wives and children turned into the streets to beg their bread? If you would be contented to be so judged, judge so of me."

They were clearly moved, as was everyone in the courtroom. A friend of King James remarked that whereas prior to the trial he would have gone a hundred miles to see Ralegh hanged, now he "would have gone a thousand miles to save his life."

The jury departed, requiring just fifteen minutes before returning with a verdict: "Guilty of treason." Although he believed the ruling had been forced on them, Ralegh took it stoically.

The clerk turned to him, reiterated the verdict, and asked, "Sir Walter Ralegh, what canst thou say for thyself, why judgment and execution of death should not pass against thee?"

"The jury have found guilty," Ralegh replied soberly, and turning to the judges, he added, "They must do as they are directed."

The judges perfunctorily noted his complaint before pronouncing the sentence. "You shall be led from hence to the place whence you came," Lord Chief Justice Popham told Ralegh, "there to remain until the day of execution," when "you shall be drawn . . . through the open streets to the place of execution" to be "hanged and cut down alive." While still living, "your body shall be opened, your heart and bowels plucked out, and your privy members cut off, and thrown into the fire before your eyes; then your head to be stricken off from your body, and your body shall be divided into four quarters, to be disposed of at the king's pleasure."

As Popham brought the trial to a close, some of the jurors were reportedly "so far touched in conscience" that they dropped to their knees to beg Ralegh's forgiveness. Having expected Ralegh to be found guilty of only the lesser charge of misprision, Coke was astonished. The famously emotionless Cecil is said to have teared up. On his deathbed, one of the judges, Sir Francis Gawdy, would say, "Never before had the justice of England been so depraved and injured as in the condemnation of Sir Walter Ralegh."

The trial would come to prove a landmark in criminal justice, with global backlash leading both to restrictions on the admission of hearsay and stronger guarantees of the rights of the accused to face their accusers—for example, the confrontation clause in the Sixth Amendment of the United States Constitution, which gives a defendant in a criminal case the right to be confronted by the witnesses against him. In the immediate aftermath of Ralegh's sentencing, however, Coke, Cecil, and Gawdy all kept their feelings to themselves.

26

DISPOSED OF AT THE KING'S PLEASURE

When word of Ralegh's lionhearted defense spread across England, wrote a courtier, "never was a man so hated and [then] so popular, in so short a time." Seemingly everyone in England with access to pen and paper sent a letter to King James pleading for a reversal of the judgment. To no avail. Ralegh was scheduled to be hanged and quartered on December 10, 1603.

The executions of the convicted Main Plot and Bye Plot conspirators began on November 29 on the Winchester Castle green. Ralegh was still in the castle at the time, in a cell overlooking the gallows. There's no record of whether he watched the proceedings that day, but it would have been difficult for him to ignore the screams, first when the condemned men were cut down from the gibbet—still very much alive—and castrated, again when their abdomens were slashed open and their organs were plucked out and tossed onto a fire along with their genitals, and once more if they were still conscious when they were quartered—hacked into four pieces that, along with their heads, would be parboiled and displayed as cautionary tales to anyone considering treason.

Of acute interest to Ralegh was Cobham's execution. Anticipating that the urgency of unburdening himself before meeting his maker would spur Cobham to confess to his lies, Ralegh had begged the court to carry out Cobham's sentence prior to his own. On December 9, Ralegh was certainly watching from his cell as the stout thirty-nine-year-old climbed the scaffold steps nonchalantly—odd in anyone's case and particularly out of character for the cowardly Cobham. He'd leveraged his social standing into an upgraded execution, a beheading rather than a hanging and quartering. Still, he would have to gird himself for the four or five seconds following the blow of the axe, when the oxygen remaining in the blood and tissue of his disembodied head would provide him with just enough consciousness to take inventory of his situation. During such a span following her decapitation in 1536, Anne Boleyn appeared to spectators to be trying to speak. And sometimes, as had been the case with the Earl of Essex two years earlier, the executioner needed more than one swing of the axe to cut off the oxygen supply.

Given the opportunity by the sheriff to say a "short farewell of the world," Cobham expressed remorse for his offense against King James before averring "upon the hope of his soul's resurrection" that his accusations against Sir Walter Ralegh were all true. Next, Cobham received a reward he must have known was coming: King James, the sheriff announced, had stayed the execution. While most of the spectators roared their approval, one man eyed Ralegh's open window and speculated that Sir Walter "had hammers working in his head to beat out the meaning of this stratagem."

"We have this day beheld a work of so great mercy," Ralegh wrote to the Privy Council, going on to plead for the same in the name of English law, "who knowing her own cruelty, and that she is wont to compound treasons out of presumptions and circumstances, does advise the king to be *misericorditer justus* [mercifully just]."

Receiving no reply, he resigned himself to die the next day, and he began preparing for death, writing a letter to Bess late into the night: "It is not God's will that I should see you any more in this life . . . My love I send you, that you may keep it when I am dead, and my counsel that you may remember it when I am no more." Rather than burden her with his sorrows—better they "go to the grave with me," he wrote—he offered her "all the thanks which my heart can conceive, or my words can rehearse for your many travails, and care taken for me, which though they have not taken effect as you wished, yet my debt to you is not the less." The letter otherwise was an exhortation:

> I beseech you for the love you bear me living, do not hide yourself many days, but by your travails seek to help your miserable fortunes and the right of your poor child. Thy mourning cannot avail me, I am but dust . . . Most sorry I am God knows that being thus surprised with death I can leave you in no better estate . . . If you can live free from want, care for no more: for the rest is but vanity . . . Love God and begin betimes to repose yourself upon him, and therein shall you find true and lasting riches, and endless comfort . . . I can say no more, time and death call me away . . . Teach me to forgive my persecutors and false accusers, and send us to meet in his glorious kingdom.

He signed off: "My dear wife farewell. Bless my poor boy. Pray for me, and let my good God hold you both in his arms. Written with the dying hand of sometime thy husband but now (alas) overthrown . . . Yours that was, but now not my own. WR"

In the morning, when the time came for him to ascend the scaffold, Ralegh learned that his execution had been stayed. King James could have had the sheriff announce the reprieve the day before, at the same time as Cobham's, but he'd evidently preferred that Ralegh spend the night staring down death. Regardless, the flood of joy left Ralegh at a loss for words, perhaps for the first time since he'd learned to speak; the best he could do was compare himself to "a man raised from the dead."

Because his sentence had merely been suspended rather than commuted, however, he now had the official status of "legally dead," meaning he would remain imprisoned indefinitely and with no more civil rights than a corpse: he couldn't hold offices, much less derive income from them, and, as was standard for convicted traitors, all his worldly possessions were forfeited to the Crown. In anticipation of a guilty verdict, he'd managed to divest himself of some of his estate and had transferred the lease on Sherborne Castle to his ten-year-old son. But without any income, his only means of paying Sherborne's £200 annual rent and tenfold expenses would be for Bess to sell off valuables that were few and far between.

On his return to the Tower of London, he also incurred the expense of constructing an additional story above his apartment

The Tower of London

so that Bess and Wat could live with him. After its completion, he might well have recouped its cost by charging admission to the countrymen he'd won over with his performance at Winchester Castle; daily they crowded outside to cheer while he took his exercise on the rooftop walkway. But because the spectacle embarrassed the new regime, the walks were banned, and for good measure, Bess was informed, it was "his Majesty's express will" that she and Wat "resort to her house on Tower Hill." Although they were allowed to visit, they could "no longer lodge hereafter within the Tower."

Still, Ralegh had hope in the rumors that King James had had an ulterior motive for staying the execution: El Dorado. In fact, James *was* interested in finding the golden city, but because he was committed to peace with the Spanish—who regarded "the pirate Guaterral" as a threat to their territories—Robyn Dudley was a better choice to lead the expedition.

Dudley was distracted, though, by news that his parents—Earl of Leicester Robert Dudley and Baroness Douglas Sheffield—had been secretly married prior to his birth in 1574, meaning he was entitled to the legitimacy he'd craved for most of his twenty-nine years. His resulting claim was contested in a defamation lawsuit filed by his father's widow, Lettice Knollys. If he was legitimate, then her marriage had been bigamous, which would not only be humiliating but would also cost her and her children their inheritance.

When the case was decided against him, a disgusted Dudley left the country, eloping with a cousin despite being already married. Ordered by King James to return to England to face charges of bigamy, he refused, choosing exile in Italy; the Italians were not only accepting of him but happy for him to use his father's title, Earl of Leicester. It probably helped that he'd offered to spearhead their colonization effort in Guiana.

By then, King James had chosen veteran explorer and privateer Charles Leigh as his El Dorado champion. When Leigh set sail in March 1604, Ralegh finally grasped that his incarceration wasn't just another temporary setback. He tried to make the best of it: he read a library's worth of books and wrote one of his own, a million-word

Ralegh in his chemistry laboratory at the Tower

historical survey that would be published in 1614 as *The Historie of the World*. Meanwhile, to indulge his passion for alchemy, he converted a onetime chicken coop at the Tower into a laboratory, leading him to produce medicines that would be regarded by many as his greatest accomplishment: King James's grandson, King Charles II, would have his physician re-create one of them to combat the Great Plague of London in 1665, and no less an authority than the father of modern chemistry, Robert Boyle (1627–1691), would regularly use a Ralegh recipe, reportedly achieving "great cures by it."

Still, this was a man who'd felt penned in by a fifteen-thousand-acre estate, and the Bloody Tower was no Sherborne Castle; moisture from the muddy ditch surrounding the building permeated the walls, leaving his rooms dank, intensifying the cold as well as the pungent, musky stench from the big cats and the occasional elephant or bear in the remnants of the zoo installed at the complex in 1235 by Henry III. The fifty-year-old Ralegh began to suffer from difficulty breathing, severe circulatory problems, and palsy. And as if he didn't already have enough incentive to get out, Bess was pregnant again, at thirty-nine.

Shortly after their son Carew was born, in February 1605, Ralegh was presented with a new path to freedom when Charles Leigh died following ten months in which he and his fellow Guiana settlers had proven incapable both of sustaining themselves and of avoiding horrific tropical illnesses. King Christian IV of Denmark stepped into the breach with a plan to send a fleet of thirteen Danish navy vessels to Guiana under Ralegh's command. All Christian lacked was approval from his brother-in-law, King James. James's response, in essence, was that England needed Ralegh in prison, and the expedition never materialized.

Meanwhile, though, a fresh, incontrovertible assay of Ralegh's 1595 Guiana ore samples yielded a finding of 2.083 percent gold, a fraction of the figure reported a decade earlier but still "very fine" and enough that Robert Cecil now had use for Ralegh. With the Privy Council behind him, Cecil advanced a two-part plan that began with Lawrence Keymis sailing to Guiana to collect additional samples. If they, too, assayed well, Ralegh would be released to lead a more substantial follow-up expedition.

The plan was opposed by, of all people, Ralegh. Sending Keymis alone, he argued, was tantamount to prospecting on behalf of Spaniards, as they "immediately would build castles and forts thereabout so that by this means it would all be lost." He lobbied instead to go along with Keymis on a single expedition. Cecil was won over, but King James feared Spanish backlash, and by late July 1607, with Ralegh's imprisonment well into its fourth year, that plan was dead too.

Cecil had another use for Ralegh, though. Setting aside any sentimentality remaining from his son's stay at Sherborne Castle in the Raleghs' care, the secretary of state set about dispossessing them of the property, which King James wanted to flip to a young knight with whom he was said to be infatuated. Studying the records, Cecil found a clerical error that invalidated Ralegh's transfer of Sherborne to his son Wat. The property, therefore, still belonged to Ralegh, who, as a convicted traitor, had to forfeit it to the Crown.

Bess fought the resulting eviction, first requesting an audience with King James, and, when ignored, contriving to cross paths with him at court, taking her sons Wat and Carew along as visual aids and pleading for his compassion. The king was unmoved, forcing her and the boys to move full-time into the house she'd rented in London.

No one was more devastated than Ralegh, who once more saw El Dorado as his only hope. Over the next year he penned and sent out proposal upon prospectus, succeeding only in sparking the interest of a fourteen-year-old maritime buff. The fourteen-year-old, however, was the king's son, Henry, Prince of Wales, an impassioned Ralegh fan who declared, "No king but my father . . . would keep such a bird in such a cage!" Henry proceeded to lobby his father to send Ralegh to El Dorado, and his timing was ideal: a new Italian expedition was being mounted by James's old nemesis, the self-titled Earl of Leicester Robyn Dudley. In his capacity as naval adviser to Ferdinando I, Grand Duke of Tuscany, Dudley had sent a preliminary expedition to Guiana that successfully established an Italian foothold, including a strong alliance with the Natives. Before Dudley could follow up, though, Ferdinando I died and was succeeded by Cosmo II, who had no interest in Guiana, creating a vacuum for England.

By then, King James had tabbed Robert Harcourt a gentleman adventurer, rather than Ralegh. Harcourt reached Guiana in May 1609 and concluded that there were "certainly mines of gold, or silver, or of both." He failed to locate them, though, in large part because of the Guianans' disappointment that he was not their old friend Sir Walter Ralegh. One of the Guianans, a future chieftain who would become well-known as Harry the Indian, convinced Harcourt to take him to England so that he might be of service to Ralegh and facilitate his return to Guiana.

Still unable to persuade his father to release Ralegh, Prince Henry did the next best thing, commissioning and underwriting an expedition helmed by onetime Ralegh protégé, Sir Thomas Roe. With two ships, a pair of pinnaces, and an army of amply supplied men—a first in the history of El Dorado exploration—Roe left England on February 24, 1610, reaching South America two months later. In canoes, he and his cohorts worked their way to the Orinoco and devoted thirteen months to a systematic search for Manoa, traversing every last waterway, negotiating no fewer than thirty-two sets of rapids and, essentially, drawing a dragnet over the Guiana Highlands. In a 1611 letter home, Roe lamented he'd found "nothing new," and, unless it had been moved, Manoa had never been there. Neither had Macureguarai, nor any other component of the El Dorado story save for the savanna.

The overwhelming evidence forced Ralegh into the nightmarish realization that over the better part of a century, shrewd men—from Diego de Ordáz to Topiawari to Ralegh himself—had simply been hoodwinked. Moreover, he had spent nearly two decades in pursuit of a chimera. While staggered, he kept himself from collapse by clutching the report's lone positive—Roe had significantly bolstered claims about Guiana's mineral wealth—and in the ensuing months he managed to interest investors in his return to Topiawari's gold mine.

Two of the foremost obstacles to his release from the Tower of London fell away early in 1612 when Cecil died of cancer at forty-eight and the now eighteen-year-old Prince Henry exacted a promise from his father to pardon Ralegh at Christmastime, and, for good measure, restore Sherborne Castle to him. A late-summer swim in the River Thames left Henry stricken with fever, however. By fall he was dead, and without his advocacy, so was Ralegh's hope of going anywhere: King James tossed Ralegh's pardon into the fire and reversed his reversal of his Sherborne decision.

Ralegh languished in the Tower for another year, but with hope that the publication of *The Historie of the World* would help his cause, particularly its message that a monarch's obligation was to care for his subjects. Ultimately the book would become a massive success, ranking among the greatest works of history since Herodotus, with ten editions in the seventeenth century alone. In the short term, however, King James was piqued by its message that a monarch's obligation was to care for his subjects rather than simply exercise his divine right as he pleased. Taking it as an indictment of his rule, he banned the book. It seemed only a matter of time until he revisited Ralegh's execution, which, in 1603, he'd merely paused.

27

TO DIE FOR THE KING AND NOT BY THE KING

THINGS CHANGED. MANY of the courtiers responsible for the 1603 treason trial died or fell out of favor with King James, and the political pendulum swung toward nationalism. The new secretary of state, Ralph Winwood, an ardent enemy of Spain, regarded Guiana as an opportunity to spark a war, with Walter Ralegh serving as England's standard bearer. To the Hispanophile king, Winwood said only that Ralegh was uniquely capable of bringing home gold, whether El Dorado existed or not.

The king's influential favorite, twenty-three-year-old knight Sir George Villiers, also backed the plan, if only because he'd been paid £1,500 to do so by Ralegh's camp—a core of friends, relatives, and investors who had never lost faith in him. For a change, James was amenable, possibly due to his recognition of Ralegh's innocence, and certainly because of the national debt, which, due to his profligate spending, had doubled, to a suffocating £700,000 since he'd assumed the throne. Of course Ralegh was amenable. As he put it, "To die for the king and not by the king is all the ambition I have in the world."

On March 19, 1616, he received a letter from the Privy Council with news that the king was "pleased to release you out of your imprisonment in the Tower . . . to make your provisions for your intended voyage." There was, of course, a catch: except for £175 that the king would contribute toward a new ship, Ralegh had to fund the entire Guiana expedition himself—yet His Majesty would receive a fifth of the proceeds. Ralegh also had the option of simply turning down the commission and going home; Villiers was willing to secure him a full pardon for another £1,500. But Ralegh wanted to go to Guiana. He had to, he thought, lest he return to the stage as an unemployed sixty-two-year-old swordsman—and £1,500 poorer. He was also confident that he would come home with heaps of gold.

Agreeing to the Privy Council's terms, he emerged from the Tower for the first time since 1603 (save for a brief relocation to Fleet Prison in 1604), stepping into a jarringly different London, an explosion of stone and mortar constructions having given uniformity and neoclassical grandeur to the warren of winding, incongruous streets he remembered. Many of his familiar and favorite sights had been drastically altered or were gone altogether: on the Strand, for example, the view of Durham House was now blocked by a two-story shopping arcade, the New Exchange, built by Robert Cecil. And the royal banqueting hall—Whitehall's answer to Mount Olympus, where Ralegh had dined privately with Queen Elizabeth—was now a hole in the ground, having been torn down to make way for architect Inigo Jones's Palladian masterpiece, the Banqueting House. But perhaps the greatest change Ralegh saw was in his own reflection, thirteen years in the Tower having furrowed his pronounced brow, grayed his beard, and hobbled him.

His wizened mien did nothing to disabuse potential investors of the notion that he was a walking anachronism: his fundraising effort fell £10,000 short of the £30,000 needed for the expedition.

He figured he could close the gap, though, by selling off all his possessions—furniture, art, the Ming dynasty porcelain, any remaining jewelry. Technically, though, they were Bess's possessions, since they were now in her name, and she was daunted by the risk of liquidating everything they had—and even more concerned by the perils of the expedition itself. Ralegh, however, was as sure of finding the gold mine as he was "of not missing his way from his dining-room to his bedchamber." And the normally understated Keymis was willing to stake his life on it. Bess consented to the sell-off, even putting on the market the last significant asset of her own, a farm in Surrey, raising another £2,500 for the venture.

Next, Ralegh went shopping, first advancing £500 to shipwright Phineas Pett to build a swift, 440-ton, thirty-six-gun flagship, then buying or bartering for another eleven vessels. Finding an able crew was more challenging. The manifold hazards of the voyage scared off all except the most experienced mariners, and they in turn balked at committing to an enterprise helmed by an unpardoned prisoner. With the ongoing Spanish campaign to convince King James to pull the plug on the enterprise, they thought, Ralegh could be back in the Tower any day. To counter that notion—and to have a fallback plan if things went awry—Ralegh revisited paying Villiers £1,500 for a pardon. Don't waste the money, Attorney General Francis Bacon advised him. "Your commission is as good a pardon for all former offences as the Law of England can afford you." Accordingly, Ralegh passed on Villiers's offer, which would prove a catastrophic mistake.

In the short term, despite Bacon's assurances, Ralegh continued to have recruiting difficulties, and the thousand men he was ultimately able to attract were, he lamented, "the scum of men," most of them "drunkards, blasphemers, and such" whose families considered them "an exceedingly good gain to be discharged of." The gentlemen volunteers he managed to sign on differed only in that they had bigger liquor budgets. His efforts to outfit the fleet were repeatedly interrupted by drunken brawls and serious injuries the crewmen inflicted on both civilians and themselves.

To control the crew, he realized, he would have to lean more heavily on friends and kinsmen than he would have preferred. His son Wat, for example. Now twenty-two and described as "his father's exact image both in body and mind," Wat was a solid candidate to command a ship. On paper. In the flesh, he was quarrelsome and impulsive. Two years earlier, in 1614, he'd had to flee England after seriously injuring his opponent in a duel fought under dodgy circumstances. Although Ralegh loved his son, even he had to admit that Wat was "a bear."

It was telling that, while weighing Wat's request to join the expedition, Ralegh was uncertain about bringing him to something as uncomplicated as a friend's dinner party. He consented only after exacting a promise from Wat to mind his manners—"Better were it to be unborn than to be ill bred," Ralegh liked to say. At the party, the two sat next to each other at the dinner table, with Wat behaving splendidly, until, halfway through the meal, he told the distinguished company the story of how he'd visited a whore that morning only to be turned away because, as she explained, "Your father lay with me but an hour ago." Incensed, Ralegh slapped Wat in the face. Although hot to retaliate, Wat recalled his promise to act with decorum, and rather than striking his father, he turned to the man seated to his other side, smacked him, and told him to pass it around the table so that it would "come to my father anon."

Ralegh had an even bigger headache at court, in Spain's ambassador to England, Diego Sarmiento de Acuña, who would soon become the First Count of Gondomar. The forty-nine-year-old was a nephew of Pedro Sarmiento de Gamboa, the conquistador Ralegh had captured in 1586 and duped into sharing Spanish intelligence on El

Dorado. The same incident had sparked Gondomar's lifelong grudge against Guaterral.

In 1613, King Philip III had needed an ambassador in London who could "keep the king of England good"—in other words, steer James away from alliances against Spain while making sure he acted in the best interests of English Catholics. At first blush, Gondomar was an odd choice for the job. Not only was he loath to live among the heretics, as he regarded Protestants, but he was also haughty, especially when in England, where he considered everyone morally inferior. And then there was his rectal fistula, a painful cavity between the bowel and the skin near the anus. As a result of the condition, everywhere he went, Gondomar required a hole to be cut into the center of his seat—in fact, he demanded it. The imperiousness as much as the eccentricity, in combination with his severe features and dagger-shaped beard, cast him as a classic villain in the eyes of Englishmen. The lone exception was King James, who considered Gondomar one of history's greatest diplomats—and a friend. The Spaniard became widely known in England as *el Maquiavelo español* for his ability to manipulate James. It was said that Gondomar could "with his facetious words and gestures pipe King James asleep"—for instance, that His Highness was regarded in the Spanish court as the English Solomon.

In 1616, Gondomar came to James to convey Spain's outrage at Ralegh's release from prison. How could the king of England on one hand profess friendship for Spain while, on the other, authorize an armed incursion into Spanish territory and the seizure of the king of Spain's ships? The latter complaint stemmed from a story making the rounds that Ralegh had boasted to Francis Bacon that he was going to take the Spanish treasure fleet. "But that would be piracy," Bacon had protested. "Oh no," Ralegh had replied. "Did you ever hear of men who are pirates for millions? They who aim at small things are

Count Gondomar and his chair

pirates." Allowing "the old pirate" to proceed, Gondomar maintained, would terminate the friendship between their countries.

James was terrified; the relationship with Spain was vital to him for several reasons, not least of which was that he stood to reap a dowry of no less than "£500,000 besides the jewels" from the marriage of his surviving son and heir, Prince Charles, to King Philip III's daughter, Infanta Maria Anna. The trouble, James confided to Gondomar, was that his hands were tied by public sentiment. The 1603 treason trial had won Ralegh a place in the hearts of his countrymen that still endured. They'd come to see him as the last vestige of a bygone golden age of explorers and adventurers, and now they were clamoring for James to allow him to pick up where he'd left off.

The king could only imagine the hue and cry if he held Ralegh back from Guiana.

As a favor to his English friend, Gondomar outlined a scenario wherein Spain might consent to the expedition: Ralegh had to be limited to just one or two ships, with Spanish escorts conducting him to his mine and then bringing him safely back to England with the gold he discovered. James wasn't sure he could get the support of his privy councillors, who, in anticipation of Spanish remonstration, had advised him to consider no course other than to wholeheartedly back the expedition. Now they would justifiably fear the Spanish escorts slitting the Englishmen's throats and absconding with the gold.

Gondomar understood: the English Solomon had an uncannily good point. The two friends soon arrived at an alternative: to go to Guiana, Ralegh would have to certify that he would neither "inflict the least injury in the world" on a Spanish subject nor take any other action that might break the peace between Spain and England. Any violation and he would pay with his head.

Ralegh was vexed. How was it possible, he asked, "to break the peace where there is no peace?" The Spaniards treated English visitors to South America as invaders practically as a rule. To comply with the requirement, he would have to sail harmoniously past the Spanish soldiers in San Thomé, who, conceivably, would merely sit and watch as the flotilla proceeded to turn up the Caroní River. They would be fully aware, though, that the *Ingleses* were heading to the gold mine where Topiawari had taken Guaterral in 1595, and which, although within several miles of San Thomé, had eluded them. What were the chances that they would sit idly while the *Ingleses* worked the legendary mine in the weeks that followed? Given the tendency for sparks to fly whenever any Spanish company came within fifty miles of any English one—much less his pugnacious bunch—Ralegh faced a challenge tantamount to threading an eyeless needle.

But seeing no room for negotiation, he agreed to the new terms, and in hope of keeping his men in line, he issued a set of "Orders to be observed by the Commanders of the Fleete and land companies" that outlined the upright conduct he expected from his company, including attending divine service mornings and evenings, "praising God every night with singing of a psalm at the setting of the watch," and refraining from blaspheming, stealing, and gambling with dice and cards. He also prohibited chasing or boarding other ships—a regulation one of his captains would flout with dire consequences.

Unfortunately, King James—via Count Gondomar—had more requirements still. First, Ralegh's backers would be required to put up a £15,000 surety bond against any transgressions on his part. Next, prior to weighing anchor, Ralegh had to supply a map of his intended route, including estimated dates of arrival at each port as well as the gold mine. Finally, he had to reveal the precise whereabouts of the mine. While James had promised to keep the location secret, it was as likely that Gondomar would manipulate him into divulging it as it was that Ralegh's ships would get wet while crossing the Atlantic. King Philip would then be able to dispatch forces to waylay the English fleet while his agents made an end run for the gold. Again, because the terms weren't up for discussion, Ralegh agreed; he could still fudge the map just enough to throw the Spaniards off his trail.

At last, on March 26, 1617, a full year after his release from the Tower, the now sixty-three-year-old Ralegh left London aboard his flagship, the *Destiny*, bound for Plymouth with two hundred men, including Wat. Joining them on the voyage up the Thames were the eighty men of the 240-ton *Star*; seventy-eight on the 150-ton *Thunder*; the 80-ton *Southampton* with twenty-nine men; a three-gun pinnace; the *Page* with a crew of ten; and Captain Edward Hastings and an indeterminate number of sailors aboard the 160-ton *Encounter*.

In Plymouth, those six vessels would be joined by seven more, among them the *Convertine,* commanded by Lawrence Keymis, and then in Guiana the fleet would expand once again, with four French ships that were crucial to the inland expedition's success. Having ruled it impossible for his force to get the gold without clashing with the Spaniards, Ralegh had looked for help to France, where he had strong ties dating back to his service with the Huguenots as a teenager during the French Wars of Religion. Several influential Frenchmen were interested in participating in the new expedition, among them onetime ambassador to England and current member of France's Council of State, Samuel Spifame, the Sieur de Bisseaux. Ralegh asked them to run interference in Guiana, distracting the Spaniards so that he and his men could work the mine. Ultimately, two of his French friends, Antoine Belle and Charles Faige, agreed.

As ever, Ralegh ran into maddening delays on the Thames. When the *Star* ran out of food two hundred miles short of Plymouth, her captain's solution was to land, procure a horse, ride the ninety miles back to London, and solicit Bess Ralegh for more funds. Walter, meanwhile, had to sell his silver to reap £300 for another ship in the same predicament.

On June 11, 1617, when the full thirteen-vessel, thousand-man fleet had finally assembled in Plymouth and was ready to sail, Ralegh calculated that he'd reduced his family's net worth to just £100, diluting the exhilaration of getting underway. Compared to its 1595 precursor, this expedition offered little of the thrill of adventure and none of the discovery. It was purely a business trip that, as he saw it, had just two possible outcomes: "perish or prosper."

28

BETTER TO HAVE BEEN HANGED

THE EXPEDITION STARTED out well enough. In Plymouth, the night before the fleet was set to depart, Ralegh's fellow West Countrymen came out in droves and threw him a lavish party. A send-off, they called it, but really it was a commemoration of his newfound place alongside local maritime heroes Sir Francis Drake and Sir John Hawkins. In the morning, when the fleet weighed anchor, the same well-wishers massed at the pier and cheered as he ascended the *Destiny*'s gangplank—with pomp added by a drummer they'd hired for the occasion. And they were electrified by the spectacle of the thirteen ships getting underway: mountains of canvas aglow in a propitious dawn, bows cleaving waves, and a thousand rugged men bound for glory.

At the helm of the *Destiny*, Ralegh might have been forgiven for pinching himself: after twenty-two years, thirteen of them spent in prison, he could once again feel the singular rapture of a ship bounding toward treasure, and he could savor the mounting distance between him and the Tower, Gondomar, James, and the other iniquities of gray terra firma. The world was, once again, in color.

Almost immediately, however, a storm barreled into the English Channel, leading to what was undoubtedly one of the most anticlimactic moments in West Country history: Ralegh was forced to retreat to Plymouth, where his well-wishers were still lingering and the drummer had only just begun to pack up his kit.

Ralegh attempted to get the fleet to sea again a day later, succeeding only insofar as avoiding a second awkward reencounter with the well-wishers. Once on the water, the ships ran into another storm that forced another retreat, this time to Falmouth, fifty miles up the coast. Ralegh waited there for twelve days before judging the conditions suitable for his third attempt to get out of England.

He should have waited a thirteenth day, at least: a gale off the southwestern tip of Cornwall hammered the fleet, nearly sinking one of the ships as they raced for refuge to Kinsale, on the southern coast of Ireland. Pending better weather, the company moved inland and stayed in Cork, where day after day of contrary winds added up to weeks, costing Ralegh half the summer, the best season for crossing the Atlantic. As July passed, his restless crewmen drank, bickered, and fought, all at a prodigious clip; the best he could say was that they hadn't killed anyone. Yet.

Finally, on the morning of August 19, 1617, almost five months after departing London, Ralegh awoke to a fresh northeasterly wind that allowed him and his men to weigh anchor. For the first time in seven weeks, they breathed in warm sea air. And plenty of it: over the next sixteen hours, they flew some fifty miles. No doubt it was exhilarating—for most of the crew. Ralegh, insofar as his journal reflects, was only counting down the miles toward his goal.

The next ten days were uneventful—until the thoughts of the *Southampton*'s captain, John Bailey, turned to booty. Off Portugal's Cape St. Vincent, despite Ralegh's emphatic prohibition of pursuing vessels in his "Orders to be observed by the Commanders of the Fleete and land companies," Bailey chased down a quartet of French merchant ships, boarded them, and relieved them of some fish oil, a fishing net, and a pinnace. Once he caught up, Ralegh reimbursed the Frenchmen for everything that had been taken, including the pinnace, which he later renamed the *Fifty Crowns* after her price.

Ralegh was out of his mind, Bailey maintained. If these Frenchmen were anything other than pirates—and, as such, fair game—then Bailey was Queen Elizabeth. Ralegh conceded that the French vessels were fitted out like men-of-war, and that their holds were full of cargo, such as Spanish apparel, that had clearly been pirated from actual merchantmen—from Spain, no less. But it didn't matter; the last thing he wanted was to pique the Spaniards.

Despite his precautions, that was exactly what happened when the self-professed French merchants went on to recount the story of the encounter and, in its many retellings throughout Europe, it became a tale of Sir Walter Ralegh's "high-seas piracy." That version of the story would eventually be corroborated by none other than Captain Bailey himself, who, infuriated by the loss of his prizes, took the *Southampton* and stormed back to England. Knowing he would have hell to pay for deserting a commander with a royal commission, he claimed he'd abandoned the fleet because of his "fear that Sir Walter would turn pirate." As an outraged Gondomar reported to King Philip III, the righteous Captain Bailey "had sailed with [Ralegh] under the belief that his intention was to discover unknown countries, but when he saw his evil object he returned."

The ambassador went on to present Philip with evidence that Ralegh was planning to sack Lanzarote—easternmost of the Canary Islands, which were under Spain's control—as a precursor to ambushing His Majesty's treasure ships. "Pray send the fleet to punish this pirate," added Gondomar, recommending that each and every one of the heretical *Ingleses* be put to death immediately save for Ralegh and his officers, who could instead be taken to Seville for a public execution. "This is the only way to treat such pirates and disturbers, and a necessary step for preservation of peace with England."

On September 6, 1617, the English fleet indeed landed at Lanzarote, where, as Ralegh recorded, he paid Spanish islanders for "a quantity of wheat, goats, sheep, hens and wine." But fearing that he and his men were part of a dangerous fleet of Barbary corsairs, the islanders withheld the provisions. Ralegh attempted to persuade Lanzarote's governor that he and his crewmen were in fact Christians with "no intent to invade any of [the Canary] islands nor to offend any of the Spanish king's subjects." He added that their water was running dangerously low—a situation that wasn't enhanced by the blistering heat and volcanic desertscape that seemed to be Lanzarote's defining features. When he failed to make headway, his men pressed him to march on the town—Teguise, five miles inland—so that they could help themselves to the provisions. But Ralegh's fundamental guiding principle on this expedition, aside from acquiring gold, was to do absolutely nothing that, as he himself put it, "would offend his Majesty."

While continuing his effort to reprovision, he sought to address the dire scarcity of water by landing men on a deserted stretch of Lanzarote far from any habitation. They found a spring, but before they could fill their casks, they were ambushed by a throng of Spanish islanders intent on preemptively attacking the supposed Barbary pirates. Three Englishmen died in the fray before the rest managed to repel the islanders.

Because of the likelihood that the islanders would return with the three hundred Spanish soldiers garrisoned in Teguise, Ralegh weighed anchor, intent on reprovisioning instead at another island, La Gomera, 350 miles southwest—"the best of all the Canaries," he proclaimed. But no sooner did he and his men land there than they again came under attack, the islanders this time fearing they were Dutch pirates.

Once again Ralegh tried to convince a local governor that he'd come only to procure victuals, that he and his men were "vassals of the King of Great Britain in perfect league and amity with the King of Spain," and so on. At length, he succeeded, except that, unbeknownst to him, in the recounting that would reach Gondomar, he'd pirated those victuals as part of his preparation for intercepting the Spanish treasure fleet. To exact compensation, Spain would impound English vessels in Seville, leading King James to vow that if the Canary Islands story were true, Ralegh and his supporters would be executed.

Troubling as it was, the incident would be inconsequential compared to the problems during the Atlantic crossing, which got underway on September 21, 1617, after two weeks in the Canaries. Again, Ralegh was bedeviled by personnel issues. He'd capitalized on the delays in departing England by divesting himself of the worst of his intractable employees; still, most of the remainder were woefully inexperienced. On the night of September 30, an entire ship's crew went to sleep without anyone standing watch, leaving their vessel to crash into another one and sink. The crewmen were rescued—"though better," Ralegh opined, "to have been hanged than saved."

Meanwhile, the fleet suffered an outbreak of calenture, a delirium-intensive fever believed to be induced by tropical heat. Fifty men on the *Destiny* alone were confined to their sleeping quarters, Ralegh among them. "I have suffered the most violent calenture for fifteen days that any man did and lived," he wrote Bess. The best the doctors could offer was that seventeenth-century cure-all, evacuation of the "superfluous humors from the whole body" via bloodletting, transpiration, enema, or vomiting.

Rest was a more effective treatment, but easier prescribed than carried out on an Atlantic crossing during hurricane season. On October 1, while the fleet was anchored in the Cape Verde Islands—nine hundred miles southwest of the Canaries—wind tore apart the heavy anchor cables as though they were made of tinsel, leaving the anchors themselves on the ocean bottom, along with the newly acquired *Fifty Crowns*. As Ralegh scrambled to get the rest of his ships out of the hurricane's path, they were hit with as much rain as he'd ever seen. "The water ran in at my neck," he recorded in his journal, "and out at my knees, as if it had been poured on me with pails."

"It pleased God to visit us with great sickness and loss of our ablest men," he added, at which point his journal entries effectively became obituary columns. Among the first to die were the surgeon and three other men integral to the expedition's success: the sailmaker, one of the quartermasters, and John Pigott, the general whom Ralegh had handpicked to be his second-in-command on land. Pigott's lieutenant soon followed him to the grave. So did the trumpeter, one of the cooks, and arguably the company's most indispensable member, master gold refiner John Fowler. Over the next few days, Ralegh lost sixteen more men.

On October 14, ten days after the fleet's departure from the Cape Verde Islands, a resplendent rainbow spanned the sky—a bad sign for seamen, whose precepts included "Rainbow in the morning, sailor take warning, a rainbow towards night is the sailor's delight." (Since rainbows result from sunlight refracting into a mass of water droplets, to observe one a westbound sailor has to have his back to the sun, which rises to the east. Therefore, a rainbow visible in the morning does in fact indicate rain ahead.) At ten the next morning, sure enough, the sky darkened. Yet unlike any dark sky the crews had ever seen, this one enveloped their ships in a mysterious "black as pitch" pall that clung to them for three days and nights, requiring the pilots to use candles to keep from crashing into one another. To the common sailors who believed that the supernatural was everywhere—seabirds were spirits of those lost at sea, for example—the explanation was, naturally, paranormal. Even the odd skeptics had to be praying now.

The pall was less troublesome, however, than its replacement, which Ralegh described as a "stark calm." On October 19, the twenty-ninth day of the Atlantic crossing, the ships traveled a total of just three miles, a rate of an eighth of a mile per hour, about the same pace as a three-toed sloth. They were still a thousand miles from South America, as far as they knew (it would be another 118 years before clockmaker John Harrison's invention of the marine chronometer allowed seamen to discover their longitude). Ralegh's 1595 fleet, in contrast, had completed the entire crossing in just twenty-two days.

The bigger problem was fresh water. Owing to the hurried departures from both Lanzarote and the Cape Verde Islands, the casks had never been filled. With nowhere left to stop for more en route to South America, the company was forced into half rations—as little as four pints daily, insufficient for typical adults, who lose an average of nearly two pints of water per day from perspiration alone. For men required to perform rigorous shipboard duties in extreme South Atlantic heat, it could mean severe dehydration with symptoms including headaches, dizziness, insomnia, irritability, and decreased blood flow, which mitigated speed, strength, and reaction time.

Those problems were minor, however, in comparison to the one that arose the following day, October 20: a waterspout—a column of mist created by the temperature disparity between the warm sea and cold air, or, to the contemporaneous seamen, a terrifying, otherworldly beast descending from the heavens and making a beeline for their ships. As much as a thousand feet tall and three hundred feet in diameter, and rotating as fast as fifty miles an hour, waterspouts can have the effect on masts and rigging of a thousand cannons fired in rapid succession—which, as it happens, is what the vortices sound like. They pose a particularly acute challenge for becalmed crews, like Ralegh's, who were unable to move their ships out of the way. Their vessels creaked and groaned, meanwhile, as though pleading with them to try anything to escape. As the behemoth roared toward the fleet, apart from clinging to whatever purchase they could find and bracing against the elemental onslaught, all Ralegh and his men could do was pray.

29

YET SHALL YOU FIND THEIR ASHES

PRAYER, IT SEEMED, helped. "Blessed be to God," Ralegh reported, the waterspout dissipated two miles shy of the fleet. Waterspouts were known to presage foul weather, however, and indeed it soon began to rain, "violently." But for the best, as the precipitation yielded three hogsheads worth of water, alleviating the drought that had afflicted the company.

In other good news, on the night of October 22, 1617, when the rain abated, the clear sky presented Ralegh and his men with a view of the Magellanic clouds, the pair of spiral galaxies orbiting the Milky Way that appear as incandescent clouds in the southern hemisphere. The spectacle had a way of convincing mariners that they were not adrift in infinite darkness, as it often seemed, but rather guided by a divine hand.

Now, though, a slew of new rainbows begged to differ. A week of storms followed, tapering off on October 30 but only to present a double rainbow, which, according to Ralegh, "put us in fear that the rains would never end." Of course the rain did end, eventually, but not before a calenture spike brought the total number of fatalities to forty-two of the *Destiny*'s two hundred crewmen. Ralegh thought he himself would add to that figure, on October 31, when he "took a

Walter and Wat Ralegh on a stamp

violent cold which cast me into a burning fever," leaving him unable to eat solid food, save stewed prunes, or do anything but lie in bed and sweat through six shirts a day for two weeks. Notwithstanding the isolation of the captain's quarters, he was forced to endure the "most filthy stench" of the horde of other invalids belowdecks. On the bright side: Wat was unaffected.

On November 11, when the stirring cry of *Land!* finally rang from the deck, Ralegh couldn't even get out of bed to take in the New World; rolling over and propping himself on a side to glance out a porthole was as much as he could manage. Ahead was Cape Wiapoco, the site of English explorer Charles Leigh's short-lived settlement (and of the modern Cabo Orange, in northern Brazil). The crossing had taken fifty-two days, a full month longer than the 1595 iteration.

Three days later, when the fleet landed at Caliana seventy miles north (now Cayenne, the capital city of French Guiana), Ralegh had recovered enough to go ashore, albeit in a chair carried by his men. Meeting the party was a group of Guianans sent by Harry the Indian, who'd gone to England with explorer Robert Harcourt in 1609 solely for the opportunity to meet the great Sir Walter Ralegh and then stayed two years as his servant in the Tower. When the English ships had first appeared on the horizon, Harry—now a powerful chieftain—had his people bring a feast of roasted fish, pistachios, plantains, and grapes to welcome Ralegh.

Although Ralegh was too ill to eat so much as a grape, the reception was deeply reassuring. It had been twenty-two years since he last stood in South America, yet as he wrote Bess, "To tell you I might here be king of the Indians now were a vanity; but my name hath still lived among them, and all offer to obey me." (Letters home had suddenly become an option when one of the captains, Peter Alley, too sick to stay on, sailed back to England.)

While the ships underwent necessary repairs in Caliana, Ralegh rested on the sandy shore, shaded by palms, cooled by gentle sea breezes, and able to enjoy the fresh and fragrant tropical air—"a very earthly paradise," he said of the country. Soon his appetite returned, and his health along with it. But he still lacked one of the most essential ingredients for the expedition's success: the four French ships. Seven months after their departures from Le Havre and Dieppe—or long since the Frenchmen should have arrived in Caliana—there was no sign of them.

In fact, the vessels' commanders—Ralegh's friends Antoine Belle and Charles Faige—had decided that it would be both more pleasant and more profitable to trade on their own account than to ply their way up the steamy Orinoco and take bullets for Englishmen for a share of gold that was far from a certainty. Accordingly they'd changed course from Guiana to the Mediterranean, where, almost immediately, they were captured by Algerian pirates. Next, as far as is known, Faige ended up in debtors' prison in Genoa, deathly ill, while Belle found his way to Rome and worked out a deal with the Spanish ambassador wherein he was given passage home and a hundred ducats (the equivalent of £50, or roughly the amount a skilled tradesman earned in three years) in exchange for his confession to having plotted with the pirate Guaterral to plunder Trinidad and Margarita.

In Caliana, Ralegh knew only that, given the elapsed time, it was improbable that Faige and Belle were coming, leaving him no choice but to proceed without them. His plan of a non-English force to engage the Spaniards wasn't dead, however. The relationship between the Guianans and the Spaniards was a powder keg, and with a little prodding—and perhaps a few munitions—he might light its fuse.

He readied the fleet for the six-hundred-mile sail up to the Orinoco Delta, where he planned to transfer from the *Destiny* to one of the five vessels with sufficiently shallow drafts to manage the labyrinth. During the voyage, however, fever leveled him again, this time leading him to question his fitness to lead the inland expedition.

Meanwhile, several of his officers raised issues of their own with the plan to ascend the Orinoco. Convinced that the Spaniards would either follow them or bottle them in, they demanded that an experienced commander stay behind to defend their flank. Due to the attrition during the Atlantic crossing, the list of available commanders who met their criteria consisted of only a few names, none of whom they trusted not to bolt at the sight of Spanish warships.

The gold mine had been Ralegh's goal for six years—since he accepted Thomas Roe's conclusion that El Dorado probably didn't exist—but it took only a few seconds for him to realize that the best way of attaining it was, paradoxically, not to go. In notifying his officers of his decision, he assured them that when they returned from the mine, they would find him waiting for them "dead or alive." If they couldn't see the ships he was to watch over, he said, "yet shall you find their ashes, for I will fire with the galleons if it come to extremity, but run away I never will."

The officers were satisfied, which presented Ralegh with a new problem: finding someone to lead the inland expedition in his stead. His designated second-in-command, John Pigott, now lay fifteen thousand feet beneath the surface of the Atlantic. Ralegh had chosen a terrific replacement for Pigott, the Cambridge man, Virginia company veteran, and "exceedingly valiant and worthy gentleman" Warham St. Leger. But St. Leger now was even sicker than Ralegh.

Another contender was the freshly promoted sergeant major, George Ralegh, Walter's nephew. George had served with distinction in the Netherlands during the Dutch attempt to gain independence from Spain (known, after its conclusion in 1648, as the Eighty Years' War). But at just a month past his seventeenth birthday, he was simply too young to be placed in command of hundreds of unruly men whom even a prodigy like Alexander the Great would have had a hard time keeping in line. In fact the post of sergeant major had already been a reach for young George; Walter had had to elevate him because of St. Leger's illness coupled with the deaths of the company's two other sergeant majors, Hart and Snedall—now both buried in Caliana.

The only other viable candidate to lead the inland expedition was Ralegh's right-hand man and devoted friend, Lawrence Keymis. The scholar-turned-explorer's leadership experience consisted only of command of ten men on the embarrassment of a mission to Guiana way back in 1596. Although courageous, he was prone to paralyzing indecision and despair. Moreover, the hardened crewmen probably wouldn't appreciate the onetime Fellow of Balliol's flair for Latin verse. On the other hand, at fifty-three, he had seniority over them. He could also be trusted to dodge the Spaniards, which was crucial. Add the totality of his Guiana experience, and Keymis was the best choice. Or so Ralegh concluded.

On December 10, George and Wat Ralegh were among the 250 soldiers under Keymis's command, who, along with 150 mariners, boarded five small ships. This inland squadron also included several landing craft and carried a full month's worth of victuals, a lesson learned in 1595. For the umpteenth time, Ralegh exhorted the officers to avoid any entanglement with Spanish settlers. "I would not, for all the world, receive a blow from the Spaniards to the dishonour of our nation," he told Keymis.

Also heavy on Ralegh's mind was Wat, an immature twenty-four, too eager to prove himself, his reason overly susceptible to hijack by his emotions. If "without manifest peril of my son and the other captains, you cannot pass towards the mine," Ralegh advised Keymis, "then be well advised how you land." If worse came to worst, they could still accomplish a great deal by stealthily collecting a basket or two of ore "to satisfy his majesty that my design was not imaginary but true."

Then Ralegh could do nothing but watch the five vessels sail off, quickly becoming indistinguishable from the hazy gray-green continent. The moment coincided with the beginning of what stood to be one of his greatest challenges: weeks upon weeks of waiting for word.

30

"VICTORY! VICTORY!"

FOR NEARLY A month, Keymis and his four hundred men faced rivers seemingly trying to tackle them. Two of their five ships ran aground, forcing their captains and the majority of the 150 mariners to stay behind to extricate them. The three other vessels, along with the rest of the mariners and all 250 soldiers, finally managed to reach Arromaia late on the afternoon of January 2, 1618.

The change to the province since Keymis's last visit, almost twenty-two years earlier, was alarming: Antonio de Berrío's stockade at San Thomé had mushroomed from a cluster of crude bamboo huts into a substantial town that included 140 houses, a church, and two convents, everything surrounded by a redoubtable stone wall and a moat. To stay within the anti-aggression parameters established by King James, Keymis now needed a means of getting past San Thomé without incident before continuing up the Orinoco to the Caroní and Topiawari's gold mine. But even if the squadron could somehow sail there undetected, Keymis thought, he would be unable to work the mine; there were so many Spaniards that they were bound to detect the English presence and send for reinforcements. The Englishmen would then be able to escape with their lives only if the freshly arrived Spanish troops were preoccupied by their new gold mine.

Accordingly, on approach to San Thomé, Keymis's best hope was that its citizens got a good, long look at his large and potent force, assumed that he was planning to attack, and promptly surrendered. But instead of white flags, Keymis saw two ominous billows of smoke. Using mortars, San Thomé's inhabitants had launched a pair of artillery shells that now shrieked toward the English squadron.

A mortar

As far as Keymis was concerned, aside from the damage that flying bombs could do, being fired on was a positive development. Ralegh had told him that if "the Spaniards begin to war on you, then let the sergeant major repel them . . . and drive them as far as he can." Now Keymis was within his rights to remove San Thomé from the equation, and he knew exactly how to go about it. Earlier in the day, he'd disembarked young Sergeant Major George Ralegh and his 250 troops four miles short of San Thomé and had them march toward the settlement in battle order, as if they had every intention of attacking. The idea, again, was to precipitate a surrender. Now that he had been fired upon, Keymis could direct them to actually attack.

By nine on what became a starry night, when George Ralegh and his troops had advanced to within half a mile of San Thomé, they were surprised by shouts of "perros ingleses!"—English dogs—from ten Spanish soldiers, who opened fire from a dark hilltop. Accounts of the ensuing conflict vary wildly—understandable, given the darkness, the clouds of gun smoke obscuring the eyewitnesses' vision, and the thunderous discharges that swallowed all other sounds. While the Spanish sources unanimously painted the *perros ingleses* as the aggressors and the English uniformly decried the Spaniards as war criminals, all parties were in general accord on the details of the critical episode that followed the initial volleys: George Ralegh gathered his pikemen and musketeers in the hope of presenting an overwhelmingly superior body against which the handful of Spaniards would be completely insane to continue fighting. At that moment, Wat Ralegh emerged from within the corps of pikemen and, exhorting his brethren to follow him, charged toward the Spaniards with "unadvised daringness," as one of his comrades put it. "Come on, my hearts!" Wat exclaimed, according to another source. A third had him shouting, "Victory! Victory!"

Before engaging the enemy at close quarters, pikemen typically waited for their musketeers to fire and dilute the threat. Now, one of the Spaniards, who would otherwise have been diving for cover from English projectiles, was able to stand his ground, level his musket, and shoot. The ball struck Wat. A second Spanish musketeer swung his weapon by the barrel, landing its stock square against Wat's head and knocking him to the ground.

Wat's comrades charged into the fray to protect him; Sergeant John Plesington drove the spiked top of his halberd—a battle-axe mounted on a shaft as tall as a man—through the second Spanish musketeer. But before any of the English soldiers could help Wat off the ground, guerrilla leader Gerónimo de Grados advanced and, per a Spanish report, dealt Guaterral's son "a sword thrust on the left side of his gullet that . . . sent the heretic to re-echo his song in Hell." Quickly, the rest of George Ralegh's force fell upon the Spaniards, killing all but Grados and one or two others, who ran in retreat to San Thomé. George and his troops chased after them—smack into gunfire from within the guardhouse. The Spaniards held the position long enough for most of their citizens to flee San Thomé through a rear exit.

Eventually, the Englishmen's numerical superiority facilitated the seizure of the guardhouse, allowing them to enter the town. They found themselves in a sandy main square and under fire all around from Spanish arquebuses poking through loopholes freshly cut into the exterior walls of the houses. In response, the Englishmen set fire to the houses, and by one in the morning of January 3, 1618, San Thomé was theirs. There was no celebration, however. Not even a measure of relief. Allowing the citizens to escape had been a serious blunder: now the Spaniards could summon reinforcements, all but negating the strategic value of having captured San Thomé.

Despite the heightened urgency of getting to the gold mine, Keymis saw fit to commemorate Wat Ralegh and three others who'd been killed in the fighting. The four men were lain on boards placed on the shoulders of their comrades, who marched around San Thomé's main square to their drummers' slow and deliberate beat, their weapons pointed toward the ground, a mark of respect on such occasions. The eulogies, if any, weren't recorded, but as the slain men were interred within the church—Wat and a second officer by the altar, the other two in the nave—the erudite Keymis could have done worse than to borrow from the scene in Shakespeare's recent *Henry V*, when King

San Thomé

Henry uses the memory of their fallen comrades to rally his troops: "The fewer men, the greater share of honour . . . And gentlemen in England now a-bed shall think themselves accurs'd they were not here."

Three weeks earlier, upon landing at Trinidad, Walter Ralegh had immersed himself in a daily routine, patrolling for any evidence of an increased Spanish military presence beyond the benign handful of soldiers at the rebuilt San José de Oruña—incoming Spanish warships, for example. He also foraged for medicinal plants and herbs to treat any wounded when the men of the inland expeditionary force arrived. Surely the most difficult part of these tasks was fighting the constant urge to scan the western horizon for the boats carrying Keymis, Wat, and company from Guiana.

Perhaps for a diversion, on January 19, 1618—a little over a month into his stay in Trinidad—Ralegh sent a ship up to Puerto de los Hispanioles to trade for tobacco. The Spaniard soldiers there, construing the action as the execution of the pirate Guaterral's rumored plan to raid San José, sent twenty musketeers to defend the port. From a hundred feet away, the Spaniards fired their arquebuses, hitting none of their targets. The volley was enough to prompt the disembarking Englishmen to reembark at once. In response, Ralegh pointedly did not retaliate.

Ten days later, however, when the Spaniards shot at a small party of men he'd sent to Piche to get tar for their ships, Ralegh could no longer hold back. With six musketeers, he jumped into his barge and rushed to the rescue, joined by the now healthy Warham St. Leger and another officer in their skiffs. The sight of the force spurred the Spaniards to retreat to the woods, but not before they'd killed one member of the tar party and captured a cabin boy. Ralegh yet again turned the other cheek, thinking instead about the men returning from the mine—or, rather, trying not to think about them.

Day after day, the view of the continent, eight miles across the Gulf of Paria, was uninterrupted by sails. There was no sign of the men at all and no news, not even a rumor via the islanders' networks. Until, on February 1, a Tivitiv trader arrived in a canoe with a report that the English squadron had captured San Thomé, killing three important Spaniards, including Fernando de Berrío's replacement as governor, Diego Palomeque de Acuña (a relative of the First Count of Gondomar, Diego Sarmiento de Acuña).

It was easy for Ralegh to dismiss the claim: the Tivitivas had deceived him before—in 1595, when they'd lured him to their village under the pretext of helping to orient his pilot, Ferdinando. And Guianans had to be considered unreliable sources in general, given that they'd sworn up and down that a great and magnificent golden city stood on the far side of the Cordillera, where Roe had since definitively established there was nothing but grass. Of course, the most compelling reason to disregard the story was that Ralegh's prime directive to Keymis had been to steer clear of San Thomé. Oddly, though, Ralegh's men heard the identical story the same day from an entirely different source, in a Nepoyo village sixteen miles east of Pelicans Bay. They were also told that two English captains had been killed in the altercation.

Forget patrols, medicinal plants, and rising tensions with Spaniards on Trinidad. Ralegh now knew he wouldn't be able to rest until he learned the truth. Repeatedly, he sent skiffs into the Orinoco Delta in search of news; just as often, they returned with no more than cassava bread and oranges. On February 13, in hope the Nepoyos had heard something new, he recorded in his journal, "I sent Sir W. St. Leger, Captain Chudley, and Captain Giles, with 60 men, to the Indian town." His journal ends there, as abruptly as if he'd died. Which was how he felt the next day, February 14, when he received a letter Keymis had written a month earlier detailing the battle in San Thomé, including the circumstances of Wat's death.

"The world hath taken end in me," Ralegh would later write in a letter to a friend at court, summing up his expedition as "the greatest and sharpest misfortunes that have ever befallen any man." Keymis had tried to soften the blow with details of Wat's "extraordinary valour and constant vigour of mind." Wat even continued to inspire his men posthumously, Keymis maintained, having said with his last breath, "Lord have mercy upon me, and prosper your enterprise!" Between the lines, however, Ralegh read, "My son, having more desire of honor than of safety, was slain."

As he wrote to Bess, "My brains are broken . . . God knows I never knew what sorrow meant until now." The Raleghs had lost a son a quarter century earlier—Damerei, as an infant; yet the grief over Wat's death almost entirely eclipsed that loss. The lone positive for Ralegh: "I shall sorrow the less because I have not long to sorrow." The reason: he would not have long to live, the attack of San Thomé almost certainly constituting his death warrant. His only hope was that, in lieu of a justification, King James would accept a mountain of gold.

Keymis was working on it. He'd already found some gold in San Thomé's treasury: a gold bar, a heavy gold chain, an ingot, and a few other gold pieces worth about two thousand Spanish reales, or £500. As for getting up the Caroní River to the mine, the problem was the escapees from San Thomé. If only he'd blockaded the town and penned them in, because now, having regrouped three miles up the Orinoco on Isla Fajardo and taken refuge in the small stockade there, they were blockading him—not only keeping him from the gold but also preventing him from venturing out to the surrounding villages to enlist the aid of Guianans.

Of even greater concern to Keymis were Spanish reinforcements: the common takeaway from the interrogations of the few Spaniards he did capture was a certainty that fresh troops would be arriving any day. Even with the recent influx of the hundred-some mariners who'd managed to loose their vessels from the shoals, such a force could obliterate his own, or at the least, obliterate his chances of working Topiawari's mine.

Late on the night of the funeral, reluctant to delay his attempt at the mine any longer, Keymis took a few men in one of the skiffs and tried to sneak past the Spaniards on Isla Fajardo. Reaching the mouth of the Caroní undetected, the party rowed upriver. The familiar thunder of Llovizna Falls grew louder as Keymis began searching for the embankment where Topiawari had taken him and Ralegh—three miles from the mouth of the river, according to the map he'd drawn that day in 1595. Surprisingly, a full four miles from the mouth of the river, he'd yet to spot the embankment.

After another mile he questioned whether he ever would. One muddy and overgrown stretch of Caroní shoreline was indistinguishable from the next, especially at night, and he might have had difficulty even at high noon. Topography changes over time along even the tamest brook. On the Caroní, each rainy season buries the malleable banks beneath millions of pounds of thrashing water for months at a time. Twenty-three such seasons had passed since Keymis had last seen the embankment, which had been unremarkable to begin with.

After he and his men had rowed another five miles, he found it. Or so he said—it's likely he'd realized there was no possibility whatsoever of finding it, but he dared not admit it to the men, his command of whom was tenuous. Instead, he improvised, directing them to another deposit he knew, likely the valley near Llovizna Falls, where, in 1595, as Ralegh wrote, "every stone that we stooped to take up promised either gold or silver." Keymis and Ralegh had seen gold in the quartz there, but, lacking any mining tools other than their daggers, they'd been unable to extract any of it.

Keymis's men must have wondered how one of England's finest mathematical minds could have underestimated the distance to the mine by 200 percent. But they were more concerned about the sunrise—just a few hours away—that could divulge their whereabouts. They scrambled ashore, surged up the bank, and pushed their way inland through towering grass. The hard sand offered them good footing, though fueled by adrenaline on top of their urgency, no doubt they could have flown through the most stubborn clay. Climbing several small hills, they reached the plains, described by Ralegh in 1595 as "without bush or stubble, all fair green grass," with birds "singing on every tree . . . a thousand several tunes" audible though the "thunder of waters."

No such details of Keymis's visit exist, nor of his attempt to open the mine, but likely he and his men swung pickaxes, surely they worked as quickly as possible, and, soon, they were electrified, unearthing veins of white quartz laced with metal that glowed wonderfully golden. Once they'd extracted enough to meet Ralegh's requirement "to satisfy his majesty that my design was not imaginary," they hurried back to the skiff and sailed downriver.

Landing back at San Thomé sometime before sunrise, Keymis displayed one of the samples as if it were a trophy. It's easy to imagine the men cheering him while marveling at the bright stripes the ore cast when reflecting the campfire. Certainly it was a nice moment for Keymis, if not the highlight of his life, sweetened by the exhilaration of having just sidestepped calamity. All at once, his twenty-three years of struggles, imprisonment, brushes with death, and preposterous reversals of fortune could be viewed as persistence rewarded. Better still, Ralegh, his illustrious mentor and guiding light, would not only be vindicated in England but rightly lionized and, if no longer able to live happily ever after, to at least to find some consolation for Wat's death.

But any such reverie on Keymis's part was undone a few hours later, when the refiner broke it to him that the samples were fool's gold at best and utterly worthless. And then Keymis himself came undone.

31

GREAT SANDS AND ROCKS

Lawrence Keymis would sooner be quartered by galloping plow horses than harm Sir Walter Ralegh, yet here he was poised to destroy him. Now that the refiner had pronounced the ore worthless, meaning that Keymis's men crossed the Atlantic and since then risked their lives more than a dozen times for nothing, he would have to admit to misleading them about the gold mine. And then he would have to convince them to go back up the Caroní in search of the gold mine he'd really been trying to find. They would probably mutiny before he was halfway through his convoluted explanation. But even if they were pleading to tangle with the Caroní again, even if they were willing to die to get the gold, the same problem remained: since the map he'd drawn in 1595 had proven to be a waste of parchment, he had no way of finding the mine.

As an alternative, he considered the hallowed Mount Iconuri mine the chieftain Putijma had tried to show him in 1595. Keymis was fully confident he could navigate his way back to Mount Iconuri, but he had no idea of the whereabouts of the mine itself, meaning he and his men might scrape away at the mountain's thousands of acres of thick underbrush and sediment for months without finding anything more than sandstone.

Then he remembered Gilbert, the pilot who'd guided him down the Orinoco during the 1596 visit to Guiana. Gilbert knew the way to the Iconuri mine, having been there with Putijma. But Gilbert was already an old man then—twenty-two years ago. In the unlikely event he was still alive, he would be as hard to find as the mine. Putijma, though, might still be around. But what if the "stones the color of gold" he'd boasted about were merely stones the color of gold?

Indecision paralyzed Keymis, until a passing remark by an Arromaian provided a new clue that enabled the mathematician all at once to transform a jumble of Guianan lore and Spanish speculation into a near certainty that he would find gold deposits, if not the motherlode, on a bank of "great sands and rocks" six miles up the Orinoco. His men had to wonder to what extent desperation or hyperactive optimism factored into his certainty; after all, he'd been willing to stake his life on his ability to find Topiawari's mine. But now, at least, there was hope.

To reach the bank of great sands and rocks, he realized he would again have to get past the Spaniards on Isla Fajardo. Rather than troubling him, the thought of the stockade made him giddy: that the Spaniards had placed a defensive fortification in proximity to the great sands and rocks bolstered his theory about gold there.

He packed forty men into a pair of boats and raced upriver, approaching Isla Fajardo, passing it, then leaving it behind, all without

incident—before running into another ambush laid by Gerónimo de Grados, the guerrilla leader who'd dealt Wat Ralegh his death blow. This time Grados had nine of his guerrillas and ten Guianan archers, and with a flurry of musket balls and arrows they wounded two Englishmen, killed seven, and forced the boats into a hasty retreat, according to a Spanish account. An English casualty report differed, recording two dead and seven wounded, with one of the latter—Captain Thomas Thornhurst, who'd been shot in the head—not dying until weeks later.

Keymis and the other survivors regrouped at San Thomé before making a second attempt a few days later with numbers sufficient to obliterate Grados's guerrillas if they dared attack again. They didn't, allowing Keymis to finally reach the storied bank. After four days of searching there—while enduring brutal heat and humidity, clouds of biting insects, and inadequate provisions—his men began grumbling that they'd just added a new entry to the long list of legendary gold deposits that proved to be nothing more than sand and rocks. If forced into a fifth day of digging, it seemed, they would mutiny.

Keymis gave most of them leave to return to San Thomé while he stayed and continued searching along with George Ralegh and sixteen others who were pained by the notion that failure would mean Wat Ralegh had lost his life in vain—and Sir Walter would too. Still unable to find any gold, those eighteen diehards rowed further upriver over the next two and a half weeks, frantically trading Natives trinkets for new clues that led them to excavate one sandy, rocky bank after the next, all the way to the Orinoco's confluence with the Guárico River, 230 miles from San Thomé. And they would have kept going, but it was now February, the driest part of the dry season, and the water was too shallow to accommodate their boats.

Keymis's simple solution was to wait a month or so for the water to rise, but a long-simmering issue within his ranks began to boil over: the entire expedition had been predicated on a certainty that the company would find the gold mine on the Caroní. In hindsight, it seemed quite clear that that belief was just speculation that had been reconfigured by Ralegh's thirteen years of imprisonment, frustrated ambition, and longing to be free. Yet Keymis's belief was unshaken. His troops, even the most fervent, now thought of him as delusional, as well as hateful, and, worse, "false to all the men." Having reached their threshold, they wanted to return to Trinidad.

Mount Iconuri, which was on the way back to Trinidad, became Keymis's last chance. Augmented by his other 370 men in San Thomé, he thought, he would have a strong enough force that any Spanish unit would give him a wide berth. But as he was about to discover, his tabulation was flawed. Back in San Thomé, during the weeks he'd been away, any time Englishmen had set foot outside the town's walls to avail themselves of the cornfields or grazing cattle, they were gunned down by Grados's guerrilla unit. They'd countered by waiting until dark and then marching a large detachment spread so far apart that Grados couldn't ambush them. In that respect, they succeeded. Grados and company turned to sniping, however, killing fourteen or fifteen of the Englishmen and sending the rest bolting back into the town. Additional forays fared no better. Together, Grados and starvation had whittled the English force to 150 men.

When Keymis and the diehards returned to San Thomé, the second week in February, they found the town in ashes, their comrades having set fire to it to facilitate their withdrawal. When Keymis caught up to them downriver, they were in no condition to march through the fifteen or twenty miles of impenetrable jungle to get to Mount Iconuri, let alone climb it. Their fitness aside, they wanted no part of starving and ducking Spanish bullets for months on end while searching for yet another fool's gold mine. The expedition had devolved into a collective referendum on Ralegh's legendary plunges into enemy fire. Perhaps, like many other military heroes, he'd simply been lucky all these years. Or was it that he, like Wat, prioritized glory over life itself? In essence, hadn't he led his own son to his grave? And though he was now in Trinidad, wasn't he leading them to theirs?

For Keymis, all that mattered now was finding gold on Mount Iconuri, whatever it took; anything was better than returning to Trinidad empty-handed. Unfortunately, when he and his men came within sight of Mount Iconuri the next day—February 9, 1618—its copious bay had been reduced by the dry season to a pool just two or three feet deep, not nearly enough to accommodate any of their boats. Accessing the shore would therefore require the men to spend hours wading through what amounted to an anaconda- and alligator-infested quagmire. Because as little as politely asking them to try would almost certainly spur them to mutiny, Keymis saw no option other than to return to Trinidad. In a letter he would send to the island in advance of the company, he told Ralegh, "The disgrace of not bringing our men to this mine will . . . rest heavy upon me in the judgements and opinions of most men." He feared Sir Walter would be chief among them.

Three weeks later, on March 2, 1618, while the 168 surviving members of the 400-man inland expeditionary force dragged themselves onto the shores of Pelicans Bay, Keymis hurried aboard the *Destiny* to make the case that he wasn't to blame for returning empty-handed. He and the men, he told Ralegh, had had "their hands full to defend themselves from firing, and the daylight and nightly alarms." Between Grados's guerrillas, the Guianans whom the Spaniards had coerced into their service, and the Spanish reinforcements due any moment, he'd had no way "to pass up the woody and craggy mountains and hills without the loss of all the commanders," and "the rest would easily enough have been cut in pieces in their retreat." But even if he'd managed to find the gold deposit, it would have been "impossible to lodge any companies at the mine for lack of victuals." The "greater error," he concluded, would have been "to discover it [for] the Spaniards."

Ralegh wasn't persuaded. Keymis's "care of losing so many men in passing through the woods," he said, "was but feigned." The issue was simply that a brilliant polymath had failed to find the mine. Which beggared credulity. Using the 1595 map, Ralegh added, "a blind man might find it." Had Keymis only "gone directly to the place" and "brought to the king but one hundred weight of the ore, though with the loss of a hundred men," the expedition would "have given his majesty satisfaction, preserved my reputation and given our nation encouragement to have returned the next year with a greater force."

For several days afterward, Keymis seemed "greatly discontented," according to Ralegh. Ultimately, Keymis returned to the captain's cabin and presented a written apology for his failure to find the mine. To Ralegh's dismay, it was largely a restatement of the case the mathematician had already made in person. He told Keymis that "he had undone me by his obstinacy, and that I would not favor or colour in any sort his former folly." When Keymis asked whether that was his "resolution," Ralegh said it was. "I know then, sir, what course to take," Keymis said and left the cabin.

Ralegh heard him trudging up to his own cabin, directly overhead, and then stepping inside before a gunshot shattered the shipboard stillness, no doubt startling the bay's eponymous pelicans into flight. Suspecting the worst, Ralegh sent a page, who quickly returned and reported that there was nothing to worry about: Captain Keymis had fired out his cabin window while cleaning his pistol. Checking again half an hour later, however, the page pieced together that Captain Keymis had in fact been trying shoot himself and failed, the bullet having merely broken a rib. Now Keymis lay face down on his bed in a pool of blood created by the dagger lodged in his heart.

Whatever sympathy Ralegh felt was subsumed by disgust. "What wonder is it that I have failed," he grumbled, "where I could neither be present myself, nor had any of the commanders I trust living, or in state to supply my place." Now, though, he was healthy enough to lead a new inland expedition and collect the gold. If he died trying, he thought, fine; his body would be with his son's, and he would at least have defended his honor. He remained confident, however, that he would find Topiawari's mine.

But even if he failed, he could still salvage the expedition. To repay George Ralegh's troops for freeing him from enslavement in San Thomé, a bright Guianan named Christoval Guayacunda had not only told them about a rich gold mine near the fortress but also given them a pair of ingots from it that had since tested as "very fine." In the worst-case scenario, as Ralegh saw it, he would follow Guayacunda to this secondary mine and extract enough of the ore to convince King James to send a greater force.

In fact, there was a far worse scenario, as he discovered when advancing the plan. The men who'd just returned from the continent—"our men weary, our boats split, our ships foul, and our victuals well-nigh spent," as one of them wrote—would have just as soon set themselves on fire as return to Guiana. The crewmen who'd been on Trinidad had even less interest in going inland, or staying on Trinidad for that matter, given what they'd heard of the imminent arrival of an armada sent by King Philip III. Sir Walter, with all due respect, could either sail home with them or get out of their way.

The expedition, Ralegh realized, had come to nothing. "As Sir Francis Drake and Sir John Hawkins died heart-broken when they failed of their enterprise, I could willingly do the like," he wrote Bess. Quickly, though, he picked himself off the ground and devised an entirely new enterprise, which was, he went on to tell her, "to contend against sorrow to comfort and relieve you."

Relieving her—and their surviving son, Carew—entailed coming home with enough gold to placate King James, and to get it, Ralegh needed buy-in from his increasingly mutinous company. Rather than pitch his plan amid their evacuation of Trinidad, he waited until after the ships had safely departed and reconvened at a Caribbean island 450 miles north, which stood to put them in a better frame of mind. Originally, the Caribs called the island *Oualie*—Land of Beautiful Waters—for its bright turquoise and crystalline bays. It would be renamed Dulcina by English settlers taken by its bountiful sugarcane and general sweetness. But the name that would stick was Nevis, a derivation of the Spanish *nieves,* or snow, of which the tropical island has none whatsoever. The three-thousand-foot volcanic peak at its center, however, was consistently capped by white clouds, making it look like a Swiss Alp.

The fleet—what was left of it, anyway—anchored off Nevis on March 12, 1618. More than a third of the original thousand men had died during the expedition, and since departing Trinidad, two of the eleven vessels had deserted, one helmed by Captain Wollaston, the other by Captain Whitney—of all people. It was Whitney whose ship had run out of provisions at the start of the expedition, forcing Ralegh to part with his own silver, reducing his net worth to £100. Wollaston and Whitney would go on to pirate in the Atlantic with moderate success, their biggest score being £3,000 worth of dry fish taken from a small fleet of French ships.

Stung by their departures but still sanguine about his prospects, Ralegh gathered the remaining captains and outlined a new plan: sail to the Azores archipelago and ambush Spain's homeward-bound treasure fleet. Essentially it was the same gambit with which the English fleet would have separated the Spaniards from their silver in the Azores in 1597 if Essex hadn't inexplicably disappeared at the critical moment. Now, with the benefit of that experience, Ralegh told his captains, he could array their ships at precisely the right choke points. It was a once-in-a-lifetime opportunity!

The captains saw a different once-in-a-lifetime prospect: death. They and their subordinates, especially those who'd been under siege in San Thomé, had had enough of the Spaniards—and Gerónimo de Grados's guerrillas were a bunch of farmers compared to the soldiers who escorted the treasure fleet. But even if the treasure galleons were defended by a solitary grandmother in a rowboat, was plundering them really an option? King James had promised Gondomar "on his faith, his hand, and his word" that if Ralegh and company returned to England with gold taken by force from Spanish subjects, England would not only return it to the Spaniards but also hand over "the authors of the crime to be hanged in the public square of Madrid."

Ralegh played a fresh card, a privateering commission from France that would authorize him to plunder Spanish ships. Before departing England, he'd written his French friends and enjoined them to convince King Louis XIII to sign off. The captains were unmoved; the same French friends had promised to join the fleet, and where were they?

As the captains and their crews began to refit and reprovision in preparation for departure, Ralegh scrambled to find an alternative plan, but one scaled-down Guiana excursion or modified treasure-fleet scheme after the next failed to gain traction. Eager either to go home or to find opportunities for enrichment without a high likelihood of death, crews peeled away.

Soon Ralegh was reduced to just four ships, including the *Destiny*, far too few to strike at the Spanish treasure fleet. From the

point of view of the three remaining captains, that ought to have been obvious to him, yet he persisted in his plotting.

By March 21, his fleet consisted of only the *Destiny*. "What shall become of me now I know not," he wrote to Secretary of State Winwood. "I am unpardoned in England and my poor estate consumed, and whether any other prince will give me bread I know not." Winwood would never receive the letter, having died five months earlier, at fifty-four, and been replaced by Robert Naunton. No fan of Ralegh's, Naunton was unlikely to take any action other than to compound his problems.

Regardless, as long as King James was in charge of England, Ralegh saw the sovereign in France—Louis XIII—as his best bet for bread. He estimated that over the next three months, by preying on Spanish commercial vessels in the *Destiny*—a ship compared to which, he maintained, "there is not better in the world"—he could come up with £100,000, a nest egg for his new life in France, which would be a refuge. And perhaps much more: he had not only his base of supporters among the Huguenots but also friends in Louis's court who'd been appalled by King James's treatment of him and were now likely to regard him as an asset. Especially intriguing was Louis himself, who was sixteen—the same age Prince Henry had been in 1610 when he commissioned Sir Thomas Roe's El Dorado expedition.

Fleeing to France had a significant two-part hitch, though: Ralegh would subject Bess and Carew to ruin, and he would betray the friends and relatives who'd underwritten a £15,000 surety bond the Crown had mandated largely to prevent him from yielding to such a temptation. As he was painfully aware, the same friends and relatives had committed their money in spite of their suspicion that if the expedition foundered, he would forsake them in name of royal favor—in France or wherever else he could get it. As much as they admired him, they understood that his personal motto, *Amore et Virtute*—with Love and Virtue—was aspirational. It really ought to have been *Aurum et Gloriam:* for Gold and Glory.

But that version of Walter Ralegh was no longer extant on March 24, 1618, when, as he wrote Bess, rather than plunder Spanish ships and seek asylum in France, he was sailing back to England to restore to her and Carew the estate he'd gambled away on Guiana. "If I live to return," he told her, "resolve yourself that it is the care for you that hath strengthened my heart." He would not have been optimistic about his prospects of living to return, however, had he heard the hushed conversations of his crewmen.

32

SIR JUDAS

SAILING THREE THOUSAND miles to Newfoundland before crossing the Atlantic might seem counterintuitive, but none of Ralegh's crewmen took issue with the route; given the prevailing wind patterns and ocean currents, it was the safest and most expedient way back to Europe. Instead the crewmen found fault with their own decision to remain aboard. Rather than plunder and revelry in the sunny Caribbean, their future now consisted of a month of gelid sailing followed by even harder labor when they reprovisioned in Newfoundland, for instance, careening—hauling the ship onto land and then scraping and burning away weeds and barnacles for up to two weeks.

Nearing the Newfoundland port of St. John's in April 1618, a group of conspirators seized all the company's guns and swords while the weapons were being cleaned and then took control of the *Destiny*—henceforth a pirate ship, they declared. To Ralegh's astonishment, they drew the support of most of the crew, including several of the gentlemen.

Intent on getting as close as he could to England, he tried convincing them to sail the ship to Killybegs, a town on the northwestern coast of Ireland that, he told them, was an ideal base of operations for plundering the Atlantic. They were willing on one condition, that he promise to obtain pardons for their past piracies. If only because he and the few crewmen who'd stood by him would be thrown overboard if he didn't, Ralegh gave his word.

Toward the end of May, the ship landed in Kinsale, Ireland, where Ralegh had many friends, which made it odd that nobody came to greet him. A year earlier, when foul weather had forced his fleet to take refuge in Ireland, the regional viscounts, earls, and barons practically trampled over one another to invite him to dinner. Their current change of heart was rooted in the story on every Irish lip—at least in aristocratic circles: Count Gondomar had recently arrived at Whitehall without an appointment and demanded to see King James at once about the English attack on San Thomé. Told that His Majesty was engaged, Gondomar said he needed only the time required to tell the king a single word. Permitted that long in the royal presence, Gondomar burst into the audience chamber, waved his arms, and exclaimed, "*Piratas! Piratas! Piratas!*" before spinning around and marching out.

The crew of the *Destiny* thus learned that Ralegh had "fallen into the grave displeasure of his Majesty." It turned out to be a lucky break for Ralegh insofar as the mutineers, fearing they would be captured and dragged to the scaffold along with him, abandoned the ship and fled. Once again in command, he sailed back to England, landing in Plymouth on June 21, 1618, a year and nine days after the locals' gala celebration of him as a latter-day Drake. They did nothing to mark his return; by consorting with him now, they risked trouble with the law.

Having been apprised of his departure from Kinsale, Bess was waiting when he hobbled ashore into what stood to be the longest embrace in history. It was curtailed, however, by her news: on June 9, desperate to keep the Anglo-Spanish peace and collect the £500,000 dowry for his son, King James had issued "a Proclamation declaring His Majesties pleasure concerning Sir Walter Rawleigh, and those who adventured with him." In it, the king decried the "horrible invasion of the town of S. Thomé" as a "malicious breaking of the peace which hath been so happily established, and so long inviolately continued." He went on to promise that Ralegh and his confederates would be tried and punished for their "scandalous and enormous outrages." And that would happen soon as possible, if James could help it, because his friend Count Gondomar was desperate to end his tour as ambassador, his rectal condition having deteriorated to the point that he needed not only a special chair but also to be carried from room to room.

Gondomar ran into an obstacle when he asked the Privy Council to make good on King James's promise to send Ralegh to Madrid for execution without a trial. Unaware of any such covenant, the privy councillors ran to James, who sheepishly confessed that Gondomar had talked him into it. It didn't matter, they said, because, according to English law, Ralegh needed a fair hearing. James demurred before assuring Gondomar that Ralegh would be handed over to the Spaniards just as soon as he had a "fair hearing"—much as the 1603 Winchester Castle trial was fair.

Devon's vice admiral had then been dispatched to Plymouth to arrest Ralegh, and, as Bess told her husband by way of welcoming him home, the lawman was due any moment. So as much as Walter had been honorable in returning to England, he had to flee as soon as possible. Fortunately, she'd been able to make the arrangements: she now had a boat captain standing by in London to spirit him to France.

Ralegh balked, spent from a homeward journey that would have been arduous enough without a prolonged fever and a return of his palsy, not to mention his grief and a mutiny. The last thing he wanted now was to be tossed about in a stifling stagecoach for a week to get to another boat, especially since he'd come to England with the intent of taking care of his family. But convinced, ultimately, that he could do a better job of that alive than dead, he joined Bess aboard the stagecoach she had at the ready and they sped toward London.

Just twenty miles into the two-hundred-mile journey, though, they crossed paths with the coach bringing none other than Sir Lewis Stukley, Devon's vice admiral, presenting Ralegh with two choices: surrender or, his fragile health notwithstanding, run. Because Stukley, as luck would have it, was a kinsman of his (a nephew of his late cousin Richard Grenville), Ralegh submitted to arrest, with Bess continuing to London to devise a means of freeing him.

Ralegh's decision paid immediate dividends: in Plymouth, rather than place him in confinement, Stukley allowed him to stay at a friend's house, where, over the next three weeks, he was able to rest and recuperate. Meanwhile, Stukley barely looked in on him; the vice admiral was preoccupied by the job of selling the *Destiny*'s impounded cargo in addition to his host of regular duties, all while scrambling to extricate himself from personal debts incurred in a series of failed ventures. Ralegh wondered if his kinsman wasn't intentionally giving him an opportunity to escape. In any case, he was afforded the time and space to work out a flight plan with Bess.

At midnight on July 23, he left his friend's house and snuck down to shore, where his longtime privateering cohort Samuel King waited in a rowboat. A survivor of the recent Guiana expedition and one of the few who hadn't turned against Ralegh, King rowed him onto Plymouth Sound. Just beyond the Plymouth fort's firing range, Bess—and, presumably, Carew—waited aboard a bark that would take the family to France.

A quarter of a mile from the bark, Ralegh began having second thoughts. By fleeing to France, he felt, he would be vindicating "those who told the king that I feigned the mine and decided to turn corsair."

He preferred to stay and fight, and if the charge could be proved, "I shall be content to suffer death."

Bess had chosen King for this job for a reason: more than just a longtime associate, he was also Ralegh's friend. As such, he knew when Ralegh's vanity was tripping him up, and he had no compunctions about saying so: Count Gondomar, he likely reminded Ralegh now, wanted him dead. If Ralegh didn't die, King James wouldn't get his desperately needed half-million-pound dowry. There was no possibility of Ralegh emerging from this entanglement with his head. But he didn't have to become entangled in the first place. He could instead, say, go to Paris with his beloved wife and, while they availed themselves of fine wine and haute cuisine, let things cool down in England—or simply change, as things are wont to do. As for Ralegh's inclination to defend himself, that was admirable, but at present he and King stood a better chance of capturing the Spanish treasure fleet in their rowboat than he did of clearing his name. Had he forgotten that he'd spent thirteen years in the Tower of London for a crime he'd had absolutely nothing to do with?

In response, Ralegh seized on the title of James's screed, "A Proclamation declaring his Majesty's pleasure concerning Sir Walter Rawleigh, and those who adventured with him." What if he could make the case that one of "those who adventured with him" was to blame for taking San Thomé? After all, he said, Keymis "followed not my directions . . . I gave no authority for it to be done." Thereby convincing himself to write a defense to send to the palace, Ralegh had King return him to Plymouth.

Having been updated by King, presumably, Bess remained on the bark, hoping that Walter would rethink his decision; even if he were to author the most compelling defense in history, there was no assurance that James would ever see it. If Walter wanted to try anyway, he could write his heart out during the voyage to France.

The following day, July 24, Bess got her wish: Ralegh changed his mind. Again he found Samuel King at midnight, and again they rowed onto the bay. But again he decided he couldn't go through with it and King returned him to Plymouth. Bess was left to hope Ralegh would change his mind once more and that, for once, she and King could prevail upon him to board the bark. Before they had a chance, however, Stukley received orders from the Privy Council to "speedily bring hither the person of Sir Walter Raleigh."

Accordingly, Ralegh once again found himself in a stagecoach bound for London, this time accompanied by Stukley. With them was a doctor, a Frenchman named Manoury whom Stukley had hired because of Ralegh's palsy and generally poor health. Bess and Samuel King went to London as well, hoping once again to be able to liberate Ralegh. Somehow.

In Stukley's coach, Ralegh was enjoying the conversation with Manoury until the gravity of his situation started to set in—and then was underscored by happenstance: the coach approached Sherborne Castle, at its peak summer splendor, close enough for him to see how well his plantations and orchards had grown. Were the Fates rubbing his nose in his shortcomings? With a sigh, Ralegh told the doctor, "All this was mine, and it was taken from me unjustly."

Two glum days and thirty-five miles later, the party stopped for the night in Salisbury, where, again, the Fates seemed to be up to something. As Ralegh learned at the coaching inn, King James was about to visit Salisbury as part of his summer progress. All at once seeing a way out of his predicament, Ralegh enlisted Manoury's aid.

Over the ensuing three days, the doctor told Stukley that his captive was sick, bedridden, and unable to eat, much less travel. In fact, Ralegh was writing—and enjoying mutton and fresh-baked bread Manoury smuggled to his room. The result was a fifty-eight-page document entitled "Sir Walter Rawleigh his Apologie for his voyage to Guiana." Intended for King James, it related Keymis's failure to follow Ralegh's direct order to steer clear of San Thomé. Although Ralegh couldn't supply Keymis's testimony, he had the next best thing, the letter the mathematician had sent him from the Orinoco; he inserted it into the "Apologie" before the secondary charge that the voyage to Guiana had been a pretext to escape the Tower. If so, he argued, "Why did I not keep my liberty once I had it?"

King James arrived at Salisbury on August 1, a day or two later. It's unknown whether he saw Ralegh's "Apologie," but it stands to reason he at least heard about it based on the royal order Stukley subsequently received: get Ralegh out of town posthaste. On a related note, with James's assurance that Ralegh was en route to Madrid to be executed, Gondomar had felt comfortable in ending his tour of England and returning home to Spain—in a triumphal procession highlighted by the king's proclamation that, in all of English history, no ambassador had ever been as loved and respected.

Gathering that exculpatory evidence ran contrary to the royal ends, Ralegh realized that Bess had been right all along: he could be of no use to his family unless he fled England. His only remaining question, he confided to Manoury, was how to go about it. The Frenchman had a surprising response: Stukley. Not only a kinsman but also an ardent admirer of Ralegh's, the vice admiral would be eager to help him escape.

Indeed, when they arrived in London, on the night of August 7, Stukley worked things out so that rather than go to the Tower, Ralegh could stay with Bess at the house she'd rented on Broad Street. And on August 9, the vice admiral met Ralegh there, bringing him a false beard and a hat with a green band that stood out enough that a passerby would likely fixate on it rather than its wearer. Stukley also had a plan for the two of them to sneak down to the docks and leave the country that night.

Ralegh's farewell to Bess and Carew, if any, wasn't recorded; the family would have to wait for a less precarious time to reunite. He and Stukley then stole down to the Thames, where trusty Samuel King was waiting in a wherry to take them to Tilbury, twenty miles downriver, to meet the yacht that would carry them to France.

Climbing aboard the wherry, Ralegh handed Stukley two of the pistols he'd brought in case things went awry—which happened as soon as the they pulled away from the bank: a large, heavily manned ship materialized from the darkness, apparently following them. Alarmed, Ralegh decided to abort the attempt. Stukley argued for staying the course, but his argument made no sense—until he revealed that its sole purpose was to stall until the wherry had gone far enough that the Crown's meager case against Ralegh was bolstered by an attempt to flee justice. Having now succeeded, Stukley placed both Ralegh and Samuel King under arrest in the name of His Majesty King James.

Through his astonishment, Ralegh managed to joke, "Sir Lewis, these actions will not turn out to your credit." Stukley begged to differ: for his services, he was set to be credited £965 from the exchequer, with still another £20 going to his confederate, Dr. Manoury. In fact, for his part in the ploy, he would become widely known as Sir Judas Stukley, and when he asked for King James's help in repairing his reputation, the monarch told him, "If I should hang all that speak ill of thee, all the trees in my kingdom would not suffice."

33

THE POWER OF THE TONGUE

On August 17, 1618, a week after his arrest, Ralegh was taken from the Tower of London and placed before the privy councillors, likely in the Star Chamber, the Palace of Westminster courtroom named for the patterns on its ceiling. Henry Yelverton, who'd succeeded Francis Bacon as attorney general, began the proceedings with a recitation of Ralegh's "impostures." Sir Walter had been licensed to "go against infidels" in Guiana and "avoid the offense of the king's friends" in search of a gold mine, Yelverton said. But really, there was no gold mine—or at least none that Ralegh had any interest in finding. Instead, Sir Walter "purposed to set war between the two kings of England and Spain."

The proof, the attorney general went on, could be found in Wat Ralegh's words to his men prior to their advance on San Thomé: "This was the mine they sought," Wat said, implying that gold had been just a pretext. Had there actually been a mine, Sir Walter would have taken miners and mining equipment to Guiana. Instead, "he desired only to have a piece of ore to blear the king's eyes." And once he'd taken San Thomé, finding little of value, he sought to plunder the Spanish treasure fleet. Two of Ralegh's captains were brought into the courtroom to corroborate the last charge. One was his friend, Warham St. Leger, who acknowledged—no doubt through gritted teeth—that, yes, Sir Walter had wanted to ambush the treasure fleet.

Next, Solicitor General Thomas Coventry rose to detail Ralegh's impostures following his return to England, beginning with his flight from justice. "If Sir Lewis Stukley had not prevented him, he had been gone," Coventry said, then tacked on a charge of sedition, claiming that Sir Walter had said "he would one day laugh at this heartily that he had so prettily abused both king and state." Sir Walter, therefore, was "now unworthy of any further continuance of his Majesty's favour"—in other words, the stay on his 1603 death sentence.

Ralegh was then allowed the floor and, with it, a chance to prove the Solomonic doctrine he held as a precept: "Life and death are in the power of the tongue." He had hope in the fact that the Privy Council had no more Henry Howards, the King James patsies who would vote for hanging even if God had appeared as Ralegh's witness and refuted every last charge. The newer councillors had shown themselves to be devotees of the rule of law willing to stand up to the king in its defense, for instance when James promised Gondomar that Ralegh would be executed without a trial.

"I do verily believe that his Majesty doth in his own conscience clear me of all guiltiness," Ralegh began, noting that during the 1603 treason trial James had said that he himself would have rued being tried by such a partisan jury. Further, Ralegh reminded them, "Justice Gawdy upon his death bed said that the justice of England was never so depraved and injured as in the condemnation of Sir Walter Ralegh." How, then, could the privy councillors now seriously consider reinstating the death sentence from that trial?

As for his alleged impostures, Ralegh said that in fact he had intended to find a mine and that he did bring excavation equipment, some £2,000 worth, as well as gold refiners, including the eminent master refiner John Fowler, whose body he'd unfortunately had to commit to the deep en route to Guiana. And not only had he trusted Captain Keymis to find the mine, so had the privy councillors: in 1607, they'd proposed sending Keymis to Guiana to do the identical job. Still, Ralegh confessed to erring in trusting Keymis to avoid San Thomé, and he allowed that St. Leger's testimony was accurate: indeed, he had advanced the idea of taking the Spanish treasure fleet. But wanting to plunder the treasure fleet, as opposed to attempting to do so, was not a capital offense. As for attempting to escape, yes, he'd done that too, though not until after he was under arrest on false charges. In response to the final alleged imposture, that he'd made "ill speeches" about the king, he admitted only to having said, "My confidence in the king is deceived." And who could blame him?

Not the privy councillors. Bringing the hearing to a close, they went to King James and told him his case was lacking. Although Ralegh was returned to the Tower, he'd succeeded in avoiding the scaffold.

But only temporarily. James essentially removed the Privy Council from the proceedings, in its stead appointing a special commission consisting of men known for their contempt of Ralegh, including Bacon and the prosecutor of the 1603 treason case, Edward Coke. Their job: find legal grounds for shipping Ralegh to Spain.

Hoping to elicit evidence of her husband's sedition, they placed Bess Ralegh under house arrest in the care of a wealthy London merchant. (Giving such public responsibilities to men of that class was typical at the time.) Living with her at her rented house on Broad Street, he failed to collect any dirt over three weeks before the special commissioners acceded to his request to return to his "many great occasions and affairs." They replaced him with another businessman, whom they instructed "not to suffer any person to have access unto her, save only such as you shall, in your discretion, think fit," and to intensify her desperation, they stripped her of basic comforts such as furniture. She was allowed to keep her writing implements, though, the idea being to spur her to incriminating communications.

Bacon, Coke, and their fellow special commissioners thought they had the opportunity they'd been waiting for when, on September 18, she received a letter from Ralegh. "I am sick and weak," he'd written, and "my swollen side keeps me in perpetual pain and unrest." If ever he could have used an update on the effort to get him to France, it was now. But in reply Bess wrote only, "I am sorry to hear amongst many discomforts that your health is so ill . . . I hope your health and comforts will mend, and mend us for God." The special commissioners wound up with nothing more incriminating than her dismay at having to sit on the floor.

They tightened the screws, moving her to the Tower of London as well. And they went to work on her husband, sending in a spy, Thomas Wilson, who posed as a Tower official. Ralegh enjoyed their ensuing conversations, yielding a book's worth of reports by Wilson that the members of the special commission scoured in search of damning statements. There was one item that had promise: Ralegh had resumed his work as a chemist. Back in 1607, Lord Chief Justice John Popham—who'd presided over the 1603 treason trial—had taken an "elixir" made by Ralegh and died within an hour. In 1618, the special commission could find no suggestion of foul play, however. As for Ralegh's current alchemy pursuit, it turned out he was developing a machine that distilled salt water so that it became potable, a solution to the age-old problem of keeping drinking water fresh over the course of long sea voyages. In sum, Wilson's reports only gave the special commissioners reason to exonerate Ralegh.

At least on treason charges. They still stood a chance of hanging him for piracy. Deposing one disgruntled crewman after the next, they heard no shortage of testimony about Ralegh's piratical intentions during the expedition. But no one had witnessed him place a blade between his teeth and swing aboard a Spanish galleon. The most serious allegations came from John Bailey, the captain of the *Southampton,* who'd deserted the fleet in 1617 after his own piratical efforts against a quartet of French merchantmen had been thwarted by Ralegh. Bailey had all the trimmings of a star witness for the Crown until Bacon and company's investigation led them to conclude that the captain had "behaved himself undutifully and contemptuously not only in flying from . . . but also in defaming his said general"—so much so that they were obliged to route Bailey to prison. If anything, in reimbursing Bailey's victims—paying the Frenchmen for everything that had been taken, including the pinnace consequently renamed the *Fifty Crowns*—Ralegh deserved a commendation for suppressing piracy.

Turning to the trespass case, the special commission verified Ralegh's claim that he'd been on the island of Trinidad at the time of the San Thomé attack, a hundred miles away as the crow flies, but effectively a world away given the maze of winding waterways. And regardless of whether Ralegh had ordered Keymis to refrain from attacking San Thomé, Bacon couldn't affirm any Spanish claim to the territory; as Ralegh had argued, building a fortress in San Thomé gave King Philip no more stake in Guiana than placing one in Limerick would give him dominion over Ireland. By the Law of Nations, if any European power did have rights to Guiana, it was England, given that Ralegh had taken possession of it in 1595 in the name of Queen Elizabeth "by virtue of a cession by all the native chiefs of the country" and maintained those relationships ever since—and King James had recognized as much, legally, in 1609, when he permitted Harcourt to found a colony there "under the seal of England."

The best the special commissioners could do, then, was to make life harder for Ralegh: they moved him from his apartment to a tiny, upper-story room in the Brick Tower, deprived him of his valet, and threatened to take away his chemicals. But as the investigation limped into its third month, court gossip had it that "the King is much inclined to hang Ralegh, but it cannot handsomely be done, and he is likely to live out his days."

On September 28, Ralegh tried to capitalize, writing to King James about how he'd been warned by his crewmen that "if I returned to England I should be undone, but I believed in your Majesty's goodness more than in all their arguments." The king now had an opportunity to display his mercy and bask in public adulation.

A week later, having received no response, Ralegh wrote a follow-up letter offering to "disclose matters of great service to the state, when much wealth and advantage will result." It would be difficult for him to do so, it went without saying, from a scaffold in Madrid.

As it happened, the Spanish no longer had any interest in executing him, as King James was informed at Royston Palace on October 15 by Gondomar's interim replacement, Julián Sánchez de Ulloa. King Philip wanted the English to handle things instead. And they should get on with it, Ulloa said. The delay was starting to upset the shaky marriage negotiations.

No need to worry, James assured him, underscoring his commitment by presenting the diplomat with a pair of gold ingots that had been stripped from Ralegh upon his arrest. James hoped that King Philip would see the ingots—originally given to Ralegh's men by Christoval Guayacunda, whom they'd freed from enslavement in San Thomé—as having been restored their rightful owners.

As soon as Ulloa left, James summoned Coke and Bacon for an update on the grounds for executing Ralegh. The best His

Majesty would be able to do, they said, was revisit the 1603 treason case in which Ralegh had been sentenced to be executed "at the king's pleasure." Were it now his pleasure, His Majesty need simply issue a warrant instructing the Lieutenant of the Tower to carry out the sentence. To preempt public outcry, they could justify the action by cataloging and publishing Ralegh's "late crimes and offenses"—the piracy, the trespass, the flight from justice, and so forth.

But James's stance on summary justice had shifted, at least in this case: for a catalog of crimes and offenses to warrant executing Ralegh, he realized, there would first have to be some sort of trial. Bacon saw another loophole: in lieu of a trial, the Privy Council could conduct a hearing that had a semblance of a legal proceeding, one wherein whatever Ralegh said in rebuttal wouldn't matter because, as a legally dead person, his defense was immaterial. While open to the idea, James was loath to give Ralegh any opportunity to speak. "It would make him too popular," he said, citing the 1603 trial, where Ralegh "by his wit turned the hatred of men into compassion for him." Once more, Bacon had an idea: if the hearing were conducted privately, the special commission could find Ralegh guilty, order his immediate execution, and simultaneously publish a report in which his oratory was edited so as to preclude public outrage.

It was settled. Sir Walter Ralegh would die. Since there was no longer any point in worrying about her, Bess Ralegh was discharged from the Tower. All that remained was the hearing with a semblance of a legal proceeding. It took place on October 24, 1618, with the special commission convening privately, probably in the Star Chamber, which Coke called "the most honourable court (our Parliament excepted) that is in the Christian world."

In the unlikely event a transcript was taken, it has since been lost. The only known reporting is a letter from interim Spanish ambassador Ulloa to King Philip III. "Walter Ralegh was taken from the Tower to the Council, where they kept him under examination from 3 o'clock in the afternoon until 7 at night," Ulloa wrote, adding that Bacon detailed "the injuries [Ralegh] had inflicted upon Your Majesty's subjects and territories, and how greatly he had abused the king's permission to discover the gold mine." Ulloa said nothing of Ralegh's defense, whether it impressed the special commissioners or, for that matter, whether they paid attention. The Spaniard related only that Bacon brought the hearing to a conclusion by telling Ralegh that as a consequence of his actions, he would die. "On hearing this," Ulloa added, "Ralegh lost consciousness." He awoke to the news that Bacon lacked the legal authority to order an execution, that a judge was required, and, per the writ of habeas corpus, the defendant had to be present for the judgment.

As Ralegh waited in the Brick Tower for such an official dispatch to the scaffold, entreaties on his behalf poured into Whitehall Palace from all over the kingdom. Among those trying to sway King James were his wife, Queen Anne, and thirteen-year-old Carew Ralegh, who not only looked like his father but also, within a year, would follow in his father's footsteps to Oxford, to Parliament, and finally to court, where he would serve as a Gentleman of the Privy Chamber for King James's son, Charles I. Now Carew wrote to James to "beg mercy from your majesty" lest he become "a fatherless child." The king did not respond.

On October 28, at eight in the morning, Ralegh received a summons to appear at the Court of King's Bench. Although burning with fever and shivering, he managed to get out of bed and pull on clothing, but to the dismay of his supporters who'd gathered outside the

Tower to cheer him on, their dashing and famously meticulous hero appeared to have been replaced by a hobbled scarecrow with a passing resemblance to Sir Walter Ralegh. His wild and overly long hair was particularly upsetting to his onetime valet, who was in the crowd. Comb it, he urged his old boss. "Let them comb it that are to have it," Ralegh said, earning a laugh. As did his subsequent request for a recommendation of a "plaster that will set a man's head on again, when it is off."

Along the route to Westminster, crowds had gathered to pay homage to the last of the illustrious Elizabethan adventurers. Surely their adulation gratified Ralegh, though just as likely, the implicit finality unnerved him. The route itself—taking him past such milestones of his rise as Durham House, Whitehall, and the Palace of Westminster—must have seemed like his life flashing before his eyes.

Ralegh at the Court of King's Bench

"My lords," intoned Attorney General Yelverton in the soaring Palace of Westminster courtroom, "Sir Walter Ralegh, the prisoner at the bar, was fifteen years since convicted of high treason, by him committed against the person of his majesty and the state of this kingdom, and then received the judgment of death, to be hanged, drawn, and quartered." He added that Ralegh had "been as a star at which the world hath gazed," but "stars may fall." Therefore, it was "his majesty's pleasure now to call for execution of the former judgment." The clerk of the Crown read the judgment before asking the prisoner whether he knew of any reason "why execution should not be awarded."

In response, Ralegh turned toward the scarlet-robed judges. "My Lords," he said, "my voice is grown weak by reason of my late sickness, and an ague [fever] which I now have."

"Sir Walter, your voice is audible enough," said Lord Chief Justice Henry Montagu, who, unlike the special commissioners, would follow the law rather than the king's whims. At least, Ralegh had good reason to hope so: Montagu was part of a long line of highly respected and accomplished jurists beginning with his grandfather, Sir Edward Montagu, who'd also served as lord chief justice, from 1539 to 1545.

"Then, my Lord, all I can say is this," Ralegh continued, "that the judgment I received to die so long since, I hope it cannot now be strained to take away my life." He explained that because "it was his Majesty's pleasure to grant me a commission to proceed in a voyage beyond the seas, wherein I had power, as marshal, on the life and death of others so, under favor, I presume I am discharged of that judgment." A legally dead man wasn't allowed to possess a toothpick, much less the power over the life and death of others. Since Ralegh was given that power, he contended, his commission itself equated to a pardon.

The judges looked at one another in stunned silence.

Ralegh dove headlong into the loophole he'd seemingly found: "For by that commission I departed the land and undertook a journey, to honor my sovereign and to enrich his kingdom with gold—"

Lord Chief Justice Henry Montagu cut in. "In a case of treason, you must be pardoned, and not implicitly. There was no word tending to pardon in all your commission, and therefore you must say something else to the purpose, otherwise we must proceed to give execution."

Ralegh's legal foundation had been pulled out from under him, but he managed to hold on to his equanimity. "If your opinion be so, my lord, I am satisfied, and so put myself on the mercy of the king, who I know is gracious." He wasn't surrendering, so much as changing tack. "As concerning that judgment which is so long past, and I think there are some could witness, nay his majesty was of the opinion that I had hard measure therein."

Montagu demurred. "Sir Walter Ralegh, you must remember yourself," he said. "You had an honorable trial, and so were justly convicted." He went on to conclude the hearing by declaring, "Execution is granted."

Ralegh still had hope that King James would demonstrate his great mercy by declining to sign the execution warrant. That hope was quashed moments later with Montagu's production of a document titled *De Warranto Speciali pro Decollatione Walteri Raleigh, Militis, A. D. 1618*—A Special Warrant for the Decapitation of Walter Raleigh, Soldier. James had signed it ahead of time in anticipation of the ruling. With it, he also demonstrated mercy: rather than subjecting Ralegh to hanging, drawing, and quartering, as per the 1603 judgment, the royal pleasure now was "to have the head only of the said Sir Walter Ralegh cut off."

Sheriffs took Ralegh into custody and led him to the nearby St. Peter's monastery gatehouse, which served as a prison. There he was to spend the night while a scaffold was erected outside, in the Old Palace Yard. He would die the following morning, October 29, 1618—a date chosen because it was London's annual celebration of Lord Mayor's Day, with a parade and boisterous public festivities that would draw away the people who might have otherwise come to the Old Palace Yard to protest.

34

TO DIE IN THE LIGHT

RALEGH TRIED TO embrace death. If, rather than fade to oblivion in a dark corner of the Tower, he could die in the light—climb the scaffold before all his countrymen, head held high, resolute in his innocence—he could achieve martyrdom, providing him both a victory over King James and a legacy that could bolster his family.

He took his first steps toward that end as the sheriffs led him out of the courtroom following the grant of execution, asking a friend among the onlookers whether he would be at the show tomorrow. Yes, the man replied, provided he could find a place in the crowd. Ralegh sympathized: "I do not know what you may do for a place . . . But for my part, I am sure of one."

He endeavored to sustain the levity in the gatehouse prison that night, as friends and kinsmen soberly filed through to say farewell. "The world itself is but a larger prison," Ralegh quipped, "out of which some are daily selected for execution." He faced his greatest challenge with his final visitor, Bess, whom he'd been unable to see for two months.

When their reunion brought them to the topic of thirteen-year-old Carew, Ralegh found discussion too painful. He'd written a fifteen-page life-instruction manual, however, that would allow his son to have at least a modicum of paternal guidance going forward, on topics such as choosing friends and a wife, avoiding flatterers—"for even the wisest men are abused by these"—and drinking: the wine lover "shall not be trusted of any man, for he cannot keep a secret."

Much of the couple's time was absorbed by housekeeping—outstanding debts, prospective sources of revenue, provisions for the widows of men who'd faithfully served him—and far too quickly, the abbey clock struck midnight, ending visiting hours. In parting, Bess related that she had held out hope until now that their allies would prevail upon King James to show mercy after all. Weeping, she said that they had managed only to get authorization for disposal. (Customarily, a traitor's body parts were distributed to the four corners of the kingdom to serve as warnings to others, with his severed head parboiled, coated in pitch, then stuck onto one of the long iron spikes atop the London Bridge gates. In this case, the remains would go to the family, a privilege typically accorded only to nobility.)

In response, Walter tried to make light of his lifelong inattentiveness: "It is well, dear Bess, that thou mayst dispose of it dead that hadst not always the disposing of it when it was alive."

After she'd left, he continued his effort to buoy her by revising a verse from a poem he'd written three decades earlier exhorting her to enjoy love before "cruel time" takes away "our youth, our joys, and all we have and pays us but with age and dust." Had he heeded his own advice, their story—"the story of our days," as he put it—would have been set at Sherborne, rather than in the mythic El Dorado and the Tower of London, and would be ongoing rather than in its final pages. But now, by adding two lines to the verse, following "the story of our days," he provided hope for a sequel:

Even such is time, that takes in trust
Our youth, our joys, our all we have,

And pays us but with earth and dust;
Who, in the dark and silent grave,
When we have wandered all our ways,
Shuts up the story of our days;
But from this earth, this grave, this dust,
My God shall raise me up, I trust.

The Raleghs part

At 7:06 a.m. on Friday, October 29, 1618, the first flecks of dawn revealed an elevated wooden platform, ten feet square, that had been constructed overnight in the Old Palace Yard, around the corner from the gatehouse prison. On it sat a 125-pound oak block topped by a pair of semicircular concavities, one on the rear to accommodate the victim's chest and, on the front, a second, smaller aperture for his head, angled downward so as to give his neck prominence and align it with the arc of the axeman's stroke. Straw had been scattered around the base of the block to absorb blood. Others saw this assembly as a scaffold; Walter Ralegh regarded it as the stage for the valedictory address he'd spent most of the night composing.

He tried out parts of the speech on Dean of Westminster Abbey Robert Tounson, who arrived shortly after sunrise to administer the Sacrament of the Holy Eucharist. San Thomé "stands upon the King of England's own ground," Ralegh said as part of his argument that the expeditionary force hadn't trespassed. But Tounson was interested only in Ralegh's salvation. As a rule, the priest knew, once a condemned man stood upon the scaffold, he confessed his crimes. Old grudges and unsettled scores, the likes of which Sir Walter was now going on about, had to be set aside so that he could beg forgiveness from his sovereign and from God, thus gaining the spectators' prayers. Trying to steer Ralegh in the same direction, Tounson explained to him that men who wound up on the scaffold simply were not innocent, and, Christ aside, "your assertion of innocency is an oblique taxing of the justice of the realm."

"I confess that by course of law I must justly die," Ralegh argued, "but you must give me leave to stand upon my innocency in the fact."

To Tounson's horror, the man whose head was about to be chopped off proceeded to devour a breakfast of fried steak and roasted eggs before enjoying a pipe of tobacco. He was making no more of his death than if it were a pleasant journey! How, the priest asked, could any man who knows God and fears Him die so cavalierly? It was easy, Ralegh said, because he was assured of "the love and favour of God . . . and his own innocency." Unlike other men who merely made outward shows of bravado, he felt joy within. Despite himself, Tounson was won over.

The rest of the world was next. Ralegh tidied his hair for a change and chose clothing that was impressive yet befitting a solemn occasion: a brown satin doublet with a white ruff, black taffeta breeches, gray silk stockings, and a black velvet cloak. In deference to the cold day and his fever, he added a nightcap beneath his hat. At eight o'clock, the outfit was completed by shackles and chains, when a pair of sheriffs led him out of the gatehouse.

In the Old Palace Yard, a barrier had been placed around the scaffold to restrict the audience size—the same reason the execution was scheduled for such an early hour. Word of the event had blazed through London, however, resulting in a "great multitude" (the most precise attendance figure available among many contemporaneous accounts) within the barrier, and even more spectators outside it, many of them sitting on horses for a better view. Yet another multitude was crammed into the balconies overlooking the yard. To make headway, the sheriffs had to push through the ever-swelling throng. Ralegh, meanwhile, was all smiles, greeting friends as though they were his party guests, impressing everyone with his calm and self-possession.

As he stepped into the shadow of the scaffold, however, he halted, gasping for breath—teetering on the brink of unconsciousness, it appeared to onlookers, who were left to wonder whether he'd been debilitated by either the sight of the abyss or the grins of his many enemies in attendance.

The sheriffs urged him to warm himself by the fire they'd built beside the scaffold in deference to the bitter day. He declined. He didn't have long before his fever overtook him, he said, and if it happened while he was on the scaffold, the crowd would think he was quaking with fear.

Climbing the steps, he saluted the many knights, lords, and others in the crowd, which included Bess, before explaining that he'd been ill. Not complaining, mind you; it was just a caveat. "If, therefore, you perceive any weakness in me," he said, "ascribe it to my sickness rather than to myself."

Reaching the top of the scaffold, he took in his surroundings, his gaze bouncing from his shackles to the guards to the waiting executioner before settling on his delighted enemies, from whom he appeared to draw strength. "His mind became the clearer," wrote one audience member, "as if already it had been freed from the cloud and oppression of the body." According to another onlooker, Ralegh was as free of apprehension "as if he'd come hither rather to be a spectator than a sufferer."

"I thank my God heartily," he told the crowd, "that he hath brought me into the light to die, and hath not suffered me to die in the dark prison of the Tower." A glance at his notes and he launched into the self-defense that was the bulwark of his valedictory: "There was a report that I meant not to go to Guiana at all, and that I knew not any mine, nor intended any such matter, but only to get my liberty . . . But it was my full intent to go for gold, for the benefit of his majesty and those that went with me."

Accustomed to repentance from the condemned, the audience was taken aback. Ralegh persisted, though, making the same arguments he had in court, but calling a new corroborating witness. "For a man to call God to witness to falsehood at any time is a grievous sin," he said. "To call God to witness to a falsehood at the time of death is far more grievous and impious . . . I do therefore call the Lord to witness, as I hope to be saved, and as I hope to see Him in his kingdom . . . within this quarter of this hour."

To listeners who accorded as much credence to *nemo moriturus praesumitur mentire* (a dying person is not presumed to lie) as they did to *sol noctu* (the sun will set at night), Ralegh's words now carried greater weight. The murmurs in the Old Palace Yard subsided, and even the pigeons hushed, it seemed, as he went on to explain the difficulties in attaining the gold mine before addressing the Crown's contention that he'd consequently decided to flee England: "I cannot deny it," he said. "I desired to save my life."

The spectators found themselves empathizing. As one of them would record, "Such was his unmoved courage and placid temper that it . . . changed the affection of his enemies who had come to witness [his death], and turned their joy to sorrow." In their new perspective, the scaffold was a sacrificial altar to King Philip III, and a national disgrace. If ever Ralegh stood a chance to incite the crowd to free him, this was the moment.

But that wasn't what he wanted. As far as he was concerned, he told them, justice had been done. King James was not responsible for his death; the blame rested squarely on the shoulders of another man: Walter Ralegh. "Of a long time, my course was a course of vanity," he explained. "I have been a seafaring man, a soldier, and a courtier, and in the temptations of the least of these there is enough to overthrow a good mind, and a good man." It was his megalomania that had impelled him toward glory that was unattainable, depriving him of sublime domesticity, his son Wat's life, and, now, his own.

He still had hope of salvation, though, and toward that end, he entreated the members of the audience to join him in prayer—to "the great God in heaven, whom I have grievously offended"—in the hope that God "would forgive me, and that he would receive me into everlasting life." They prayed with him, and afterward he turned away from them. "I have a long journey to go," he said, "and therefore will take my leave."

The crowd watched in stunned silence as he shed his cloak, doublet, and hat, giving them away to nearby spectators, at the same time shaking hands. The executioner was moved to take off his own cloak and place it in front of the block to provide cushioning for Ralegh's knees. He also offered a blindfold, which Ralegh declined, asking instead whether he could inspect the axe. Rubbing a thumb along the edge of the blade, he said, "It is a sharp and fair medicine, to cure me of all my diseases."

He turned and kneeled before the block, fitting his chest into the rear concavity—until he noticed the executioner kneeling beside him.

October 29, 1618, in the Old Palace Yard

It would be impossible to do the deed, the executioner explained, without Sir Walter's forgiveness. Ralegh complied, gathering the man into an embrace.

At length, the executioner rose and took up the axe. Ralegh laid his neck across the block and extended his hands, a signal to proceed. Nothing happened. The axeman still couldn't bring himself to do it.

"What dost thou fear?" Ralegh demanded. "Strike, man, strike!"

35

HE WAS A MORTAL

In Spain, Gondomar was so eager to have his moment of triumph that he'd importuned English diplomats to send confirmation of Ralegh's execution in advance of Secretary of State Naunton's official dispatch. The former ambassador would be disgusted to read that his enemy "died with such high spirits as if he was going to a wedding."

On the scaffold in the immediate aftermath, the executioner gathered up Ralegh's head by the bloodied, silver hair and displayed it to the crowd. His duty now was to exclaim, "Behold the head of a traitor." But he couldn't speak.

A spectator filled the silence: "We have not another such head to be cut off." It was a precursor to the tributes that would spread throughout England, through all classes of people, on waves of commiseration and admiration—and rage. As another onlooker cried out, "I wish such [a head] were on Master Secretary's shoulders," an editorial on Naunton's inability to think for himself rather than let King James do it for him. Still another spectator predicted that in death, Ralegh would "do more harm to the faction that procured it than he ever did in his life."

The executioner carefully placed Ralegh's head in a red velvet bag and brought it to Bess, who stood by in a black mourning coach drawn by a pair of white horses. On receipt of her husband's body, shrouded in his black cloak, she raced away before King James could reconsider his grant of authorization for disposal.

She would go on to have Walter's head embalmed, and she would keep it with her for the rest of her life, twenty-five years in which she didn't remarry. His body was buried in front of the main altar at the Church of St. Margaret, Westminster, in a grave initially marked only by his coat of arms. When time permitted, an inscription was added:

> Within the Chancel of this Church was interred the body of the great Sir Walter Raleigh, on the day he was beheaded, in Old Palace Yard, Westminster, October 29, 1618. Reader, should you reflect on his errors, remember his many virtues; and that he was a mortal.

Incidentally, he was also right about the gold. In 1627, Robert Harcourt, the same explorer sent by King James to find El Dorado in 1609, led a new expedition to Guiana. He met with such failure that to pay his resulting debts, he had to sell Ellenhall, the Staffordshire village that had been owned by his family for generations. Over the following century, such notables as the Spanish soldier Nicholas Martenez and the German doctor Nicolas Horstmann were among dozens of additional El Doradans drawn to the New World by new golden-city rumors, their fruitless expeditions costing the lives of hundreds of their men. The key, perhaps, was a much smaller force: in 1857, a lone German prospector stumbled on a fifteen-pound gold nugget in Caratal—now known as El Callao—five miles from the spot to which Ralegh had dispatched his cousin Butshead in search of Macureguarai. The nugget led to the discovery of one of the largest gold deposits in history. Soon El Callao became the world leader in annual gold production, with as much as 11,300 pounds a year. By 1920, the end of its heyday, it had yielded a total of more than 200,000 pounds.

As for the reports of a golden city in the region, they've long since been relegated to folklore, but El Dorado can be found by anyone who goes to El Callao today. It's a small town forty miles south with a bar called La Copa de Oro—the Golden Cup—whose patrons can often be heard toasting to health and love, as well as to money.

ACKNOWLEDGMENTS

This chronicle of Walter Ralegh's quest would have been a mere couple-paragraphs-long aside in a spy novel if my literary agent, Richard Abate, hadn't produced a nonfiction book contract seemingly from thin air. Having Richard for an agent is, for a writer, like having a magic wand. Better, really, because if I had a magic wand, I'd be conjuring up cheesecakes all the time.

In addition to Richard, I'm forever grateful to Ben George, who, in editing *Paradise of the Damned*, exhibited Ralegh-level forethought, brilliance, perseverance, and, when it came to the glut of exposition, swordsmanship. Still, the book would have belonged in the fiction section if not for corrections by U.S. Naval Academy history professor Virginia Lunsford. And without her feedback, it would have belonged in a dumpster.

I'm also hugely indebted to the following: first—and foremost—reader Joan Kretschmer; 100.00 percent pure gold publicist Alyssa Persons; the best marketing manager this side of Topiawari, Anna Brill; el hombre dorado of production editors, Mike Noon; the Sir Francis Drake of audio producers, Jen Patten; Lord High Admiral Craig Young; and the finest editorial assistant in the Seven Seas if not the universe, Maya Guthrie. Thanks also to Anna Beer, Nelson Cortes, Jr., Harry Camp, Darcy Glastonbury, Sue Jones, Andy

Maddux, Judy Seelbach, Henry Thomson, Malcolm Thomson, Matthew Thomson, Trouser Thomson, Jeffrey Ward, Don Winslow, and anyone else who has read this far.

Please send questions or comments to kqthomson@gmail.com.

A NOTE ON THE SOURCES

Paradise of the Damned was assembled from the journals, memoirs, and correspondence of Walter Ralegh, Robert Dudley, Bess Ralegh, Antonio de Berrío, and Lawrence Keymis, among others, whose words have been reprinted herein exactly as they were written or transcribed four centuries ago, save for minor amendments to spelling, period conventions, and the like that might hinder modern readability. (Maybe a bit more than minor in Bess Ralegh's case; see the endnotes for her original efforts.) Because the objective of much of their writing was to simultaneously attract backers and dupe rivals, this book also utilized a good ton's worth of grains of salt supplied by their contemporaries, including Thomas Birch, Dudley Carleton, Robert Cecil, John Chamberlain, Juan de Castellanos, Richard Hakluyt, Raphael Holinshed, Samuel Purchas, Fray Pedro Simón, Henry Sidney, Rowland Whyte. Equally instrumental was the exhaustive and insightful work of historians Edward Edwards, V. T. Harlow, John Hemming, Robert Lacey, Joyce Lorimer, Charles Nicholl, William Oldys, Paul Sellin, William Stebbing, Richard Schomburgk, Robert Schomburgk, and Raleigh Trevelyan.

Finally, it's hard to overstate the utility of the United Kingdom's National Archives, which seemingly never fails to yield a five-hundred-year-old wine patent when you need one. Also invaluable is the archives' currency converter—at nationalarchives.gov.uk/

currency-converter—which lets you input a sum for any year since 1270 and see its present-day purchasing power. With the £1,000 Ralegh earned from his wine patent in 1590, for example, he could have bought either 121 horses, 537 cows, 2,941 stones of wool, or 555 quarters of wheat, or he could have paid a skilled tradesman to administer the patent for sixty-six years.

SELECTED BIBLIOGRAPHY

Acosta, Joaquín. *Compendio histórico del descubrimiento y colonización de la Nueva Granada en el siglo décimo sexto.* Paris: Beau, 1848.

Anderson, Charles Loftus Grant. *Old Panama and Castilla Del Oro: A Narrative History of the Discovery, Conquest and Settlement by the Spaniards of Panama, Darien, Veragua, Santo Domingo, Santa Marta, Cartagena, Nicaragua, and Peru.* Boston: Page, 1914.

Andrews, Kenneth R. *Elizabethan Privateering: English Privateering during the Spanish War, 1585–1603.* Cambridge: Cambridge University Press, 1964.

Arciniegas, Germán. *The Knight of El Dorado: The Tale of Don Gonzalo Jiménez de Quesada and His Conquest of New Granada, Now Called Colombia.* New York: Viking, 1942.

Bassett, Fletcher S. *Legends and Superstitions of the Sea and of Sailors in All Lands and at All Times.* Belford: Clarke, 1885. Kindle.

Beer, Anna. *My Just Desire: The Life of Bess Raleigh, Wife to Sir Walter.* New York: Ballantine, 2003.

Bell, P. L. *Venezuela, a Commercial and Industrial Handbook.* Washington, DC: U.S. Government Printing Office, 1922.

Beveridge, William. *Prices and Wages in England.* London: Frank Cass & Co., 1965.

Birch, Thomas. *Memoirs of the Reign of Queen Elizabeth: From the Year 1581 Til Her Death. In which the Secret Intrigues of Her Court, and the Conduct of Her Favourite, Robert Earl of Essex, Both at Home and Abroad, are Particularly Illustrated.* London: A. Millar, 1754.

Birch, Thomas, and Robert Folkestone Williams. *The Court and Times of James the First: Illustrated by Authentic and Confidential Letters, from Various Public and Private Collections,* vol. 1. London: Henry Colburn, 1848.

Bowen, Catherine Drinker. "The Lion and the Throne: The Trial of Sir Walter Ralegh." *The Atlantic,* December, 1956.

Brigham, Clarence S., ed. *British Royal Proclamations Relating to America 1603–1783.* New York: Burt Franklin, 1911.

Britton, John, and Edward Wedlake Brayley. *Memoirs of the Tower of London: Comprising Historical and Descriptive Accounts of that National Fortress and Palace.* London: Hurst, Chance, 1830.

Brushfield, Thomas Nadauld. *Raleghana.* London: Bonham Norton, 1906.

Camden, William. *Annales Or, the History of the Most Renowned and Victorious Princesse Elizabeth, Late Queen of England.* London: Benjamin Fisher, 1635.

Carew, George, and Thomas Roe. *Letters from George Lord Carew to Sir Thomas Roe: Ambassador to the Court of the Great Mogul, 1615–1617.* London: Camden Society, 1860.

Carleton, Dudley. *Dudley Carleton to John Chamberlain, 1603–1624; Jacobean letters.* New Brunswick, NJ: Rutgers University Press, 1972.

de Castellanos, Juan. *Elegías de varones ilustres de Indias.* Originally published in 1589; version cited herein: Madrid: Imprenta y Estereotipía de M. Rivadeneyra, 1852.

del Castillo, Bernal Díaz. *Historia verdadera de la conquista de la Nueva España* (The True History of the Conquest of New Spain). First published in 1568. Ann Arbor, University Microfilms, 1966.

Cayley, Arthur. *The Life of Sir Walter Ralegh, Knt.* London: Cadell and Davies, 1806.

Chamberlain, John, and Norman Egbert McClure. *The Letters of John Chamberlain.* Philadelphia: American Philosophical Society, 1939.

Cobbett, William et al. *Cobbett's Complete Collection of State Trials and Proceedings for High Treason and Other Crimes and Misdemeanors from the Earliest Period to the Year 1783.* London: R. Bagshaw, 1809.

Collins, Arthur, and Henry Sidney. *Letters and Memorials of State in the Reigns of Queen Mary, Queen Elizabeth, King James, King Charles the First. etc.* London: Osborne, 1746.

Creighton, Charles. *A History of Epidemics in Britain: From A.D. 664 to the Extinction of Plague.* Cambridge: Cambridge University Press, 1891.

Cunningham, George Godfrey. *Lives of Eminent and Illustrious Englishmen: From Alfred the Great to the Latest Times, on an Original Plan.* Glasgow: A. Fullarton, 1837.

Dictionary of National Biography, 1885–1900, vol. 55. London: Smith, Elder, 1898.

Disraeli, Benjamin, and Isaac Disraeli. *Curiosities of Literature.* Boston: W. Veazie, 1860.

Edwards, Edward. *Letters of Ralegh.* London: Macmillan, 1868.

Edwards, Edward. *The Life of Sir Walter Ralegh.* London: Macmillan, 1868.

Eliot, Sir John. *The monarchie of man.* London, Chiswick, 1879.

Gallay, Alan. *Walter Ralegh: Architect of Empire.* New York: Basic, 2019.

de Gamboa, Pedro Sarmiento. *The History of the Incas.* Translated by Brian S. Bauer and Vania Smit. Austin: University of Texas Press, 2009.

Gardiner, Samuel R. "The Case Against Sir Walter Ralegh," in *The Fortnightly*. London: Chapman and Hall, 1867.

Gardiner, Samuel Rawson. *History of England from the Accession of James I to the Outbreak of the Civil War, 1603–1642, vol.* 3. London: Longmans, Green, 1895.

Gardiner, Samuel Rawson. *Prince Charles and the Spanish Marriage: 1617–1623, vol. 1.* London: Hurst and Blackett, 1869.

Green, Matthew. *London: A Travel Guide through Time*. London: Penguin, 2016.

Hakluyt, Richard. *The Principal Navigations, Voyages, Traffiques & Discoveries of the English Nation Made by Sea Or Overland to the Remote & Farthest Distant Quarters of the Earth at Any Time Within the Compasse of These 1600 Yeares, vol. 7.* London: J. Dent, 1926.

Harcourt, Robert. *A Relation of a Voyage to Guiana*. London: W. Welby, 1613.

Harington, Sir John. *Nugae Antiquae*, vol. 1. Middle Row, Holdborn: Vernor and Hood, Poultry, and Cuthell and Martin, 1804.

Harlow, V. T., ed. *The Discoverie of Guiana* by Sir Walter Ralegh. London: Argonaut Press, 1928.

Harlow, V. T., ed. *Ralegh's Last Voyage*. London: Argonaut Press, 1932.

Hearne, Thomas, and John Aubrey. *Letters Written by Eminent Persons in the Seventeenth and Eighteenth Centuries*. London: Longman, Hurst, Rees, Orme, and Brown, 1813.

Hemming, John. *The Search for El Dorado*. New York: E. P. Dutton, 1979.

Her Majesty's Stationery Office. *Calendar of State Papers, Domestic Series, of the Reign of James I, 1611–1618*. London: Her Majesty's Stationery Office, 1858.

Her Majesty's Stationery Office. *Calendar of the Cecil Papers in Hatfield House, vol. 4, 1590–1594*. London: Her Majesty's Stationery Office, 1892.

Holinshed, Raphael. *Holinshed's Chronicles of England, Scotland and Ireland*, vol. 3. London: Johnson, 1808.

Howard, Henry, Earl of Northampton; Robert Cecil, Earl of Salisbury; and David Dalrymple. *The Secret Correspondence of Sir Robert Cecil with James VI. King of Scotland*. London: A. Millar, 1766.

Howell, T. B., Esq. *A Complete Collection of State Trials, vol. II*. London: Longman, Hurst, Rees, Orme, and Brown, 1816.

Howes, Edmund, and John Stow. *The Annales, or Generall Chronicle of England*. London: Thomas Adams, 1615.

von Humboldt, Alexander. *Personal Narrative of Travels to the Equinoctial Regions of America*. London: H. G. Bohn, 1853.

Jonson, Ben. *Notes of Ben Jonson's Conversations with William Drummond of Hawthornden*, January 1619. London: Shakespeare Society, 1842.

Keymis, Lawrence. *A Relation of the second Voyage to Guiana performed and written in the yeere 1596*. London: Thomas Dawson, 1596.

Lacey, Robert. *Sir Walter Ralegh*. London: Phoenix, 1971.

Latham, Agnes M. C. "Sir Walter Ralegh's Cynthia." *Review of English Studies* 4, no. 14 (1928).

Latham, Agnes, and Joyce Youings. *The Letters of Sir Walter Ralegh*. Exeter: University of Exeter Press, 1999.

Leng, Robert; William Tite; Edward Harley, Earl of Oxford; and John Bruce. *Documents Relating to Sir Walter Raleigh's Last Voyage*. London: Camden Society, 1864.

Little, Benerson. *The Sea Rover's Practice: Pirate Tactics and Techniques, 1630–1730*. Washington, DC: Potomac, 2007.

López de Gómara, Francisco. *General History of the Indies*. London, 1625.

Lorimer, Joyce, ed. *Sir Walter Ralegh's Discoverie of Guiana*. England: published for the Hakluyt Society by Ashgate, 2006.

Maclean, John. *Letters from Robert Cecil to Sir George Carew*. London: Camden Society, 1854.

Mandeville, John. *The Travels of Sir John Mandeville*. London: Penguin, 2005.

Marcus, Geoffrey Jules. *A Naval History of England: The Formative Centuries*. London: Longmans, 1961.

Markham, Clements R. *Expeditions into the Valley of the Amazons, 1539, 1540, 1639*. First published in 1859; this edition: Anatiposi Verlag, 2023.

Mohs, Friedrich. *Treatise on Mineralogy: Or, the Natural History of the Mineral Kingdom*. Edinburgh: A. Constable, 1822.

Moses, Bernard. *The Spanish Dependencies in South America*. London: Smith, Elder, 1914.

"Newes of Sr Walter Rauleigh," November 17, 1617. British Museum, Ayscough's Cat. No. 3272.

Nicholl, Charles. *The Creature in the Map: A Journey to El Dorado*. Chicago: University of Chicago Press, 1997.

Nicholls, Mark, and Penry Williams. *Sir Walter Raleigh*. London: Continuum, 2011.

Nichols, John. *The Progresses, Processions and Magnificent Festivities of King James the First, His Royal Consort, Family and Court, Etc.* London: J. B. Nichols, 1828.

Ojer, Pablo. *Don Antonio de Berrío: Gobernador del Dorado*. Venezuela: Universidad 323 Católica "Andrés Bello" Facultad de Humanidades y Educación, Instituto de Investigaciones Históricas, 1960.

Oldys, William. *The Works of Sir Walter Ralegh, Kt.* Oxford: University Press, 1829.

de Oviedo y Valdés, Gonzalo Fernández. *Historia general y natural des las Indias, islas y Tierra-firme del Mar Océano*. Seville: José Amador de Los Rios, 1535–1537.

Paré, Ambrose. *The Workes of That Famous Chirurgion Ambrose Parey*. London: R. Coates and W. Dugard, 1649.

Purchas, Samuel. *Purchas His Pilgrimes*. Glasgow: James MacLehose and Sons, 1907; originally published in 1625.

Ralegh, Carew. *Observations upon Some Particular Persons and Passages in a Book Lately Make Publick; Intituled, A Compleat History of the Lives and Reignes of Mary Queen of Scotland, and of Her Son James, the Sixth of Scotland, and the First of England, France and Ireland.* London: printed for Ga. Bedell and Tho. Collins and Sidney, 1656.

Ralegh, Walter. *The Discoverie of the Large, Rich, and Beautiful Empire of Guiana by Sir Walter Ralegh, Knight.* Included in Schomburgk's edition of *The Discovery,* citation below.

Ralegh, Walter. *The Historie of the World.* First published London: Walter Burre, 1614; herein: Oxford: University Press, 1829.

Ralegh, Walter. "Instructions to His Son and to Posterity," c. 1610. In Oldys, *Works,* vol. 8.

Ralegh, Walter. "Nature that Washed her Hands in Milk." poetryfoundation.org/poets/sir-walter-ralegh.

Ralegh, Walter. "Sir Walter Ralegh's Journal of His Second Voyage to Guiana." In Schomburgk, *Discovery.*

Rowse, A. L., *Ralegh and the Throckmortons.* New York: Macmillan & Co., 1962.

Schomburgk, Richard. *Travels in British Guiana, vol. I.* Translated by Walter Roth. Georgetown, British Guiana: Daily Telegraph Office, 1922–1923.

Schomburgk, Robert H., ed. The Hakluyt Society, *The Discovery of the Large, Rich, and Beautiful Empire of Guiana by Sir Walter Ralegh, Knight.* New York: Burt Franklin, 1848.

Schuller, Rodolfo R. *The Ordáz and Dortal Expeditions in Search of Eldorado: As Described on Sixteenth Century Maps.* Washington, DC: Smithsonian Institution, 1916.

Scott, Walter. *A Collection of Scarce and Valuable Tracts on the Most Entertaining Subjects: Reign of King James I.* London: T. Cadell and W. Davies, 1809.

Sellin, Paul R., and Donald Carlisle. "Assays of Sir Walter Raleigh's Ores from Guayana, 1595–1596." *Ben Jonson Journal* 18, no. 2 (November 2011).

Sellin, Paul R. *Treasure, Treason and the Tower.* Abingdon, Oxon: Taylor and Francis, 2016.

Shaw, William Arthur. *The History of Currency, 1252–1894.* New York: Putnam, 1896.

Silverberg, Robert. *The Golden Dream.* Athens: Ohio University Press, 1967.

Simón, Fray Pedro. *The Expedition of Pedro de Ursua & Lope de Aguirre in Search of El Dorado and Omagua in 1560–1.* Translated by William Bollaert. London: Hakluyt Society, 1861.

Simón, Fray Pedro. *Noticias historiales de las conquistas de Tierra Firme en las Indias Occidentales.* Bogotá: M. Rivas, 1882.

Stebbing, William. *Sir Walter Ralegh: A Biography.* Oxford: Clarendon, 1891.

Stuart, King James. *Daemonologie*. Printer to the Kings Majestie, 1597.

Summerson, John Newenham. *Architecture in Britain, 1530 to 1830*. New Haven: Yale University Press, 1993.

Tittler, Robert, and Norman Jones. *A Companion to Tudor Britain*. Malden, MA: Wiley-Blackwell, 2004.

Trevelyan, Raleigh. *Sir Walter Raleigh: Being a True and Vivid Account of the Life and Times of the Explorer, Soldier, Scholar, Poet, and Courtier—The Controversial Hero of the Elizabethan Age*. New York: Henry Holt, 2004, Kindle edition.

Van Heuvel, Jacob Adrien. *El Dorado: Being a Narrative of the Circumstances which Gave Rise to Reports, in the Sixteenth Century, of the Existence of a Rich and Splendid City in South America, to which that Name was Given, and which Led to Many Enterprises in Search of it; Including a Defence of Sir Walter Raleigh, in Regard to the Relations Made by Him Respecting It, and a Nation of Female Warriors, in the Vicinity of the Amazon, in the Narrative of His Expedition to the Oronoke in 1595*. New York: J. Winchester, 1844.

Warner, George F., ed. *The Voyage of Robert Dudley to the West Indies, 1594–1595*. London: Hakluyt Society, 1899.

Weir, Alison. *The Life of Elizabeth I*. New York: Random House, 2013.

White, Peter, and Alan Cook. *Sherborne Old Castle, Dorset: Archaeological Investigations 1930–90*. London: Society of Antiquaries of London, 2015.

Whitehead, Charles. *The Life and Times of Sir Walter Ralegh*. London: N. Cooke, Milford House, Strand, 1854.

Whitehead, Neil L., ed. *The Discoverie of the Large, Rich and Bewtiful Empyre of Guiana*. Manchester: Manchester University Press, 1998.

Wood, Michael. *Conquistadors*. Oakland: University of California Press, 2001.

NOTES

Epigraph

vii "Happiness is only to be found in El Dorado . . .": Ralph Delahaye Paine, *The Book of Buried Treasure: Being a True History of the Gold, Jewels, and Plate of Pirates, Galleons, Etc., which are Sought for to this Day* (London: Macmillan, 1911), 347.

1. The Golden Man

3 Juan Martín de Albujar: the Albujar story herein is derived primarily from Albujar's account as related in *The Discoverie of the large and bewtiful Empyre of Guiana* by Sir Walter Ralegh (full citation below), meanwhile incorporating *The Expedition of Pedro de Ursua & Lope de Aguirre in Search of El Dorado and Omagua in 1560–1*, by Fray Pedro Simón and translated by William Bollaert (London: Hakluyt Society, 1861), and Juan de Castellanos's *Elegías de varones ilustres de Indias* (originally published in 1589; version cited herein: Madrid: Imprenta y Estereotipía de M. Rivadeneyra, 1852), 433–455.

5 Aztecs: the practice of removing still-beating-hearts is detailed in Bernal Díaz del Castillo, *Historia verdadera de la conquista de la Nueva España* (The True History of the Conquest of New Spain), first published in 1568 (Ann Arbor, University Microfilms, 1966), 316.

5 "manoa" means lake: John Hemming, *The Search for El Dorado* (New York: E. P. Dutton, 1979), 153.

5 gold bars "in heaps . . .": Francisco López de Gómara, *General History of the Indies* (London, 1625), ch. 120.

5 chief who annually coated his body in turpentine before rolling in gold dust: Joaquín Acosta, *Compendio histórico del descubrimiento y colonización de la Nueva Granada en el siglo décimo sexto* (Paris: Beau, 1848), 199.

6 Amyris plants and Calophyllum trees: Robert H. Schomburgk, ed., The Hakluyt Society, *The Discovery of the Large, Rich, and Beautiful Empire of Guiana by Sir Walter Ralegh, Knight* (New York: Burt Franklin, 1848), 21, footnote 1.

6 seventh month: there is considerable discrepancy over the length of Albujar's stay in Manoa. Seven months is Ralegh's figure, based upon a deposition of Albujar's confessor Berrío found in San Juan. In the seminal work *Noticias historiales de las conquistas de Tierra Firme en las Indias Occidentales*, published in 1625, historian Fray Pedro Simón reported that Albujar stayed for as many as ten years in Manoa, during which time he "had a wife, houses, land and slaves who served him, and so much freedom to be able to leave and be absent for as long as he wanted, as the most important Indian in the Province." Fray Pedro Simón, *Noticias historiales de las conquistas de Tierra Firme en las Indias Occidentales* (Bogotá: M. Rivas, 1882), 357. The Albujar story seems to have begun thirty-six years earlier, when, in his *Elegías de varones ilustres de Indias*, Juan de Castellanos, who wrote that Albujar was a contemporary of his in Margarita, who had merely spent seven years in captivity among poor Guianan tribesmen.

7 *Nemo moriturus praesumitur mentire*: www.legalaffairs.org/issues/November-December-2002/review_koerner_novdec2002.msp.

8 200,000 pounds: P. L. Bell, *Venezuela, a Commercial and Industrial Handbook* (Washington, DC: U.S. Government Printing Office, 1922), 301.

8 copper on the Statue of Liberty: sixty-two thousand pounds per the National Park Service, nps.gov/stli/index.htm (note that gold is more than twice as dense as copper).

8 $100 billion: the average yearly wage of a laborer was about £5 per J. I. Andrés Ucendo and R. Lanza García, "Prices and Real Wages in Seventeenth-Century Madrid," *Economic History Review* 67, no. 3, 2014, 607–626. Gold was £3 per ounce: measuringworth.com/datasets/gold/result.php. Accordingly, an ounce of gold was worth 60 percent of the average annual wage, a present-day equivalent of $30,000 per ounce for as much as 3.5 million ounces, or $105.6 billion.

8 "Ralegh": in letters and official documents from that pre-universal-spelling era, he is referred to as *Rawley, Raghley, Rawleghe, Raulie, Raleh, Raughley, Rawlley,* and *Wrawley*, and sixty variations thereof, including *Raleigh*.

8–9 human chain: Juan de Castellanos, *Elegias de Ilustres Varones de Indias* (Madrid, 1847), Parte I, Elegia I, Canto 4, cited in V. T. Harlow, ed., *The Discoverie of Guiana* by Sir Walter Ralegh (London: Argonaut Press, 1928), xlvii.

9 "infinite numbers of souls . . .": Ralegh, *Discoverie*, 135.

9 "dominions may be exceedingly enlarged . . .": Ralegh, "Of the Voyage to Guiana," 136.

2. Those Dainty Hands Which Conquered My Desire

10 twenty-seven-year-old: William Stebbing, *Sir Walter Ralegh: A Biography* (Oxford: Clarendon, 1891), 6: "If the inscription on [Ralegh's] National Portrait Gallery picture, '1588, aetatis suae 34,' and that on Zucchero's in the Dublin Gallery, 'aet. 44, 1598,' be correct, his birth must have been not in 1552 [as has been widely speculated], but about 1554."

10 patent for the sale of wine and licensing of vintners: Arlene Spencer, "Wine Licenses Issued by Royal Prerogative: A Golden Ticket, During Elizabeth I, Until It Wasn't: TNA E 351 3100 Series Wine Licenses," at https://globalmaritimehistory.com/wine-licenses-issued-by-royal-prerogative-a-golden-ticket-during-elizabeth-i-until-it-wasnt-tna-e-351-3100-series-wine-licenses/.

10 "to seek new worlds for gold, for praise, for glory": Walter Ralegh, "The 21st (and last) Book of the Ocean to Cynthia": poeticous.com/sir-walter-raleigh/the-ocean-to-cynthia.

11 distinguished himself at Oxford: *Athenae Oxonienses*, ii. 236 at quod.lib.umich.edu/cgi/t/text/text-idx?c=eebo;idno=A71277.0001.001.

11 in France on behalf of persecuted Protestants: William Camden, *Annales Or, The History of the Most Renowned and Victorious Princesse Elizabeth, Late Queen of England* (London: Benjamin Fisher, 1635), 117.

11 "put to the sword": Raphael Holinshed, *Holinshed's Chronicles of England, Scotland and Ireland*, vol. 3 (London: Johnson, 1808), 165.

11 Six hundred defenders: per the commander Lord Grey, in *Irish Correspondence of Elizabeth*, vol. lxviii, 29, excerpted in Edward Edwards, *The Life of Sir Walter Ralegh* (London: Macmillan, 1868), 42.

12 "Outward beauty is a true sign . . .": Count Baldesar Castiglione, *The Book of the Courtier* (originally published in 1528, version excerpted herein: London: Duckworth, 1902, translation from Italian by Leonard Eckstein Opdycke), 294.

12 Body Extraordinary: Robert Tittler and Norman Jones, *A Companion to Tudor Britain* (Malden, MA: Wiley-Blackwell, 2004), 63.

12–13 "buried in oblivion": Stebbing, *Sir Walter Ralegh*, 1.

13 "It nearly always happens . . ." Castiglione, *Book of the Courtier*, 22.

13 Sir Thomas Hoby's 1563 translation of *The Book of the Courtier*: John R. Hale, *England and the Italian Renaissance: The Growth of Interest in its History and Art* (Madden, MA: Blackwell), xviii.

13 "no man is esteemed for colorful . . .": quoteland.com/share/Sir-Walter-Raleigh-Quotes/44793/.

14 "a plashy place": Thomas Fuller, *The History of the Worthies of England*, vol. 1. (London: John Nichols, 1811), 287.

14 the queen's bedsheets (which might yield information about her menstruation): Tracy Borman, *Elizabeth's Women: Friends, Rivals, and Foes Who Shaped the Virgin Queen* (New York: Bantam, 2010), 223–224.

14 seal: British Museum item number 1904,0113.2: www.britishmuseum.org/collection/object/H_1904-0113-2.

14 her affinity for tall, dark, and handsome: John Aubrey, *Brief Lives* (first published 1898; herein: Woodbridge: Boydell, 1982), 253.

15 gone through books: Robert Naunton, *Fragmenta Regalia* (London: A. Murray, 1870), 31.

15 "taken with his elocution . . ." and subsequent reasons for Elizabeth's enchantment: Naunton, *Fragmenta Regalia*, 47.

16 "came a storm . . .": Sir John Harington, *Nugae Antiquae*, vol. 1 (Middle Row, Holdborn: Vernor and Hood, Poultry, and Cuthell and Martin, 1804), 362.

16 "She did fish for men's souls . . .": Harington, *Nugae Antiquae*, vol. 1, 358.

16 "life's joy" and "soul's heaven above": Walter Ralegh, "Fortune Hath Taken Thee Away, My Love": poetryfoundation.org/poems/50022/fortune-hath-taken-thee-away-my-love.

16 secretly written Shakespeare's plays: William James Rolfe, ed., *Shakespeare's Sonnets* (New York: American Book, 1905), 250.

16 "Those eyes which set my fancy on a fire . . .": Ralegh, "The 21st (and last) Book of the Ocean to Cynthia."

16 "said to love this gentleman now . . .": W. B. Rye, *England as Seen by Foreigners* (1865), excerpted in Robert Lacey, *Sir Walter Ralegh* (London: Phoenix, 1971), 51.

16 patent: "to discover, search, find out and view such remote heathen and barbarous lands, countries and territories, not actually possessed of any Christian prince, nor inhabited by Christian people," March 25, 1584, letters patent excerpted in Schomburgk, *Discovery*, xxvvii.

16 "my true fantasy's mistress": Walter Ralegh, "Fortune Hath Taken Thee Away, My Love": poetryfoundation.org/poets/sir-walter-ralegh.

17 November 8, 1584: All dates herein are per the Julian calendar England used until the adoption of the "New Style" Gregorian calendar in 1752, when Wednesday, September 2 was followed by Thursday, September 14, synching the English with the rest of the Western world.

18 ten to twelve: Anna Beer, *My Just Desire: The Life of Bess Raleigh, Wife to Sir Walter* (New York: Ballantine, 2003), 38.

18 rejoice in it, as she did: Alison Weir, *The Life of Elizabeth I* (New York: Random House, 2013), 261.

18 free of loyalties and agendas: Beer, *My Just Desire*, 60.

18 an act of treason for a person of royal blood: 1536 Treason Act: Danby Pickering, *Statutes at Large*, vol. 4 (Cambridge: Cambridge University Press, 1762), 447.

18 November 19, 1591: A. L. Rowse, *Ralegh and the Throckmortons* (New York: Macmillan & Co., 1962), 148.

18 The right corsets and dresses: medievalists.net/2013/12/birth-control-and-abortion-in-the-middle-ages.

18 Queen Elizabeth suspected nothing: Beer, *My Just Desire*, 49.

18 two and three in the afternoon on March 29, 1592: Rowse, *Ralegh and the Throckmortons*, 160.

18 Ralegh's family tree: one of his ancestors, Sir John de Ralegh, married the daughter of Sir Richard d'Amerie, who married Elizabeth, daughter of Gilbert Earl of Gloucester by Joan D'Acres, daughter of King Edward I, "which Gilbert was descended of Robert Earl of Gloucester, son of King Henry I": Charles Whitehead, *The Life and Times of Sir Walter Ralegh* (London: N. Cooke, Milford House, Strand, 1854), 2.

19 First Earl of Salisbury Robert Cecil, biographical information: historyofparliamentonline.org/volume/1558-1603/member/cecil-robert-1563-1612.

19 "If any such thing were [true,] . . .": Walter Ralegh, "To Robert Cecil from Chatham, 10 March [1592]," in Agnes Latham and Joyce Youings, *The Letters of Sir Walter Ralegh* (Exeter: University of Exeter Press, 1999), 62–63.

20 "courtyard": Beer, *My Just Desire*, 58.

3. England or India or Elsewhere

21 "left behind her . . ."—a letter to Cecil meant to be shared with the queen: "To Sir Robert Cecil [from Durham House], [c. 26 July, 1592]," in Latham and Youings, *Letters*, 70.

22 "Her love hath end . . .": Walter Ralegh, "The 21st (and last) Book of the Ocean to Cynthia."

22 it would collect dust for three centuries: Agnes M. C. Latham, "Sir Walter Ralegh's Cynthia," *Review of English Studies* 4, no. 14 (1928): 129–134. http://www.jstor.org/stable/508141.

22 captured the *Madre de Dios*: Richard Hakluyt, *The Principal Navigations, Voyages, Traffiques & Discoveries of the English Nation Made by Sea Or Overland to the Remote & Farthest Distant Quarters of the Earth at Any Time Within the Compasse of These 1600 Yeares, vol. 7* (London: J. Dent, 1926), 570

22 John Newenham Summerson, *Architecture in Britain, 1530 to 1830* (New Haven: Yale University Press, 1993), 33.

22 "more than ever any man . . .": Walter Ralegh, "To Lord Burghley From the Tower, 13 September, 1592," in Latham and Youings, *Letters*, 78–79.

23 1572: Pedro Sarmiento de Gamboa, *The History of the Incas* (Austin: University of Texas Press, 2009), translated by Brian S. Bauer and Vania Smith, xiii.

23 Don Pedro Sarmiento de Gamboa, and the circumstances of his capture: Stephen Clissold, *Conquistador, the Life of Don Pedro Sarmiento de Gamboa* (London: D. Verschoyle, 1954), 183–189.

23 introducing him to Queen Elizabeth: Clissold, *Conquistador*, 22.

23 conversing in Latin: Alan Gallay, *Walter Ralegh: Architect of Empire* (New York: Basic, 2019), 161.

23 learned in order to avail himself of New World intelligence: Schomburgk, *Discovery*, xvi.

23 "Prevention is the daughter of intelligence": quotefancy.com/quote/1549297/Walter-Raleigh-Prevention-is-the-daughter-of-intelligence.

23 the Thames dried up: G. A. Cole and T. J. Marsh, "The impact of climate change on severe droughts: Major droughts in England and Wales from 1800 and evidence of impact" (Bristol: Environmental Agency, 2006), 23.

23 one in ten: Charles Creighton, *A History of Epidemics in Britain: From A.D. 664 to the Extinction of Plague* (Cambridge: Cambridge University Press, 1891), 353–354.

23 1592–1593 London Plague: Creighton, 351–352.

24 27 percent of English babies: ourworldindata.org/child-mortality-in-the-past.

24 "Sir Walter Ralegh was one that, it seems . . .": Arthur Cayley, *The Life of Sir Walter Ralegh, Knt.* (London: Cadell and Davies, 1806), 205.

24 December 13, 1592: letter to Lord Burghley and others in Agnes Latham and Joyce Youings, *Letters*, 85.

24 December 22: Sir Arthur Throckmorton, Throckmorton Diary, vol. 1 (n.p.) at https://discovery.nationalarchives.gov.uk/details/r/c257099c-5016-452c-9328-f946571a05c6.

24 "esteemed fame more than conscience": Ben Jonson, *Notes of Ben Jonson's Conversations with William Drummond of Hawthornden*, January 1619 (London: Shakespeare Society, 1842), 46.

25 suddenly limited means—as is manifest from Ralegh's will: A. M. C. Latham, "Sir Walter Ralegh's Will," *Review of English Studies* 22, no. 86 (1971), 129–136.

25 £40,000: Schomburgk, *Discovery*, xxxi.

25 forty-three years: H. O. Lancaster, *Expectations of Life: A Study in the Demography, Statistics, and History of World Mortality* (New York: Springer, 1990), 8.

25 two years longer than commoners: S. Ryan Johansson, "Medics, Monarchs and Mortality, 1600–1800," *Discussion Papers in Economic and Social History*, no. 85, October 2010 (University of Oxford): 15, table 2.

25 tended to perish ten years sooner: Johansson, "Medics, Monarchs, and Mortality."

26 reconnaissance of Guiana's Atlantic coast: Alden T. Vaughan, "Sir Walter Ralegh's Indian Interpreters, 1584–1618," *William and Mary Quarterly* 59, no. 2 (2002): 341–376.

26 two Natives of Trinidad and two more from the continent: Salazar, "Account of the occurrences in the Island of Trinidad," excerpted and translated from Spanish to English in Harlow, *Discovery*, 117.

27 "dissevered from him" and subsequent: "Lady Ralegh to Sir Robert Cecil," in Edwards, *The Letters of Sir Walter Ralegh* (London: Macmillan, 1868), 398.

27 twenty-four men had died: Vaughan, "Sir Walter Ralegh's Indian Interpreters," 341–376.

27 "toward the sunset": Bess Ralegh's actual words—converted herein per orthography, which would not catch on for another half century—were "I hope for my sake you will rather draw sur watar towardes the est than heulp hyme forward touard the soonsett": letter from Bess Ralegh to Robert Cecil, September 8, 1594, in *Calendar of the Cecil Papers in Hatfield House, vol. 4, 1590–1594* (London: Her Majesty's Stationery Office, 1892) at british-history.ac.uk/cal-cecil-papers/vol4/pp556-575.

27 "England or in India or elsewhere": Walter Ralegh, "To Sir Robert Cecil [from Durham House] 20 September 1594" in Latham and Youings, *Letters*, 119.

27 Charles Howard: historyofparliamentonline.org/volume/1558-1603/member/howard-charles-i-1536-1624.

28 Robert Dudley biographical information: George F. Warner, ed., *The Voyage of Robert Dudley to the West Indies, 1594–1595* (London: Hakluyt Society, 1899), preface.

29 In his own account of their discussion: Robert Dudley, "Robert Dudley's Voyage to the West Indies 1594–1595," in Warner, *Voyage of Robert Dudley*, 67–68.

29 "he had order to do from Queen Elizabeth": Abram Kendall, "Robert Dudley's Voyage to the West Indies 1594–1595, Narrated by Abram Kendall, Master," in Warner, *Voyage of Robert Dudley*, 84.

29 "A person of stature . . ." quote by Sir William Dugsdale in Warner, *Voyage of Robert Dudley*, xii.

29 Kenilworth Castle in Warwickshire: www.english-heritage.org.uk/visit/places/kenilworth-castle/history-and-stories/.

30 Thomas Heaton: Ralegh letter, "To Sir Robert Cecil [from Durham House], 20 September 1594," in Latham and Youings, *Letters*, 119.

30 a nose for prizes: Kenneth R. Andrews, *Elizabethan Privateering: English Privateering during the Spanish War, 1585–1603* (Cambridge: Cambridge University Press, 1964), 251.

31 "our servant Sir Walter Ralegh": Public Records Office State Papers 12/250 no. 46, excerpted in Raleigh Trevelyan, *Sir Walter Raleigh: Being a True and*

Vivid Account of the Life and Times of the Explorer, Soldier, Scholar, Poet, and Courtier—The Controversial Hero of the Elizabethan Age (New York: Henry Holt, 2004), Kindle edition, 4452.

31 "trusty" or "well-beloved": Patent Roll 26 Eliz. pt. 1 38–40. Public Records Office C66 112512, excerpted in Trevelyan, *Sir Walter Raleigh*, 445.

31 "This wind breaks my heart" and subsequent details of Christmas, including Ralegh's presence at Sherborne: Walter Ralegh, "To Sir Robert Cecil from Sherborne, 26 December 1594": Latham and Youings, *Letters*, 122.

31 "bound to the wars": Walter Ralegh, "To Sir Robert Cecil from Sherborne, 26 December 1594": Latham and Youings, *Letters*, 122.

32 £150 a year: "300 marks," he put it. T. B. Howell, Esq., *A Complete Collection of State Trials, Vol. II* (London: Longman, Hurst, Rees, Orme, and Brown, 1816), 26.

32 "In the winter of my life . . .": Ralegh, *Discoverie*, iv.

4. The Unlucky Bastard

33 thirteen years old when he matriculated at Oxford: Foster, *Alumni Oxonienses, 1500–1714*, cited in Warner, *Voyage of Robert Dudley*, iii.

33 "my lawful son": Warner, *Voyage of Robert Dudley*, vii.

34 the *Happy Entrance*, the *Carcass*: Forces.net, "12 Bonkers Names For Royal Navy Ships": forces.net/services/navy/12-bonkers-names-royal-navy-ships.

34 most of the crewmen were impressed, and other details of the Dudley expedition draw on the narration by Captain Wyatt, "Robert Dudley's Voyage to the West Indies, 1594–1595," in Warner, *Voyage of Robert Dudley*, 1–66.

34 An average swimmer can swim two miles per hour: https://swimminglevel.com/swimming-times/1-mile-times.

35 Landing in Falmouth, and details of the fleet's retreat: "Sir William Brown to Robert Sidney," July 24, 1597, in Arthur Collins and Henry Sidney, *Letters and Memorials of State in the Reigns of Queen Mary, Queen Elizabeth, King James, King Charles the First (etc.)* (London: Osborne, 1746), 57.

36 "misfortune": Dudley, 68.

36 bad luck: maritimemuseum.co.nz/collections/top-20-sailing-superstitions.

36 "two great and rich galleons": Wyatt, 88.

36 December 22: Kendall, 82.

36 "Indian stuff": *Calendar of the Manuscripts of the Most Hon. the Marquis of Salisbury, K. G., etc. preserved at Hatfield House* (Hereford: Eyre and Spottiswoode, 1895), 357.

36 Imprisonment for debt: Kenneth R. Andrews, *Elizabethan Privateering: English Privateering During the Spanish War, 1585–1603* (Cambridge: Cambridge University Press, 1966), 145.

37 squint in one eye: Lacey, *Sir Walter Ralegh*, 75.

38 "seemed to swim in a sparkling sea of fire . . .": Richard Schomburgk, *Travels in British Guiana, vol. I*, translated by Walter Roth (Georgetown, British Guiana: Daily Telegraph Office, 1922–1923), 12.

38 a Spanish ship laden with firearms: Stebbing, *Sir Walter Ralegh*, 112.

38 Even while at sea, his existence was lavish: Stebbing, *Sir Walter Ralegh*, 135.

5. All That Glisters

40 January 31, 1595: Wyatt, 21.

40 "fiercest storm in nearly a century": Wyatt, 14.

41 Arawak . . . as opposed to Carib: Joyce Lorimer, ed., *Sir Walter Ralegh's Discoverie of Guiana* (England: published for the Hakluyt Society by Ashgate, 2006), lxvii.

41 undeserving of Christian commiseration: Schomburgk, *Discovery*, 33, note 1.

41 "Carib" and "Cannibal": Alexander von Humboldt, *Personal Narrative of Travels to the Equinoctial Regions of America* (London: H. G. Bohn, 1853), 85.

41 "A fine shaped and a gentle people . . .": Dudley, 70.

41 insect repellent: Jessica Boddy, "Is Body Paint a Good Insect Repellent? The Answer Lies in This Field of Sticky Mannequins." *Popular Science*, January 21, 2019, popsci.com/body-paint-insect-repellent/.

41 skin color, facial tattoos: Schomburgk, *Travels in British Guiana, vol. I*, 174–175.

41 "Calcuri": Wyatt, 47.

42 "unaccustomed, God knows . . .": Wyatt, 24.

42 "Robertus Duddeleius, Anglus . . .": Wyatt, 26.

42 "God save our Queen Elizabeth": Wyatt, 28.

43 "it was very full of pelicans": Dudley, 70.

43 forty to sixty lit matches, and the story of the sentinel: Wyatt, 25.

43 witch-burning statistics: Nachman Ben-Yehuda, "The European Witch Craze of the 14th to 17th Centuries: A Sociologist's Perspective," *American Journal of Sociology* 86, no. 1 (1980): 1–31.

43 "detestable slaves of the Devil": King James VI [of Scotland, soon to become James I of England], *Daemonologie* (Printer to the Kings Majestie, 1597), xi. gutenberg.org/cache/epub/25929/pg25929-images.html.

43 Scottish witch-hunting: J. Goodare, ed., *The Scottish Witch-Hunt in Context* (Manchester: Manchester University Press, 2002).

43 2.5 million witches: United States Census Bureau, "U.S. Population Estimated at 334,233,854 on Jan. 1, 2023" at census.gov/newsroom/press-releases/2022/new-years-day-population.html.

43 witches and sea devils: Wyatt, 14.

44 "All is not gold that glistereth": Dudley, 70.

44 "much to be esteemed": Dudley, 73.

44 Robert Cecil would be incensed: Trevelyan, *Sir Walter Raleigh*, 4528.

6. A Canoeful of Gold

45 a week into his 3,100-mile journey: data and other logistical information from Ralegh's records in *The Discoverie of the Large, Rich, and Bewtiful Empyre of Guiana,* unless noted.

45 deck boards or atop cargo or wherever they could find space: Roger M. McCoy, "Life at Sea in the 16th Century," *New World Exploration*, June 26, 2016, newworldexploration.com/explorers-tales-blog/life-at-sea-in-the-16th-century.

46 Damp sleeping berth conditions: Masefield, *On the Spanish Main* (New York: Macmillan, 1906), 217.

46 Ralegh's cabin: Stebbing, *Sir Walter Ralegh*, 135.

46 the third of crewmen who were literate: David Cressy, "Levels of Illiteracy in England, 1530–1730," *Historical Journal* 20, no. 1 (March 1977): 13.

46 Budockshed: Sir William Pole, *Collections Towards a Description of the County of Devon* (London: Sir John-William de la Pole, ed., 1791), 334–335.

46 Devonian: Hayes L. Whiddon Jr., *The Whiddon Heritage* (Bloomington, IN: AuthorHouse, 2009), Kindle ed., 18.

46 "most valiant and honest": Ralegh, *The Discoverie of the Large, Rich, and Beautiful Empire of Guiana by Sir Walter Ralegh, Knight,* included in Schomburgk, *Discovery,* 17.

47 Robert Calfield, a thirty-seven-year-old, a.k.a. Caulfield, born March 20, 1557, per West Yorkshire Archive Service; Wakefield, Yorkshire, England; Yorkshire Parish Records; New Reference Number: WDP53/1/1/1.

47 their candles started fires: Mark Cartwright, "The Capture of the Treasure Ship Madre de Deus," worldhistory.org, June 23, 2020.

47 "All the mariners came to him . . .": Robert Cecil letter to Thomas Heneage cited in Trevelyan, *Sir Walter Raleigh*, 3720.

48 a duel as the solution to John Gilbert's childish excuses: *Calendar of State Documents*, R. Domestic, 1591–1594, 477.

48 On rations: *A Descriptive Catalogue of the Naval Manuscripts in the Pepysian Library at Magdalene College,* Cambridge, vol. 1, ed. J. R. Tanner (Naval Records Society, 1903), 165–167.

48 Dudley's men were unwilling to go; and details of Thomas Jobson's inland expedition: Dudley, 73–75.

48 Thomas Jobson biographical information: Warner, *Voyage of Robert Dudley*, ix.

49 "boat people": Beth A. Conklin, *American Anthropologist* 97, no. 4 (1995): 815–816.
49 fifty feet: Schomburgk, *Discovery*, 49, footnote.
49 men barely over five feet tall: Schomburgk, *Travels in British Guiana, vol. I*, 93.
49 the expression "as dirty as a Warao": Schomburgk, *Travels in British Guiana, vol. I*, 88.
49 chigoe fleas: Schomburgk, *Travels in British Guiana, vol. I*, 94–95.
50 "By force . . .": Dudley, 74.
50 "great town called El Dorado": Dudley, 74.
51 "almost dead from famine . . ." and following: Dudley, 75.

7. Oyster Trees

52 sturdier rudders: Lawrence V. Mott, *The Development of the Rudder: A Technological Tale* (College Station: Texas A&M University Press, 1997), 142.
52 barge, and subsequent details of Trinidad coastal reconnaissance voyage: Ralegh, *Discoverie*, 2.
53 Cantyman: Ralegh, *Discoverie*, 5.
54 "a seat of Indians": Ralegh, *Discoverie*, 12.
54 £3 per twenty-eight-gallon barrel: William Beveridge, *Prices and Wages in England* (London: Frank Cass & Co., 1965), 234.
54 a skilled tradesman earned in a year: https://www.nationalarchives.gov.uk/currency-converter/#currency-result.
55 mangroves that appeared to sprout the prized mollusks: Ralegh, *Discoverie*, 3.
55 André Thevet's account and *The Natural History, Volume XII*: Ralegh, *Discoverie*, 3.
55 Ralegh is universally credited today as the discoverer of what became known as Pitch Lake, the largest natural deposit of asphalt in the world: www.destinationtnt.com/pitch-lake/.
55 Dudley had already seen it: Dudley, 86.
55 April 4, according to Spanish sources: Charles Nicholl, *The Creature in the Map: A Journey to El Dorado* (Chicago: University of Chicago Press, 1997), 94.
55 "to enter into terms of peace": Ralegh, *Discoverie*, 13.
56 Nine came aboard: Pedro de Salazar, "Account of the occurrences in the Island of Trinidad . . .," in the Archivo General de Indias, Sevilla; excerpted in Harlow, *Discover*, 117.
56 "a few draughts made them merry": Ralegh, *Discoverie*, 13.
57 Berrío had invited Whiddon's men: Ralegh, *Discoverie*, 5.
58 "the ways and passages": Ralegh, *Discoverie*, 5–6.
58 story Ralegh heard a few years earlier: Ralegh, *Discoverie*, 25.
58 "I have arrived at this port . . .": "Berrío to the King, Margarita, 11 July 1595," in *Pablo Ojer, Don Antonio de Berrío: Gobernador del Dorado* (Venezuela: Universidad

Católica "Andrés Bello" Facultad de Humanidades y Educación, Instituto de Investigaciones Históricas, 1960), 113–114, translated in Hemming, *Search for El Dorado*, 163; in Berrío's chronology, which was reported long after the facts, he sent de la Hoz only after receiving Ralegh's letter, which soldiers had brought him. Conceivably Ralegh had sent the letter with the first Spanish soldiers he encountered—before inviting them aboard.

59 bacon torture: Ralegh, *Discoverie*, 7.

59 nineteen Spaniards: Salazar report in Harlow, *Discovery*, 117.

59 "put them to the sword": Ralegh, *Discoverie*, 14.

59 lieutenant-colonel: Deposition of Robert Calfield [here: "Cawefield"] by Robert Cecil: *Calendar of the Manuscripts of the Most Hon. the Marquis of Salisbury, K. G., etc. preserved at Hatfield House, Hertfordshire, Part IV* (London: Eyre and Spottiswoode, 1892), 230.

59 Franciscan convent: Nicholl, *Creature in the Map*, 98.

60 "abode not any fight . . ." and subsequent: Ralegh, *Discoverie*, 14.

60 "dismissed": Ralegh, *Discoverie*, 14.

60 reports of Spanish officials: Salazar report in Harlow, *Discovery*, 118.

61 Alvaro Jorge biographical information: Lorimer, *Sir Walter Ralegh's Discoverie of Guiana*, 47.

62 "almost dead of famine . . .": Ralegh, *Discoverie*, 14.

62 "A great casique [chieftan] of the north . . .": Ralegh, *Discoverie*, 15.

62 "place of the hummingbird": Nicholl, *Creature in the Map*, 100.

62 "handled these caciques with great courtesy . . .": "Reports from a Spanish agent relating to Sir Walter Ralegh's plans to uncover a gold mine in Guiana 1612": "Documentos sobre Walter Raley y sus piraterias en Guayana, in Julian Paz, *Catalogo de manuscritos de America existentes en la Biblioteca Nacional*, at Biblioteca Nacional, Madrid, 1868418; transcription and translation by Joyce Lorimer in Lorimer, *Sir Walter Ralegh's Discoverie of Guiana*, 296–305.

8. If the Snows of the Andes Turned to Gold

63 the corners of his mouth appeared to have sagged: portraits of Berrío, e.g., at the Museo Nacional de Colombia.

64 "a gentleman of great assuredness . . .": Ralegh, *Discoverie*, 15.

64 Construction of a fort: Salazar report in Harlow, *Discovery*, 118.

64 "deliver up the said General Berrío . . .": Salazar report in Harlow, *Discovery*, 118.

64 His captive had married into the quest, other Berrío biographical information: Harlow, *Discovery*, lxx.

64 Gonzalo died, leaving María and Antonio his fortune: "Letter from Antonio de Berrio to the King, describing his Third Journey (26 October 1591)," translated and reprinted in Harlow, *Discovery*, 95.

64 Typically such licenses: Hemming, *Search for El Dorado,* 51.

65 Ralegh read: Ralegh, *Discoverie,* v.

65 Dalfinger's story: Harlow, *Discovery,* xlvii–xlviii.

65 Welsers, and additional Dalfinger background: Bernard Moses, *The Spanish Dependencies in South America* (London: Smith, Elder, 1914), chap. iv.

65 "[Conquistadors] are the sort of men. . .": Gonzalo Fernández de Oviedo y Valdés, *Historia general y natural des las Indias, islas y Tierra-firme del Mar Océano* (Seville, José Amador de Los Rios, 1535–1537), 222–223, excerpted and translated in Hemming, *Search for El Dorado,* 49.

66 bloodbath: Hemming, *Search for El Dorado,* 35.

66 Cindahuas people: Hemming, *Search for El Dorado,* 36.

66 seventy-five horses: nationalarchives.gov.uk/currency-converter/#currency-result and using mid-16th century price of gold of about £2.5 per ounce per www.measuringworth.com/datasets/gold/result.php.

66 poisoned arrow: Bernard Moses, *Spanish Dependencies in South America,* 68.

66 Diego de Ordáz's and Alonso de Herrera's stories: Harlow, *Discovery,* xlviii.

66 "A father with an ugly daughter . . .": José de Acosta, *Historia natural y moral de las Indias,* bk. 4, chap. 12 (originally published in 1590), excerpted and translated in Hemming, *Search for El Dorado,* 11.

66 waterfalls: Rodolfo R. Schuller, *The Ordáz and Dortal Expeditions in Search of Eldorado: As Described on Sixteenth Century Maps* (Washington, DC: Smithsonian Institution, 1916), 4.

67 poisoned: Robert Silverberg, *The Golden Dream* (Athens: Ohio University Press, 1967), 59.

67 plagued by vampire bats: Hemming, *Search for El Dorado,* 48.

67 through his mouth: Oviedo, *Historia general y natural des las Indias,* 240, excerpted and translated in Hemming, *Search for El Dorado,* 49.

67 plumed helmets, damask breeches, and other details of Hohermuth's force: Hemming, *Search for El Dorado,* 55.

68 "suffering as much misery and privation . . .": Philipp von Hutten, "Zeitung aus India," in *Johann George Meusels Historich-Litterarisches Magazin* 5 (Bayreuth and Leipsig, 785), excerpted in Hemming, *Search for El Dorado,* 62.

69 "Thus golden and resplendent . . ." and subsequent details from the 1535 reporting: Joaquín Acosta, *Compendio histórico del descubrimiento y colonización de la Nueva Granada en el siglo décimo sexto* (Paris: Beau, 1848), 199, translation by Google Translate.

69 anoint themselves with turtle-fat: Humboldt, *Personal Narrative of Travels,* 46.

69 Having served under his older half brother Francisco Pizarro, and other Gonzalo Pizarro biographical information: Hemming, *Search for El Dorado,* 9–16.

69 The Sumacans: Harlow, *Discovery,* liii.

70 "the thorns and matted underwood . . .": Clements R. Markham, *Expeditions into the Valley of the Amazons, 1539, 1540, 1639* (first published in 1859; this ed.: Anatiposi Verlag, 2023), 17.

70 "It seemed as if a charnel-house . . .": a Spanish eyewitness per Edwards, *Life of Sir Walter Ralegh*, 166.

70 "giving good treatment to the Indians . . ." and subsequent: Hemming, *Search for El Dorado*, 69.

70 *El Requierimento*: Charles Loftus Grant Anderson, *Old Panama and Castilla Del Oro: A Narrative History of the Discovery, Conquest and Settlement by the Spaniards of Panama, Darien, Veragua, Santo Domingo, Santa Marta, Cartagena, Nicaragua, and Peru* (Boston: Page, 1914), appendix.

70 1,925 pounds of fine gold: Hemming, *Search for El Dorado*, 84.

70–71 Michael Wood, *Conquistadors* (Oakland: University of California Press, 2001), 18.

71 "to advance like fish . . .": Pedro de Aguado, *Recpolicacíon historial* (Lisbon, 1581), excerpted and translated in Hemming, *Search for El Dorado*, 74.

71 as many deaths as on any expedition in the history of New World exploration: Hemming, *Search for El Dorado*, 72.

71 Don Quixote: Germán Arciniegas, *The Knight of El Dorado: The Tale of Don Gonzalo Jiménez de Quesada and His Conquest of New Granada, Now Called Colombia* (New York: Viking, 1942), 273.

71 stream of Muisca tributes: Hemming, *Search for El Dorado*, 151.

71 Philipp von Hutten: Harlow, *Discovery*, lviii.

72 golden statues the size of boys: Hemming, *Search for El Dorado*, 134.

73 benefited from Spanish tutelage: Juan Ginés De Sepúlveda, *Democrates Alter, Or, on the Just Causes for War Against the Indians*, 1544: https://www.college.columbia.edu/core/content/democrates-alter-or-just-causes-war-against-indians-0.

73 "land of gold": Juan Álvarez Maldonado, *Relación de la Jornada y descubrimiento del Río Manu* (1572), excerpted and translated in Harlow, *Discovery*, lxv.

73 Pedro Maraver de Silva, biographical information: Pedro Simón, *The Expedition of Pedro de Ursua & Lope de Aguirre in Search of El Dorado and Omagua in 1560–1*, translated by William Bollaert (London: Hakluyt Society, 1861), l.

74 "who were so rich . . .": Fray Pedro Simón, *Noticias historiales de las conquistas de Tierra Firme en las Indias Occidentales* (Bogotá: M. Rivas, 1882): translation by Harlow, *Discovery*, lxvi.

74 1576, detail of Silva's second expedition: Simón, *Expedition of Pedro de Ursua & Lope de Aguirre*, li.

75 Albujar lived in Manoa for seven years: Castellanos, *Elegías*, 433–455.

75 "gente pobre": Castellanos, *Elegías*, 433.

9. The El Doradans

76 it was their point of origin: "Letter from Antonio Berrio to the King . . . 26 October 1591" from the Archivo General de Indias, Sevilla, reprinted and translated in Harlow, *Discovery*, 95–105.

76 "For the greatness, for the riches . . .": Ralegh, *Discoverie*, 13.

76 deposition of Albujar: Ralegh, *Discoverie*, 5.

76 a hundred men, and subsequent details of Berrío's first expedition, including his remarks: "Letter from Berrio to the King . . . 24 May 1585" from the Archivo General de Indias, Sevilla, reprinted and translated in Harlow, *Discovery*, 91. This narrative also draw on Ralegh's accounts in the *Discoverie*, and Simon's in *Setima Noticia Historiale de last Conquistas de Tierra Firme.*

77 the water's resemblance to black tea: earthobservatory.nasa.gov/images/144147/a-blackwater-river-meets-the-sea.

77 "I crossed the plains, passing mighty rivers . . ." and subsequent Berrío quotes from his 1584 expedition: Berrío, "Letter from Antonio de Berrio to the King, describing his Third Journey," in Harlow, *Discovery*, 95.

78 spring of 1585 . . . and Berrío second El Dorado expedition chronology: Harlow, *Discovery*, lxx–lxxvi.

79 March 19, 1590 . . . and details of Berrío's third expedition: "Letter from Berrío to the King, in which he treats of his adventures during the First, Second, and Third Journeys, and of the Ill Welcome which he received in Margarita (1 January 1593.)," in Harlow, *Discovery*, 98–105.

79 Native baskets called *pacara:* Schomburgk, *Discovery*, 75, note 2.

80 Salto La Llovizna: Lonely Planet Guide, "Parque La Llovizna": lonelyplanet.com/venezuela/ciudad-guayana/attractions/parque-la-llovizna/a/poi-sig/1017440/1007056.

80 "great store of plates of gold" and subsequent: Ralegh, *Discoverie*, 36.

80 symbols of high lineage: Joyce Lorimer, ed., *Sir Walter Ralegh's Discoverie of Guiana*, xi, 61, footnote 3.

80 Beginning with Columbus: Hakluyt Society, *Select Documents Illustrating the Four Voyages of Columbus: Including Those Contained in R.H. Major's Select Letters of Christopher Columbus* (London: Hakluyt Society, 1930), 16.

81 in cahoots with his chief El Dorado rival, Francisco de Vides: Ralegh, *Discoverie*, 37.

82 letter to King Philip: letter from Berrío to the King, October 26, 1591, in Harlow, *Discovery*, 96.

82 £50,000: William Arthur Shaw, *The History of Currency, 1252–1894* (New York: Putnam, 1896), 316.

83 "from a province not passing a day's journey off . . .": letter from Domingo de Vera included and translated to English in Schomburgk, *Discovery*, 81.

83 "many eagles of gold . . .": Rodrigo Caranca letter, included and translated to English in Schomburgk, *Discovery*, 83.

83 "The devil himself . . .": "Letter from Berrío to the King, 24 November 1593," excerpted in Harlow, *Discovery*, lxxxiv.

84 "the east from the west": Ralegh, *Discoverie*, 34.

85 "stricken into a great melancholy and sadness" and subsequent excerpts of conversation between Ralegh and Berrío: Ralegh, *Discoverie*, 41.

85 commemorate the completion of one expedition: Hemming, *Search for El Dorado*, 9.

85 "This city is the greatest and the finest . . .": letter from Pizarro to Charles V excerpted in Bob Bridle, ed., *Explorers: Tales of Endurance and Exploration* (London: DK, 2010), 115.

10. He Who Doesn't Die Will Go Crazy

88 "four goodly entrances": Ralegh, *Discoverie*, 45.

89 barras, and other problems, according to Berrío: Ralegh, *Discoverie*, 42.

90 on or about April 18–May 18, according to Ralegh's *Discoverie*, but the dates for the inland voyage in the memoir seem to be a month late; otherwise Ralegh would have spent nearly two months on Trinidad. Also, Spanish accounts of incidents Ralegh reports on Guiana are dated one month earlier than the *Discoverie* records them. In addition, the rainy season comes much later than usual. The mathematical and logistical case for the earlier date is detailed by Paul R. Sellin in *Treasure, Treason and the Tower* (Abingdon, Oxon: Taylor and Francis, 2016).

90 "draw but five foot": Ralegh, *Discoverie*, 35.

91 Ferdinando: Ralegh, *Discoverie*, 47.

91 a hundred pounds of cassava bread to get a knife: Ralegh, *Discoverie*, 40.

91 one shirt, one knife, and one hatchet: in Ralegh's *Discoverie* manuscript but edited out of the published version: Joyce Lorimer, *Sir Walter Ralegh's Discoverie of Guiana*, xi.

91 *Arawabiecie*: Schomburgk, *Travels in British Guiana, vol. I*, 81.

91 flocks of red ibis, white egret: Schomburgk, *Travels in British Guiana, vol. I*, 82.

92 the worst of the four channels, the Caño Pedernales: Sellin, *Treasure, Treason and the Tower*, Kindle ed., 67.

92 "All the pictures my imagination had painted . . .": Schomburgk, *Travels in British Guiana, vol. I*, 92.

93 mud flats: Sellin, 37.

93 "very young, and of no judgment": Ralegh, *Discoverie*, 36.

93 "*Quien se va à Orinoco* . . .": Schomburgk, *Discovery*, 46, footnote.

93 follow the currents back toward the Gulf: Schomburgk, *Discovery*, 46, footnote.

94 walking palms: bbc.com/travel/article/20151207-ecuadors-mysterious-walking-trees.

94 as long as thirty feet: nationalgeographic.com/animals/reptiles/facts/green-anaconda.

94 860 volts: Emma Goldberg, "New Electric Eel Is Most Shocking Yet," *New York Times*, September 10, 2019, nytimes.com/2019/09/10/science/new-electric-eel-shock.html.

94 bats: vampyrum spectrum information (converted from Newtons): gbif.org/species/144104655.

95 howler monkey, general information: nationalgeographic.com/animals/mammals/group/howler-monkeys/.

95 Howler monkey vocal chamber information: M. A. Schön, "The Anatomy of the Resonating Mechanism in Howling Monkeys," *Folia Primatol* (Basel) 15, no. 1–2 (1971): 117–132.

95 white witches: genent.cals.ncsu.edu/biggest/.

95 embodiment of a lost soul: inaturalist.org/guide_taxa/1312961.

11. Upon the Hard Boards

97 "lie in the rain and weather . . ." and subsequent Orinoco Delta narrative and quotations: Ralegh, *Discoverie*, 11.

98 Tivitivas counted on their inaccessibility: Sellin, *Treasure, Treason and the Tower*, 77.

98 "labyrinth of rivers": Ralegh, *Discoverie*, 46.

98 Little Venice: pbs.org/frontlineworld/stories/venezuela/facts.html.

98 name derived from *tigüe-tigüe*—or, possibly, from *tibtibe*, a Lokono word for "mollusk": Neil L. Whitehead, ed., *The Discoverie of the Large, Rich and Bewtiful Empyre of Guiana* (Manchester: Manchester University Press, 1998), 158, footnote 159.

100 hunting dogs trained: Schomburgk, *Discovery*, 48, footnote.

100 "half dead with fear": Ralegh, *Discoverie*, 48.

100 Caño Guinamorena: Sellin, *Treasure, Treason and the Tower*, 81.

100 *lodo*: Sellin, *Treasure, Treason and the Tower*, 82.

100 "like rooks upon trees": Ralegh, *Discoverie*, 50.

101 ballast: William Falconer, *An Universal Dictionary of the Marine* (Good Press, 1780), Kindle ed., 854.

102 "As goodly a river . . .": Ralegh, *Discoverie*, 53.

102 "the world's third most powerful river . . ." and related data: Patricia Miloslavich, Alberto Martín, Eduardo Klein, Yusbelly Díaz, Carlos A. Lasso, Juan José Cárdenas, and Oscar M. Lasso-Alcalá, "Biodiversity and Conservation of the Estuarine and Marine Ecosystems of the Venezuelan Orinoco

Delta" (Caracas: Universidad Simón Bolívar, Departamento de Estudios Ambientales), 67.

103 "Nothing emboldens them sooner . . .": William Dampier, *A New Voyage Round the World* (first published by James Knapton, London, in 1697, cited herein from the collection of his works titled *Dampier's Voyages,* edited by John Masefield [London: E. Grant Richards, 1906], 169).

104 "the world would laugh": Ralegh, *Discoverie,* 54.

104 "We saw birds of all colours . . .": Ralegh, *Discoverie,* 54 (with bird identifications in footnote).

104 pale blue: Ralegh describes the birds "watched," once a synonym for pale blue per Lorimer, *Sir Walter Ralegh's Discoverie of Guiana,* 107, footnote 2.

104 Caño Guara: Sellin, *Treasure, Treason and the Tower,* 88.

105 "Just four reaches more": Ralegh, *Discoverie,* 57.

105 reaches: Schomburgk, *Discovery,* 56, note 2.

106 "On both sides of the river . . ." and subsequent description: Ralegh, *Discoverie,* 57.

106 "a very proper young fellow": Ralegh, *Discoverie,* 58.

106 162 pounds per square inch: sciencefocus.com/nature/top-10-which-animals-have-the-strongest-bite/.

107 pickup truck: 2002 Florida State University study: fsu.edu/indexTOFStory.html?lead.erickson.

12. Patience Conquers Pain

109 he could manufacture his own philosopher's stone: Matthew Lyons, *The Favourite* (London: Constable & Robinson, 2011), Kindle ed., 3587–3620.

109 member of Parliament, other Gifford biographical information: historyofparliamentonline.org/volume/1558-1603/member/gifford-george-1552-1613.

110 "would have been less, both for himself and his posterity . . .": John Chamberlain to Sir Dudley Carleton, June 10, 1613, in Chamberlain, *The Letters of John Chamberlain,* vol. I, 457, cited in Lyons, 4399.

110 "A youth must have seen his blood flow . . .": twelfth-century courtier Roger of Hoveden cited in Dr. Matthew Green, *London: A Travel Guide through Time* (London: Penguin) 2016, 101.

110 *dolor patientia vincitur* and information pertaining to Gifford's Tower of London stay: John Britton and Edward Wedlake Brayley, *Memoirs of the Tower of London: Comprising Historical and Descriptive Accounts of that National Fortress and Palace* (London: Hurst, Chance, 1830), 319; possibly this is a truncation of Seneca's adage, *Libentur feras, quod necesse est: dolor patientia vincitur.*

111 Gifford took nine of the men: Ralegh, *Discoverie,* 56.

111 "try the uttermost of their strengths": Ralegh, *Discoverie,* 58.

112 "Nothing on earth could have been more welcome . . ." and subsequent: Ralegh, *Discoverie,* 58.

112 a combination of pressure, intense heat: goldrefiners.com/what-does-a-gold-refiner-do.

112 the gentleman: Salazar, "Account of the occurrences in the Island of Trinidad," excerpted and translated from Spanish to English in Harlow, *Discovery*, 119.

112 "good quantity of ore and gold": Ralegh, *Discoverie*, 59.

113 "some thing or other": Ralegh, *Discoverie*, 61.

113 "used them for the satisfying . . .": Ralegh, *Discoverie*, 60.

114 "Nothing got us more love . . .": Ralegh, *Discoverie*, 62.

114 "such things as they desired . . .": Ralegh, *Discoverie*, 62.

114 "if we waded them over the shoes . . .": Ralegh, *Discoverie*, 60.

114 sediment: earthobservatory.nasa.gov/images/6215/ciudad-guayana-venezuela.

115 "The party shot endureth the most insufferable torment . . .": Ralegh, *Discoverie*, 70–71.

115 Matamata turtles: Smithsonian's National Zoo and Conservation Biology Institute: nationalzoo.si.edu/animals/matamata-turtle.

116 "very wholesome meat": Ralegh, *Discoverie*, 63–64.

116 eighty to 140 paces: Schomburgk, *Travels in British Guiana, vol. I*, 236.

13. True Remedies of Poisoned Arrows

117 "above all things" and details of the Ralegh-Toparimaca summit: Ralegh, *Discoverie*, 64.

118 "Jaguar Island": Whitehead, *The Discoverie*, 168, footnote 78.

118 piwari, the recipe, and its effects on the women: Schomburgk, *Discovery*, 65, footnote.

118–119 "beat the bones of their lords . . ." and subsequent details of wine: Ralegh, *Discoverie*, 53.

119 "It was very strong, with pepper . . .": Ralegh, *Discoverie*, 64.

120 "perfect red" and other descriptions of the scenery: Ralegh, *Discoverie*, 69.

120 "Almost every tree . . .": Schomburgk, *Travels in British Guiana, vol. I*, 114.

120 the conquistadors had tried to obtain the cure: Ralegh, *Discoverie*, 71.

120 head to toe in quilted cotton padding: Hemming, *Search for El Dorado*, 70.

120 "There was nothing whereof I was more curious . . .": Ralegh, *Discoverie*, 70.

121 urari-yè: Ralegh, *Discoverie*, 72.

121 modern remedy for strychnine poisoning: Jenna Otter and Joseph L. D'Orazio, "Strychnine Toxicity," National Library of Medicine: ncbi.nlm.nih.gov/books/NBK459306/.

122 Taj Mahal is 39,500 cubic meters: wonders-of-the-world.net/Taj-Mahal/Dimensions-of-the-Taj-Mahal.php.

122 the appearance of winged ants: Schomburgk, *Travels in British Guiana, vol. II*, 87.

122 "dark and dismal clouds . . .": Schomburgk, *Travels in British Guiana, vol. II,* 88.
122 "vivid summer lightning that . . .": Schomburgk, *Travels in British Guiana, vol. II,* 87.
122 sixty-five feet: britannica.com/place/Orinoco-River/Climate.

14. Called for by Death

123 "great anchor": Ralegh, *Discoverie,* 17.
124 *Topuremacka,* in the Macusi language: Schomburgk, *Discovery,* 78, footnote 1.
124 best manufacturers of the urari poison: Schomburgk, *Discovery,* 71, footnote 1.
124 elaborately crafted six-foot-long wooden blowpipes: "Blowpipe (1884.140.905)," Pitt Rivers Museum of Anthropology and World Archeology: web.prm.ox.ac.uk/weapons/index.php/tour-by-region/oceania/americas/arms-and-armour-americas-43/index.html.
124 "[Ralegh] embraced them, and made show of much love . . .": "Extract from Francis Sparry's Petition to King Philip II of Spain, c. 1600" (Archivo General de Indias, Indiferente Generale, Legajo 747), cited and translated from Spanish to English in Nicholl, *Creature in the Map,* 339.
125 "too delicious for a subject to taste of": William Oldys, *The Works of Sir Walter Ralegh, Kt.* (Oxford: University Press, 1829), vol. 1, 200, footnote h.
125 Los Negros: Sellin, *Treasure, Treason and the Tower,* 179.
125 "the wisest of al the Orenoqueponi . . .": Ralegh, *Discoverie,* 78.
126 "barred over with small plates . . .": Ralegh, *Discoverie,* 74.
126 "a little of the powder . . .": Ralegh, *Discoverie,* 74.
126 "like a dog": Ralegh, *Discoverie,* 93.
126 "her Majesty's greatness, her justice, her charity . . ." and Ralegh's subsequent discussion with Topiawari: Ralegh, *Discoverie,* 74–78.
127 "inward feeling of the loss of his country . . .": Ralegh, *Discoverie,* 76.
128 *orejones:* Museo Larco, "Mohica Gold Ear Ornaments": museolarco.org/en/exhibition/permanent-exhibition/online-exhibition/gold-and-jewelry/mochica-old-ear-ornaments/.
129 "far to go . . .": Ralegh, *Discoverie,* 77.
129 "great roar and fall" and Ralegh's subsequent details of the Caroní: Ralegh, *Discoverie,* 78–81.
129 "as broad as the Thames at Woolwich": Ralegh, *Discoverie,* 80.
130 "one stone's cast": Ralegh, *Discoverie,* 80.
131 "it was not possible by the strength of any men . . .": Ralegh, *Discoverie,* 81.

15. Very Fine

132 "smoke that had risen over some great town . . ." and subsequent details of the cataracts: Ralegh, *Discoverie,* 81.

132 orchids: Schomburgk, *Discovery*, 81–82, footnote 1.

133 pilot: Jimmie Angel Historical Project: www.jimmieangel.org/Rio.html.

133 Ralegh had read about such creatures . . . in Mandeville: Ralegh, *Discoverie*, 86.

133 "showing nothing of neck or head . . .": John Mandeville, *The Travels of Sir John Mandeville* (originally published in 1356; this edition: London: Penguin, 2005), 72.

133 "fable": Ralegh, *Discoverie*, 85.

134 "ill footman": Ralegh, *Discoverie*, 82.

134 "the whole vault of heaven . . ." and subsequent: Schomburgk, *Travels in British Guiana, vol. I*, 97.

135 "the golden parts of Guiana": Ralegh, *Discoverie*, 91.

135 "be buried there": Ralegh, *Discoverie*, 92.

135 destruction of entire nations of people: Walter Ralegh, "Of the Voyage for Guyana": Sloane Manuscripts at the British Library, 1133, fol. 45, reprinted in Schomburgk, *Discovery*, 135.

135 "in their just defensive wars . . .": Ralegh, "Of the Voyage for Guiana," 135.

136 "desire nothing of the gold or treasure . . .": Ralegh, *Discoverie*, 94.

137 "Most of the gold which they made in plates . . ." and subsequent: Ralegh, *Discoverie*, 96.

137 Ralegh would tell Queen Elizabeth . . . Bartholomew Columbus: Ralegh, *Discoverie*, 117.

138 "never saw a more beautiful country . . .": Ralegh, *Discoverie*, 82.

138 Spanish spy: Anonymous, "News of the gold mine reconnoitered by Raley thanks to the directions of an old cacique," translated from Spanish in Lorimer, *Sir Walter Ralegh's Discoverie of Guiana*, 299–302.

138 Of the spy, all that's known: "Archbp. Abbot to the King," July 23, 1612, in *Calendar of State Papers, Domestic Series, of the Reign of James I, 1611–1618* (London: Her Majesty's Stationery Office, 1858), 138.

139 "muy fino," or very fine gold; twenty or twenty-two karats: Sellin, *Treasure, Treason and the Tower*, 6553.

139 old miners' rule of thumb: Sellin, *Treasure, Treason and the Tower*, 4381.

139 Brick hardness: Friedrich Mohs, *Treatise on Mineralogy: Or, the Natural History of the Mineral Kingdom* (Edinburgh: A. Constable, 1822).

139 "quarz": Cambridge Dictionary: dictionary.cambridge.org/dictionary/german-english/quarz.

139 "did not dare to attempt such a thing . . ." and subsequent details of the second Ralegh-Topiawari summit: Ralegh, *Discoverie*, 94.

140 "declaring to him that there was much gold": extract from a report by the Licenciate Pedro de Liaño to the king (March 25–April 12, 1596), translated and reprinted in Harlow, *Discovery*, 120–125.

140 "at the root of the grass": "To the Earl of Salisbury [from the Tower, 1611], in Latham and Youings, *Letters*, 322.

140 "Having learned what I could . . .": Ralegh, *Discoverie*, 97.

16. Stones the Color of Gold

142 "stones the color of gold . . ." and subsequent details of the expedition's stay with Putijma: Ralegh, *Discoverie*, 97–98.

143 Upata grasslands: Lorimer, *Sir Walter Ralegh's Discoverie of Guiana*, 183, footnote 1.

143 "great fishes as big as a wine pipe" and subsequent details of the excursion with Putijma: Ralegh, *Discoverie*, 99.

143 wine pipe: Simon Difford, "Casks—barrel, butt, punchon, pipe, barrique, hogshead": Difford's Guides for Discerning Drinkers: diffordsguide.com/encyclopedia/481/bws/casks-barrel-butt-punchon-pipe-barriquehogshead.

144 "diamonds and other previous stones . . .": Ralegh, *Discoverie*, 102.

144 "It appeared like a white church tower . . .": Ralegh, *Discoverie*, 101.

144 Walter Reilly: Wikipedia, "Mount Roraima": en.wikipedia.org/wiki/Mount_Roraima.

144 Arthur Conan Doyle's 1912 novel *The Lost World*: Universidad de Barcelona, "Tourism Is Threatening Arthur Conan Doyle's Lost World," *Science Daily*, September 6, 2016: sciencedaily.com/releases/2016/09/160906085543.htm.

145 Monkey Falls: Sellin, *Treasure, Treason and the Tower*, 4964.

145 "drunk as beggars": Ralegh, *Discoverie*, 102.

145 "surpass all description . . .": Ralegh, *Discoverie*, 102, footnote 1.

145 "a small quantity satisfied us . . .": Ralegh, *Discoverie*, 103.

145 "heartily afraid": Ralegh, *Discoverie*, 105.

146 Sean Gallagher, Jonisha Pollard, and William L. Porter, "Locomotion in Restricted Space: Kinematic and Electromyographic Analysis of Stoopwalking and Crawling," *Gait and Posture* 33, no. 1 (January 2011): 71–76.

146 Raleana: Lawrence Keymis, *A Relation of the second Voyage to Guiana performed and written in the yeere 1596* (London: Thomas Dawson, 1596), online at www.perseus.tufts.edu/hopper/, unpaginated.

146 "Putijma pointed to . . .": Keymis, "*Relation of the second Voyage to Guiana*."

146 "Our hearts were cold . . .": Ralegh, *Discoverie*, 105.

147 "the bitterest of all our journey . . .": Ralegh, *Discoverie*, 106.

148 "all very sober, and melancholy . . ." and Ralegh's other reporting of the evacuation of the galliot: Ralegh, *Discoverie*, 107.

17. To Offend and Enfeeble the King of Spain

149 "There was never to us a more joyful sight . . ." and subsequent: Ralegh, *Discoverie*, 107.

149 forty-seven feet: Clyde L. MacKenzie Jr., Luis Troccoli, Luis B. Leon S., "History of the Atlantic Pearl-Oyster, Pinctata imbricata, Industry in Venezuela and Colombia, with Biological and Ecological Observations," *Marine Fisheries Review* 65, no. 1, 1–20.

149 "Pearl Age" and pearl valuation: Dr. Akitsugu Sato and Dr. Laurent E. Cartier, "The Value of Pearls: A Historical Review and Current Trends," *GemGuide*, April 26, 2022.

150 "to offend and enfeeble . . .": Public Records Office State Papers 12/250 no. 46, excerpted in Trevelyan, *Sir Walter Raleigh*, 4452.

150 "to await the enemy to the last man . . ." and other details of the Margarita defense: "Simon de Bolivar to the King (at Margarita, 8 July 1595)," Archivo General de Indias, Sevilla; excerpted in Harlow, *Discovery*, 127–128.

150 resemblance to the pomegranate: Adrien Gay, *Grenade Warfare: School of the Grenadier, a Guide for Hand Bombers and Rifle Grenadiers* (Atlanta: E. W. Allen, 1918), 2.

151 substantial cash rewards: Benerson Little, *The Sea Rover's Practice: Pirate Tactics and Techniques, 1630–1730* (Washington, DC: Potomac, 2007), 195.

151 The results of Ralegh's attempts to land boats on the islet: Sellin, *Treasure, Treason and the Tower*, 211.

151 ransom of 1,400 ducats for Berrío: "Simon de Bolivar to the King (at Margarita, 8 July 1595)," 128.

151 dreary wasteland of scrub and cacti: Trevelyan, *Sir Walter Raleigh*, 4925.

152 "devilish road" and subsequent excerpts from the Spanish official reporting of the Cumaná raid: "Report sent by Francisco de Vides, Governor of Cumana, to the Contador, Simon de Bolivar, to the Island of Margarita, of the events in the said City of Cumana on Friday the twenty-third of June of this present year one thousand five hundred and ninety-five . . .": Archivo General de Indias, Seveilla, included in full and translated in V. T. Harlow, *Discovery of Guiana*, 130–131.

155 Off the coast of Cape San Antonio, and subsequent details of the reunion with Preston's fleet: Hakluyt, *Principal Navigations*, 183.

155 They'd even done well in Cumaná: Richard Hakluyt, *Principal Navigations*, 211.

155 peak hurricane season: Anantha R. Aiyyer and Chris Thorncroft, "Climatology of Vertical Wind Shear over the Tropical Atlantic," *Journal of Climate* 19, no. 12 (June 15, 2006).

18. Kings of Figs and Oranges

156 "Sur hit tes trew I thonke the leveng God . . .": letter from Bess Ralegh to Robert Cecil, "Cecil Papers: September 1595": british-history.ac.uk/cal-cecil-papers/vol5/pp380-396.

156 "come home well and rich": letter from Robert Cecil to Thomas Heneage, September 9, 1595, in "Cecil Papers: September 1595": british-history.ac.uk /cal-cecil-papers/vol5/pp358-380.

156 "Sir Walter Rawley is returned . . .": letter from Rowland White to Robert Sidney, September 25, 1595, excerpted in Nicholl, *Creature in the Map*, 266.

157 "making known to that nation her virtues . . .": letter from Rowland White to Robert Sidney, September 27, 1595, excerpted in Nicholl, *Creature in the Map*, 266.

157 "honorable" and "profitable," and subsequent argument for colonization of Guiana: Ralegh, "Of the Voyage for Guyana," in Schomburgk, *Discovery*, 138–149.

157 "kings of figs and oranges": Walter Ralegh, "A Discourse Touching a Marriage Between Prince Henry of England, and a Daughter of Savoy," 1611, in Oldys, *Works*, vol. 8, 246.

157 "marcasite, and of no riches or value": Schomburgk, *Discovery*, xi.

157 assayers . . . beyond reproach: Paul R. Sellin and Donald Carlisle, "Assays of Sir Walter Raleigh's Ores from Guayana, 1595–1596," *Ben Jonson Journal* 18, no. 2 (November 2011).

157 0.0033 percent gold is high average, and additional analysis of the assayers' findings: Sellin and Carlisle, "Assays of Sir Walter Raleigh's Ores from Guayana, 1595–1596."

158 four pence: Ronald Sheppard and Edward Newton, *The Story of Bread* (Boston: Charles Branford, 1957), 167.

158 too soft and effete: Stebbing, *Sir Walter Ralegh*, 120.

158 purchased the ore from the Barbary Coast: Ralegh, *Discoverie*, xi.

158 "malicious slanders . . ." and subsequent: Ralegh, *Discoverie*, 7.

158 *ra leah*: A. D. Mills, *Dictionary of English Place-Names* (Oxford: Oxford University Press, 1991), 42.

159 "a desolate place" and subsequent from Ralegh: "To Sir Robert Cecil from Sherborne 10 November 1595" in Lathan and Youings, *Letters*, 125.

159 available record: "The Lord Admiral to Robert Cecil," in Marquess of Salisbury, Robert Cecil et al., *Calendar of the Manuscripts of the Most Hon. the Marquis of Salisbury, K.G., &c. &c. &c., Preserved at Hatfield House, Part VI* (Hertfordshire, London: H. M. Stationery Office, 1895), 85–86.

159 attending church daily: H. M. G, de L'Isle and Dudley MSS, excerpted in Rowse, *Ralegh and the Throckmortons*, 196–197.

160 "company were all slain . . .": Keymis, *A Relation of the second Voyage to Guiana* (London: Thomas Dawson, 1596), unpaginated.

160 Vera was able to rile up King Philip: "Copy of a letter from Domingo Vera (while in Spain) to the King, setting forth the burning of S. Joseph de Oruña,

the capture of Berrio, and other proceedings (1595)": Archivo General de Indias, included and translated in Harlow, *Discovery*, 124–125.

161 speech about the marvels of Manoa: Harlow, *Discovery*, xci.

161 Seville contributed five ships, and ensuing popularity of the expedition: Edwards, *Life of Sir Walter Ralegh*, 177.

161 set sail February 23, 1596: Schomburgk, *Discovery*, 17.

161 "from a province not passing a day's journey off . . .": letter from Domingo de Vera included and translated to English in Schomburgk, *Discovery*, 81.

162 "many eagles of gold . . .": Rodrigo Caranca letter, included and translated to English in Schomburgk, *Discovery*, 83.

162 "an eagle that weighed 27 pounds . . .": Rodrigo Caranca letter, in Schomburgk, *Discovery*, 83.

162 "giant all of gold . . .": "The report of Domingo Martines of Iamaica [sic], Concerning the Dorado," in Schomburgk, *Discovery*, 84.

162 "would fill up those plains with Indians . . .": Rodrigo Caranca letter, in Schomburgk, *Discovery*, 81.

162 "You may perceive in by this relation that is no dream . . .": "To Sir Robert Cecil from Sherborne, 12 November 1595," [Ralegh wrote November 13, but there is some evidence he was one day off] in Latham and Youings, *Letters*, 126–127.

162 "if I be thought unworthy . . .": "To Robert Cecil from Sherborne, 26 November 1595," in Latham and Youings, *Letters*, 132–133.

162 [Cecil listed as] one of the enterprise's principals: John Harwood Hill, *The Chronicle of the Christian Ages: Or, Record of Events Ecclesiastical, Civil and Military, from the Year 1 to the End of 1858* (Uppingham: n.p., 1859), 1597.

163 1595 raids on Cornwall port cities, and other national security concerns: Anna Beer, *Patriot or Traitor: The Life and Death of Sir Walter Ralegh* (London: One World, 2018), 125–126.

163–164 "returned a beggar, and withered": Ralegh, *Discoverie*, v.

19. Headless Men

165 £500: Rowland Whyte letter to Sir Robert Sidney, Sidney Papers, vol. I, 377, excerpted in Schomburgk, *Discovery*, 153.

165 "travels fit for boys less blasted . . .": Ralegh, *Discoverie*, iii–x.

165 "a country that hath yet her maidenhead . . .": Ralegh, *Discoverie*, 115.

165 "whatsoever Prince shall possess it . . .": Ralegh, *Discoverie*, 11.

166 three editions: Neil L. Whitehead, *The Discoverie*, 1.

166 "eyes in their shoulders . . .": Ralegh, *Discoverie*, 85.

167 "men with mouths on their breasts" and reports of men similar to the Ewaipanoma: Schomburgk, *Discovery*, 85, footnote 2.

167 "he never would yield . . .": Keymis, *Relation of the second Voyage to Guiana,* unpaginated (about halfway through).

167 Vides let his rival sit, and subsequent details of Berrío's fourth expedition: "Extract from a report by the Licentiate Pedro de Liaño to the King (25 March–12 April 1596)," reprinted and translated in Harlow, *Discovery,* 120–122.

168–169 "The Indians our friends . . ." and Keymis's subsequent remarks about his expedition: Keymis, *Relation of the second Voyage to Guiana* (unpaginated).

170 "the time of our return promised . . .": Keymis, *Relation of the second Voyage to Guiana,* unpaginated (about halfway through).

170 military school: Biblioteca Nacional Madrid, folios 8r, 11r, cited in Sellin, *Treasure, Treason and the Tower,* 193.

171 "the richest and most plentiful": Keymis, *Relation of the second Voyage to Guiana,* unpaginated (about three-eighths through).

172 "the hope of following this voyage would be buried": Keymis, *Relation of the second Voyage to Guiana,* unpaginated (about five-eighths through).

172 Columbus: Andrzej Grzybowski, "The history of antitobacco actions in the last 500 years": pubmed.ncbi.nlm.nih.gov/17288236/.

172 John Hawkins: Edmund Howes and John Stow, *The Annales, or Generall Chronicle of England* (London: Thomas Adams, 1615), appendix.

172 the famous story . . . seeing Ralegh smoking a pipe: Trevelyan, *Sir Walter Raleigh,* 103.

173 "Thus have I emptied your purse . . .": Keymis, *Relation of the second Voyage to Guiana,* unpaginated (about halfway through).

173 "He certified me of the headless men . . .": Keymis, *Relation of the second Voyage to Guiana,* unpaginated (about three-quarters through).

20. How Can We Fire on Our Brothers?

175 "[I have come] to expel you . . ." and details of Santiago's attempt: Simón, *Noticias historiales, Primera Parte,* 363–364.

176 "It's Santiago and them": Simón, *Noticias historiales,* 363.

177 470 of his charges to San Thomé: "Letter from Domingo de Ybarguen (y Vera) to His Majesty giving account of the Journey for Eldorado. Dated from this Island of Trinidad, 27 October 1597": from the Archivo General de Indias, Sevilla, included and translated in Harlow, *Discovery,* 108–112.

178 "voracious for human flesh": Simón, 363.

178 second wave of a hundred soldiers: "Letter from Domingo de Ybarguen (y Vera) to His Majesty . . . Trinidad, 27 October 1597," 110.

178 "a long series of hardships": "Letter from Domingo de Ybarguen (y Vera) to His Majesty . . . Trinidad, 27 October 1597," 110.

180 eggs by the hundreds: Cleveland Clinic, "Tungiasis": my.clevelandclinic.org/health/diseases/24162-tungiasis.

180 "as light as if they were made of straw": Simón, *Noticias historiales*, 363.

180 wives armed themselves with butcher's knives: Simón, *Noticias historiales*, 371.

181 Berrío fell extremely ill, and other details of Berrío's final days: "Letter from Domingo de Vera 27 October 1597," reprinted and translated to English in Harlow, *Discovery*, 108–113.

182 "slothful": "Royal warrants to governors and others in the West Indies to stop trade with the enemy, and to investigate charges against Fernando de Berrio, Governor of Trinidad," November 14, 1600, cited in Harlow, *Discovery*, xciii, footnote 3.

182 Fernando de Berrío: biographical information Gertrude Carmichael, *The History of the West Indian Islands of Trinidad and Tobago, 1498–1900* (London: A. Redman, 1961), 28.

182 as many as twenty expeditions: Valeriano Sánchez Ramos, "Don Fernando de Berrio y Ourña, Gobernador del Dorado," *Farua: Revista del Centro Virgitano for de Estudios Historicos*, no. 8 (2005): 105–142.

21. Ralegh Hath Made Me Love Him

183 largest fleet: Trevelyan, *Sir Walter Raleigh*, 5375.

184 ninety-six English and twenty-four Dutch ships, and other details of the fleet: Stebbing, *Sir Walter Ralegh*, 126.

184 June 1, 1596: N. A. M. Rodger, *The Safeguard of the Sea: A Naval History of Britain, 660–1649* (New York: W. W. Norton, 1999), 284.

184 a blustery June 20, and other details of the Cádiz incursion are derived from Ralegh's reporting, except where noted: Walter Ralegh, "Relation of the Cadiz Action," reprinted in Oldys, *Works*, vol. 8, 667–674.

185 "the utter overthrow of the whole armies . . .": Ralegh, "Relation of the Cadiz Action," 667.

186 fortress information: guiadigital.iaph.es/bien/inmueble/22813/cadiz/cadiz/castillo-de-san-lorenzo-de-puntales.

188 "interlaced and deformed with splinters": Ralegh, "Relation of the Cadiz Action," 673.

189 "heaps of soldiers . . .": Ralegh, "Relation of the Cadiz Action," 672.

189 The *San Matéo* and the *San Andrés* crews also tried to burn their ships: Walter Ralegh, "To Arthur [Gorges] from Cadiz, 21 June 1596," in Latham and Youings, *Letters*, 149.

189 Spanish merchants willing to pay two million ducats: "Journall of all the Particularities that fell out the Voyage under the Charge of the Lords Generals,

MS. Lamb," ccl. fol. 357, excerpted in Edwards, *Life of Sir Walter Ralegh*, 218.

189 £1,769 and higher shares of other officers: Anonymous, *Calendar of State Papers, Domestic Series, of the Reign of Elizabeth, 1595–1597* (Outlook, 2020), no. 266 (nos. 94–96).

189–190 "I hope her most excellent Majesty . . .": Walter Ralegh, "To Robert Cecil From Aboard Ship Off Cadiz, 7 July [1596]," in Latham and Youings, *Letters*, 151–152.

190 "Sir Walter Ralegh's service was so much praiseworthy . . .": June 30 letter from Sir George Carew excerpted in Edwards, *Life of Sir Walter Ralegh*, 220.

190 "Sir Walter Ralegh did in my judgment, no man better . . .": Sir Anthony Standen to Lord Burghley, Cadiz, July 5, 1596; in MS. Harl. 6845, fol. 101, verso. (British Museum), excerpted by Edwards, *Life of Sir Walter Ralegh*, 221.

22. The Carving of the Queene's Meate

191 burning down nearly half the city: *Colección de documentos inéditos para la historia de España* (Spain: Academia de la Historia, 1860).

191 It was supposed to be a national enterprise, and Queen Elizabeth's analysis: Cott Manuscripts E IX, f337, at British Library, cited by Trevelyan, *Sir Walter Raleigh*, 5549–5558.

192 taken ill at military school and died: Biblioteca Nacional Madrid, folios 8r, 11r, cited in Sellin, *Treasure, Treason and the Tower*, 193.

192 "Opinion upon the Spanish Alarum": reprinted in Oldys, *Works*, vol. 8, 676.

193 "Many of them are missing . . .": Herault de Maisse, *The Discreet Ambassador De Maisse: A Journal*, in *The Spectator*, October 24, 1931, archive.spectator.co.uk/article/24th-october-1931/32/the-discreet-ambassador-de-maisse-a-journal-transl.

193 teeth . . . were black: Ben Johnson, Elizabeth I—A Life In Portraits, Historic UK: historic-uk.com/HistoryUK/HistoryofEngland/Elizabeth-I-Life-in-Portrait/.

193 due to the surge in sugar importation: Rebecca Larson, "Queen Elizabeth's Rotten Teeth," *Tudors Dynasty*, December 13, 2017: tudorsdynasty.com/queen-elizabeths-rotten-teeth/.

193 "very youthful still in appearance . . .": Thomas Platter, "Travels in England," 1599, translated by Clare Williams (1937), reprinted in *Travel Narratives from the Age of Discovery: An Anthology* (Oxford: Oxford University Press, 2006), 400.

194 "Sir Walter Ralegh was brought by [Cecil] to the Queen" and subsequent excerpts from letter: "Rowland Whyte to Sir Robert Sydney" June 2, 1597, in Collins and Sidney, *Letters and Memorials*, 54.

194 what Rowland Whyte didn't know: Lacey, *Sir Walter Ralegh,* 238.

194 colonel general and subsequent Essex biographical information: Robert Lacey, *Robert, Earl of Essex: an Elizabethan Icarus* (London: Weidenfeld & Nicolson, 1971).

195 The Spaniards were too well entrenched, and details of the Ferrol plotting: Stebbing, *Sir Walter Ralegh,* 135.

195–196 Durham House details: Beer, *Patriot or Traitor,* 118.

196 dining companions: "Rowland White, Esq; to Sir Robert Sidney," April 19, 1597, in Collins and Sidney, *Letters and Memorials,* 42–43, and June 2, 1597, in Collins and Sidney, *Letters and Memorials,* 55.

196 went to a play together, Shakespeare play, *Richard II:* "Letter to Sir Robert Cecil from Weymouth, 6 July 1597," in Latham and Youings, *Letters,* 158–160.

197 the English fleet sailing to Ferrol, and other strategizing: *Domestic Correspondence of Queen Elizabeth,* June 15, 1597, cited in Edwards, *Life of Sir Walter Ralegh,* 233

197 "within a day's journey . . .": M. Thomas Masham, "The Third Voyage Set Forth by Sir Walter Ralegh to Guiana," in Hakluyt, *Principal Navigations,* 879.

197 "some mines inland": "Questions put to Francis Sparry," in Lorimer, *Sir Walter Ralegh's Discoverie of Guiana,* 272.

197 One of Cecil's spies: letter from "Giles Harwick to [Sir Robert Cecil] 10/20 Nov. 1597," in Lorimer, *Sir Walter Ralegh's Discoverie of Guiana,* 267.

198 "sufficient" mine: "Captain Jo. Stanley to Sir Robert Cecil," September 22, 1598, in Calendar of the Cecil Papers in Hatfield House, vol. 8, 1598, at british-history.ac.uk/cal-cecil-papers/vol8/pp348-373.

23. They Did Not Deign to Take Off Their Hats

199 July 13, 1597: the narrative of this episode draws heavily on accounts by Earl of Essex Robert Devereux and Arthur Gorges along with Ralegh's letters, all cited below.

199 "raised and enraged . . ." and subsequent details of the storm: Ralegh, "To Sir Robert Cecil from Plymouth, 18 July 1597," in Latham and Youings, *Letters,* 160–163.

199 120 ships: letter from Rowland Whyte, Esq., to Sir Robert Sydney, April 23, 1597, in Collins and Sidney, *Letters and Memorials,* 44.

199 the case of one Ralegh's gentleman volunteers: Trevelyan, *Sir Walter Raleigh,* 5845.

200 totaled: Robert Devereux, Earl of Essex, "The Voyage to the Iles of Azores," in Samuel Purchas, *Purchas His Pilgrimes, vol. 20* (Glasgow: James MacLehose and Sons, 1907; originally published in 1625), 25.

200 little more than barnacles: the Spanish lost just four ships, and only one of any consequence, a galleon carrying £50,000 worth of cochineals and other goods from Havana: *Domestic Correspondence of Queen Elizabeth*, vol. ccxxvi, 21, excerpted in Edwards, *Life of Sir Walter Ralegh*, 243, and Robert Monson, "Narrative of the Island Voyage," in Cotton MS Titus, B. viii, fol. 127, 229, excerpted in *Exmouth and Its Neighbourhood, Ancient and Modern* (Gwydir Place: W. M. Bounsall, 1868), 193.

200 Elizabeth lit into Essex, and details of their contretemps: letter from Rowland Whyte, Esq., to Sir Robert Sydney, November 5, 1597, in Collins and Sidney, *Letters and Memorial*, 74–75.

201 Essex demanded a duel, etc.: Rowland Whyte, Esq; to Sir Robert Sidney, December 21, 1597, in Collins and Sidney, *Letters and Memorials*, 77.

201 deeming such violence puerile: Susan Brigden, *New Worlds, Lost Worlds: The Rule of the Tudors 1485–1603* (New York: Viking, 2000), 317.

201 court-martial, and other reporting on the Azores expedition: Sir Arthur Gorges, "A Larger Relation of the . . . Iland Voyage," in Samuel Purchas, *Purchas His Pilgrimes, vol. 20* (Glasgow: James MacLehose and Sons, 1907; originally published in 1625), 34–129.

202 December 21, 1597 . . . House of Lords: Sir Simon D'Ewes Journal of Queen Elizabeth's Parliaments, fol. 1708, 539–540, cited in Oldys, *Works*, 311.

202 took off their hats: Trevelyan, *Sir Walter Raleigh*, 6065.

202 "My fortune at Court . . .": "Remembrancer's Roll" fol. 253 of Michaelmas Term, 7th James I, R. H. excerpted in Edwards, *The Letters of Sir Walter Ralegh*, 466–467.

202 "made mad with intricate affairs . . .": Walter Ralegh, "To Sir Robert Cecil from Plymouth, 30 October 1597," in Latham and Youings, *Letters*, 172–173.

202 Gilbert Talbot: Thomas Secombe, "Talbot, Gilbert (1553–1616)," *Dictionary of National Biography, vol. 55* (London: Smith, Elder, 1885–1900).

202 the Dutch . . . December of 1597: A. Cabeliau, "Account of a Journey to Guiana and the Island of Trinidad," translated and reprinted: British Guiana Boundary Arbitration, British Case, App. vol. 1, 18–22, reprinted in Harlow, *Ralegh's Last Journey*, 128–133.

203 "made by Sir Walther Halley": Cabeliau, "Account of a Journey to Guiana," 130.

203 Charles of Sudermania . . . was willing to commit twelve fully victualed vessels: Hist. MSS Comm, Marquis of Salisbury MSS (Hatfield Papers), Part VIII, p. 363, excerpted and cited in Harlow, *Discovery*, ci.

203 "Go and be hanged!" and details of the Elizabeth-Essex shouting match: Thomas Birch, *Memoirs of the Reign of Queen Elizabeth: From the Year 1581 Til Her Death. In which the Secret Intrigues of Her Court, and the Conduct of Her*

Favourite, Robert Earl of Essex, Both at Home and Abroad, are Particularly Illustrated (London: A. Millar, 1754), 384.

204 "as crooked in her mind . . .": Birch, *Memoirs of the Reign of Queen Elizabeth*, 463.

204 "Governor Don Fernando . . .": Cabeliau, "Account of a Journey to Guiana," 130.

205 Nonsuch Palace in Surrey, and details of Essex's encounter with Elizabeth: Birch, *Memoirs of the Reign of Queen Elizabeth*, 433.

205 "contemptuous disobedience": Birch, *Memoirs of the Reign of Queen Elizabeth*, 434.

205 eight-pound axe: rounded up from seven pounds and fifteen ounces: Geoffrey Abbott, *Execution: A Guide to the Ultimate Penalty* (London: Summersdale, 2012).

205 It failed to uncouple the earl's head and body, and the following account of the execution: Birch, *Memoirs of the Reign of Queen Elizabeth*, 484.

205 "sorry that I was not with him . . .": Reporting from "Sir Walter Ralegh's Speech Immediately before he was beheaded," in V. T. Harlow, *Ralegh's Last Voyage* (London: Argonaut Press, 1932), 310.

206 "worse than cat and dog": letter from Ralph Adderley to Walter Bagot on the June 9, 1600, excerpted in John Pope-Hennessy, *Sir Walter Ralegh in Ireland* (London: K. Paul, Trench, 1883), 131.

206 "a sweet and comfortable recreation . . .": Privy Council, excerpted in Green, *London*, 15.

206 bull tossed a wounded dog: diary of Josh Evelyn, excerpted in Green, *London*, 13.

207 letters patent for "the Conquest and Planting of Guiana": British Library, Harleian MSS, 35, f. 402 and seqq. Translated from French and excerpted in V. T. Harlow, *Ralegh's Last Voyage*, 7.

207 As long as Tyrone was making trouble in Ireland: Ralegh, "Ralegh to George, Lord Carew (—?, 1618)," reprinted in Harlow, *Ralegh's Last Voyage*, 251–252.

207 the governor of Jersey: "Rowland Whyte, Esq; to Sir Robert Sidney," August 23, 1600, in Collins and Sidney, *Letters and Memorials*, 112.

207 "laboured like a mule": Walter Ralegh, "To Robert Cecil from London, 7 September 1601," in Latham and Youings, *Letters*, 211.

24. The Greatest Lucifer That Hath Lived in Our Age

208 "the greatest Lucifer . . .": letter from Henry Howard to King James excerpted in Robert Lacey, *Sir Walter Ralegh*, 274.

208 Ralegh reflexively replied: Lacey, *Sir Walter Ralegh*, 274.

209 "if the like offer . . .": Earl of Northampton, Henry Howard, Earl of Salisbury, Robert Cecil, Dalrymple, David, *The Secret Correspondence of Sir Robert Cecil with James VI. King of Scotland* (London: A. Millar, 1766), 47.

209 "The mind of man is that part of God . . .": Ralegh, "To Sir Robert Cecil, 24 January 1597," in Latham and Youings, *Letters*, 154–156.

209 "support a person whom most religious men . . .": letter from Sir Robert Cecil to King James: "Correspondence of King James VI of Scotland Respecting His Succession to the Throne of England," *Camden Old Series*, July 1861, 19.

209 "My martyr": Lacey, *Sir Walter Ralegh*, 269.

209 ringing bells, joyous song: Catherine Drinker Bowen, "The Lion and the Throne: The Trial of Sir Walter Ralegh," *The Atlantic*, December, 1956.

210 Burghley House information: burghley.co.uk/about-us/the-house.

210 "Virtue followeth oftest noble blood": King James VI of Scotland, *The Basilicon Doron of King James VI* via *Dictionaries of the Scots Language*: dsl.ac.uk/entry/dost/oft.

210 "loathsome to the eye . . .": King James I, "His Counterblast to Tobacco," 1604, Document Bank of Virginia, https://edu.lva.virginia.gov/dbva/items/show/124.

211 "my little beagle": *Historic Houses of the United Kingdom: Descriptive, Historical, Pictorial* (London: Cassell, 1892), 55.

211 "On my soul, man . . .": Aubrey, *Brief Lives*, 264.

211 "Would to God that had been put to trial . . .": Aubrey, *Brief Lives*, 264.

211 "Discourse touching a War with Spain and the protecting of the Netherlands": in Walter Raleigh, *The Works of Sir Walter Ralegh, Kt: Miscellaneous works* (Oxford: The University Press, 1829), 299.

211 lost his job as captain of the guard: Collins and Sidney, *Letters and Memorials*, 346, note.

211 "wise with a wise prince . . .": Walter Ralegh, *The Historie of the World* (first published London: Walter Burre, 1614; herein: Oxford: University Press, 1829), 40.

212 Ralegh had recruited him: William Cobbett et al., *Cobbett's Complete Collection of State Trials and Proceedings for High Treason and Other Crimes and Misdemeanors from the Earliest Period to the Year 1783* (London: R. Bagshaw, 1809), 2.

213 no more interest in giving defendants a fair trial than Romans . . .: Lacey, *Sir Walter Ralegh*, 296.

213 Pre-1696 rules for the defendants' legal representation, or lack thereof: John H. Langbein, "The Prosecutorial Origins of Defence Counsel in the Eighteenth Century: The Appearance of Solicitors," *Cambridge Law Journal* 58, no. 2 (July 1999): 314–365.

214 "I am now made an enemy and a traitor . . .": "To Lady Ralegh [from the Tower, on or shortly before July 27, 1603]," in Latham and Youings, *Letters*, 247–249.

214 "rather a cut than a stab": "Lord Cecil to Sir Thomas Parry," August 4, 1603, Thomas Birch and Robert Folkestone Williams, *The Court and Times of James*

the First: Illustrated by Authentic and Confidential Letters, from Various Public and Private Collections, vol. 1 (London: Henry Colburn, 1848), 13.

214 "perfectly whole": note from a lieutenant to Cecil, July 30, 1603, excerpted in Greg Wilkinson, "Sir Walter Raleigh: deliberate self-harm in the Tower of London, 1603," *British Journal of Psychiatry* 213, no. 5 (2018).

25. The Horriblest Traitor That Ever Lived

215 1603 plague: Ian Munro, "The City and Its Double: Plague Time in Early Modern London," *English Literary Renaissance* 30, no. 2 (2000): 241.

215 "brought alive through such multitudes . . .": letter from William Waad to Robert Cecil, 1603, *Domestic Correspondence of James I*, vol. 4, 36, excerpted in Edwards, *The Life of Sir Walter Ralegh*, 386.

216 judges' attire: https://www.judiciary.uk/about-the-judiciary/the-justice-system/history/.

216 powdered wigs: Claire Barrett, "Shaved Heads and Syphilis: A Brief History of Wigs," HistoryNet, June 30, 2020, historynet.com/shaved-heads-and-syphilis-a-brief-history-of-wigs/.

217 the practice of judicial recusal: Richard E. Flamm, "History of and Problems with Federal Judicial Disqualification Framework," *Drake Law Review*, May 2010, 751–753.

217 "Not guilty" and, unless noted, all dialogue from the treason trial, from the trial transcript: "The Trial of Sir Walter Raleigh, knt. at Winchester, for High Treason: 1 James I. 17th of November, A. D. 1603," T. B. Howell, Esq., *A Complete Collection of State Trials, vol. 2* (London: Longman, Hurst, Rees, Orme, and Brown, 1816), 2.

217 King James reportedly joked: Carew Ralegh, *Observations upon Some Particular Persons and Passages in a Book Lately Make Publick; Intituled, A Compleat History of the Lives and Reignes of Mary Queen of Scotland, and of Her Son James, the Sixth of Scotland, and the First of England, France and Ireland* (London: printed for Ga. Bedell and Tho. Collins and Sidney, 1656), 7.

217 greatest legal mind: Lacey, *Sir Walter Ralegh*, 297.

217 "We will never see his like . . .": Amy Louise Erickson, "Review of Widows, by Jan Bremmer and Lourens van den Bosch," *History Workshop Journal*, no. 45 (1998): 297.

219 To *thou* a person: Lacey, *Sir Walter Ralegh*, 299.

219 "so worthily, so wisely, so temperately . . .": David Jardine, *Criminal Trials*, vol. 1 (London: Nattali and Bond, 1832), 461.

219 "Never any man spoke so well in times past . . .": letter from Sir Dudley Carleton to Mr. John Chamberlain, November 27, 1683, reprinted in Cobbett, *Cobbett's Complete Collection of State Trials*, 48.

220 "a great satisfaction . . .": Stebbing, *Sir Walter Ralegh*, 218.

220 "No man shall be condemned of treason unless . . .": 5 and 6 Edward VI, c. 11, s. 12: *Statutes at Large From Magna charta to 1800*: n.p., 1763, at archive.org/details/statutesatlarge24britgoog.

220 "At the mouth of two witnesses . . .": Deuteronomy, 17:6: biblehub.com/deuteronomy/17-6.htm.

221 English common law: Peter Mirfield, "The Right to Confront One's Accusers: Did Sir Walter Raleigh Die for Nothing?," *Singapore Journal of Legal Studies*, 2019, 423–439.

221 only the Catholics: Lacey, *Sir Walter Ralegh*, 302.

222 "would have gone a thousand miles to save his life": Henry William Dulcken, ed., *Worthies of the World* (London: Ward, Locke, 1880), 14.

223 "so far touched in conscience . . .": Francis Osborne, *The Works of Francis Osborn, Esq.*, 9th ed. (London: A. and J. Churchil, 1701), 334.

223 even Coke was surprised: Anonymous, *Observations upon Sanderson's History of Queen Mary and King James* (1656), cited in Stebbing, *Sir Walter Ralegh*, 230.

223 Cecil teared up: Trevelyan, *Sir Walter Raleigh*, 7633.

223 "Never before had the justice of England . . .": "Proceedings at the Privy Council against Sir Walter Raleigh," in Robert Leng, William Tite, Earl of Oxford, Edward Harley, and John Bruce, *Documents Relating to Sir Walter Raleigh's Last Voyage* (London: Camden Society, 1864), 7–13.

223 landmark in criminal justice: Eric D. Green, Charles R. Nesson, Peter L. Murray, *Problems, Cases, and Materials on Evidence* (New York: Aspen Law & Business, 2000), 407.

223 Sixth Amendment: archives.gov/founding-docs/constitution-transcript.

26. Disposed of at the King's Pleasure

224 "never was a man so hated . . .": Dulcken, *Worthies of the World*, 14.

224 The hangings began November 29 . . . and details of the subsequent executions at Winchester Castle: relation of Sir Dudley Carleton quoted in George Godfrey Cunningham, *Lives of Eminent and Illustrious Englishmen: From Alfred the Great to the Latest Times, on an Original Plan* (Glasgow: A. Fullarton, 1837), 363–364.

225 Anne Boleyn: Adam Taylor, "Off with Her Head! Did Anne Boleyn Really Try to Speak after Being Beheaded?," *Neuroscience News*, April 25, 2019.

225 "had hammers working in his head . . .": Dudley Carleton, *Dudley Carleton to John Chamberlain, 1603–1624; Jacobean letters* (New Brunswick, NJ: Rutgers University Press, 1972), 51.

225 "We have this day beheld a work of so great mercy . . .": Ralegh letter "To the Lords Commissioners for the Trial [From Winchester, 9 December 1603]," in Latham and Youings, *Letters*, 266–267.

226 "It is not God's will that I should see you any more in this life . . .": Ralegh letter "To Lady Ralegh [From Winchester, 4-8 December 1603]," in Latham and Youings, *Letters*, 263–265.

227 "a man raised from the dead": Ralegh letter "To Lord Cecil [from Winchester on or Shortly After 10 December 1603]," in Latham and Youings, *Letters*, 268.

227 Sherborne Castle's £200 annual rent—actually £200 16s 1d: Peter White and Alan Cook, *Sherborne Old Castle, Dorset: Archaeological Investigations 1930–90* (London: Society of Antiquaries of London, 2015), 3.

228 Londoners crowding outside the Tower walls every day: Gallay, *Walter Ralegh: Architect of Empire*, 429.

228 his Majesty's express will: HMC, *Eighth Report Appendix I*, 88b; British Library, Add. MS 11402, fo. 112, excerpted in Mark Nicholls and Penry Williams, *Sir Walter Raleigh* (London: Continuum, 2011), 230.

228 report that his parents had been secretly married: Warner, *Voyage of Robert Dudley*, xli.

228 defamation suit: Robert Dudley, Earl of Leicester, *Household Accounts and Disbursement Books of Robert Dudley, Earl of Leicester, vol.* 6 (Equatorial Guinea: Cambridge University Press, 1995), 29.

230 In the 1660s, King Charles II . . . Robert Boyle: Lacey, *Sir Walter Ralegh*, 315.

230 "great cures": Aubrey, *Brief Lives*, 797.

230 zoo installed by Henry III in 1235: "The Tower of London Menagerie" on Historic Royal Palaces, History and Stories: hrp.org.uk/tower-of-london/history-and-stories/the-tower-of-london-menagerie/#gs.q2x0p4.

230 Charles Leigh, expedition information: "Captain Charles Leigh, His Voyage," in Samuel Purchas, *Purchas His Pilgrimes, vol. 16*, 309–323.

230 2.038%: Sellin and Carlisle, "Assays of Sir Walter Raleigh's Ores from Guayana, 1595–1596."

231 "immediately would build castles . . ." and subsequent excerpts: Walter Ralegh, "To the Earl of Salisbury [from the Tower, c. July] 1607," in Latham and Youings, *Letters*, 297–298.

231 King James wanted to flip [Sherborne]: John Chamberlain to Sir Dudley Carleton, January 10, 1608, in John Nichols, *The Progresses, Processions and Magnificent Festivities of King James the First, His Royal Consort, Family and Court, Etc.* (London: J. B. Nichols, 1828), 214.

231 Bess fought: Carew Ralegh, "The Humble Petition of Carew Ralegh, Esq., only Son of Sir Walter Ralegh, late deceased," in Walter Scott, *A Collection of Scarce*

and Valuable Tracts on the Most Entertaining Subjects: Reign of King James I (London: T. Cadell and W. Davies, 1809), 454.

231 The king was unmoved: Carew Ralegh, "Humble Petition of Carew Ralegh," 454.

232 "No king but my father . . .": E. Littell, *Littell's Living Age, Second Series, Volume IX* (Boston: Littell, Son and Company, 1855), 604.

232 Dudley as adviser to Grand Duke of Tuscany Ferdinando I: Michele Paolo, "An Italian Colony in America: A Forgotten Attempt," *Italics Magazine*, June 24, 2020.

232 "certainly mines of gold, or silver . . .": Robert Harcourt, *A Relation of a Voyage to Guiana* (London: W. Welby, 1613), 40.

232 Roe left for Guiana on February 13, 1610—and details of the expedition, Harlow, *Ralegh's Last Voyage*, 13–14.

232 "nothing new": letter from Thomas Roe to Robert Cecil dated February 28, 1610 [but probably 1611], reproduced in James A. Williamson, *English Colonies in Guiana and on the Amazon, 1604–1668* (Oxford: Clarendon, 1923), 55–57.

233 Prince Henry exacted a promise from his father: Stebbing, *Sir Walter Ralegh*, 259.

233 ten editions: Lacey, *Sir Walter Ralegh*, 325.

27. To Die for the King and Not by the King

234 Sir George Villiers . . . paid £1,500: "Observations on Sanderson's History of King James," cited in Stebbing, *Sir Walter Ralegh*, 294.

234 "good gold cheap": "To the Earl of Salisbury [from the Tower, c. July] 1607," in Latham and Youings, *Letters*, 297.

234 national debt of £700,000, King James's profligate spending: Julian Goodare, "The Debts of James VI of Scotland," *Economic History Review* 62, no. 4 (2009): 931.

234 "To die for the king . . .": "To Sir Ralph Winwood from the Tower [Early 1616]," in Latham and Youings, *Letters*, 335–336.

235 "His Majesty being pleased to release . . .": March 19 letter from Privy Council to Ralegh excerpted in Thomas Nadauld Brushfield, *Raleghana* (London: Bonham Norton, 1906), 49.

235 another £1500: according to Carew Ralegh, cited in Schomburgk, *Discovery*, 169.

235 Fleet Prison: the National Archive E407/56, fo. 99, bill of lieutenant of the Tower for January to March 1604, cited in Nicholls and Williams, *Sir Walter Raleigh*, 234.

235 Durham House . . . royal banqueting hall: Lacey, *Sir Walter Ralegh*, 341.

236 "of not missing his way from his dining-room . . .": John Maclean, *Letters from Robert Cecil to Sir George Carew* (London: Camden Society, 1854), 71.

236 advance of £500: Geoffrey Jules Marcus, *A Naval History of England: The Formative Centuries* (London: Longmans, 1961), 180.

236 "Your commission is as good a pardon": Carew Ralegh letter to James Howell in *Howell's Letters*, vol. 2, 371 (edition of 1678), excerpted in Edwards, *The Life of Sir Walter Ralegh*, 590.

236 "the scum of men" and other descriptions of crew: Walter Ralegh, "Sir Walter Raghley's Large Apologie for the ill successe of his enterprise to Guiana," in Harlow, *Ralegh's Last Voyage*, 317.

237 "his father's exact image both in body and mind": Stebbing, *Sir Walter Ralegh*, 300.

237 "quarrelsome and impulsive": Fred B. Trombly, "Masks of Impersonality in Burghley's 'Ten Precepts' and Ralegh's 'Instructions to his Son,'" *Review of English Studies* 66, no. 275 (2015): 480–500.

237 in 1614, Wat had had to flee England: letter from Sir George Carew to Sir Thomas Roe in Robert Tyrwhitt, *Notices and remains of the family of Tyrwhitt* (n.p., 1858), 10.

237 "a bear": Aubrey, *Brief Lives*, 268–269.

237 "Better were it to be unborn than to be ill bred": Walter Ralegh, "Instructions to His Son and to Posterity," Oldys, *Works*, vol. 8, 560.

237 "Your father lay with me but an hour ago," and dinner party story: Aubrey, *Brief Lives*, 268–269.

238 "keep the king of England good" and subsequent Gondomar biographical information: Francis Hamilton Lyon, *Diego Sarmiento de Acuña* (Oxford: B. H. Blackwell, 1909), 5.

238 one of history's greatest diplomats: Lyon, *Diego Sarmiento de Acuña*,72.

238 "with his facetious words and gestures . . .": Sir Robert Cotton, *Count Gondamor* [sic]*'s Transactions during His Embassy in England* (Cornhill: John Garfield, 1659), iv.

238 the English Solomon: John Robert Moore, "The Contemporary Significance of Middleton's Game at Chesse." *PMLA* 50, no. 3 (1935): 761–768.

238 "But that would be piracy . . .": Samuel Rawson Gardiner, *Prince Charles and the Spanish Marriage: 1617–1623, vol. 1* (London: Hurst and Blackett, 1869), 56.

239 "the old pirate": Stebbing, *Sir Walter Ralegh*, 304.

239 No less than £500,000: King James told his negotiator, Sir John Digby, "You are to demand two millions of crowns, and you are not to descend lower than so many crowns as may make the sum of £500,000, besides the jewels.": *Foreign Correspondence*, Spain, vol. lv. fol. 139. R.H., cited by Edwards, *Life of Sir Walter Ralegh*, 676.

240 "inflict the least injury in the world": Harlow, *Ralegh's Last Voyage*, 37.

240 "to break the peace where there is no peace . . .": Stebbing, *Sir Walter Ralegh*, 327.

241 "Orders to be observed by the Commanders of the Fleete and land companies": Harlow, *Ralegh's Last Voyage*, 121–126.

241 March 26, 1617—alternatively, per *The Annals of Mr. W. Camden, in the Reign of King James I*, March 28—per Schomburgk, *Discovery*, 173, note 1.

241 240-ton and twenty-five-gun *Star*, and specs of fleet: "Newes of Sr Walter Rauleigh," November 17, 1617, at the British Museum, Ayscough's Cat. No. 3272; excerpted in Harlow, *Ralegh's Last Voyage*, 152.

242 "perish or prosper": Walter Ralegh, "To Sir Richard Boyle from Rostellan, Co. Cork, 28 June 1617," in Latham and Youings, *Letters*, 342–343.

28. Better to Have Been Hanged

243 hired a drummer: Plymouth Municipal Records, cited in Trevelyan, *Sir Walter Raleigh*, 9348.

243 Thirteen ships, one thousand men, other details of the fleet: George Carew, Thomas Roe, *Letters from George Lord Carew to Sir Thomas Roe: Ambassador to the Court of the Great Mogul, 1615–1617* (London: Camden Society, 1860), 116.

244 at six in the morning of August 19, and other dates, distances, and reporting on the voyage: Walter Ralegh, "Sir Walter Ralegh's Journal of His Second Voyage to Guiana," reprinted in Schomburgk, *Discovery*, 174.

245 The French sailors did write home: Cottington to "Winwood; Madrid, Oct. 21 (O.S.), 1617," in *Spanish Correspon. James I, 1617*, excerpted in Edwards, *Life of Sir Walter Ralegh*, 607.

245 "fear that Sir Walter would turn pirate": Sir George Carew, *Letters from George Lord Carew to Sir Thomas Roe* (London: Nichols, 1860), 129.

245 "had sailed with him [Ralegh] . . ." and subsequent excerpts from letter: "Gondomar to the King of Spain, 22nd October, 1617," translated to English and reprinted in Harlow, *Ralegh's Last Voyage*, 153.

246 "a quantity of wheat, goats, sheep . . ." and subsequent: Ralegh, "Sir Walter Raleigh's Journal," reprinted in Hakluyt, *Discovery*, 180.

246 "no intent to invade any of those islands . . .": Ralegh, "Sir Walter Raleigh's Journal," 182.

246 "would offend his Majesty": Ralegh, "Sir Walter Raleigh's Journal," 181.

246 "The best of all the Canaries": Ralegh, "Sir Walter Raleigh's Journal," 183.

247 "vassals of the King of Great Britain . . .": Ralegh, "Sir Walter Raleigh's Journal," 184.

247 official report: "Correspondence with the governor of Lancerota": Edwards, *Life of Sir Walter Ralegh*, 607.

247 "though better . . . to have been hanged": Ralegh, "Sir Walter Raleigh's Journal," 186.

247 "I have suffered the most violent calenture . . .": "To Lady Ralegh from Cayenne, 14 November 1617," in Latham and Youings, *Letters*, 345.

247 Ambrose Paré, *The Workes of that Famous Chirurgion Ambrose Parey* (London: R. Coates and W. Dugard, 1649) 28.

248 "the water ran in at my neck . . .": Ralegh, "Sir Walter Raleigh's Journal," 167.

248 "It pleased God to visit . . .": Ralegh, "Sir Walter Raleigh's Journal," 190.

248 "Rainbow in the morning . . .": Schomburgk, *Discovery*, 192, footnote 2.

248 Since rainbows result from sunlight: Joe Rao, "Rainbows: How They Form & How to See Them," LiveScience, March 15, 2011, livescience.com/30235-rainbows-formation-explainer.html.

248–249 "black as pitch": Ralegh, "Sir Walter Raleigh's Journal," 191.

249 seabirds were spirits: Fletcher S. Bassett, *Legends and Superstitions of the Sea and of Sailors in All Lands and at All Times* (Belford: Clarke, 1885), Kindle ed., 2974–2976.

249 "stark calm": "Sir Walter Raleigh's Journal," 193.

249 Speed of a three-toed sloth: www.themeasureofthings.com/results.php?comp=speed&unit=mph&amt=.7

249 two pints per day: https://www.ncbi.nlm.nih.gov/books/NBK236237/.

249 the temperature differential between the warm sea, and other waterspout facts: Zahra Ahmed, "8 Facts About Waterspouts at Sea," www.marineinsight.com/?s=8+Facts+About+Waterspouts+at+Sea, and education.nationalgeographic.org/resource/waterspout/.

29. Yet Shall You Find Their Ashes

251 "Blessed be God": Ralegh, "Sir Walter Raleigh's Journal," 193.

251 "violently": Ralegh, "Sir Walter Raleigh's Journal," 193.

251 "put us in fear that the rains would never end": Ralegh, "Sir Walter Raleigh's Journal," 196.

251 forty-two of the *Destiny*'s two hundred crewmen: "To Lady Ralegh from Cayenne, 14 November 1617," in Latham and Youings, *Letters*, 346.

251–252 "a violent cold . . .": Ralegh, "Sir Walter Raleigh's Journal," 197.

252 "most filthy stench": Ralegh, "Sir Walter Raleigh's Journal," 199.

253 Harry, Ralegh's onetime Tower servant: Edwards, *The Life of Sir Walter Ralegh*, 611.

253 "to tell you I might here be king . . .": "To Lady Ralegh from Cayenne, 14 November 1617," in Latham and Youings, *Letters*, 346.

253 "a very earthly paradise": Ralegh, "Newes of Sr Walter Rauleigh," 152.

253–254 rather than rendezvous with Ralegh in England: letter by James Hancock: "Letter from a member of the Expedition during a stay at Falmouth (16th June, 1617)," reprinted in Harlow, *Ralegh's Last Voyage*, 143.

254 as far as is known, they safely reached Genoa, and subsequent (sketchy) details of Faige and Belle: Samuel R. Gardiner, "The Case Against Sir Walter Ralegh," in *The Fortnightly* (London: Chapman and Hall, 1867), 609.

254 amount a skilled tradesman earned in three years: nationalarchives.gov.uk/currency-converter/#currency-result.

254 he confessed to having worked for the infamous corsario: "Anthony Belle's Examination at Madrid, taken by Diego Brochero (10th March, 1618)," translated and reprinted in Harlow, *Ralegh's Last Voyage*, 126–127.

254 powder keg: Pedro Simón, *Noticias historiales de Venezuela* (Venezuela: Biblioteca Ayacucho, 1992), chap. 30.

255 "dead or alive . . .": Ralegh, "Sir Walter Rawleigh his apologie for his voyage to Guiana," reprinted in Oldys, *Works*, vol. 8, 490.

255 Sir Warham St. Leger biographical information: Douglas Richardson, *Royal Ancestry: A Study in Colonial and Medieval Families* (Salt Lake City, UT: the author, 2013), vol. 4, 538, Saint Leger 21. Warham Saint Leger.

255 "exceedingly valiant and worthy gentleman": Ralegh, "To Sir Ralph Winwood from St Christophers, 21 March 1618," in Latham and Youings, *Letters*, 349.

255 served long with distinction: Ralegh, "To Sir Ralph Winwood from St Christophers, 21 March 1618," in Latham and Youings, *Letters*, 349.

255 seventeenth birthday: the baptismal register of Withycombe Raleigh, a civil parish in East Devon, lists "George the sonne of mr George Rauleigh . . ." per T. N. Brushfield, MD, *Raleghana* (reprinted from the "Transactions of the Devonshire Association for the Advancement of Science, Literature, and Art," 1896 vol. 28, 272–312), 16.

256 "I would not, for all the world . . .": Ralegh, "Apologie," 490.

256 "without manifest peril of my son . . .": Ralegh, "Apologie," 490.

256 "to satisfy his majesty . . .": Ralegh, "Apologie," 494.

30. "Victory! Victory!"

257 late in the afternoon: "Depositions of the Inhabitants relating to the Capture of S. Thomé," translated and reprinted in Harlow, *Ralegh's Last Voyage*, 193.

257 January 2, 1618, and Keymis inland expedition time line: Ralegh, "Apologie," 492.

257 140 houses, a church and two convents: Schomburgk, *Discovery*, 210.

258 Keymis's best hope: Harlow, *Ralegh's Last Voyage*, 60.

258 "repel them . . .": Ralegh, "Apologie," 325.

259 "perros ingleses": Walter Ralegh, "To [Lord Carew, Late July/Early August 1618]," in Latham and Youings, *Letters*, 366.

259 "unadvised daringness . . .": "A Letter Written by Captaine Charles Parker," reprinted in Harlow, *Ralegh's Last Voyage*, 231.

259 "Come on, my hearts!": King James, "A Declaration of the Demeanor and Carriage of Sir Walter Ralegh, Knight . . . ," reprinted in Harlow, *Ralegh's Last Voyage*, 335–356.

259 "Victory! Victory!": King James, "Declaration," in Harlow, *Ralegh's Last Voyage*, 335–356.

259 a Spanish soldier parried Wat's sword: Ralegh, "Apologie," 326.

259 John Plesington: Ralegh, "Apologie," 491.

260 "a sword thrust . . ." and details of the battle: Pedro Simón, *Noticias historiales de Venezuela* (Venezuela: Biblioteca Ayacucho, 1992), 387.

260 Wat Ralegh's corpse was paraded . . . and details of the funerals: Pedro Simón, *Noticias historiales de Venezuela*, 389–390.

261 "The fewer men, the greater share of honour . . .": William Shakespeare, "The Life of King Henry the Fifth" (London: Macmillan, 1890), 20.

262 believing that the pirate Guaterral: Pedro Simón, *Noticias historiales de Venezuela*, 436.

262 a relative of the First Count of Gondomar: Schomburgk, *Discovery*, 209.

263 "The world hath taken end in me" and subsequent excerpts: Walter Ralegh, "To Sir Ralph Winwood from St. Christophers, 22 March 1618," in Latham and Youings, *Letters*, 347–348.

263 "extraordinary valour": "Keymis's letter, dated the eighth of January, from Oronoko," reprinted in Oldys, *Works*, vol. 1, 507.

263 "My son, having more desire of honor . . ." and subsequent: Walter Ralegh, "To Sir Ralph Winwood from St. Christophers, 22 March 1618," in Latham and Youings, *Letters*, 347–348.

263 "My brains are broken . . ." and other lines from Walter Ralegh's letter to Bess Ralegh: "To Lady Ralegh from St. Christophers, 22 March 1618," in Latham and Youings, *Letters*, 353.

264 in San Thomé's treasury: Simón, *Noticias historiales de las conquistas de Tierra Firme en las Indias Occidentales*, 398.

264 the Spaniards' certainty that reinforcements would be arriving: Edwards, *The Life of Sir Walter Ralegh*, 642.

265 "every stone that we stooped to take . . .": Ralegh, *Discoverie*, 82.

265 "without bush or stubble . . .": Ralegh, *Discoverie*, 82.

266 "to satisfy his majesty that my design . . .": Ralegh, "Apologie," 490.

266 Keymis displayed one of the samples: Samuel Jones letter to the Privy Council March 22, 1618, reprinted in Harlow, *Ralegh's Last Voyage*, 232–237.

31. Great Sands and Rocks

267 Keymis was fully confident: the story of Keymis post-Caroní efforts to find gold is cobbled together from Fray Pedro Simón's Narrative of Ralegh's Expedition,

Samuel Jones's March 22, 1618, letter to the Privy Council, among other accounts, both English and Spanish, cited below.

268 "great sands and rocks": and the logistics of Keymis's search along the Orinoco: "Fray Pedro Simón's Narrative of Ralegh's Expedition, translated from *Setima Noticia Historiale de las Conquistas de Tierra Firme*," chaps. 13–14, in Harlow, *Ralegh's Last Voyage*, 162–189.

269 according to a Spanish source: "Fray Pedro Simón's Narrative of Ralegh's Expedition," 178.

269 English casualty reporting: Ralegh, *Apologie*, 326.

270 "deluded": Samuel Jones letter to the Privy Council March 22, 1618, reprinted in Harlow, *Ralegh's Last Voyage*, 237.

270 "false to all the men": "A Letter Written by Captaine Charles Parker," reprinted in Harlow, *Ralegh's Last Voyage*, 231.

270 his 370 men in San Thomé: "Depositions of the Inhabitants relating to the Capture of S. Thomé," reprinted and translated in Harlow, *Ralegh's Last Voyage*, 193–209.

270 "thick and impassable woods": Ralegh, "To Sir Ralph Winwood from St Christophers, 21 March 1618," in Latham and Youings, *Letters*, 350.

271 "The disgrace of not bringing our men to this mine . . .": Keymis letter to Ralegh, February 9, 1618, in Cambridge University Library Mss Ee 50–52, 3; excerpted in Trevelyan, *Sir Walter Raleigh*, 9837–9841.

271 "their hands full to defend themselves from firing . . ." and subsequent parts of conversation between Ralegh and Keymis, except where noted: Ralegh, "Apologie," 327–328.

272 Captain Keymis had merely fired his pistol: Ralegh, "To Sir Ralph Winwood from St Christophers, 21 March 1618," in Latham and Youings, *Letters*, 349.

273 "What wonder is it that I've failed": Ralegh, "Apologie," 317.

273 "our men weary . . .": Samuel Jones letter to the Privy Council March 22, 1618, 237.

273 "As Sir Francis Drake . . ." and subsequent excerpts from letter: Walter Ralegh, "To Lady Ralegh from St. Christophers, 22 March 1618," in Latham and Youings, *Letters*, 354.

274 Oualie, Nevis history: Vincent K. Hubbard, *Swords, Ships & Sugar: History of Nevis* (Corvallis, OR: Premiere, 2002), 20–23.

274 £3,000 worth of dry fish: Harlow, *Ralegh's Last Voyage*, 85.

275 "on his faith, his hand, and his word": Gondomar to Philip III, June 14, 1618, Madrid Palace Library, excerpted in Samuel Rawson Gardiner, *History of England from the Accession of James I to the Outbreak of the Civil War, 1603–1642, vol.* 3 (London: Longmans, Green, 1895), 132.

275 prospective French commission: Samuel Jones letter to the Privy Council March 22, 1618, in Harlow, *Ralegh's Last Voyage*, 232–237.

276 "What shall become of me now . . .": Walter Ralegh, "To Sir Ralph Winwood from St Christophers, 21 March 1618," in Latham and Youings, *Letters*, 351.

276 "there is not better in the world . . ." and subsequent: Walter Ralegh, "To Lord Carew from Plymouth, [c. 11] June 1618," in Latham and Youings, *Letters*, 358.

276 authorization from French Admiral Charles de Montmorency: Ralegh, "To King James from the Tower, 4 October 1618," in Latham and Youings, *Letters*, 374.

277 he would foresake them: Edwards, *Life of Sir Walter Ralegh*, 643.

277 £15,000 surety bond: Lacey, *Sir Walter Ralegh*, 360.

277 As he was painfully aware: Walter Ralegh, "To Sir Ralph Winwood from St Christophers, 21 March 1618," in Latham and Youings, *Letters*, 351.

277 "provide somewhat for you . . .": Walter Ralegh, "To Lady Ralegh from St. Christophers, 22 March 1618," in Latham and Youings, *Letters*, 354.

32. Sir Judas

278 sail to Newfoundland to reprovision and refit, and subsequent details of the return journey: Walter Ralegh, "To Lord Carew from Plymouth [C. 11] June 1618," in Latham and Youings, *Letters*, 356–361.

278 Killybegs: Walter Ralegh, "To Lord Carew from Plymouth, [c. 11] June 1618," in Latham and Youings, *Letters*, 357–358.

279 on every Irish lip: Oldys, *Works*, 510.

279 "Pirates! Pirates! Pirates!": James Howell, 1618 letter "To Sir James Crofts, Knight, at St. Osith," in *The Familiar Letters of James Howell* (London: D. Nutt, 1892), 23.

279 "fallen into the grave displeasure of his Majesty" and reaction of the conspirators: Ralegh, "To Lord Carew from Plymouth, [c. 11] June 1618," in Latham and Youings, *Letters*, 358.

279 "our dear brother the King of Spain" and subsequent: "A Proclamation declaring His Majesties pleasure concerning Sir Walter Rawleigh, and those who adventured with him," June 9, 1618, in Clarence S. Brigham, ed., *British Royal Proclamations Relating to America 1603–1783* (New York: Burt Franklin, 1911), 9.

280 carried from room to room: Lyon, *Diego Sarmiento de Acuña*, 65.

281 Stukley was a nephew: Edwards, *Life of Sir Walter Ralegh*, 654.

281 Lewis Stukley biographical information: John Knox Laughton, "Stucley, Lewis," *Dictionary of National Biography, 1885–1900, vol. 55* (London: Smith, Elder, 1898), 122.

281 Captain Samuel King: the escape attempt draws on "Captain Samuel King's Narrative of Sir Walter Ralegh's Motives and Opportunities for conveying himself out of the kingdom," 1618, in the British Museum, per Oldys, who excerpts it in *Works*, vol. 1—see p. 513—but no longer discoverable at the museum.

281 "by those who told the king that I feigned the mine . . .": Ralegh, "To Lord Carew from Plymouth, [c. 11] June 1618," in Latham and Youings, *Letters*, 357.

282 "I shall be content to suffer death": Walter Ralegh, "To Lord Carew from Plymouth, [c. 11] June 1618," in Latham and Youings, *Letters*, 360.

282 "followed not my directions": Ralegh, "To [Lord Carew, Late July/Early August 1618]," in Latham and Youings, *Letters*, 364.

282 "I gave no authority for it to be done": Ralegh, "To Lord Carew from Plymouth, [c. 11] June 1618," in Latham and Youings, *Letters*, 358.

283 "speedily bring hither the person of Sir Walter Raleigh . . .": ACP Colonial 1613-80 (July 23, 1618), 19–30, excerpted in Trevelyan, *Sir Walter Raleigh*, 10,239.

283 peak summer splendor: Edwards, *The Life of Sir Walter Ralegh*, 657.

283 "All this was mine . . .": Manoury, as quoted by Francis Bacon, "Declaration . . .," in Harlow, *Ralegh's Last Voyage*, 348.

284 "Why did I not keep my liberty once I had it?": Ralegh, "Apologie," 498.

284 no ambassador had ever been as loved: Lyon, *Diego Sarmiento de Acuña*, 72.

284 Broad Street: Beer, *My Just Desire*, 204.

285 "Sir Lewis, these actions . . .": Benjamin Disraeli, *Curiosities of Literature* (London: F. Warne, 1881), 121.

285 £965: "Dec. 29. To Sir Lewis Stukeley, for performance of his service and expenses in bringing up hither, out of Devonshire, the person of Sir Walter Ralegh, £ 965 6s.3d," in *Pells Order Book, 1618*, cited by Edwards, *The Life of Sir Walter Ralegh*, 673, footnote 2.

285 "If I should hang all that speak ill . . .": "Stucley, Lewis," *Dictionary of National Biography, 1885–1900*, 123.

33. The Power of the Tongue

286 "impostures" and other Yelverton remarks from the October 17 hearing: "Proceedings at the Privy Council against Sir Walter Raleigh," in Robert Leng, William Tite, Earl of Oxford, Edward Harley, and John Bruce, *Documents Relating to Sir Walter Raleigh's Last Voyage* (London: Camden Society, 1864), 7–13.

287 "If Sir Lewis Stukley had not prevented him, he had been gone . . ." and other remarks by Thomas Coventry in "Proceedings at the Privy Council against Sir Walter Raleigh."

287 "Life and death are in the power of the tongue": Walter Ralegh, "Instructions to His Son," in Oldys, *Works*, vol. 8, 564.

287 "I do verily believe that his Majesty . . ." and Ralegh's remarks at the August 17 hearing: "Proceedings at the Privy Council against Sir Walter Raleigh."

288 such public responsibilities were routinely placed: Edwards, *Life of Sir Walter Ralegh*, 684.

288 "many great occasions and affairs . . .": *Registers of the Privy Council*, James I, vol. 3, 510–512, excerpted in Edwards, *Life of Sir Walter Ralegh*, 685.

288–289 "not to suffer any person . . .": *Registers of the Privy Council*, James I, vol. 3, 510–512, excerpted in Edwards, *Life of Sir Walter Ralegh*, 685.

289 "I am sick and weak . . .": Ralegh, "To Lady Ralegh from the Tower, 18 September 1618," in Latham and Youings, *Letters*, 370.

289 "I am sorry to hear amongst many discomforts . . ." (orthography applied): Stebbing, *Sir Walter Ralegh*, 352.

289 moving her and her writing implements to the Tower of London: October 15, 1681, letter from Naunton to Wilson cited in Edwards, *Life of Sir Walter Ralegh*, 688.

289 machine that distilled salt water: Lacey, *Sir Walter Ralegh*, 320.

290 "behaved himself undutifully . . .": "Proceedings at the Privy Council relating to Captain Bayly's desertion," in *Acts of the Privy Council January, 1618–June, 1619*," excerpted in Harlow, *Ralegh's Last Voyage*, 155–156.

290 "by virtue of a cession by all the native chiefs . . .": Walter Ralegh, "To Lord Carew from Plymouth, [c.11] June 1618," in Latham and Youings, *Letters*, 358–359.

291 They made life harder for Ralegh: Stebbing, *Sir Walter Ralegh*, 348.

291 "the King is much inclined to hang Ralegh . . .": October 3, 1618, letter from Harwood to Carleton excerpted in Stebbing, *Sir Walter Ralegh*, 345–346.

291 "spent my poor estate . . ." and subsequent: "Sir Walter Ralaighes Letter to King James at his returne from Guiana," reprinted in Harlow, *Ralegh's Last Voyage*, 277–278.

291 "disclose matters of great service . . .": Walter Ralegh, "To King James from the Tower, 4 October 1618," in Latham and Youings, *Letters*, 373–376.

291 Spanish no longer wanted him put to death, and subsequent Philip III status update: "King of Spain to Sanchez de Ulloa," translation in *Domestic Correspondence of James I*, vol. 99, 74, excerpted in Edwards, *Life of Sir Walter Ralegh*, 688.

291 King James was informed at Royston Palace on October 15: "Naunton to Wilson," October 15, 1618, cited in Edwards, *Life of Sir Walter Ralegh*, 688.

291 a pair of gold ingots that had been stripped from Ralegh: "An Inventory of Such Things as Weare Found on the Body of Sir Walter Rawley, Knight, the 10th Day of August, 1618," reprinted in Edwards, *Letters*, 496.

292 revisit the 1603 treason case, and idea of report "late crimes and offenses": "The Commissioners to the King (18th October 1618)," in Harlow, *Ralegh's Last Voyage*, 295–296.

292 James's stance: "The King's Reply," in Harlow, *Ralegh's Last Voyage*, 296.

292 "it would make him too popular" and subsequent: "The King's Reply," in Harlow, *Ralegh's Last Voyage*, 296.

292 "The most honourable court . . .": Edward P. Cheyney, "The Court of Star Chamber," *American Historical Review* 18, no. 4 (July 1913): 745.

293 letter interim Spanish ambassador Julián Sánchez de Ulloa wrote: DIHE, I, 198, excerpted and translated in Martin Hume, *Sir Walter Ralegh* (New York: Alfred A. Knopf, 1926), 282.

293 Carew Ralegh biographical information, "Carew Ralegh (1605–1666)," *Dictionary of National Biography, vol.* 55 (London: Smith, Elder, 1885–1900), 187.

293 "beg mercy from your majesty": Carew Ralegh, *Carew Ralegh to King James;* Edwards, *Letters*, 488.

294 "Let them comb it . . .": "John Pory to Carleton," October 31, 1618, *Calendar of State Papers, Domestic, Cor.*, 1611–18, 588.

294 the route to Westminster: Lacey, *Sir Walter Ralegh*, 373.

295 "Sir Walter Ralegh, the prisoner at the bar . . ." and subsequent excerpts from the Westminster hearing: "The bringing Sir Walter Ralegh to Execution," in *Hargrave's State Trials, vol.* 8, reprinted in Cayley, *The Life of Sir Walter Ralegh, Knt.*, 161.

295 raised bench: Green, *London*, 136.

296 *De Warranto Speciali pro Decollatione Walteri Raleigh, Militis, A. D. 1618:* Oldys, *Works*, vol. 8, 773.

297 October 29—a date chosen . . . Lord Mayor's Day: Thomas Hearne, John Aubrey, *Letters Written by Eminent Persons in the Seventeenth and Eighteenth Centuries* (London: Longman, Hurst, Rees, Orme, and Brown, 1813).

34. To Die in the Light

298 "I do not know what you may do for a place . . .": Stebbing, *Sir Walter Ralegh*, 372.

298 "The world itself is but a larger prison . . .": Benjamin Disraeli and Isaac Disraeli, *Curiosities of Literature* (Boston: W. Veazie, 1860), 461.

298 his final visitor, Bess—and details of the visit: "John Chamberlain to Sir Dudley Carleton, October 31, 1618," in John Chamberlain and Norman Egbert McClure, *The Letters of John Chamberlain* (Philadelphia: American Philosophical Society, 1939), 179–180.

299 "for even the wisest man . . .": Walter Ralegh, "Instructions to His Son and to Posterity," c. 1610, reprinted in Oldys, *Works*, vol. 8, 557–570.

299 parboiled, coated in pitch: Green, *London: Travel Guide through Time*, 47.

299 "It is well, dear Bess . . .": "John Chamberlain to Sir Dudley Carleton, October 31, 1618," in Chamberlain and McClure, *Letters of John Chamberlain*, 180.

299 amending the last verse: V. B. Heltzel, "Ralegh's 'Even Such Is Time,' *Huntington Library Bulletin* 10 (1936): 185–188.

299 "cruel time" took "our youth, our joys . . .": Walter Ralegh, "Nature that Washed her Hands in Milk": poetryfoundation.org/poets/sir-walter-ralegh.

300 "But from this earth, this grave, this dust . . .": "Verses said to have been found in his Bible in the Gatehouse at Westminster," in Oldys, *Works*, vol. 8.

301 "stands upon the King of England's own ground" and subsequent details of Tounson's effort to administer the Sacrament of the Holy Eucharist: "Dr. Robert Tounson, Dean of Westminster, to Sir John Isham, Bart," in Edward Edwards, *Letters of Ralegh* (London: Macmillan, 1868), 489–492.

301 Once a condemned man stood on the scaffold: Andrew Fleck, "At the Time of His Death: Manuscript Instability and Walter Ralegh's Performance on the Scaffold," *Journal of British Studies* 48, no. 1 (2009): 4–28.

301 "your assertion of innocency . . ." and subsequent conversation: Tounson letter in Edwards, *Letters of Ralegh*.

302 shackles and chains: Sir John Eliot, *The monarchie of man* (London, Chiswick, 1879), 158.

302 "great multitude": Edwards, *Life of Sir Walter Ralegh*, 698.

303 "his mind became the clearer . . .": Eliot, *Monarchie of man*, 158–159.

303 "as if he'd come hither rather to be a spectator": "Mr. Thomas Lorkin to Sir Thomas Puckering, Bart.," reprinted in Harlow, *Ralegh's Last Voyage*, 311–315

303 "I thank my God heartily . . ." and subsequent excerpts from Ralegh's scaffold speech: "Sir Walter Ralegh's Speech Immediately before he was beheaded," in Harlow, *Ralegh's Last Voyage*, 305–311.

304 "Of a long time, my course was a course of vanity . . .": "Archbishop Sancroft's transcript," in Tanner MSS, Bodleian Library, excerpted in Edwards, *Life of Sir Walter Ralegh*, 704

35. He Was a Mortal

307 "died with such high spirits . . .": E. J. Sánchez Cantón, "Ejecución de Sir Walter Raleigh," in undated *Bolétin de la Real Academia de la Historia*, 126–129, excerpted in Trevelyan, *Sir Walter Raleigh*, 10,625.

307 "do more harm to the faction that procured . . .": Pory to Carleton, October 31, 1618.

308 "Within the Chancel of this Church . . .": Edwards, *Life of Sir Walter Ralegh*, 706.

308 Harcourt had to sell Ellenhall: Edward William Harcourt, *The Harcourt Papers, vol. 1* (Oxford: James Parker, 1878), 103.

308 such notables as the Spanish soldier Nicholas Martenez . . .: Jacob Adrien Van Heuvel, *El Dorado: Being a Narrative of the Circumstances which Gave Rise to Reports, in the Sixteenth Century, of the Existence of a Rich and Splendid City in South America, to which that Name was Given, and which Led to Many Enterprises in Search of it; Including a Defence of Sir Walter Raleigh, in Regard to the Relations Made by Him Respecting It, and a Nation of Female Warriors, in the Vicinity of the Amazon, in the Narrative of His Expedition to the Oronoke in 1595* (New York: J. Winchester, 1844).

308 fifteen-pound gold nugget: Nichol, *Creature in the Map*, 198.

308–309 El Callao gold production: Bell, *Venezuela, a Commercial and Industrial Handbook*, 301.

309 to money, health and love: "Salud, amor, pesetas y tiempo para disfrutarlos," or "Health, love, money and time to enjoy them," pesetas being a colloquial name for the coin worth one-fifth of a peso.

ILLUSTRATION CREDITS

Page 7: El Hombre Dorado (Illustration by Theodor de Bry, source: Gotthard Arthus, *Americae Pars VIII* [Viduae & filiorum, 1599])

Page 8: Walter Ralegh's signature (Wikimedia Commons)

Page 11: Sir Walter Ralegh (Illustration by James Posselwhite, Wikimedia Commons)

Page 15: Ralegh "cast and spread his new plush cloak on the ground whereon the Queen trod gently." (Wilbur F. Gordy, *American Beginnings in Europe* [New York: Charles Scribner's Sons, 1912])

Page 17: Queen Elizabeth I (Queen Elizabeth I, print, Crispijn de Passe the Elder, Wikimedia Commons)

Page 19: Bess Throckmorton (Portrait of Elizabeth Throckmorton, c. 1591, artist unknown, Tudorplace.com)

Page 28: Sir Robert Cecil ("Robert Cecil, 1st Earl of Salisbury," Wikimedia Commons)

Page 30: Robert Dudley (Wyatt, ed., *The Voyage of Robert Dudley to the West Indies, 1594–1595* [London: Hakluyt Society, 1899])

Page 53: *Niña*, *Pinta*, and *Santa María* (Mary Hield, *Glimpses of South America* [London: Cassell, 1882])

Page 56: No caption (Trinidad and Tobago stamp, Wikimedia Commons)

Page 57: Antonio de Berrío (Wikimedia Commons)

Page 60: Ralegh moves on San José de Aruña (Illustration by Theodor de Bry, Gotthard Arthus, *Americae Pars VIII* [Viduae & filiorum, 1599])

Page 61: Ralegh liberates the five Trinidadian chieftains (Unknown artist, "Sir Walter Raleigh sets at Liberty Five Indian Kings," 1768, engraving, Yale Center for British Art)

Page 68: Poisoned arrows (Illustrator Seymour M. Stone, in Cyrus Townsend Brady, *South American Fights and Fighters: And Other Tales of Adventure* [London: Hodder & Stoughton, 1910])

Page 71: Nonsuch Palace (Illustration by H. W. Brewer, in *The Builder*, vol. 66, January–June 1894)

Page 74: The execution of Atahualpa ("The execution of the Inca Emperor Atahuallpa on the stake, ordered by Pizarro," engraving with etching after E. Chappel, Wellcome Collection)

Page 84: Ralegh and Berrío (*The Historical Scrap Book* [London: Cassell, 1886])

Page 86: Gonzalo Jiménez de Quesada (R. B. Cunninghame Graham, Robert Bontine, *The Conquest of New Granada* [London: W. Heinemann, 1922])

Page 92: No caption (George Cubitt, *Pizarro; Or, The Discovery and Conquest of Peru* [London: Wesleyan Conference Office, 1878])

Page 95: No caption ("Jaguar fishing on banks of Orinoco," illustration from Thomas Frost, *Half-hours with the Early Explorers* [London: Cassell, Petter, Galpin, 1873], 196)

Page 99: Late Tivitiva chieftain (Illustration by Theodor de Bry, Gotthard Arthus, *Americae Pars VIII* [Viduae & filiorum, 1599])

Page 101: Treehouses (John George, *Uncivilized Races of Men in All Countries of the World* [Hartford: J. B. Burr, 1870])

Page 107: The "largarto" attack (Illustration by Theodor de Bry in Johann Ludwig Gottfried, *Newe Welt Und Americanische Historien* [Frankfort: Merian, 1655])

Page 119: Winemaking (Girolamo Benzoni, *History of the New World* [London: Hakluyt Society, 1857])

Page 127: Ralegh meets with Topiawari (Illustration by Theodor de Bry, source: Gotthard Arthus, *Americae Pars VIII* [Viduae & filiorum, 1599])

Page 159: Sherborne Castle (Illustration by John Preston Neale in John Preston Neale, *Views of the Seats of Noblemen and Gentlemen in England, Wales, Scotland and Ireland,* vol. 4, held and digitized by the British Library)

Page 160: El Escorial (*The Illustrated History of the World, for the English People* [London: Ward, Lock, 1882])

Page 163: Ralegh's map of Guiana ("America map from *Grand Voyages* [1596] by Theodor de Bry," Wikimedia)

Page 166: Ewaipanoma (Illustration by Levinus Hulsius. Walter Ralegh, *Deß Goldreichen Königreichs Guianæ in America oder newen Welt* [Levini Hulsii, 1601])

Page 169: No caption (Charles K. True, *The Life and Times of Sir Walter Ralegh* [London: Wesleyan Conference Office, 1881])

Page 173: Ralegh's servant misinterprets smoking ("Sir Walter Raleigh Being Doused," artist unknown, Wikimedia Commons)

Page 174: A Carib (Mary Hield, *Glimpses of South America* [London: Cassell, 1882])

Page 195: Robert Devereux, the Second Earl of Essex (*The Illustrated History of the World, for the English People* [London: Ward, Lock, 1882])

Page 196: Durham House (left), Salisbury House, and Worcester House on the Thames (Durham House, Salisbury House and Worcester House on the Thames, print, after Wenceslaus Hollar, Wikimedia Commons)

Page 201: No caption (*The Historical Scrap Book* [London: Cassell, 1886])

Page 206: King James I (*Cassell's History of England: From the Wars of the Roses to the Great Rebellion* [London: Cassell, 1905])

Page 210: Burghley House (Shutterstock)

Page 218: Sir Edward Coke (*Cassell's History of England: From the Wars of the Roses to the Great Rebellion* [London: Cassell, 1905])

Page 227: The Tower of London (Illustration by Wenceslaus Hollar [1607–1677], Metropolitan Museum of Art collection, Wikimedia Commons)

Page 229: Ralegh in his chemistry laboratory at the Tower (*Cassell's History of England: From the Wars of the Roses to the Great Rebellion* [London: Cassell, 1905])

Page 239: Count Gondomar and his chair (Thomas Scott, *The Second Part of Vox Populi* [Netherlands: A. Janss, 1624])

Page 252: Walter and Wat Ralegh on a stamp (1934) (Author)

Page 258: A mortar (Shutterstock)

Page 261: San Thomé (Charles K. True, *The Life and Times of Sir Walter Ralegh* [London: Wesleyan Conference Office, 1881])

Page 268: No caption (Shutterstock)

Page 276: No caption (Shutterstock)

Page 294: Ralegh at the Court of King's Bench (*Cassell's History of England: From the Wars of the Roses to the Great Rebellion* [London: Cassell, 1905])

Page 300: The Raleghs part ("Raleigh Parting from His Wife" by E. Lutz, no recorded date, Wellcome Collection via Wikimedia Commons)

Page 305: October 29, 1618, in the Old Palace Yard (Wikimedia Commons)

INDEX

Page numbers in italics indicate an illustration.

ABOUT THE AUTHOR

Keith Thomson is the author of the nonfiction book *Born to Be Hanged,* as well as several novels, including *Pirates of Pensacola* and the *New York Times* bestseller *Once a Spy.* The former Columbia history major also writes nonfiction for the *New York Times, Garden & Gun,* and the *Huffington Post* on a range of topics, including national security and piracy. He lives in Birmingham, Alabama.